THE LGBTQ+ HISTORY BOOK

THE LGBTQ+ HISTORY BOOK

DK LONDON

PROJECT ART EDITOR
Anna Scully

SENIOR EDITORS
Camilla Hallinan, Laura Sandford

EDITORS
John Andrews, Alethea Doran, Joy Evatt,
Lydia Halliday, Scarlett O'Hara, James Smart,
Dorothy Stannard, Rachel Warren Chadd

ILLUSTRATIONS
James Graham

PICTURE RESEARCHERS
Sarah Hopper, Jo Walton

JACKET DESIGN
Stephanie Cheng Hui Tan

JACKET DESIGN DEVELOPMENT MANAGER
Sophia MTT

PRODUCTION EDITOR
Robert Dunn

SENIOR PRODUCTION CONTROLLER
Poppy David

MANAGING ART EDITOR
Anna Hall

MANAGING EDITOR
Carine Tracanelli

ASSOCIATE PUBLISHING DIRECTOR
Liz Wheeler

ART DIRECTOR
Karen Self

DESIGN DIRECTOR
Phil Ormerod

PUBLISHING DIRECTOR
Jonathan Metcalf

DK DELHI

PROJECT ART EDITOR
Anjali Sachar

SENIOR EDITOR
Dharini Ganesh

ART EDITORS
Mridushmita Bose, Nobina Chakravorty

ASSISTANT ART EDITOR
Mitravinda V K

ASSISTANT EDITOR
Aashline R. Avarachan

SENIOR MANAGING EDITOR
Rohan Sinha

MANAGING ART EDITOR
Sudakshina Basu

DTP DESIGNERS
Rakesh Kumar, Mrinmoy Mazumdar,
Rajdeep Singh, Vikram Singh

PRODUCTION EDITOR
Jaypal Singh Chauhan

PRE-PRODUCTION MANAGER
Balwant Singh

PRODUCTION MANAGER
Pankaj Sharma

SENIOR JACKETS COORDINATOR
Priyanka Sharma Saddi

EDITORIAL HEAD
Glenda Fernandes

DESIGN HEAD
Malavika Talukder

original styling by
STUDIO 8

First published in Great Britain in 2023 by
Dorling Kindersley Limited
DK, One Embassy Gardens, 8 Viaduct Gardens,
London, SW11 7BW

The authorised representative in the EEA is
Dorling Kindersley Verlag GmbH. Arnulfstr. 124,
80636 Munich, Germany

Copyright © 2023 Dorling Kindersley Limited
A Penguin Random House Company
10 9 8 7 6 5 4 3 2 1
001–333661–Apr/2023

A CIP catalogue record for this book
is available from the British Library.
ISBN: 978-0-2415-9626-5

Printed and bound in Europe

For the curious
www.dk.com

This book was made with Forest Stewardship Council ™
certified paper – one small step in DK's commitment to a
sustainable future. For more information go to
www.dk.com/our-green-pledge

Leabharlann
Contae na Mídhe

CONTRIBUTORS

PROF MICHAEL BRONSKI, CONSULTANT EDITOR

Michael Bronski (he/him), an independent scholar, journalist, and writer, has been active in gay liberation as a political organizer, writer, publisher, and theorist since 1969. He is the author of numerous award-winning books, most recently *A Queer History of the United States for Young People* (2019). He is Professor of the Practice in Activism and Media in the Studies of Women, Gender and Sexuality at Harvard University, US.

DR KIT HEYAM, CONSULTANT EDITOR

Kit Heyam (they/he) is a writer and academic specializing in queer literature and history, as well as a trans awareness trainer and queer heritage practitioner. They are the author of *The Reputation of Edward II, 1305–1697: A Literary Transformation of History* (2020) and *Before We Were Trans: A New History of Gender* (2022).

PROF VALERIE TRAUB, CONSULTANT EDITOR

Valerie Traub (she/her) is a Distinguished University Professor of English and Women's Studies at the University of Michigan, US, where she teaches courses on 16th- and 17th-century sexuality, gender, and race in British literature and culture, as well as queer and feminist theory. Among her many books are *Thinking Sex with the Early Moderns* (2015).

JON ASTBURY

Jon Astbury (they/them) is a historian, curator, editor, and lecturer. They co-curated *Out and About!*, an exhibition of the Bishopsgate Institute's LGBTQ+ archives at the Barbican, London, in 2022. They have contributed to *The Architecture Book* (2022) in Dorling Kindersley's *Big Ideas Simply Explained* series.

HANNAH AYRES

Hannah Ayres (she/her) is a PhD researcher based in the Sociology Department at the University of Warwick, UK. She has taught on modules that discuss sexuality, gender, research methods, media, human nature, and more. Hannah has also helped to produce guidance on inclusive teaching for trans and gender-diverse students at the University of Warwick.

NICK CHERRYMAN

Nick Cherryman (they/them) holds an MA in Gender, Sexuality, and Culture from the University of Manchester, and are currently doing their PhD in Gender Studies. Their multidisciplinary approach explores gender, media, culture, and feminist/queer theory. Nick regularly performs as drag artist Ibi Profane, and can be found on Instagram at @IbiProfane.

ABIGAIL MITCHELL

Writer, editor, and cultural historian Abigail Mitchell (she/her) is a postgraduate researcher at the University of Southampton, UK, exploring the history of the Essex witch trials through the lens of queer theory. She has edited or contributed to several Dorling Kindersley titles, including *The Feminism Book* (2019), *The Black History Book* (2021), and *Migrations* (2022).

MELISSA MARTIN

Melissa Martin (she/her) is currently studying for a PhD in Social Science at Cardiff University, UK. Her research interests include the sociology of medicine, disability studies, queer and crip theories, ethnography, and participatory action research.

ADDITIONAL CONTRIBUTORS

Alishia Alexander, Prof Howard Chiang, Dr Kashish Dua, Dr Beverley Duguid, Dr Michael Erdman, Joy Evatt, Dr Nicole Froio, Dr Samar Habib, Prof Dominic Janes, Mie Astrup Jensen, Kahu Kutia, Ugla Stefanía Kristjönudóttir Jónsdóttir, Yentl Love, Ailish McAlpine-Green, Prof Robert Mills, Cheryl Morgan, Adebayo Quadry-Adekanbi, Prof Carlos Rojas, Prof Cherene Sherrard-Johnson, Prof Gregory D. Smithers, Prof Ruth Vanita, Dr Stephanie Yingyi Wang, Dr Jonathan Ward

CONTENTS

SUBCULTURES AND PUBLICITY

SEXOLOGY AND SEXUAL IDENTITIES

PROTESTS, PRIDE, AND COALITION

INTRODU

CTION

The words we now use for the LGBTQ+ community would be as alien to the people of the ancient world as the concept of an LGBTQ+ community itself. Historians looking for evidence of same-sex desires, gender variance, or intersex experiences have found it in many places – from art, poetry, and drama to diaries, letters, and court records – but portrayed completely differently from modern LGBTQ+ life. As American historian David Halperin has observed, for most historical societies the idea of a conceptual divide between the heterosexual and homosexual did not exist, making it problematic to describe people from the past in these terms.

Historians who study LGBTQ+ experience routinely encounter the same questions: how did past figures understand gender and sexuality? Can and should we give them the modern label of LGBTQ+, based on our interpretations of their actions? Historians are also required to present their findings under a certain burden of proof. How can we be sure that Alexander the Great and Hephaestion were not simply intimate friends? Does it matter whether the 19th-century American women living together in "Boston marriages" had what we would call

sex? The demand for "proof" of sex acts has excluded some people from LGBTQ+ history – particularly in debates about the erotic nature of women's "romantic friendship" and in identifying the history of asexuality. Yet contemporary scholarship has moved towards a broader idea of "what counts", such as American historian Judith Bennett's term "lesbian-like" to describe women whose primary relationships were to each other.

Archival challenges

Studying LGBTQ+ history comes with a particular challenge, familiar to anyone researching marginalized

Queerness has an especially vexed relationship to evidence. Historically, evidence of queerness has been used to penalize and discipline queer desires, connections, and acts.
José Esteban Muñoz
Cuban-American academic (1967–2013)

people. Traditional archives – museum collections, court records, library archives – can present a skewed picture of the past, as LGBTQ+ histories are typically only mentioned in relation to prosecution, scandal, or supposed abnormality. This is no accident, as over time such institutional archives have been curated by societies hostile to the existence of LGBTQ+ people. Prior to the 19th century, much of the extant evidence was created not by LGBTQ+ people themselves, but by others who condemn – and obscure – them. The historian must learn to "read against the grain", finding the silences in the archive into which queer possibility can be read. Many LGBTQ+ historians prefer to call their work "queer history", because "queer" suggests a challenge to the status quo, a breaking with tradition, and a resistance to rigid definitions and fixed identities.

What is LGBTQ+ history?

A number of countries around the world now celebrate LGBTQ+ History Month, including the UK and Hungary in February; Germany and Cuba in May; and the US, Canada, and Australia in October. These celebrations usually centre around the recent history of

LGBTQ+ rights movements, and shine a spotlight on historical LGBTQ+ figures. However, the scope of LGBTQ+ history is far beyond what such celebrations could convey. It is a potentially infinite project, full of endless avenues for exploration and interpretation. It is, importantly, not a story of linear progress from intolerance to equality, no matter how politically useful such a claim might be. Crucially, LGBTQ+ history is not a single story at all – it is many conflicting and contrasting histories that overlap and interact in surprising ways.

This book is not an exhaustive catalogue of important LGBTQ+ stories, but a cross-section over time and place that seeks to move away from histories of individuals to expose larger societal structures and ideologies. It includes queer theory as part of LGBTQ+ history because it not only explains how we have come to understand sexuality and gender in the 20th and 21st centuries, but also has provided a theoretical underpinning for much recent political activism.

Transing history

No book of LGBTQ+ history would be complete without the stories of transgender, intersex, and other

The longing for community across time is a critical feature of queer historical experience.
Heather Love
American queer theorist

gender-nonconforming people. They can be complicated histories: accounts of cross-dressing; of living as another gender; of gender deviance; and of those who were considered between sexes or a third gender are often tied up both in each other and in stories of same-sex desire. For earlier histories, this book describes such gender subversion as "transing gender" to indicate how people were acting in relation to gender norms, rather than giving them an ahistorical label. As with the history of sexuality, we aim to shift the lens for transing gender from individual identities to wider social practices. There is considerable variation in these practices around the world, many of which were –

and in places still are – threatened and prosecuted by religious or political forces.

Changing terminologies

Over time, people have used a number of words to describe what we now call LGBTQ+ experiences – from sodomites and sapphists to mollies, tribades, urnings, and *berdaches*. This book also uses the modern language of homosexual, lesbian, transgender, non-binary, cisgender, and queer (used in its academic contexts, or where it is a person's chosen identity), as well as terms from non-English contexts. We describe transgender people as assigned male or female at birth and presenting/living as men/women. Our use of these terms reflect the differences in how we conceive gender and sexuality from people of the past, but aim not to obscure the things that we have in common.

Many of the historians who study this history are themselves LGBTQ+. The pursuit of queer history is, therefore, often a search for ancestry and legitimacy, a need for proof that LGBTQ+ people have, as the protest chant goes, always been here. What American historian Carolyn Dinshaw has called a "queer desire for history" is at the very heart of this project. ∎

EARLY EXPLOR

BEFORE 1300 CE

ATIONS

Niankhkhnum and Khnumhotep, both seemingly men, are buried together like a married couple.

Sappho is born on Lesbos; her love poetry makes the island's name synonymous with same-sex desire.

A Roman court case shows that the castrated *galli* are considered neither men nor women.

***c. 2400* BCE**

***c. 630* BCE**

77 BCE

***c. 2000* BCE**

336–323 BCE

7–1 BCE

The Sumerian *Epic of Gilgamesh* depicts a homoerotic relationship between its hero, Gilgamesh, and Enkidu.

Alexander the Great rules the kingdom of Macedon, with his beloved Hephaestion serving as his general.

Emperor Ai of Han rules in China; he lavishes gifts upon his male favourite, Dong Xian.

A ny attempt to identify the first lesbian, or gay man, or transgender person to ever live would be both unsuccessful and unenlightening. If we assume that sexuality and gender are, at least in some way, innate, it stands to reason that humans have always had the potential for same-sex desires, and have wanted to express their gender in ways that did not match their presumed sex. The understandings the first humans had about their gender and sexuality are completely out of our reach; even archaeological discoveries of seemingly same-sex lovers buried together, or "female" bodies buried in "male" poses, can only tell us so much. Our modern interest in discovering traces of LGBTQ+ existence can lead us down ahistorical paths. In 2021, for

example, news reports described the finding of 1,000-year-old remains in Finland as proof of "non-binary" ancestors, when researchers had actually found a body with intersex characteristics.

Types of evidence

Some archaeological finds from the ancient world have suggested that same-sex partnerships existed and that society might have accepted these partnerships. One of the earliest examples is ancient Egyptian manicurists Niankhkhnum and Khnumhotep, buried together around 2400 BCE and depicted like a married couple in their tomb painting. We also have examples of legendary pairs from mythology, who were depicted as homoerotic partners or even unequivocally as lovers – such as

Enkidu and Gilgamesh from the Sumerian *Epic of Gilgamesh* and the ancient Greek heroes from the *Iliad*, Achilles and Patroclus.

Some of the most famous examples of homoeroticism in the ancient world come from court records of male rulers, for whom it seems to have been acceptable to have relationships with male favourites. This is particularly true for the Han emperors of China (206 BCE–220 CE), but court records also name Abbasid caliph al-Amin (r. 809–813), who preferred the company of enslaved men to women. Ancient poetry and treatises are another key source of evidence, from the poems of the Greek poet Sappho to the Indian sex manual, the *Kama Sutra*, which describes sexual acts between male and female same-sex couples,

The apostle **Paul's Letter to the Romans** condemns homoerotic sexual relations as unnatural.

Antinous, beloved by the Roman emperor Hadrian, drowns in the Nile; Hadrian creates a cult dedicated to his beauty.

The Latin "**sodomia**" is used for the first time by French theologian Hincmar of Reims, describing "unnatural" acts.

57 CE

130 CE

860 CE

c. **100–** *c.* **200** CE

786–809 CE

1277

The *Kama Sutra* is written in India, featuring sex acts between same-sex partners.

Abbasid caliph Al-Rashid rules from Baghdad; his court poet Abu Nuwas is known for his homoerotic poems.

The first recorded execution for sodomy in Western Europe takes place in Basel (now in Switzerland).

---

as well as marriage-like bonds between male partners, called *parasparaparigraham*.

These ancient partnerships, despite appearing to be what we would now class as homosexual, were viewed in different ways. In ancient Greece, the male partners were expected to be between an older and a younger man, with the younger taking a passive sexual role. Similarly, in ancient Rome, a distinction was made between the active, penetrating partner, and a man who was passive or receptive. The former was acceptable, the latter considered shameful.

Understanding gender
Ancient societies explored gender in a variety of ways. Some of their own terminology seems to convey the idea of crossing gender lines, or existing outside a binary gender system – as in the "men–women" temple workers of the Sumerian goddess Inanna (who could, according to hymns, change one gender to another), the "woman-boy" of ancient Egypt, and the "third nature" in the *Kama Sutra*. These descriptions seem to focus on lived gender expression rather than a person's genitalia.

Conversely, the ancients also had a lot to say about sex organs. Both ancient Greece and Rome built statues to the intersex god/dess Hermaphroditos, and Rome in particular was familiar with ideas of changing sex. Roman physicians wrote about what we would now call intersex conditions; priests called *galli* underwent castration and lived as women; and the emperor Nero supposedly hired a surgeon to operate on his new wife Sabina, who was assigned male at birth.

Religious persecution
The advent of Christianity had a far-reaching effect on attitudes towards what it considered sexual sin. In the 1st century CE, the apostle Paul's Letter to the Romans condemned homoerotic lust, and from about the 4th century, Christian thinkers began to characterize the Biblical fall of Sodom and Gomorrah as the result of same-sex behaviour. By the 5th century, the Church had begun to condemn sex outside marriage, and by the 12th century, same-sex intercourse was being prosecuted in Christian kingdoms as a crime against nature. By the early 13th century, this crime was punishable by death. ∎

WHEN HEROES LOVE
THE EARLIEST EVIDENCE FOR LGBTQ+ PEOPLE (*c.*2400 BCE)

IN CONTEXT

FOCUS
Archival challenges

BEFORE
***c.*2600 BCE** Ur-Nanshe, master musician of Mari, ancient Sumer, is depicted with breasts, wearing a fringed robe.

AFTER
700 BCE The *Iliad*, the ancient Greek epic that includes the story of Achilles and Patroclus, is written by a poet traditionally named as Homer.

***c.*400 BCE** The Greek historian Ctesias writes the *Persica*, which blames the downfall of the neo-Assyrian empire on the "effeminacy" of King Sardanapalus (Ashurbanipal).

1849 The *Epic of Gilgamesh* is found in the library of Ashurbanipal at Ninevah.

1964 In Saqqara, Egypt, workmen discover the tomb of Niankhkhnum and Khnumhotep.

Evidence of **people's relationships and behaviour** in early history is open to **many different interpretations**.

Historians tend to demand a **higher standard of proof for LGBTQ+ history** than for history of heterosexual behaviour and cisgender experience.

Until recently, the possibility of **same-sex relationships or gender transgression** in antiquity was **not even considered**.

Looking at the **archaeological and written evidence** again, it is possible to interpret it as evidence of **same-sex behaviour and gender nonconformity**.

It is difficult to know what ancient people thought about issues such as gender and sexuality, from the limited evidence available. Historians have had to base their understanding on these sparse archaeological findings.

In the 15th century, when Europeans began colonizing large parts of the world, they found many cultures had flexibility around sexuality and gender. It is likely that this behaviour had existed for centuries, though this is hard to prove without written records.

Heroic pairings

There are many ancient tales about men who were close friends and showed each other great affection,

See also: Gender and sexuality in ancient Greece 20–23 ▪ Gender and sexuality in ancient Rome 30–35 ▪ Male–male love poetry 80–81 ▪ Defining "homosexual" and "heterosexual" 106–07

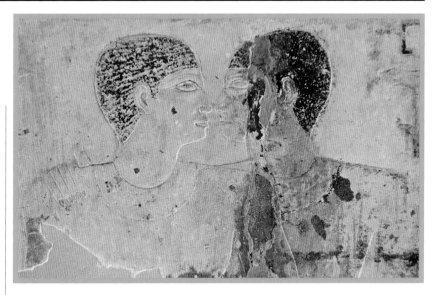

Niankhkhnum and Khnumhotep embrace in this wall painting in their tomb at Saqqara. An image such as this would usually only feature in the tomb of a married couple.

such as Gilgamesh and Enkidu, legendary heroes from the Sumerian *Epic of Gilgamesh*, ancient Greek warriors Achilles and Patroclus from Homer's *Iliad*, and David and Jonathan from the Hebrew Bible. However, none of these stories mentions the exact nature of the men's relationship.

More specific evidence concerns Niankhkhnum and Khnumhotep, two ancient Egyptians buried together in Saqqara in about 2400 BCE. Manicurists to King Nyuserre Ini, the two men are depicted in an intimate embrace. Many historians believe they were in a romantic relationship; many others believe they were brothers.

Understandings of gender

Even when written sources do exist, translation can be problematic. The Second Book of Kings in the Bible tells how King Josiah expelled "male prostitutes" from the temple of the goddess Asherah. These may have been transfeminine priests like the Roman *galli* in the temples of Cybele. However, Christian translators may have sought to portray all other religions as sex-obsessed and probably had little understanding of gender fluidity. The Hebrew word *qedešah* has been translated as sex worker, but this is now disputed; they may have been cisgender men with no sexual function in the cult.

The *Maxims of Ptahhotep* is a guide to etiquette for Egyptian men dated about 1991 BCE. It advises readers to avoid relations with an effeminate boy. A literal translation of the Egyptian text is "woman–boy". Similar terms appear in the work of the Sumerian princess and High Priestess of the Moon, Enheduanna. She describes the goddess Inanna as having the power to turn men into women and vice versa. We cannot be sure what she means, but we have evidence that Inanna's temple workers, the *gala*, were employed as singers and spoke a dialect usually reserved for women. In the archives of the British Museum in London, UK, there is a fragment of a statue of a *gala* dating from *c.* 2000 BCE. Its inscription reads "Silimabzuta, the man–woman of Inanna".

The Inca language, Quecha, has a similar term, *quariwarmi*, which translates as men–women. We don't know whether it describes gender, sexuality, or both. But these cultures all recognized that some people existed outside gender norms. ▪

You loved him and embraced him as a wife; and it is he who will repeatedly save you.
Epic of Gilgamesh
Gilgamesh's mother interpreting her son's dreams about Enkidu

To turn man into woman and woman into man are yours, Inanna.
Enheduanna
"Passionate Inanna"

NEVER BURY MY BONES APART FROM YOURS, ACHILLES

GENDER AND SEXUALITY IN ANCIENT GREECE (c. 800–30 BCE)

IN CONTEXT

FOCUS
Early evidence

BEFORE
c. 2000 BCE The Sumerian
Epic of Gilgamesh describes
a homoerotic friendship
between Gilgamesh and
the wild man Enkidu.

AFTER
1st century CE The Warren
Cup, a silver Roman drinking
vessel produced in the eastern
Mediterranean, depicts two
male same-sex couples.

5th century CE Letters from
monastic communities in Egypt
refer to concerns about women
members showing "physical
desire" for other women.

1973 Two AMAB skeletons
dating to c. 800 BCE, and lying
in an intimate embrace, are
found at Teppe Hasanlu, Iran.

The first work of literature in the pre-Classical period of ancient Greece was Homer's *Iliad*, written around 800 BCE. Central to this tale is the relationship between the legendary warriors Achilles and Patroclus.

Five centuries later, under Alexander the Great, Greek territory included modern-day Egypt, the Middle East, Persia (now Iran), and the Himalayas. After his death in 323 BCE, the empire split into four Hellenistic kingdoms. The kingdoms sustained Greek influence in the ancient world for centuries, even after the Roman conquest. It was the ancient Greeks who first defined "democracy", in the Classical period (510–323 BCE), though this extended only to male citizens; women and

See also: The earliest evidence for LGBTQ+ people 18–19 ▪ Sappho of Lesbos 24–27 ▪ Gender and sexuality in ancient Rome 30–35 ▪ Intersex rights 48–53 ▪ Same-sex narratives in Urdu poetry 96–97

Ancient Greek pederastic relationships

Younger man
Known as the *eromenos* ("the beloved")
Passive partner in the relationship

Older man
Known as the *erastes* ("the lover")
Active partner in the relationship

enslaved people were not able to participate in civic life. There were many enslaved people of many races and ethnicities at this time, in Greek households and labouring for the state. In the home, enslaved people of any gender were seen as acceptable sexual partners for the men who enslaved them.

Pre-Classical desire

Evidence for the acceptability of same-sex relationships between non-enslaved women as well as men includes a series of odes written by the poet Alcman in the 7th century BCE. Performed by choirs of unmarried young women in Sparta, the poems celebrate the beauty and erotic allure of their fellow girls, and of older women, suggesting that female homoerotic desire was widely recognized. This is supported by an image on a plate from Thera, Greece (*c.* 500 BCE) in which two women exchange garlands, while one

touches the other's chin (a "chin chuck") – common depictions of desire used for both different-sex and same-sex couples.

Sappho (*c.* 630–*c.* 570 BCE), who wrote poetry about same-sex desire between women, was known all over ancient Greece. In the 3rd century BCE, the Hellenistic poet Nossis acknowledges both Aphrodite as her patron goddess and Sappho as her inspiration.

By the sixth century BCE, the adherents of the cult of Orpheus, a famous poet and musician in Greek myth, popularized erotic love between men throughout the Greek world. The cult idealized an afterlife full of homosocial and homoerotic interactions for its male followers. Frescoes at tombs across the Greek world appear to support this belief, with paintings from the "Tomb of the Diver" in Paestum, Italy, depicting same-sex couples in a variety of intimate poses. The couples followed

the practice of pederasty – a term derived from the Greek *paides* (children) and *eros* (love) – with one man older (and bearded), and the other man younger (and unbearded).

The concept of pederasty is a complex and debated aspect of Greek civic life. Sources generally agree that a pederastic relationship was shared between an adult man, known as the *erastes*, and a male youth, known as the *eromenos*. Like a teacher and his pupil, the relationship was seen to aid the social transition from youth to man and citizen. Ancient Greek literature suggests a young man could be desired as an *eromenos* from the onset of puberty, similar to the age at which girls were thought suitable for marriage. Some sources maintain that by the time they had developed a full beard, young men were considered too old to be sexually attractive to other males, with the most desirable age being 16.

Sexual identities

In Classical Greece, the modern idea of fixed sexual identities such as "gay" or "straight" did not exist. »

Nothing is sweeter than desire. All other delights are second. From my mouth I spit even honey.
Nossis
Fragment of a poem

People may have considered an act "same-sex" or "opposite-sex", but individuals were not identified in terms of these acts, even if their preference was clear. Men were expected to marry and father children, but outside marriage there was little discrimination between sex with women or with boys. Men retained respectability so long as they were the "active" participant (penetrator), regardless of who they had sex with. A man who took the passive role (was penetrated) was thought "womanlike" and ridiculed.

In the few Greek texts we have concerning sex between women, male disapproval stems from women being "active participants" during intercourse. This was thought to transgress gender norms.

Achilles and Patroclus

In male same-sex social life, relationships often showed no real separation between platonic (a friendship not involving sex) and

A marble statue depicting the god/dess Hermaphroditos displays breasts and a penis. Part of an ancient Greek cult, there were many similar statues, some also bearded.

erotic intimacy. While the original text of Homer's *Iliad* does not make the nature of the shared bond between the warriors Achilles and Patroclus explicit, the deep affection between the pair led ancient philosophers to assume that the two shared a sexual relationship.

In a surviving fragment of *Myrmidons*, one of a trilogy of plays about Achilles by the dramatist Aeschylus (*c.*525–*c.*456 BCE), Achilles mourned the death of Patroclus by reflecting on the "sweet intercourse of thighs" that the two shared. Philosophers of the time debated not whether the two were sexually intimate, but rather which role in their pederastic relationship each of the characters played – *eromenos* or *erastes*.

Plato on sexuality

The ancient Greek philosopher Plato (*c.*428–347 BCE) writes in his *Symposium*, a collection of drinking-party speeches on the nature of love, that Achilles and Patroclus were lovers but debates the roles they took – *eromenos* or *erastes*. He goes on to discuss the relationship between the Athenian Pausanias and his lover, the poet Agathon. While originally in a pederastic relationship, they continued as lovers even after the younger Agathon reached maturity. This practice also appears in the work of Aristotle (384–322 BCE), the Greek philosopher and pupil of Plato, where he claimed that if a boy has a pleasing character as well as looks, a pair might continue the relationship. In Plato's *Symposium*, the Greek comic playwright Aristophanes

Depicted with a beard, Patroclus is the *erastes* to his youthful *eromenos* Achilles in this image on a 5th-century drinking vessel. Achilles is pictured tending to Patroclus's wound.

explains sexual preferences with an allegory in which humans were originally made up of two heads, four arms, four legs, and two sets of genitals. These were either male–male, male–female, or female–female. Fearing their power, Zeus, King of the gods, split them in half. Humans have searched for their original other half ever since, leading to different sexual preferences.

In Plato's *Laws*, however, Plato criticizes same-sex intercourse as prioritizing pleasure above self-

Yea, by Ganymedes of the fair locks, O Zeus in heaven, thou too hast loved.
Callimachus
Ancient Greek poet, 3rd century BCE

control, contradicting the natural order where sex is between women and men in order to procreate.

Mythological tales

The stories that the ancient Greeks told about their gods and goddesses demonstrate an awareness of same-sex attraction for men and women. In fact, all major male deities – apart from Ares, god of war – are depicted with male lovers in various myths. One of the most famous is Zeus and Ganymede, a Trojan prince. Zeus was so infatuated that he appeared in the form of an eagle and flew Ganymede up to Mount Olympus, so that the prince could be by his side for ever as a cup bearer. He remains visible in the stars to this day, represented by the constellation Ganymede and the astrological sign Aquarius.

Stories of romantic relationships between women are less common, but the seduction of the nymph Callisto by Zeus was interpreted in Classical and Hellenistic literature as evidence of Callisto's sapphic inclinations. When his advances were refused, Zeus disguised himself as the goddess Artemis, after which Callisto willingly became intimate with her/him.

Romantic and sexual relationships between military heroes also feature in tales of the Sacred Band of Thebes, a legendary military unit from the fourth century BCE. The unit was allegedly formed of 150 male couples, and credited with victories against Sparta's far larger forces. While reports of the unit may not be historically accurate, homoerotic relationships between soldiers were well known, and may have been encouraged to forge loyalty, making the existence of the Sacred Band more plausible.

Gender nonconformity

Greek mythology also explored the concept of gender identity. Statues of Aphrodite from Cyprus suggest the existence of a cult of a "bearded Aphrodite", or Aphroditos, in which the goddess is depicted with breasts, a penis, and sometimes a beard. In the Classical Period, depictions of the god/dess Hermaphroditos were popular; today they would probably be identified as intersex.

The god Dionysus was also the basis of a cult – said to have been raised as a girl, he is also described as "womanlike", and wearing "women's garments", in a display of early gender nonconformity.

… inflame the soul, the heart, the liver, the spirit of Gorgonia … with love and affection for Sophia.
Fragment of a Hellenistic spell

Petitioning the gods

In 30 BCE, Hellenistic Egypt came under Roman rule, yet its Greek culture endured. Archaeologists have discovered magic charms from the second century CE intended to influence romantic relationships, including same-sex partners. Written on lead or papyrus, the spells named a deity, often a goddess, and the effect the charm should have on the victim. Spells to ensnare same-sex partners include a fragment commissioned by a man called Serapiakos, in which he asks that the heart and soul of a man named Ammoneios will burn for him. ∎

Alexander the Great embraces Hephaestion for a kiss in this 17th-century tapestry hanging in Hampton Court Palace, UK.

Alexander and Hephaestion

Alexander the Great (356–323 BCE) was ruler of the ancient Greek kingdom of Macedon – one of the largest empires in history. Modern historians are divided over the nature of his relationship with his friend Hephaestion, though their intimacy is clear from ancient sources. According to the historian Arrian (c. 86–160 CE), they placed garlands on the alleged grave of Achilles and Patroclus, symbolizing their romantic relationship, and

Alexander told the Persion Queen Sisygambis that "[Hephaestion] too is Alexander". A letter attributed to the philosopher Diogenes (c. 404–323 BCE) accuses Alexander of being "held fast by Hephaestion's thighs".

On Hephaestion's death, Alexander wept for days over his beloved's body and extinguished the Persian sacred flame, an act usually reserved for the death of the king.

YOU WHOM OF ALL WOMEN I MOST DESIRE

SAPPHO OF LESBOS (c. 630–c. 570 BCE)

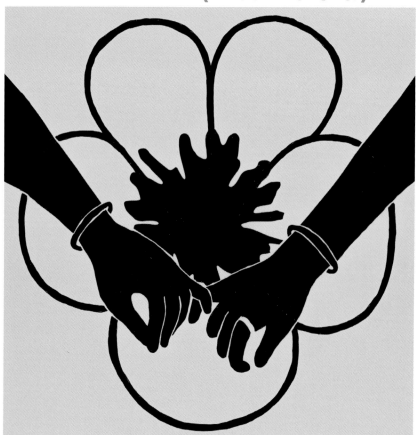

The majority of the works composed by Sappho of Lesbos – one of ancient Greece's most celebrated lyric poets – are lost to us. The Library of Alexandria in Egypt is believed to have contained nine volumes of her work, but fewer than 1,000 lines survive, mostly in fragments. Reasons for the loss may include fire caused by Roman forces besieged in the city in 48 BCE, destruction by the Christian Church after the 4th century CE due to the poetry's erotic imagery, and the natural decay of the papyrus on which it was written.

Although only one complete poem remains – the 28-line "Ode to Aphrodite", addressed

See also: Gender and sexuality in ancient Greece 20–23 ▪ Early modern lesbianism 74–79 ▪ Same-sex narratives in Urdu poetry 96–97 ▪ Sapphism 98 ▪ The diaries of Anne Lister 102–03

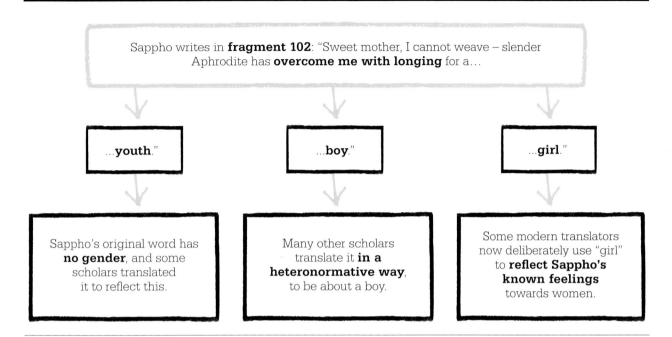

Sappho writes in **fragment 102**: "Sweet mother, I cannot weave – slender Aphrodite has **overcome me with longing** for a…

…**youth**."

…**boy**."

…**girl**."

Sappho's original word has **no gender**, and some scholars translated it to reflect this.

Many other scholars translate it **in a heteronormative way**, to be about a boy.

Some modern translators now deliberately use "girl" to **reflect Sappho's known feelings** towards women.

to the Greek goddess of love and beauty – Sappho's name has lived on, becoming synonymous with love between women. Sappho's legacy lies not only in her poetic works but in her status as an icon for lesbians around the world.

Lesbian origins

The term "lesbian" is derived from Lesbos – an island close to the west coast of present-day Turkey – and is the adjective used to describe its inhabitants. However, the word's etymology as a description of sexuality is complicated. The ancient Greek verb *lesbiazein* meant "to defile" – or, more accurately, "to act like a woman of Lesbos". According to the Dutch scholar Erasmus (*c*. 1466–1536), the women of that island were known for sexual licentiousness, and in particular for engaging in fellatio; a "lesbian" was therefore someone who engaged in this act.

While Sappho's name is now closely identified with lesbianism, many scholars would find it anachronistic to apply that label to the poet – "sapphic" and "lesbian" were not used as terms for women-loving women until at least the 17th century. In Sappho's lifetime, sexuality and sexual identity were not viewed along gender lines; instead of thinking of people as

Someone will remember us, I say; even in another time.
Sappho
Fragment 147

"homosexual" or "heterosexual" (both 19th-century terms), they were concerned with whether a person – masculine or feminine – took a more sexually active or sexually passive role when engaging in sexual acts.

Sapphic verses

Sappho's work is known for her celebration of female beauty, and for its declarations of love for other women. In one string of fragments, she sings of a lover named Atthis, who she loved long ago. In fragment 16, she yearns to see her former lover Anactoria – "her lovely step, her sparkling glance, and her face".

Few real men are mentioned by name in Sappho's lyrics – most of the male figures are mythological. By contrast, Sappho gives the personal names of 14 women, some of whom seem to have been actual Lesbos residents. Sappho herself is not the only woman on Lesbos to experience same-sex desires. In »

> Eros the melter of limbs (now again) stirs me – sweetbitter unmanageable creature who steals in.
> **Sappho**
> **Fragment 130**

Sappho embraces fellow poet Erinna (left) in a garden on Lesbos, from an 1864 painting by Simeon Solomon – a gay British artist whose work explored both male homosexuality and lesbianism.

fragment 213, she describes Archeanassa and Gorgo, both women, as "yoke-mates" (wives).

Sappho's verses were lauded in her own lifetime, after which they they first formed part of an Athenian collection (around the 5th century BCE) and later an Alexandrian collection (in the 3rd or 2nd century BCE), as the Egyptian capital built a repository of Greek literature. Sappho was praised by the 4th–5th-century Greek philosopher Plato, who described her as "Sappho the lovely", in reference to her poetry. From at least the 5th century BCE, images of Sappho appeared on vases, often with her

holding a lyre – a traditional depiction of a poet. She also became a popular character for Greek playwrights, with at least five comedies written about her in the 4th century BCE. In these works, however, Sappho was often lampooned as having an excessive sexual interest in men.

A changing legacy

Sappho's reputation in antiquity is so diverse that some scholars believe there were two women by

that name on Lesbos. While Sappho the poet was celebrated, some writers also told of a Sappho who was a *hetaira* (a courtesan), associating her with sexual licentiousness. Over the next millennium, the depiction of

Sappho of Lesbos

Born to an aristocratic family in Mytilene, on the Greek island of Lesbos, around 630 BCE, Sappho grew to be a celebrated lyric poet – someone who sang verses accompanied by a lyre (a harp-like instrument). There are ancient allusions to Sappho having a husband, although he is never named. One name does appear in the 10th-century CE *Suda*, a Byzantine lexicon – a kind of encyclopedia – but only as a ribald joke. It calls him "Kerkylas who came from Andros", which translates as "Mister Penis, hailing from the island of Man".

Many historians also believe that Sappho was a mother. In fragment 132, she mentions a girl called Cleïs (also thought to be the name of Sappho's mother), who is described with a Greek word that could mean "daughter", "child", or "slave".

Sappho's date and cause of death are uncertain. The 4th-century BCE Greek dramatist Menander probably created the legend that she died by suicide, jumping from the White Rock of Leukas because of her unrequited love for the mythological ferryman Phaon.

Sappho varied in any given period. The diverse biographical strands included her suicide due to unrequited love for a man, her heterosexual whorishness, and her lesbianism. In the 1st century BCE, the Roman poet Ovid brought those different strands together when he included Sappho in his *Heroides*: poems in letter form about (mostly legendary) women spurned by the men they loved. The poem "Sappho to Phaon" describes Sappho's feelings for women as well as men. In the letter, she foregoes her previous love of women when she meets and falls for Phaon, a mythical ferryman given youth and beauty by the goddess Aphrodite.

During the early medieval period in Europe, Sappho's popularity waned, but the Renaissance led to a renewed interest in her work, with Sappho celebrated as a talented female poet. French writer Christine de Pizan praises her wisdom and grace in the feminist *Le Livre de la cité des dames* (*The Book of the City of Ladies*), published in 1405. She was also identified as a "tribade" – the Roman name for a lesbian – in 15th-century Latin commentaries

on Venetian editions of *Heroides*. This association with sex between women was gradually suppressed as vernacular translations began to replace Latin and Greek texts.

The image of Sappho continued to change to fit the political and intellectual mores of the period. In the 18th century, she was cast as a heterosexual woman, whose embrace of her sexual desires proved her downfall. At the same time, the terms "sapphic" and "lesbian" were used to identify and condemn female–female sex.

During the 19th century, some European Classical scholars countered the homosexual reading of Sappho by depicting a chaste version. German scholar Ulrich von Wilamowitz-Moellendorff imagined Sappho as a school mistress – a teacher surrounded by students for whom she felt only platonic affection. At the same time, many British female writers – among them Christina Rossetti, Felicia Hemans, and Caroline Norton – found inspiration in Sappho, but as a woman spurned by her (male) lover.

Reclaiming Sappho
At the end of the 19th century, a growing "sapphist" movement began to revere the lyric poet as a lover of women and reclaim her as a paragon of lesbian desire. This aspect was picked up by lesbian artists in the early 20th century, such as the writer Radclyffe Hall, who, in her poem "Ode to Sappho" calls Sappho "Immortal Lesbian!".

Sappho was claimed by the feminist movement of the late 1960s and 1970s, and feminist

Papyrus fragment 44 of Sappho's poetry describes the wedding of the Greek mythological figures Hector and Andromache. It was found in an ancient rubbish dump and published in 1914.

Beloved Lesbian! we would dare to claim
By that same tear fond union with thy lot;
Yet 'tis enough, if when we breathe thy name
Thy soul but listens, and forgets us not.
Radclyffe Hall
"Ode to Sappho", 1908

Classical scholars began to revisit her work from new perspectives. More and more feminist academics have rejected the 19th-century myth of Sappho as a pure schoolmistress, and lesbian feminist poets and writers, such as American Rita Mae Brown and British novelist Jeanette Winterson, have cited her in their own work as a role model, both as a lesbian and a poet.

New papyrus fragments of Sappho's work are still being discovered. However, opinion remains divided over the provenance of the most recent fragments – from the "Brothers Poem", published in 2014.

Interest in Sappho and her work remains high both in academic and LGBTQ+ circles, with "sapphic" still used as a popular label for women and non-binary and trans people who are attracted to women. The sapphic pride flag has pink stripes at the top and bottom and a violet in the centre – the flower being associated with Sappho, who, in fragment 94, describes her former lesbian lover as wearing "crowns of violets and roses". ∎

THE PASSION OF THE CUT SLEEVE

FAVOURITES IN HAN CHINA (206 BCE–220 CE)

IN CONTEXT

FOCUS
Same-sex imperial favourites

BEFORE
4th century BCE Alexander the Great and the nobleman Hephaestion emulate the Greek heroes (and lovers) Achilles and Patroclus.

AFTER
1307–1312 CE England's Edward II loses his nobles' support after favouring Piers Gaveston, said to be his lover.

c. 1579–1625 Scotland and England's James VI and I has relationships with three of his male courtiers.

1624–63 Ana Njinga of Ndongo and Matamba (now Angola) rules as a king, wears men's clothes, and keeps a harem of wives.

c. 1644–62 Christina of Sweden dresses in men's clothes and has an intimate relationship with a countess.

Emperor Ai of Han is **in love with his male favourite**, Dong Xian.

One day, **the emperor awakes** to find Dong Xian still **sleeping on top of his sleeve**.

Rather than disturb Dong Xian when he has to leave, Emperor Ai **has the sleeve cut off**.

The "cut sleeve" becomes a **symbol of devotion**, and later a term describing homosexual love in China.

One of the China's oldest euphemisms for homosexuality, the "passion of the cut sleeve", dates back to the Han dynasty of 206 BCE–220 CE. This was considered the golden age of ancient China and, through the development of the Chinese civil service and the Silk Road, it laid foundations for later dynasties' cultural and economic growth. The story of the passion of the cut sleeve dates to the reign of Emperor Ai of Han (or Aidi), who ascended to the imperial throne in 7 BCE at the age of 20.

According to the *Hanshu* ("Book of Han"), Aidi had a male favourite named Dong Xian, whom he loved. Dong Xian was 19 years old, a court official, and married to a woman when he met the emperor, but none of that proved an obstacle. Dong's family soon moved into the imperial palace at Chang'an (modern Xi'an) to live alongside Aidi and his wife. Aidi ordered

See also: Homoeroticism and the French Renaissance 60–61 ▪ Gender transgression in modern China 134–35 ▪ LGBTQ+ activism in Asia 254–55 ▪ Chinese *lala* communities 276–77

In this 1651 illustration by Chinese artist Chen Hongshou, Aidi has his sleeve cut off to avoid waking his lover, Dong Xian.

luxurious new quarters to be built for his beloved, and showered him with expensive gifts.

According to the *Hanshu*, Aidi woke one day to find Dong sleeping on his sleeve, and decided to have it cut off rather than pull it away. After this sign of great devotion, it became fashionable for men at court to wear a cut sleeve.

Dong and Aidi

Aidi favoured Dong by promoting him to commander of the armed forces, one of the most powerful positions within the imperial regime. The emperor also gave titles to Dong's family. When he became seriously ill, the dying Aidi even attempted to name Dong as his heir, but this was seen as an abuse of his imperial power.

Aidi's advisers and the Grand Empress Dowager Wang (the mother of Aidi's predecessor) instead conspired to install her nephew, Wang Mang, beginning the short-lived Xin dynasty (9–23 CE). Dong Xian and his wife died by suicide, either at the prompting of the new regime or in fear of it.

Han tradition

Aidi was not the only Han emperor to have a male favourite. The position was common enough that several were recorded in a chapter of Han historian Sima Qian's *Shiji* ("Records of the Grand Historian") for their skills and accomplishments. According to Sima Qian, Emperor Gaozu (r. 202–195 BCE), the first Han ruler, favoured a "young boy" named Ji, while Emperor Hui (r. 195–188 BCE) had a favourite named Hong. Ji and Hong were both included in the chronicle for their good looks, and for the way other men at court tried to emulate their fashions.

Emperor Wen (r. 180–157 BCE) had three favourites. Two were eunuchs – Zhao Tan, who was skilled in observing the stars, and Beigong Bozi, "a worthy and affectionate man" – while the third, Deng Tong, was a boatman who had appeared to the emperor in a dream. The emperor searched for the man, found him, and showed

> Boys… clad like officials… were constantly in the emperor's bedchamber.
> **Sima Qian**
> **Chinese historian (*c.* 145–87 BCE), describing Emperor Hui's favourites**

him favour; in return, Deng Tong reportedly nursed the ailing ruler through his illness by sucking the pus from his wounds.

Aidi was the last Western Han emperor, but the dynasty did not end with his reign. After the Xin interregnum, the Han capital moved from Chang'an to Luoyang under the Eastern Han (25–220 CE). Male favourites became less prominent under the Tang dynasty, and ceased to be recorded after the end of the Song dynasty in the 13th century, due partly to religious influences from the West. ▪

The bitten peach

An even older story than that of the cut sleeve, the euphemism of the "bitten peach" is also used in China.

According to a cautionary tale by philosopher and statesman Han Fei, Mizi Xia was a beautiful and well-loved courtier of Duke Ling of Wey (r. 534–492 BCE). One day, while walking in the garden, he bit into a peach; finding it delicious, he offered the rest to the duke. At the time, the duke saw this as a loving gesture, but after he fell out of love with Mizi Xia, he saw the gift of the half-eaten peach as an insult.

Whether or not Mizi Xia ever existed, his name later became synonymous with male beauty, and the bitten peach became an allusion to homosexual love.

EVERY
WOMAN'S MAN
AND EVERY
MAN'S WOMAN

GENDER AND SEXUALITY IN ANCIENT ROME (*c.*240 BCE—476 CE)

IN CONTEXT

FOCUS
Acceptance of sexual differences

BEFORE
4th–5th centuries BCE In ancient Greece, pederasty – intimate relations between men and adolescent boys – develops as part of the education of young men.

AFTER
15th–16th centuries The rediscovery of the Classical world during the Renaissance leads to a greater awareness of same-sex relations.

1969 Italian film director Federico Fellini makes *Satyricon* – based on a work of the same name by the Roman author Petronius – which openly features male same-sex attraction.

2018 In London, busts of Hadrian and Antinous form part of the British Museum's "Desire, love, identity: LGBTQ histories trail".

Juventius, to kiss your eyes is sweet as honey. I will not be satisfied with thirty million kisses.
Catullus

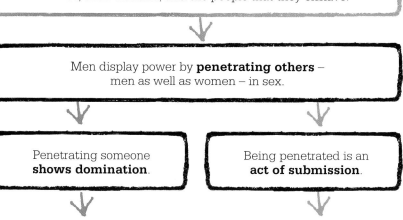

Roman male citizens have **complete power** over their wives, their children, and the people that they enslave.

⬇

Men display power by **penetrating others** – men as well as women – in sex.

⬇ ⬇

Penetrating someone **shows domination**.

Being penetrated is an **act of submission**.

⬇ ⬇

A powerful man penetrates but should never be penetrated.

A ncient Rome was a deeply patriarchal society, where the male citizen controlled his wife, those he enslaved, and his family in all household matters, including love and sex. Yet Romans did not disapprove of same-sex relations or gender crossing. Written records of Roman life first appear around 240 BCE. They provide much evidence – of varying reliability – for diversity in matters of sexuality and gender. Over Rome's long history, attitudes changed significantly as its society evolved and absorbed influences from its multicultural empire.

Phallic dominance
The Romans recognized the ancient Greek reverence for love between men, but their approach was less spiritual and more hedonistic. A vital element of Roman ideology was the power of the penis. Sexual penetration was an exercise in domination. Although moderation and self-control in most things, including sex, were held as virtues, many privileged Romans did not follow this path. The more people you penetrated, the more powerful a man you were.

Who you penetrated mattered. A Roman man was expected to have sex with his wife and produce children. He could also do anything he wanted with those he enslaved. But penetrative sex with another male Roman citizen was a different matter. Being penetrated was perceived as shameful for that man.

Phallic bronze pendants were worn by Romans to ward off evil spirits. The phallus was seen as a symbol of power, potency, and prosperity.

See also: Ancient Greece 20–23 ▪ Sappho of Lesbos 24–27 ▪ Renaissance Italy 58–59 ▪ Defining "homosexual" and "heterosexual" 106–07

The Warren Cup, now in the British Museum, London, is named after an American collector who bought it in 1911. Edward Perry Warren was known as an advocate of the ancient Greek ideal of love between men.

Despite this social disgrace, Roman documents talk of sex between men, suggesting that some Roman men sought and enjoyed penetration. The Romans tended to assume that such men were effeminate, and used many words to describe them. A *mollis* was a "soft man"; a *pathicus* was someone easily dominated by others; and a *cinaedus* (originally a kind of Greek dancer) was openly effeminate. Roman men regularly used *cinaedus* as an insult, and no Roman would admit to being one.

Same-sex tolerance

Graffiti at the Roman town of Pompeii, and frescoes found in its brothels and baths, provide evidence of the popularity of various same-sex practices. Roman erotic poetry, particularly the work of Catullus (*c.* 84–*c.* 54 BCE), also attests to same-sex acts. Many of Catullus's poems are addressed to his mistress, Lesbia, but others involve a young man called Juventius, with whom

he seems equally keen to have sex. One of the best-known depictions of sex between men from the Roman Empire is the Warren Cup, a silver drinking vessel made somewhere between 15 BCE and 15 CE. On one side, it is decorated with a bearded older man penetrating a male youth. On the opposite side, a young beardless man penetrates a boy. Sex between older and younger men – idealized in the ancient Greek *erastes* and *eromenos* relationship – was tolerated, and some wealthy Romans, including emperors, were known to have enslaved boys castrated before puberty to maintain their youthful looks.

Most Roman emperors engaged in same-sex relations. The Roman historian Suetonius (69–*c.* 122 CE) claimed that of the first 12 emperors only Claudius (10 BCE–54 CE) had sex exclusively with women. The 14th emperor, Hadrian (76–138 CE), was said to have no interest in women, including his wife, Vibia Sabina.

Gender transformations

Romans were open to the possibility of changing sex and aware of biological traits – known then as "hermaphroditism" and today as intersex – that do not fit binary ideas of "male" and "female". The most prominent "hermaphrodite" in Roman history was Favorinus (*c.* 85–155 CE), a philosopher and orator, and a favourite of Hadrian. Contemporary records suggest that, although clearly male at birth, he never went through puberty, and throughout his life his skin remained smooth and his voice high-pitched.

The Roman physician Galen (129–*c.* 216 CE), believed – like the Greek philosopher Aristotle – that a woman was a man who had not »

Hadrian and Antinous

The son of a Roman senator, Hadrian became a trusted ally of the emperor Trajan (53–117 CE) and married his grandniece, Vibia Sabina. Trajan was childless, and Hadrian was adopted as the imperial heir – possibly at the instigation of Trajan's wife, Pompeia Plotina.

Hadrian admired Greek culture, including the custom of an older man and a younger man forming a close, often sexual relationship. He was particularly attracted to one of his pages, Antinous – a boy born in 110 CE in Bithynia, in present-day northwest Turkey. As Antinous grew older, his relationship with the emperor blossomed.

In 130 CE, as the imperial family toured Egypt, Antinous drowned in the Nile. Hadrian was heartbroken and deified his young lover. As many as 28 temples across the empire were dedicated to the god Antinous – part of a cult that lasted more than 200 years.

After Antinous's death, Hadrian ordered thousands of statues and busts to be made of his lover and displayed throughout the empire. This bust dates from 130–138 CE.

An erotic fresco from a Pompeiian bathhouse includes a threesome of two men and one woman, with one man penetrating the other. To the right, two women touch each other intimately.

including the satirists Martial (c. 38–c. 103 CE) and Juvenal (c. 55–c. 127 CE), Cybele worship continued throughout the Roman Empire until Rome adopted Christianity in the 4th century CE. The Emperor Claudius made Cybele's spring festival an official part of the Roman religious calendar, and the day on which new *galli* were castrated (24 March) became a public holiday.

Roman rulers and gender

Gender crossing was openly displayed in the Roman imperial household. The emperors Caligula (12–41 CE) and Nero (37–68 CE) were both known to cross-dress. When Nero's beloved wife Poppaea Sabina died in childbirth, his courtiers offered him a replacement – a young person known as Sporus but renamed Sabina by Nero. Sabina, although assigned male at birth, was extremely feminine. Nero gave his new wife maids, clothes, jewellery, and even a noblewoman to teach her deportment. Suetonius – admittedly

[The *galli*] say they are not men … they want to pass as women.
Firmicus Maternus
Christian Roman polemicist on pagan religions, c. 348 CE

fully developed in the womb and could potentially develop further after birth. At puberty, it was suggested, a girl's sexual organs might extend out of her body, turning her into a boy. Roman scholar Pliny the Elder (23–79 CE) and 2nd-century CE Greek author Phlegon of Tralles both wrote about such transformations. Modern science suggests that what Pliny and Phlegon recorded were probably cases of the intersex trait known today as 5-alpha reductase deficiency. People exhibiting this trait do not grow a penis and testicles until puberty and are usually assigned female at birth.

The Romans also recognized that gender could change from male to female. This was most notably embodied in the *galli* – a priestly cult based around the goddess Cybele. In the 3rd century BCE, with Hannibal's Carthaginian forces occupying Italian soil, the Romans sought the help of Cybele, the patron goddess of Aeneas, their legendary Trojan ancestor.

A diplomatic mission was sent to Cybele's original home, Phrygia (in present-day Turkey), and returned with a holy statue, representing the goddess. Cybele was accompanied by her followers, the *galli*, who underwent ritual castration and then lived as women. According to the Jewish historian Philo of Alexandria (c. 20 BCE–c. 50 CE), the *galli* chose this path because they wanted to become women, although some may have felt pressurized to do so, perhaps through poverty.

Records of a court case from 77 BCE reveal that a *gallus* called Genucius was not allowed to inherit money from a friend's will because *galli* were seen as neither men nor women. Their castration – an affront to Roman manhood – meant they could never enjoy the rights of a Roman citizen, but the court case shows that the existence of more than two genders was accepted in Roman law. Although the *galli* were viewed with disgust by most Roman men, not the most trustworthy source – claimed Nero offered a reward to any surgeon who could make Sabina a complete woman. Suetonius used the Latin word *transfigurare* – the first known use of the prefix "trans" in connection with gender surgery.

Roman historians told a similar, if unreliable, story about Elagabalus, who became emperor in 218 CE, aged just 14, and was assassinated four years later. The emperor, it was claimed, loved cross-dressing, flirted with palace guards, married a man famous for his outsized penis, obsessively depilated their body hair, and allegedly offered a reward to any surgeon who could give them a vagina. The truth is hard to discern as the Roman sources were written after the emperor's death and may have been an attempt to "justify" the assassination of Elagabalus.

Incomplete histories

Evidence in Roman sources for people who were assigned female at birth but embrace a degree of masculinity is scarce. The satirist Lucian of Samosata (120–*c.* 180 CE) wrote about a person called Megillos, who lived as a man and had a wife but was apparently assigned female at birth. Megillos is fictional, but Phlegon of Tralles

Women transforming into men is not an idle story.
Pliny the Elder
Natural History, 77 CE

recorded possible evidence of those who would be called trans men today in his book *On Marvels*. Two stories describe men who gave birth. These people are likely to have been assigned female at birth but accepted as men by Roman society.

Roman burial sites have yielded some archaeological evidence of people who would be classified as trans today. In 2002, a dig at Catterick in Yorkshire, UK, revealed a 4th-century CE skeleton that appeared male but was buried with jewellery often associated with *galli* priestesses. A 1979 dig at Harper Road in London found a burial that appeared to be of a woman, but in 2016, DNA testing of the skeleton revealed XY chromosomes (the combination that usually determines maleness assigned at birth), despite its shape being closer to the shape usually considered female.

The problem with such finds is that the lives of these people are unknown. Grave goods can be misleading, and determining sex from a skeleton is not guaranteed to

A funerary relief from the 2nd century CE shows a *gallus* dressed and adorned as a Roman woman and surrounded by objects related to the cult of the goddess Cybele.

be accurate. The burial at Harper Road could have been of a feminine man, a trans woman, or an intersex person. However, while individual cases of sexual and gender fluidity in Rome are contested, the weight of evidence of such behaviour suggests that Roman society was just as diverse as most modern societies.

Women's secret desires

While their history is less well documented, women in ancient Rome doubtless engaged in a variety of sex acts together. The Romans had a word for a woman who enjoyed sex with another woman – *tribas* – which meant someone who rubbed something, or someone. This later inspired the English term "tribade", which was used from the 17th century to denote a woman who loved women.

Archaeologists have found evidence of Roman dildos, made of stuffed leather. The poet Martial wrote an epigram about a woman called Bassa, whom he claimed both rubbed and used a dildo with other women. Martial, and other Roman men who wrote about sex between women, saw such acts as absurd and debasing. There are no records of what Roman women thought. ∎

I was born with a body entirely like that of all women, but I have the tastes and desires of a man.
Megillos
from *Dialogues of the Courtesans*

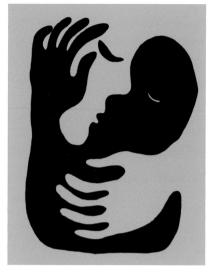

WHO DOES WHAT, WHERE, WHEN, AND WHY, WHO KNOWS?

THE *KAMA SUTRA* (*c.* 100 CE—*c.* 200 CE)

IN CONTEXT

FOCUS
Hindu view of same-sex acts

BEFORE
1st century BCE — 1st century CE The Sanskrit medical texts *Charaka Samhita* and *Sushruta Samhita* give descriptions of different types of same-sex acts and gender nonconformity.

AFTER
***c.* 13th century** *Jayamangala*, a Sanskrit commentary on the *Kama Sutra* written by Yashodhara Indrapada, recognizes same-sex desire, though it is described in derogatory terms.

***c.* 14th century** A Sanskrit version of the Hindu *Padma Purana* epic text and some manuscripts of the Bengali *Krittivasa Ramayana* describe two widows who, with the help of a priest, make love and produce a child.

The first-ever treatise on the enjoyment of sexual acts, the *Kama Sutra* is an ancient Hindu text focused on *Kama*, meaning "love" or "desire". *Sutra* translates as "thread" or "manual", and applies to a text into which a thread of teachings are woven.

In Hinduism, there are four main goals in life and *Kama* is one of these, as well as being the name of the god of desire – a figure similar to Eros in the pantheon of the ancient Greek gods.

Intimate arts

The *Kama Sutra* is divided into seven parts and 36 chapters. It encourages a skilful enjoyment of life and begins by stating that everyone should study this book, including young men, young women, and courtesans. The book lists 64 arts that everyone should cultivate, including dancing, reading, writing, drawing, playing music, cookery, flower arrangement, martial arts, learning poetry by heart, and gymnastics.

Abridged versions of the *Kama Sutra* generally highlight its second part, which covers 64 positions of heterosexual intercourse and other types of intimacy, including kisses,

An erotic carving at Khajuraho Hindu temple complex in Madhya Pradesh, India, depicts three women intimately involved with a man, but also with each other.

love-bites, love-slaps, poking, and scratching. Further chapters cover other areas of intimacy, including ideas for a girl to woo a man, and instructions to a husband on how to win his bride's confidence, such as not having intercourse for the first three nights, but conversing with her and gradually caressing her. There are also chapters on how to treat sex workers.

The "third nature"

Chapter nine of the *Kama Sutra* concerns the "third nature" (sometimes mistranslated as

See also: Gender and sexuality in ancient Greece 20–23 ▪ Gender and sexuality in ancient Rome 30–35 ▪ Same-sex narratives in Urdu poetry 96–97

"third sex"), or men who desire men. These men may be feminine-appearing (often mistranslated in the past as "eunuchs") or masculine-appearing. Feminine-appearing men can easily find male lovers, but masculine-appearing ones can find partners by working, the text suggests, as masseurs or hairdressers. This advice is followed by a graphic description of how to flirt with and make advances to a client, stimulate the penis in eight ways, and perform oral sex, an act compared with sucking a mango.

The text remarks that men who are not classified as the "third nature" may have oral sex with young male servants or actors. Two men who are friends and trust each other may mutually take one another, referred to by the term *parasparaparigraham*. *Paraspara* means "mutual", while *parigraha* has various interpretations, including "take", "accept", and "seize", which could relate to sexual intercourse. French Indologist Alain Daniélou (1907–94) translated it as "get married". Used throughout the text, *parasparaparigraham* is most frequently used to indicate

It [same-sex activity] is to be engaged in and enjoyed for its own sake as one of the arts.
Kama Sutra

There are also third-nature citizens, sometimes greatly attached to one another … who get married together.
Kama Sutra

an ongoing marriage-like bond or a union that is outside a fully sanctified marriage.

Sex between women

The word *paraspara* is also used in the *Kama Sutra* to describe sexual enjoyment between women. The text refers briefly to a self-willed woman (*svairini*) playing a man's role, possibly with another woman, and to women using their fingers or making use of vegetables as dildos on each other.

Beyond its mentions of same-sex activities such as anal sex and the use of dildos, the *Kama Sutra* treats oral sex as the primary form of sex between men and between women. There are also a few passing mentions of bisexual behaviour. The text states that some commentators disapprove of these same-sex practices but notes that they should consider factors of time, place, and different inclinations.

The *Kama Sutra*'s broad acceptance of same-sex relations as part of human experience is summed up by its conclusion: "Who does what, where, when and why, who knows?" ▪

Composition of the *Kama Sutra*

Composed in Sanskrit between *c.*100 CE and *c.*200 CE, probably in the prosperous city of Pataliputra (present-day Patna in Bihar, northeast India), the *Kama Sutra* is traditionally attributed to the sage Vatsyayana. Little is known about him, though a statement at the end of the *Kama Sutra* says he wrote the work after studying texts about *Kama* by earlier scholars. These included Auddalaki, Babhravya, and Charayana – whose texts no longer exist. It also says that he was celibate and in a state of contemplation while writing the *Kama Sutra*.

The statement also asserts that anyone who studies the *Kama Sutra* and practices *dharma* (duty and harmony with the universe), *artha* (wealth), and *kama* (desire) will overcome the senses to achieve *siddhi (*fulfilment) and *moksha* (liberation). Those who use the text simply for indulgence will not attain fulfilment.

Paintings discovered in Juna Mahal Palace, Rajasthan, India, show sexual and wooing techniques described in the *Kama Sutra*.

THE LORD RAINED UPON SODOM AND GOMORRAH BRIMSTONE AND FIRE

THE EARLY CHRISTIAN CHURCH
(4TH–6TH CENTURIES CE)

IN CONTEXT

FOCUS
Early Christian views of same-sex relations

BEFORE
5th or 6th century BCE
The biblical Book of Genesis takes its final form.

***c.*57** CE Jesus's apostle Paul condemns male and female homoeroticism in his Letter to the Romans.

79 CE A volcanic eruption destroys Pompeii, in southern Italy. Erotic art later found in the ruins attests to same-sex practices in the Roman Empire.

AFTER
11th century The Church develops the concept of "sodomy" to describe all non-reproductive sexual acts.

13th century Secular authorities in Europe begin to criminalize sodomy.

Early Christian writers used several passages from the Bible to condemn homoerotic behaviour. Key among these was the story of the destruction of Sodom in the Book of Genesis – a disaster believed by some to have been a punishment for same-sex relations among the city's inhabitants. This interpretation has contributed to homophobic readings of the narrative, but the biblical text itself is imprecise about the nature of the deeds that led to Sodom's downfall.

Sins of Sodom
Genesis 19 tells how two angels arrived in Sodom to investigate the city's sins. The patriarch Lot offered

See also: Gender and sexuality in ancient Rome 30–35 ▪ Sodomy and the medieval Catholic Church 42–45 ▪ The Spanish Inquisition 64–65 ▪ Erotic friendship in America and Europe 92–95 ▪ The trial of Oscar Wilde 124–25

Initially, Jewish and early Christian theologians suggest that the story of Sodom's destruction is **a message about the sin of inhospitality** rather than homoeroticism.

Hebrew and Christian scriptures also include **prohibitions** of male and occasionally female **homoerotic relations**.

Sodom's sins are **identified as homoeroticism** by some of the early Church Fathers.

But the Bible also features **celebrations of intense same-sex love** that have been a source of inspiration for later Christians seeking **historical precedents** for homoerotic passion.

to accommodate them in his home within the city, but before Lot's household went to bed, Sodom's inhabitants surrounded the house and called on Lot to deliver his guests "that we may know them" (Genesis 19:5). Prioritizing the wellbeing of his guests, Lot offered his two daughters in their place. Threatened with violence, Lot and his family were escorted out of the city by the angels. Subsequently, Sodom and the nearby city of Gomorrah, which was also deemed sinful, were annihilated when God rained down "brimstone and fire" – a biblical expression that symbolizes divine anger – as a punishment for the wrongdoing of its citizens.

The meaning of the Sodomite mob's desire to "know" Lot's guests has attracted much speculation. While the Hebrew word translated as "know" can have sexual

connotations in the scriptures, many modern commentators, in a return to early Jewish readings of the Sodom story, agree that the city's wickedness did not concern homoeroticism but rather the sins of inhospitality and rape.

Supporting evidence

The modern interpretation of the Genesis passage is bolstered by comparisons with a biblical narrative describing the rape of a Levite's concubine. Judges 19 tells how a member of the Hebrew tribe of Levi, his concubine, and his servant sought lodging in Gibeah and an old man in the city offered to host the party. But Gibeah's

This 13th-century depiction of the collapse of Sodom shows Lot and his daughters fleeing. Lot's wife, ignoring the angels' warning to not look back at the city, is turned into a pillar of salt.

inhabitants knocked on the old man's door and asked him to bring the Levite to them so they could "abuse him". The old man refused the request, offered up his own daughter and the Levite's concubine as alternatives, and begged them not to commit this "unnatural" crime on his guest. The concubine was handed over to the men, who abused her all night and left her dead on the old man's doorstep.

Reading the Genesis and Judges stories together, two similarities stand out. First, both can be read as imparting a lesson about hospitality: the tales narrate breaches of the obligation of host to traveller. Second, each story revolves around sexual violence or its threatened use as a means of exerting power over strangers. After all, if the Sodomites had accepted Lot's offer to deliver his daughters instead of the angels, the girls would have been raped. And in Judges, one of the women offered to the mob ends up being raped and killed.

In both cases, the cities' inhabitants were guilty not of homoeroticism but of inhospitality, a sin manifested respectively in »

acts of attempted or actual rape. Consequently, the primary message Judaism took from Genesis 19 was a concern that outsiders should be treated fairly and without hostility.

Retribution and apocalypse

Elsewhere in the Hebrew scriptures, Sodom's destruction was sometimes cited as an example of sudden divine retribution. However, these references did not concern same-sex copulation or desire specifically. The prophets Isaiah, Jeremiah, and Ezekiel compared the sins of Sodom and Gomorrah with the sins of Judah or Jerusalem, but they made no explicit reference to sexual activity in this context.

Christian scriptures contain just one direct reference to sexual immorality as the cause of Sodom and Gomorrah's downfall, in a short epistle attributed to the apostle Jude. The Book of Revelation,

An image from a 14th-century Bible shows God raining down fire after the Sodomites attack and an interpretation of the story in which demons gloat over same-sex couples embracing.

To flee from burning Sodom is to refuse the illicit fires of the flesh.
Gregory the Great

which concludes the canonical Christian Bible and was written by apostle John the Divine in the 1st century CE, also makes passing reference to Sodom. Here, the city's fiery fate is interpreted as prefiguring both the burning of Babylon as part of the global apocalypse at the end of time, and the fiery torments of the damned in hell following God's final judgement. But neither of these references explicitly represents homoeroticism as the target of divine anger.

Other prohibitions

Separate from the Sodom story, the Hebrew Book of Leviticus includes two passages that appear to prohibit same-sex acts. One passage condemns men who "lie with mankind as with womankind" as an "abomination" (Leviticus 18:22), while the other announces that men guilty of this crime be put to death (Leviticus 20:13). Although there seems to have been no direct connection between Levitical laws and the sins of Sodom, these Judaic prohibitions sometimes inspired

legislation that made sodomy a capital offence in medieval Christian states.

Christ's apostle Paul referred in his biblical writings to those who abandoned "natural use" by engaging in homoerotic acts. Paul's Letter to the Romans has enjoyed particular prominence among Christian theologians as a pretext for condemning same-sex erotic behaviour. It also contributed to a heightened awareness among early Christians of female as well as male homoeroticism.

Homoeroticism

During the first millennium of Christianity, many writers tried to make sense of biblical references to homoeroticism and to the Sodom story. But there was initially no consensus among Christians about the nature of the sins of Sodom, which were variously identified as inhospitality, pride, gluttony, self-indulgence, and carnality.

However, a homophobic interpretation eventually came to predominate, in which Sodom epitomized the affront to God of unbridled homoerotic lust. This reading first emerged in the 4th and 5th centuries CE, in the writings of the "Church Fathers", such as John Chrysostom and Augustine of Hippo, who established the doctrinal foundations of Christianity.

In the 6th century, another Church Father, Gregory the Great, who eventually became pope, described the biblical Sodomites as being possessed by "depraved" thoughts and "perverse" pleasures. Gregory's language has been taken to refer to same-sex desires specifically and his remarks proved to be influential. Gregory enlisted the Sodom narrative within his broader teachings on *luxuria*, a Latin term which roughly corresponds to

> The soul of Jonathan was knit with the soul of David, and Jonathan loved him as his own soul.
> **1 Samuel 18:1**

the English word "lust". Defined by early Christians as a sin of intense, disorderly desire that fatally distracts humanity from the love of God, *luxuria* was identified by Gregory as one of the seven deadly sins that every Christian should spurn.

Bonds of love

Early Christian readings of the Bible that interpreted Sodom's doom as being triggered by expressions of same-sex desire and lust were not inevitable. Alongside the laws and narratives inspired by these interpretations, Hebrew scriptures also included celebrations of love, intimacy, and passionate friendship between same-sex couples.

The most significant of these was the account, in the Book of Samuel, of the close relationship between Jonathan and David. Jonathan was son of Saul, King of Israel, while David was his potential rival for the throne. The biblical text describes how, after fighting together against the Philistines, the pair formed a covenant of love, Jonathan even going so far as to give his clothes and armour to David because he "loved him as his own soul" (1 Samuel 18:1). When Jonathan was later slain in battle, David lamented the loss of his "brother", whose love was "extraordinary, surpassing the love of women" (2 Samuel 1:26).

While early Christians generally interpreted such statements in platonic terms, as expressions of passionate but not necessarily erotic same-sex attachment, readers of the Bible from the 16th century on have sought to highlight the homoerotic dimensions to these relationships. At his 1895 trial for gross indecency, Anglo–Irish poet and playwright Oscar Wilde cited Jonathan and David as a positive example of the "love that dare not speak its name" – a pure, noble form of affection between two men.

As such, despite biblical passages playing a key role in early Christian condemnations of homoeroticism, they have also provided value in the search for queer forefathers in later centuries. ∎

The intense love between Jonathan and David is captured in this 1642 work by the Dutch artist Rembrandt. David weeps in Jonathan's arms before fleeing from Saul's wrath.

Ruth and Naomi are shown embracing in this 1856 oil painting by Dutch artist Ary Scheffer, implying a romantic love between them.

Ruth and Naomi

The biblical Book of Ruth describes how Naomi, who was living with her husband in the land of Moab, decides to return home following the death of her husband and sons. She sends her two daughters-in-law, Ruth and Orpha, who have outlived their husbands – Naomi's sons – to their mothers in order to find new husbands. While Orpha returns home, Ruth remains behind, pledging never to leave Naomi: "For where you go I will go" (Ruth 1:16). Ruth's pledge to Naomi was sometimes celebrated by early Christians as an archetype of virtuous love and female fellowship.

Although the biblical text does not explicitly indicate a romantic interest between the pair, artistic depictions of the episode in later centuries sometimes show Ruth tenderly touching or embracing her mother-in-law. Since the story describes a loving relationship and a lifelong commitment between women, Ruth's words have featured in some female–female marriage ceremonies.

THIS TYPE OF LOVE REBELS AGAINST NATURE

SODOMY AND THE MEDIEVAL CATHOLIC CHURCH (5TH CENTURY–1500)

IN CONTEXT

FOCUS
Persecution under sodomy laws

BEFORE
240 BCE–400 CE Sex between older and younger males is tolerated in ancient Rome.

4th century CE Christian theologians interpret the biblical account of Sodom's destruction as punishment for homoerotic lust.

AFTER
1533 The Buggery Act, making sodomy punishable by death, is introduced during the reign of Henry VIII of England.

1540–1700 The Spanish Inquisition, set up to root out heresy, prosecutes sodomy. Perpetrators over the age of 25 are sentenced to death.

1967 The UK legalizes consensual same-sex acts.

From at least as early as the 5th century CE, the Roman Catholic Church deemed forms of sexual activity other than those to do with procreation within marriage as "unnatural" or "unspeakable". Known as "sodomy" from the 11th century – though often given euphemisms – such acts included same-sex relations between men, or sometimes women, and any sexual act that did not have the potential for reproduction.

Medieval poets depicted sodomy as unnatural. The anonymous 12th-century Latin poem *"Quam pravus est mos"* ("A Perverse Custom") accuses men who prefer boys to girls of a type

See also: Gender and sexuality in ancient Rome 30–35 ▪ The early Christian Church 38–41 ▪ The Spanish Inquisition 64–65 ▪ The criminalization of sodomy 68–71

of love that "rebels against nature" since even wild beasts, it says, avoid "evil caresses".

To reinforce gender binaries among those who would today identify as lesbians or trans men, writers sometimes cited interpretations of the myth of Iphis and Ianthe, in the Roman poet Ovid's *Metamorphoses*. Iphis is born female but raised male, and is transformed by the goddess Isis into a man in order to marry Ianthe. A 14th-century French verse rendition instead depicts a depraved woman in men's attire using an "artificial member" to have sex with her female lover. The author condemns the behaviour as being "against law and against nature".

Categorizing sexual acts

It was notoriously difficult to categorize specific sex acts as "sins against nature". An 860 CE treatise by French theologian Hincmar of Reims includes the first recorded use of the Latin word *sodomia* (derived from a city that is punished in the Hebrew Bible – Genesis 18: 20–21 – for "sinfulness") in relation

In the 12th and 13th centuries, sexual sins are split into two categories:

Natural sins are **potentially procreative** (can lead to pregnancy), and take place in the right "vessel".	Unnatural sins are **not procreative** and take place in the wrong "vessel".
They include **adultery**, **fornication**, the **deflowering** of a virgin, **incest**, and **rape**.	They include **masturbation**, **heterosexual anal intercourse** (or other acts not conducive to procreation), **sodomy**, and **bestiality**.

to acts deemed unnatural. From the 11th century, sodomy could be used more narrowly to refer to sex acts between males, or specifically to anal intercourse. Around 1050, Italian monk Peter Damian wrote his "Book of Gomorrah", a letter designed to persuade the Pope to stop the spread of sodomy, which

he perhaps rightly alleged was rife among the clergy. He included four sex acts under the category of *sodomia*: masturbation, mutual masturbation, intercourse between the thighs, and anal intercourse.

Punishments

The classification of same-sex relations as unnatural was reinforced during the sacrament of confession and by ecclesiastical and secular law courts. Priests were issued with penitentials outlining the penance appropriate to particular sins.

Penitentials were also produced for religious women. Even female hermits were thought vulnerable to temptation. Aelred of Rievaulx, a 12th-century English monk, »

A carving in the 12th-century cloister of Girona Cathedral, Spain, shows devils sodomizing two men while other sinners are cooked in a cauldron – a graphic warning to all who saw the frieze.

wrote a treatise addressed to his spiritual sister, a recluse, in which he said that fellowship with a man was not the only danger to her chastity, since that "abominable sin" that inflames a woman with passion for a woman "meets with more relentless condemnation than any other crime".

People who would now be called intersex were also warned of the dangers of sex-role inversion. Peter the Chanter, a 13th-century French theologian, urged "hermaphrodites" to adhere to a single sexual role for life, or, if unable to do that, to commit to lifelong celibacy.

Hidden abuse

Euphemistic indictments of the "sin not fit to be named" may have been a way of directing attention away from the clergy's abuse of boys and young men in their charge. In 1440, an inspection of religious houses by the Bishop of Lincoln, in eastern England, turned up the case of a canon, John Alforde, who was found to have been lying with "secular youths" in the dormitory at Markby Priory. Another canon from Leicester, whose partners included two choristers, was charged with "that damnable and hateful sodomitic vice" by the bishop's inspectors. Cases of sodomy

Punishments advised in the penitential attributed to Theodore of Canterbury, *c.*700 CE	
Sin	**Punishment**
A woman fornicating with another woman	Do penance for 3 years.
A man fornicating with a virgin	Fast for 4 years.
A man fornicating with another man's wife	Fast for 4 years (2 wandering in grief, plus 2 more years fasting for 40-day periods and 3 days each week).
A man fornicating with an effeminate male or with another man or with an animal	Fast for 10 years.
Murder	Do penance for 7–10 years.
An effeminate male fornicating with another effeminate male	Do penance for 10 years; if unintentional, fast for 4 years, if habitual, fast for 15 years.
A man fornicating with his mother, sister, daughter, or brother	Fast for 12 years (15 if brother).
Whoever ejaculates seed into the mouth	"The worst evil": repent until death.

were not always consensual, as the testimony of Italian priest Donato Piermaria Bocco shows. He raped boys with impunity until his case came to court in 1507, revealing the brutality and breadth of such crimes.

Put to death

Initially punished within the ranks of the clergy, sodomy was increasingly treated as a crime in wider society and, as the Middle

An illustrated chronicle depicts the burning of Richard Puller von Hohenburg and Anton Mätzler in Zurich, Switzerland, in 1482.

Ages drew to a close, was generally pursued with greater vigour by secular authorities than by the Church. The earliest documented execution for "sodomitical vice" in Western Europe was in Basel in 1277. In what is now south Germany and German-speaking Switzerland, men who were accused of sexual acts with other men were considered to be committing "heresy", since this kind of sexual deviance was associated with paganism. In 1482, officials in Zurich ordered Richard Puller von Hohenburg and his servant Anton Mätzler to be burned at the stake for such heresy, even though Puller's confession was extracted under torture. He refused to repeat it before his execution.

People accused of gender nonconformity expressed in a sexual relationship were also put to death. In 1477, in Germany, Katherina Hetzeldorfer was tried and then drowned for living as the "husband" of a woman. The record of the trial includes a detailed description of the dildo-like "instrument" that the accused allegedly used to have their "manly will" with their partner.

In England, there are no records of executions taking place for the crime of "buggery" until after the Reformation, when King Henry VIII broke from the Catholic Church to form the Church of England. The Buggery Act of 1533 moved responsibility for punishing sodomy from ecclesiastical courts to the state. Sodomy remained punishable by death in the UK until 1861, but the last executions were in 1837.

Same-sex unions

Despite the heavy penalties and censure, people often found opportunities to form intimate same-sex partnerships, or at least to acknowledge the possibility.

A woman who takes up devilish ways and plays a male role in coupling with another woman is most vile.
Hildegard of Bingen
German abbess, poet, and composer
(1098–1179)

Rituals celebrating male–male love as a mode of voluntary kinship were not uncommon in medieval Europe. Distinct from marriage but using some of its language, "wed" or "sworn" brotherhood was immortalized in courtly literature.

A popular 12th-century French romance, *Amys and Amylion*, tells the story of two identical young nobles, biologically unrelated, who swear an oath of everlasting allegiance, "in well, woe, word, and deed". While they subsequently take wives, and one has children,

the narrative concludes with Amylion being cured of leprosy by the blood of Amys's children. The pair live together for the rest of their days, die on the same day, and share a grave.

Such stories chimed with religious celebrations of idealized friendship. Aelred of Rievaulx, who warned female recluses of threats to their chastity, also wrote a treatise on "spiritual friendship" that developed a formula for same-sex intimacy. Distinguishing between earthly, carnal, and what he called "sublime" love, Aelred deemed it perfectly acceptable for men to express their depth of feeling for other males using passionate and even erotic language, as long as this language did not lead to physical expression.

The extent to which these expressions of love provide evidence of same-sex behaviour is a matter of debate. Yet these examples show that despite the many voices condemning sodomy as a sin and crime, medieval people were sometimes able to express their relationships in terms that could be described as profoundly romantic. ∎

The effigy of Sir William Neville and Sir John Clanvowe's shared grave depicts the knights facing each other, their shields overlapping.

United in death

Loving same-sex unions were occasionally celebrated publicly in the form of funerary monuments. Some male pairs – and more rarely female couples – elected to be buried in a shared grave. Little is known about the forms of intimacy behind these decisions to remain together even in death, but the monuments testify to a depth of feeling.

In 1391, two English knights, Sir William Neville, the constable of Nottingham Castle, and Sir John Clanvowe, a poet, died a

few days apart in Galata, near Constantinople (modern-day Istanbul). The pair, who had fought together in the Hundred Years' War, were buried together in a nearby church.

The marble effigy shows the two men with their respective coats-of-arms "impaled" – a fusion suggesting an embrace and more commonly used to depict marital unions. A chronicle from the time records that Neville died of "inconsolable grief" following the loss of Clanvowe, "for whom his love was no less than for himself".

I DIE OF LOVE FOR HIM

THE ABBASID CALIPHATE (750–1258 CE)

IN CONTEXT

FOCUS
Same-sex desire and Islam

BEFORE
610 CE The Prophet Muhammad receives his first revelations from God, which are later recorded in the Qur'an.

632 Muhammad dies, having converted most of the Arabian Peninsula to Islam.

632 The Rashidun dynasty succeeds the Prophet, and expands north, west and east.

661 The Umayyads take over the growing caliphate from their capital, Damascus. They are overthrown by the Abbasids in 750.

AFTER
1258 The Mongols sack Baghdad and raze the House of Wisdom.

1261 The Abbasid Caliphate is re-established in Cairo, with a purely religious function, by the Mamluks.

From their grand Baghdad palaces, the Abbasids led an Islamic Golden Age, battling rivals such as the Byzantines and Seljuks and promoting learning and culture. Evidence of same-sex relationships can be found in the lives of caliphs (rulers) and the writings of their scholars and poets.

The fourth Abbasid caliph, al-Hadi (r. 785–786), whose short reign ended with his death aged 22, was said to have suspected two of his concubines of being lovers. After confirming his suspicions by having a servant spy on them, al-Hadi apparently beheaded the pair.

Al-Hadi was succeeded by Harun al-Rashid (r. 786–809), who developed Bayt al-Hikma (House of Wisdom), an extraordinary institution of learning that brought together some of the world's greatest scholars and fostered a flourishing of the arts, sciences, and literature.

Al-Rashid was more tolerant of same-sex acts, and one of the poets at his glittering court, Abu Nuwas, wrote some of the finest homoerotic poetry in all of Arabic literature. According to a tale in the story collection *The Thousand and One Nights*, al-Rashid once discovered him having sex with young men. Abu Nuwas greeted the caliph with drunken insolence, enraging him, but al-Rashid eventually pardoned the poet and rewarded him for his wit.

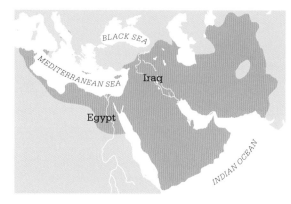

The Abbasid Caliphate (750–1258) was a cosmopolitan empire that stretched from Iraq to North Africa and Central Asia. Trade reached as far as Britain and Japan, and the Abbasids led the world in astronomy, cartography, medicine, and mathematics.

KEY

The caliphate c. 850

See also: Gender and sexuality in ancient Greece 20–23 ▪ Favourites in Han China 28–29 ▪ The early Christian Church 38–41 ▪ Ottoman gender and sexuality 62–63 ▪ LGBTQ+ Muslims 278–79

Al-Amin's favourites

Al-Rashid's son al-Amin (r. 809–813) spent his time in the intimate company of enslaved men, neglecting his wife and concubines. He became so distracted that his mother, Zubaida, began dressing enslaved girls in male clothing and cutting their hair short. Her efforts paid off, and when al-Amin began to be seen with these escorts, it triggered a fashion for women at court to wear their hair short and dress in male clothing.

Al-Amin's reign was short-lived. A power struggle led to rebellions and then civil war, and he was deposed by his half-brother, al-Ma'mun (r. 813–833). Accounts suggest that the caliph spent the last moments before his defeat playing chess with his eunuch and lover, Kauthar. Al-Amin was executed, but there is no evidence that his sexuality contributed to

Two men embrace in an illustrated manuscript of al-Hariri of Basra's 12th-century story collection *Maqamat* (*The Assemblies*). While the pair appear to have an easy intimacy, there's no indication their embrace was sexual.

Al-Ma'mun sends an envoy to the Byzantine emperor Theophilos. The two rulers shared scholarship, but also fought wars in Anatolia and Sicily.

the conflict – indeed, one of al-Ma'mun's advisors, chief judge Yahya ibn Aktham, was said to favour men.

Al-Ma'mun the rationalist

Al-Ma'mun followed a rationalist Islamic school of thought, known as al-Mu'tazila. His patronage of Bayt al-Hikma led to substantial advances in fields such as geology, philosophy, astronomy, and medicine.

Al-Ma'mun's views set him against many traditional scholars who believed holy texts should be the only source of knowledge. He set up a *mihna* (religious inquisition), which banned conservative ideas that suggested the Qur'an, the holy book of Islam, represented eternal, "uncreated" truth. He discouraged interpretations such as that of Ahmad ibn Hanbal, a prominent jurist and collector of *hadiths* (sayings of the Prophet) who claimed that both the "doer

> Kauthar is my religion, my cosmos, my infirmity, and my doctor.
> **Al-Amin**
> **on his favourite eunuch, Kauthar**

and the done to" in a sexual act between men should be killed. Instead, under his rule, scholars such as al-Jaheth felt free to write treatises extolling the sexual benefits of enslaved men or describing same-sex sexual behaviour in the animal world.

A legacy of openness

Al-Ma'mun's intellectual openness and relatively tolerant approach to sexuality informed Abbasid attitudes in the centuries that followed. Works of literature documenting the period, like *The Thousand and One Nights*, reveal non-moralistic approaches to gender and sexual variance. In Abu al-Faraj al-Isfahani's 10th-century poetry collection *Kitab al-Aghani* (*The Book of Songs*), one story tells of a renowned court singer, named Bathal, who sang that there was nothing more delectable than sex with another woman. The listening al-Ma'mun disagreed, stating that heterosexual intercourse was better, but then asked her to continue with her performance. ▪

I WANT TO BE LIKE NATURE MADE ME

INTERSEX RIGHTS (1296)

T he rights of intersex people –
individuals with variations
in their sex characteristics,
including gonads, genitals, and
chromosomes, that do not fit binary
ideas of "male" and "female" – have
exercised physicians and lawmakers
since ancient times. While the
existence of intersex people has long
been widely acknowledged, most
societies, anxious to satisfy cultural
and legal demands, have compelled
them to adopt either a female or a
male identity and adhere to it for life.
By the 13th century, Italian and
French surgeons had developed
illustrated manuals to standardize

A Roman fresco from Capua in the
3rd century CE depicts Hermaphroditus,
who was born to Hermes and Aphrodite
and later merged with the lovestruck
nymph Salmacis in a single body.

the "proper" form of the body to help
physicians decide the degree to
which a person was masculine or
feminine. In *Chirurgia Magna* (*Great
Surgery*), published in 1296, Italian
surgeon Lanfranco da Milano
recommended corrective surgery of
atypical genitalia, to return bodies
to their "natural form". He advocated
cauterizing the vagina of intersex
people deemed to be male, and
amputating "added flesh" in those
considered to be female. This
marked a turning point in the
treatment of intersex people.

Ancient precedents

The earliest recorded debates about
the nature and status of intersex
people date from ancient Greece.
Originally known as hermaphrodites
(after the myth of Hermaphroditus,
who had male and female sexual
characteristics), intersex babies
were often viewed as bad omens
and sometimes sacrificed. At the
same time, great minds attempted
to explain their existence. The
physician Hippocrates (460–370 BCE)
is reported to have theorized that
hermaphrodites existed in the

centre of a male–female spectrum.
In *The Symposium* (*c.* 385–370 BCE),
the philosopher Plato, in the spirit
of poetic myth-making to explain
the fluidity of gender and sexual
attraction, suggested that there
were three original sexes – male
(*andros*), female (*gune*), and
androgynous (*androgynos*). His
pupil Aristotle hypothesized that
hermaphrodites formed when twins
of different sexes failed to develop
separately and their genitalia
merged. He claimed that a "true"
hermaphrodite did not exist. In
Rome in the 2nd century CE, the
Greek surgeon Galen supported
Hippocrates' idea of a sex continuum
but asserted that female genitals
were inverted male genitals.

Attitudes and expectations

Across much of the ancient world,
people born with intersex variations
were expected to conform to one
sex, setting a precedent that
persisted until the 20th century. In
ancient China, for example, everyone
was expected to express the gender
(name, clothing, and familial and
sexual relationships) that aligned
with either their male or female sex
attributes. Anyone suspected of
violating gender norms was reported
to the authorities and forced to
conform. Some civilizations

*… nor perfect boy nor
perfect wench; neither
and both they seem.*
Ovid
Roman poet (43 BCE–17 CE)

See also: Ancient Greece 20–23 ▪ Ancient Rome 30–35 ▪ Hijras and British colonialism 108–09 ▪ Transgender rights 196–203 ▪ Kathoey in Thailand 220–21 ▪ Indigenous American Two-Spirit people 258–61

I am both
man and woman.
Thomas(ine) Hall

differed – India, for example, has recognized a third gender, called hijras, since ancient times.

The Abrahamic religions (Judaism, Christianity, and Islam) fiercely maintained a binary perspective, not least because of their many laws based on gender. Judaism required people who were outwardly *androgynos* (intersex) to align with men, and *tumtum* (people with indiscernible genitalia) to follow laws for men and women.

The medieval Church asserted that God made man and woman for the sole purpose of procreating,

which was allegedly threatened by genitalia that did not fit binary ideas of gender. To avoid sodomy (non-procreative sexual acts), hermaphrodites were expected to choose a male or female identity according to their predominating sexual characteristics.

Islam also acknowledged a range of sex categories but Islamic laws needed to differentiate between men and women for purposes of inheritance, religious rituals, and many aspects of daily life. Muslim jurors attributed a "provisional sex" to anyone who did not present femininely or masculinely.

Subjected to scrutiny

The causes of hermaphroditism set out by Hippocrates and Aristotle continued to be debated in Europe until the 17th century, but deciding the "correct" sex remained the main concern of physicians. They, along with midwives, were frequently called upon to examine atypical bodies in trials. The courts required practitioners to observe the body's outward appearance, perform

An enforced physical examination of English intersex person Thomas(ine) Hall, who was working in the American colonies in the 1620s, determined that they were "both male and female".

physical examinations, and assess the "maleness" or "femaleness" of the sex organs in response to sensory stimuli. The judge would ultimately declare the person male or female, a decision that could affect their livelihood, and ascertain whether they had practised sodomy by engaging in acts not in keeping with that sex. If they had, they were generally condemned to death.

Nonetheless, intersex people were sometimes exempted from charges of sodomy. In 1629, Thomas(ine) Hall, who was serving in the English army in the American colonies, was summoned by the court to confirm their true identity. Hall, who had changed identities throughout their life, proclaimed, "I am both man and woman," which »

Herculine Barbin

Born in southwest France in 1838, Herculine Barbin was raised as a girl but developed masculine characteristics during puberty. As an adult, she became a headmistress and fell in love with a female teacher, but the love affair was ended when doctors discovered she had a small vagina, a small penis, and testicles inside her body.

After a court case to decide her sex that Barbin described as a "ridiculous inquisition", she was reclassified as male.

As a result, she fell into poverty and depression. Barbin died by suicide in 1868, at the age of 29, leaving memoirs beside her bed.

In the 20th century, French philosopher Michel Foucault rediscovered Barbin's writings and published them with commentary in his 1978 book *Herculine Barbin*. In 2005, in honour of Barbin's story, Canadian activist Joëlle-Circé Laramée established Intersex Day of Remembrance or Intersex Solidarity Day on 8 November, Barbin's birthday, to highlight issues faced by intersex people.

Laws based on **religious teachings** insist on a **gender binary**.

Individuals are **designated male or female** depending on their outward sex characteristics.

Intersex people who do not fit this binary **are viewed as a problem**.

In the Middle Ages, intersex people are **required to choose one sex** and **maintain this for life** to avoid charges of sodomy.

In the modern era, **medical practice for intersex people** is based on maintaining **male and female sex categories**.

Intersex activists seek the right to **bodily autonomy** and an **end to non-consensual medical interventions** in infancy and childhood.

the court agreed was the case after examining Hall. In France, in 1601, Marie (Marin) le Marcis was accused of sodomy after assuming a male identity and marrying a woman. Marin was sentenced to death for cross-dressing, sodomy, and other crimes after physicians declared them female. However, a physician named Jacques Duval probed Marin's body, appealed the judgement, and convinced the court that Marin was a hermaphrodite.

Art and medicine

Curiosity about the human body spread with the popularization of medical texts, such as French surgeon Ambroise Paré's 1573 *Des Monstres et Prodiges* (*Monsters and Marvels*). The intersex body, a popular subject in the art of ancient Greece and Rome, reappeared in Renaissance art, as subjects of curiosity and erotic titillation. Flemish painter Jan Gossart's *The Metamorphosis of Hermaphrodite and Salmacis* (*c.* 1520) depicts Hermaphrodite as a young man resisting the embrace of the nymph Salmacis while in the background the two figures are shown united in one body. The life-size *Sleeping Hermaphroditus*, a Roman statue that was resurrected in the 17th century by Italian artist

Gian Lorenzo Bernini, who added a marble mattress and pillow, is startlingly forthright, combining a sensuous depiction of a body with curvy hips, breasts, and a phallus.

When hermaphroditism was depicted in art and medical books, people struggled to make sense of it. They continued to ask how hermaphrodites should be categorized. In 1628, English judge Edward Coke issued legal treatises that acknowledged the existence of hermaphrodites but required them to live their lives according to one gender role.

Surgical interventions

From the 18th century, theories concerning intersex people centred on the gonads (ovaries and testes). Scientists and doctors argued that "true" sex was determined only by the presence of ovarian or testicular tissue in the body, and that a "true" hermaphrodite had both gonadal tissues. They argued that secondary characteristics that developed in puberty proved sex certainty. These included increased body hair, muscular build, and a deeper voice for males, and breasts, wider hips, and menstrual cycles for females.

We are genetically deselected, selectively aborted, prenatally treated.
Mauro Cabral Grinspan
Argentinian intersex and trans activist

Gender – how someone looked, behaved, and believed themselves to be – was also considered.

In the mid-20th century, Dr John Money founded the world's first Gender Identity Clinic, in the US. Under his guidance, surgeons began to "correct" bodies to fit into the sex and gender binaries. Surgery was generally performed on intersex infants with parental consent. Doctors would create a penis or vagina, and then instruct the parents to raise their baby accordingly, often advising them to conceal the diagnosis and treatment their child had received. The approach proved problematic. Long-term damage often occurred, and children sometimes grew up identifying differently from their assigned sex.

Assertive action

By the late 20th century, intersex people across the world were beginning to challenge society's attitudes. Forming support groups, organizing conferences, and publishing newsletters, they demanded bodily autonomy, acceptance, legal recognition, access to information, adequate medical care, and protection from discrimination.

In 1996, American intersex activists Morgan Holmes and Max Beck led a landmark protest outside a medical conference in Boston, Massachusetts, to denounce non-consensual infant surgeries. The "Hermaphrodites with Attitude" demonstration had a huge impact on intersex recognition, leading to a change in medical protocols,

Activist Pidgeon Pagonis outside Chicago's Lurie Children's Hospital in 2018 calls for needless genital surgery on intersex infants to end. In 2020, the hospital ended most such surgery.

human rights protections, and to laws banning surgeries on children under 15 in many countries.

Intersex people continue to challenge outdated attitudes. As a group, they identify across a continuum, ranging from intersex to man, woman, non-binary, transgender, and many other identities. People with intersex bodies sometimes use descriptors that take in both intersex and transgender, such as the umbrella term "Two-Spirit" in Indigenous American communities. Equally, some intersex people do not identify as part of the LGBTQ+ community.

Despite advances, intersex children and adults are often still stigmatized. In order to protect people with intersex traits or status, campaigners continue to fight for informed medical care, counselling, and support. They demand equal access to public services and an end to discrimination in all areas of life, including work, education, and sports. To achieve these aims, it is essential that policymakers consult those affected when developing research and legislation that impact on their rights. ∎

The right to be X

In 2002, at the age of 48, Australian intersex activist Alexander (Alex) MacFarlane applied for a new passport that recognized their intersex identity. When Australia's Department of Foreign Affairs and Trade claimed that its computer system would only allow it to record applicants as either male or female, MacFarlane argued that this would run the risk of them committing fraud.

After months of pressure, the department agreed to include an "X" option on passports for Australians whose birth certificate records their sex as indeterminate, as MacFarlane's did (MacFarlane is believed to have been the first Australian to be issued with such a birth certificate). In 2003, MacFarlane also became the first person in Australia – and perhaps in the world – to have "X" as the gender marker printed on their passport.

RENAIS
AND
RETRIB
1300–1699

SANCE

UTION

The Black Death kills a third of Europe's population; some see it as God's punishment for sexual transgression.

1347–51

The Gutenberg press spurs book-printing in Europe, which soon fuels the spread of information from classical and contemporary sources about LGBTQ+ issues.

1450s

The Inquisition prosecutes more than 800 men for sodomy in Spain and more than 500 in Portugal.

1530–1630

1432

The Office of the Night is established in Florence to crack down on same-sex acts between men.

1492

Christopher Columbus reaches the Americas, launching a new age of global invasion, in which European colonizers persecute Indigenous peoples and punish non-heterosexual acts.

1533

Henry VIII's Buggery Act criminalizes sodomy in England. The king uses it to charge monks with sexual immorality and seize assets from monasteries.

The singling out of sodomy as a crime and the inclusion of same-sex sexual acts – of concern to the Christian Church from the 4th century CE – intensified in Europe in the Middle Ages, sparking systematic persecutions. From the 13th century, prosecuting sodomy had become not only the purview of the Church, but a matter for civil law. The criminalization of same-sex acts – mostly those between men – was codified in laws such as the English Buggery Act of 1533. Such laws had far-reaching effects as the major European powers invaded and colonized other parts of the world.

Prosecution and persecution went hand in hand in zealous campaigns to eradicate sodomitical vice. In Renaissance Italy, the Officers of the Night in Florence arrested and tried two-thirds of the city's male inhabitants for sodomy between 1459 and 1502, and from 1530 to 1630 more than 800 men were prosecuted for the same reason by the Spanish Inquisition.

The heavy hand of the law did not only crack down on relations between men. Both female same-sex relations and gender variance could be punished under sodomy laws – as in the case of Eleno/a de Céspedes, a seemingly intersex man in Spain who, after marrying a woman, was accused in 1588 of female sodomy, witchcraft, and bigamy and mocking the sacrament of marriage.

Printed possibilities

Despite widespread persecution, the 14th–17th centuries cannot simply be categorized as a time of hidden and forbidden desires. From the 15th century, the arrival of the printing press meant that texts could be widely disseminated; consequently, the presses brought pornography to the masses, with frank, bawdy, and titillating descriptions of all kinds of sexual acts – among them same-sex ones. The 17th century saw a number of erotic works, written by men, which were set in convents and depicted same-sex sexual acts between nuns, simultaneously mocking the Church and attempting to arouse readers.

From the 16th century onwards, a growing number of works about female–female desire were authored by women themselves. Scottish poet Mary Maitland wrote about wishing to marry another woman in her "Poem 49" of 1586, and others such as Welsh poet Katherine Philips and Breton poet Anne de

Describing Istanbul, the Ottoman bureaucrat and writer Latifi highlights its thriving sex industry and seductive male sex workers.

1570s

The Merrymount Colony in New England is attacked by some Puritans for its liberal practices, including tolerance of same-sex acts.

1627

A dramatic court case in London ends the marriage of AFAB cross-dresser James Howard and Arabella Hunt.

1682

English writer Aphra Behn's "To the Fair Clorinda" contains clear references to same-sex desire.

1688

1586

Mary Maitland writes her "Poem 49", for which she is considered the first named lesbian poet since Sappho.

1660s

The memoirs of the seigneur de Brantôme describe the alleged sexual licentiousness and gender play in the earlier French court.

1687

The Great Mirror of Male Love contains a number of stories about the phenomenon of "boy love" in Edo Japan.

Rohan followed suit in the 17th century, writing passionately about other women. At the same time that these poets were exploring their same-sex desires, physicians were publishing treatises that attempted to explain such desires as a medical problem. Some women suffered demeaning examinations by doctors and midwives intent on uncovering genital "abnormalities".

Beautiful boys

Taking cues from ancient Greece and Rome, men celebrated male beauty – and specifically the beauty of young men – in poetry and the arts, from Michelangelo's statue of David in Florence to English poets Richard Barnfield's beloved "fair boy" and William Shakespeare's "fair youth". The practice of an older man taking a younger partner was not limited to Christian Europe. In the Ottoman Empire, poets wrote of *gulamlar*, the beardless boys who entertained bearded men; and during Japan's Edo period an older warrior would take on a young man as both his apprentice and lover.

Colonial suppression

From 1492, European powers began to colonize other continents. Travel writers seeking to describe what they viewed as pagan and uncivilized behaviours portrayed the people of the Americas and the East as sexually transgressive: Andalusian scholar Leo Africanus described North African "witches" who seduced other women, and French writers similarly wrote of passions between women in the Ottoman Empire. While their characterization by European travellers was coloured by prejudice, it is true that non-Christian societies had markedly different approaches to gender and sexuality. Among the Indigenous peoples of the Americas, for example, many societies seemed to have no issue with same-sex relationships, and had terms in their languages for gender variance, as with the cross-dressing *xochihua* of the Nahua.

Indigenous attitudes towards gender and sexuality were not understood by the colonizing powers, who mischaracterized and prosecuted any gender variance or same-sex relations. The invaders punished what they perceived as unnatural and sinful acts, but also used Indigenous sexual practices and beliefs to justify brutal and murderous acts of conquest. ∎

58

INFINITE BEAUTY
RENAISSANCE ITALY
(14TH–16TH CENTURIES)

IN CONTEXT

FOCUS
Renaissance male sexuality

BEFORE
5th century BCE In ancient Greece, pederasty – an acknowledged relationship between an older and a younger man – becomes an established custom.

1360s Homer's *Iliad*, depicting the love between Achilles and Patroclus, is translated from Greek into Latin by Italian monk Leontius Pilatus.

AFTER
1623 In the first printed edition of Michelangelo's poems, many of the pronouns referring to the subject of the poet's desire are changed from male to female. The pronouns are restored in an English translation in 1878.

1890 The Zanardelli penal code is adopted in Italy and decriminalizes same-sex acts.

2016 Italy recognizes same-sex civil unions.

The Italian Renaissance was an era of cultural rebirth – celebrated in particular for its art and architecture – spanning the 14th to the 16th centuries. Italy at that time was also renowned for the widespread practice of sodomy. As defined by the Catholic Church, sodomy was any "unnatural" sexual behaviour, but it usually referred to sex between men.

The city of Florence garnered a reputation as both the cradle of the Renaissance and the capital of sodomy. According to records from 1459 to 1502, an estimated two-thirds of men in Florence were prosecuted by the city-state for sodomy by the age of 40. Among these were some of the period's most enduring figures, including polymath Leonardo da Vinci and painter Sandro Botticelli.

The practice of sodomy became one of the most turbulent political and moral issues of Renaissance Italy. From 1325, it was a crime that could carry severe punishment, including castration or death.

Power relations
Despite its prevalence, sodomy was acceptable to men of this era only when it conformed to a strict power dynamic, involving an "active" partner, usually over the age of 19, and a younger, "passive" boy or youth. This dynamic was considered vital to the expression of maleness. An active role, regardless of the gender of the passive participant, confirmed a man's virility. A passive role conferred femininity and even dishonour – although this was

Painter Giovanni Antonio Bazzi, seen here in his self-portrait (1508), was known as "Il Sodoma" ("the sodomite") because he loved young men. He called himself by this name with pride.

See also: Gender and sexuality in ancient Greece 20–23 ▪ Gender and sexuality in ancient Rome 30–35 ▪ The early Christian Church 38–41 ▪ Sodomy and the medieval Catholic Church 42–45

accepted as part of a stage of youth and could be redeemed once a man came of age. There was no concept of homosexuality as an identity, and sexual relationships between two older men were far less common or acceptable. It was also not unusual for men to engage in relations with men for a short period of time, and later marry a woman.

This type of relationship between an older and a younger man could be interpreted as pederasty – a concept from ancient Greece, in which a socially acknowledged and educational bond would be made between the two men. However, although Renaissance culture featured a revival of interest in classical thought, it would be a mistake to assume that this led

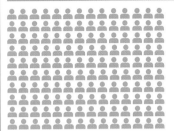

Prosecutions for sodomy in Renaissance Florence

The male population of Florence in the last four decades of the 15th century was around 20,000.

An average of 400 men a year during this time were accused of sodomy.

An average of 55–60 men a year were convicted for sodomy.

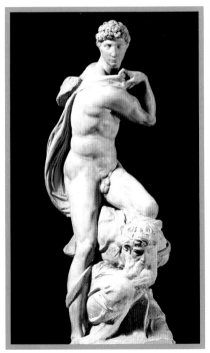

Michelangelo's statue *The Genius of Victory* (c. 1534) is said to be modelled on Tommaso dei Cavalieri, who was approximately 40 years his junior.

to sodomy being fully accepted in Renaissance society. The cultural output of the era idealized male beauty, but this did not mean sex between men was widely tolerated.

Instead, the rediscovery of classical thought offered a means by which men could explore and convey same-sex desires. Artworks often signalled taboo desires in commonly understood visual codes. Famous for his 1504 statue of David, symbol of youth and beauty, the painter and sculptor Michelangelo later expressed his love for young Tommaso dei Cavalieri through drawings, poems, and letters. One of his gifts to dei Cavalieri was his drawing *The Rape of Ganymede*, depicting a well-known Greek myth in which Zeus falls in love with and abducts a young boy as his lover and cup-bearer.

The Renaissance also saw new Latin translations of the works of the Greek philosopher Plato, along with attempts to harmonize his ideas of spiritual transcendence with Christian thought. In Platonic texts, interpretations of love between men varied. Typically, close bonds between men were held up as a transcendental form of love,

higher than the lustful love usually reserved for women. But in Italian Renaissance society, in which physical love between men was so common, presenting male–male love as a means of closeness to God proved increasingly contentious.

Persecuting sodomy

In 15th-century Florence, the "rooting-out" of sodomy became a symbol for a campaign against all of society's ills. Increased calls for crackdowns by the Church and public authorities led to the formation in 1432 of the Office of the Night – a dedicated court of six men, elected annually, tasked with finding and convicting sodomites. Operating until 1502, this court was aided by anonymous tips that people were encouraged to drop into purpose-built letterboxes. Taverns and other sites considered to be meeting places for sodomites were closed, and even discussions of sodomy could arouse suspicion.

An estimated 17,000 men were incriminated by the Office of the Night. The fact that only 3,000 were convicted perhaps reflects the socially ambiguous and ambivalent role of sexual relationships between men in Renaissance Italian society. ▪

A THOUSAND NAUGHTY CONCEITS AND LUSTY WORDS

HOMOEROTICISM AND THE FRENCH RENAISSANCE (15TH–17TH CENTURIES)

IN CONTEXT

FOCUS
Homoeroticism and gender play at court

BEFORE
1451 The marriage of French King Louis XI and Charlotte of Savoy marks the beginning of French involvement in Italy, which eventually leads to an invasion in 1494.

1462 Italian scholar Marsilio Ficino founds a group known as the Platonic Academy which becomes central to the period's reinterpretation of Neoplatonic philosophy.

AFTER
1660s Philippe I, the brother of King Louis XIV, has male lovers and wears women's clothing at court.

1791 During the French Revolution, the first Penal Code, informed by Enlightenment thinking rather than religion, does not explicitly condemn same-sex acts.

According to **Neoplatonic philosophy**, non-romantic and non-sexual **love between men** is the only form of **true, transcendental love**.

15th-century French philosophers **attempt to reconcile Neoplatonic philosophy** with traditional Christian understandings of **love between a man and a woman**.

This creates complexities and contradictions that allow a culture of **relative experimentation around sexuality and gender** to develop.

From the late 15th century until the French Revolution, the sexual reputation of France transformed from one of conservatism to one of relative freedom and experimentation. While the Catholic Church had historically defined what was deemed sexually acceptable, the influence of the Italian Renaissance brought with it the introduction of Neoplatonic philosophy, reframing considerations of sex and love in both intellectual and public spheres.

French philosophers grappled with how to reconcile classical understandings of sexuality with Christianity. Neoplatonism's presentation of male homosocial love as the highest and most spiritual form of true love made many uncomfortable, as did frequent allusions to same-sex attraction. What followed was an attempt to reframe a philosophy that had been created largely without women in mind, treating them as worthy objects of desire rather than as

See also: Gender and sexuality in ancient Greece 20–23 ▪ Renaissance Italy 58–59 ▪ Early modern lesbianism 74–79 ▪ Revolutionary France 100–01

A 17th-century portrait of Henri III, whose feminine style fuelled rumours about his sexuality. His opponents suggested that he engaged in sodomy.

temptresses who ensnared men with so-called "false beauty". Efforts were also made to categorize "good" and "bad" desires.

The royal court's reputation for sexual ambiguity was perceived as increasingly damaging to the realm. Both the court and the monarch were expected to be emblematic of the masculine virtues of power, potency, aggression, and emerging ideas of opposite-sex desire.

Brantôme's gossip
The sexual exploits of Francis I (r. 1515–47) were the subject of much court gossip, chronicled extensively by soldier and traveller Pierre de Bourdeille, seigneur de Brantôme. Brantôme's writings, first published in the 17th century and later in 1924 as *The Lives of Fair and Gallant Ladies*, offer glimpses into court life, and few of those mentioned are spared from association with some sort of illicit sex. Brantôme recounts

how noblemen in the court were pressured to take mistresses. The lives of women at court were part of a closed network to which Brantôme had little access; regardless, he blithely speculated about their same-sex relationships and spread rumours about the king.

Gender, politics, and power
The reign of Henri III, from 1574 to 1589, became a focus for the playing out of masculinity and social bonds between men. Henri failed to produce an heir, and was seen as overreliant on the counsel of his Italian mother, Catherine de Medici. His apparent lack of interest in war or sports and his enjoyment of parties led him to be seen as passive, weak, and effeminate. Many people were quick to connect these traits with sodomy, with fears stoked by the way Henri behaved in court. He was known for cross-dressing, wearing feminine clothing, make-up,

and jewellery. He was also famous for the intense relationships that he had with his *mignons* ("darlings" or "dainty ones") – men who emulated his effeminate style. It is not known whether these relationships were sexual, but Henri's opponents spread rumours of his sodomy nonetheless.

In 1589, with no further heirs, the reign of the House of Valois came to an end. Once it had been supplanted by the House of Bourbon, attempts were made to bring the court's sexual reputation and the king's image back under control, especially by Henri IV, who was known for his many mistresses. But until the French Revolution, the court continued to be a site of gender and sexual subversion, with varying degrees of scandal. ▪

The cross-dressing Mademoiselle Chevalier d'Éon in a 1787 fencing match. A diplomat, spy, and soldier, d'Éon lived openly as a man for the first half of their life and then as a woman.

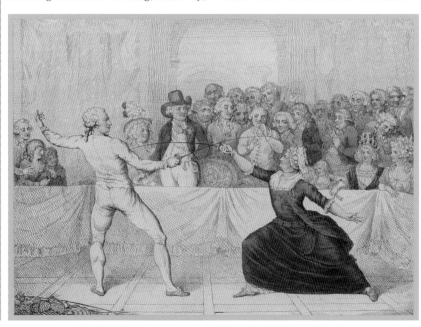

A NIGHTINGALE AMONG THE BEAUTIFUL
OTTOMAN GENDER AND SEXUALITY (15ᴛʜ–18ᴛʜ CENTURIES)

IN CONTEXT

FOCUS
Same-sex desire

BEFORE
1170–1200 Persian poet Nizāmī Ganjavī writes his *Khamsah* – five poems that have a major impact on later Ottoman Turkish love poetry.

1258–73 Jalāl al-Din Rūmī, a Sufi mystic and Persian poet, dictates the verses that form his *Masnavi* – a great influence on subsequent Ottoman poets.

***c.*1300** Osman I founds the Ottoman Empire in northwest Anatolia, present-day Turkey.

1453 Sultan Mehmet II captures Constantinople, capital of the Byzantine Empire, and makes it the Ottoman capital with a new local name – Istanbul.

AFTER
1839 The Gülhane Edict marks the start of Tanzimat, a period of reforms that begins to stigmatize same-sex acts.

In the heyday of classical Ottoman poetry, between the 15th and 18th centuries, same-sex desire was one element of an adult male's palette of pleasures, rather than a fixed identity. The literature of this period includes many examples of male authors' love and lust for younger men (the "beloveds") alongside their desire for women. As there are no substantial legal or autobiographical accounts of homoeroticism at the time, prose and poetry provide the greatest evidence of Ottoman men's affections for boys and other men.

Ottoman Turkish lacks grammatical gender, so the gender of the poets' objects of affection could be ambiguous, but other cues make it clear that these muses were both beardless boys and adolescent and adult women. Such poetry stemmed from a long tradition in Islamic literatures and often borrowed or adapted tropes from both Arabic and Persian poetry.

Although Islamic legal dictates forbade intercourse between two men, there was a clear distinction between love and sex. Expressing feelings of friendship, closeness, and

Ottoman Turkish identities and gender roles

Bearded men (*erkekler*)	Adult men for whom love of both women and beardless men is permissible.
Women (*zenler, kadýnlar, nisvan*)	Those assigned female at birth, for whom love and desire of bearded and beardless men is permissible.
Beardless men (*gulamlar*)	Young men – usually enslaved men, servants, or subjects – for whom love of both women and bearded men is permissible.
Gulampareler	Bearded men who love beardless youths.
Zenpareler	Bearded men who love women and girls.
Köçekler	Dancers assigned male at birth who adopt feminine clothing and behaviour in their performances.

See also: The Abbasid Caliphate 46–47 ▪ Male–male love poetry 80–81 ▪ Same-sex narratives in Urdu poetry 96–97 ▪ Changing Ottoman society 104–05 ▪ LGBTQ+ Muslims 278–79

love for one another was not illicit. The male–male emotions described sometimes encapsulated ideas of faithfulness, piety, and political loyalty and appear in works about religious mysticism or appropriate courtly conduct. At other times, there was explicit reference to physical pleasure.

A broad spectrum of tastes

Despite the legal constraints on male–male sexual acts and consuming alcohol, there was a thriving sex industry in Istanbul's wine houses where young men – often dancers – sold their services to older men. Latifi, a 16th-century

A 17th-century image for the Ottoman poet Atai's *Hamse* (*Quintet*) depicts a group of seated, bearded men seducing a beardless youth (bottom left).

Ottoman bureaucrat, poet, and chronicler, wrote: "Teasing, smiling and uttering sweet words, In this, male prostitutes surpass females".

For Ottomans during this era, sex was just one of many physical, mental, and emotional urges. Manuals on sex and sex acts were not uncommon, and Ottoman paintings attest to an interest in intercourse between men. Some explicit writings demonstrate that sexual roles, especially penetration, and relationships often mirrored established codes of age, hierarchy, class, and ethnic or religious difference, but these were not fixed. At times, men could fulfil new roles as they wished, or as they aged or advanced socially.

The love poetry of adult men highlights their erotic lives, but it eclipses the experiences and

A bearded man converses with a beardless youth in an illustration from a work by the 16th-century Ottoman poet Bâkî, whose themes included love.

emotions of women and people defying the gender binary. Texts written overtly by a woman for a woman are scarce in the historical sources. What is present are rare mentions, by men, of women who loved and lusted for other women, or of dancers, beauties, and sex workers who combined both masculine and feminine roles. This evidence contrasts sharply with Western European accounts – which are probably exaggerated – of widespread love and sex between women in the Ottoman lands.

Not unchallenged

The tolerance and encouragement of love between males did not go unchallenged. Occasionally, those who sought to restrict or obliterate it on grounds of its perceived immorality had the upper hand. Whatever their claims and successes, however, same-sex desire remained an undeniable thread in the everyday life of the Ottoman Empire. ▪

THE ABOMINABLE VICE WILL BE ELIMINATED

THE SPANISH INQUISITION (1478)

IN CONTEXT

FOCUS
Persecution for sodomy

BEFORE
506 The Visigothic Code imposes the death penalty for men convicted of sodomy.

1138 Portugal becomes independent of Spain but retains harsh punishments for sodomy, including death.

1184 The first Inquisition is established in Languedoc, France, primarily to repress the spread of Cathar heresy.

AFTER
1536 The Portuguese Inquisition is abolished after the Liberal Revolution of 1820.

1834 The Spanish Inquisition is abolished, six years after the last execution resulting from its investigations.

1979 Spain decriminalizes same-sex acts, after an era of it being punished under dictator Francisco Franco.

Beginning in France in the 12th century, a series of harsh investigations and intrusive institutions were set up by the Catholic Church to prosecute breaches of canon law and actions by individuals that were viewed as heresy or apostasy.

The Inquisition soon spread across Europe and the Americas. Its most infamous manifestation was the Spanish Inquisition, which was instigated in 1478 by King Ferdinand II and Queen Isabella of Spain. It is estimated that this Inquisition

prosecuted around 150,000 people, with between 3,000 and 5,000 people executed, until it was abolished in the 19th century.

The Spanish Inquisition emerged during the final years of Spain and Portugal's Reconquista, a campaign to recapture areas of the Iberian Peninsula ruled by Muslims, which led to the violent expulsion or execution of Muslims and Jews. Aiding this campaign, the Inquisition focused on those known as "New Christians" who had been forced to convert but were suspected of practising their original faiths in secret.

Persecuting sodomy
Courts of the Inquisition soon began to address concerns over violations of social order by "Old Christians" too, including sexual practices that were deemed "unnatural", such as sodomy.

Sodomy was used as a catch-all term for acts including anal sex, bestiality, oral sex, and sex with

The banner of the Spanish Inquisition is shown in this 1722 engraving. The Inquisition was independent from the Church and was responsible to the Spanish Crown.

See also: Sodomy and the medieval Catholic Church 42–45 ▪ Renaissance Italy 58–59 ▪ Colonial Latin America 66–67 ▪ The criminalization of sodomy 68–71

A victim of the Spanish Inquisition is forced to wear a conical hat in an act of public humiliation known as auto-da-fé. This might preface execution by being burned at the stake.

dildos, so opposite-sex as well as same-sex acts could be prosecuted. Sodomy was usually considered to lie outside the jurisdiction of Inquisitorial forces. In some cases, the Inquisition felt it dangerous to make the public aware that these "vices" even existed. A notable exception is the Inquisition in Aragon, which prosecuted more than 800 sodomy cases between 1570 and 1630.

A well-known case of the Inquisition in Toledo is that of Eleno/a de Céspedes, a formerly enslaved man who historians believe was what we might now call intersex or transgender. Assigned female at birth, Céspedes was arrested in 1588 for sodomy with a woman. His case was deemed to be a case of witchcraft and passed to the Inquisition. Witnesses testified that Céspedes was a man, but

medical examiners declared him to be a woman. To avoid ruling on such complexities, the Inquisition instead charged Céspedes with bigamy for not documenting the death of his former husband before remarrying.

New World colonization

Spain and Portugal's colonization of the Americas led to encounters with new religions and attitudes to sexuality that were perceived as threatening to the Church. While many Indigenous people were punished under civil law, the Inquisition remained focused on those it had persecuted in Europe, such as Portuguese Jews.

Spain's colonial Inquisition was formally established in 1571 in Mexico City, capital of its vast new American territories. The cases it tried give glimpses of same-sex desire in the country, though cases of sodomy were still only allowed to by tried by civil law. ▪

Love letters

The Inquisition relied on a climate of fear and the complete cooperation of citizens in reporting heretical behaviour, but gathering evidence strong enough to prosecute sometimes proved difficult.

In Portugal, in 1664, musician and instrument maker Manuel Viegas passed to the Vicar of Silves a collection of explicit love letters he had received from Francisco Correa Netto, a sexton at Silves Cathedral. Viegas had decided to marry a woman named Maria Nunes, and to turn in his jealous former lover. The Vicar promptly handed the letters over to the Inquisition in Évora, which began an investigation. Despite the letters and claims from several people that Correa Netto was a "sodomite", their inability to obtain proof of anal penetration, and the careful wording of the letters, meant that he was never arrested or tried. Five of Correa Netto's letters to Viegas have been preserved. They are the oldest surviving homoerotic letters in a modern European language.

My love and bounty: my feelings cannot rest an hour, either by day or night, without bringing to mind your companionship and your sweet words…
Francisco Correa Netto
Letter to Manuel Viegas, 1664

CHRISTIAN GUILT IS STILL VERY STRONG

COLONIAL LATIN AMERICA (16TH–19TH CENTURIES)

IN CONTEXT

FOCUS
Suppression of Indigenous genders and sexualities

BEFORE
1451 Pope Nicholas V allows the Papal Inquisition to prosecute sodomy.

1478 The Spanish Inquisition is established; it will try more than 800 people for sodomy between 1570 and 1630.

1492 Sponsored by Spain, explorer Christopher Columbus lands in the Bahamas, and New World colonization begins.

AFTER
1883 The Tierra del Fuego gold rush in Chile leads to the Selk'nam genocide and the displacement and deaths of many other Indigenous people.

1980s The HIV/AIDS virus spreads in Latin American homosexual communities; some conservative and religious sectors claim it reflects "divine intervention".

In the early 16th century, Spain and Portugal divided the "New World" of the Americas into dominions over which they each had control. Established in 1535, the Viceroyalty of New Spain included what is now Mexico, Central America, northern areas of South America, the Caribbean, and parts of the southwestern and central United States. It ended in 1821 after the Mexican wars for independence. The Portuguese colonization of Brazil began in 1500 and ended in the early 19th century. The pursuit of land and resources was the primary driver for this aggressive expansion, but so too was the desire to impose Christianity and European ideas of social, cultural, and moral acceptability on its numerous Indigenous populations.

European moral guidelines
As the conquerors established new political hierarchies, they enforced concepts of "normal" sexuality and gender, and used them to justify the subjugation, othering, and slaughter of many Indigenous populations. Sodomy, the "nefarious

Spain and Portugal **dominate the Indigenous peoples** of the New World through **war**, **enslavement**, and **disease**.

Domination includes the **imposition of European values** promoting **heterosexuality**.

Non-heterosexual Indigenous practices and **non-normative genders** are **deemed sinful** and **brutally suppressed**.

See also: The earliest evidence for LGBTQ+ people 18–19 ▪ Sodomy and the medieval Catholic Church 42–45 ▪ Intersex rights 48–53 ▪ The criminalization of sodomy 68–71 ▪ Indigenous American Two-Spirit people 258–61

Accused of sodomy, Panamanians were thrown to the dogs of conquistador Vasco Núñez de Balboa – portrayed here by Protestant artist Theodor de Bry.

Mexico, there are also accounts of *muxhe* – individuals assigned male at birth who dress and take on roles associated with women.

Contemporary records most commonly mention same-sex relations between Indigenous men, but also briefly mention female–female sex. Temple life in Mexico was often depicted as involving relationships between older and younger men. Lords in Ecuador and Peru were also said to have kept adolescent boys for sexual purposes.

"Justifying" persecution

During the 1550–51 Valladolid debate in Spain – the first European moral debate to discuss the rights of Latin America's Indigenous people – officials "justified" their brutal conquest by pointing to Indigenous people's practices of cross-dressing and sodomy. The colonizers thought that sodomy would spread unless it was excised via enslavement and death. Aspects of such thinking still fuel prejudices today. ▪

sin", and other non-heteronormative acts and identities were condemned as *contra natura* ("against nature").

Mass killings of the Indigenous populations has meant that what is known of their sexual practices and attitudes comes almost entirely from European sources, usually in relation to criminal cases. Christian morality influenced these writings and the terms used, but they offer some evidence of the variety of identities colonizers encountered.

Fluid sexualities

In the 16th century, Franciscan friar Bernardino de Sahagún published an ethnographic work called *The Florentine Codex*, written with the involvement of the Nahuas, the Indigenous people of what is now central Mexico. The work includes translations for Nahuatl terms, such as *xochihua* ("flower-bearer") – an androgynous, cross-dressing figure – and *patlache*, which was translated both as women who have sex with women and as "hermaphrodites". The words *cuino* or *puto* were both used to mean a passive sodomite.

Hundreds of Indigenous communities may have included people of non-normative genders. The *berdache*, now known as Two-Spirit people, adopted the dress and social status of the opposite sex. Among the Machu living in present-day Argentina and Chile, colonizers encountered the *machi weye* – healers and religious leaders who defy the idea of a gender binary by travelling between male and female identities, or entirely outside them. *Machi weye* were said to have made a "pact with the devil". From Zapotec cultures of Oaxaca,

For the Zapotecs, there are four genders: woman, man, lesbian, and *muxhe*.
Elvis Guerra
Mexican Zapotec poet and *muxhe*

CRUEL, INDECENT, AND RIDICULOUS

THE CRIMINALIZATION OF SODOMY (1533)

From around 1450 to 1800, the criminalization of same-sex acts (under the term "sodomy") surged in Europe. In England in 1533, a year before Henry VIII broke with the Roman Catholic Church, sodomy became a civil offence under the Buggery Act; it had previously come under Catholic ecclesiastical law. Sodomy at the time was defined as anal sex with penetration and the emission of semen, and applied not only to sex between men, but also to sex between men and women, as well

See also: Sodomy and the medieval Catholic Church 42–45 ▪ The Spanish Inquisition 64–65 ▪ The decriminalization of same-sex acts 184–85

Henry VIII's pursuit of monks for sodomy – but in reality to line the royal coffers – was known and later mocked, as in this illustration from 1850.

as bestiality. Men, however, were usually targeted. From the 13th century, the Church had decreed that civil authorities could also prosecute sodomy, which became punishable by death.

Political motives

After Henry VIII broke with the Catholic Church, the Buggery Act proved expedient for tackling his mounting debts. Discrediting monasteries by charging monks with sexual immorality enabled him to acquire the monasteries' wealth. Accusations of masturbation, termed "voluntary pollution", were enough to have monasteries closed.

Mary I, Henry VIII's daughter, who succeeded him in 1553, restored Catholicism, and repealed the Buggery Act, preferring sodomy to be judged by ecclesiastical courts. Her successor, the Protestant queen Elizabeth I, re-enacted the

Act in 1564, but little is known about the number of prosecutions in the 16th and 17th centuries. One notorious case was that of Mervyn Touchet, 2nd Earl of Castlehaven, who was convicted of rape and sodomy and beheaded in 1631.

Moral backlash

When William III and Mary II acceded to the throne in 1689, public attitudes had shifted against the liberalism of the preceding Restoration period (1660–85). The Society for the Reformation of Manners, founded in 1691, was among several groups that aimed to suppress what they deemed as immoral and "lewd" activities. It targeted brothels, sex work, and same-sex acts. It was especially active in the 1720s, with a series of raids on "molly houses" (same-sex meeting places), and its accusations led to a marked increase in arrests for sodomy and "attempted sodomy".

At least 10 men were hanged for sodomy in 18th-century England, and the pillory, a more frequent punishment, could result in death, »

The trial of Mervyn Touchet

In 1631, Anglo-Irish aristocrat Mervyn Touchet, 2nd Earl of Castlehaven, went on trial for the rape of his wife and two counts of sodomy in a case brought before the Privy Council, Charles I's advisers, by the earl's eldest son and heir, James. The earl was convicted of both crimes, sentenced to death, and beheaded – the only English MP ever to be executed for a non-political crime.

At his trial, the earl had stated that, because his servant Giles Broadway had taken part in the sodomy, Broadway could not be called to testify against him. But the Privy Council ruled that a participant in a crime could be a legal witness until convicted, as sodomy would otherwise "seldom or never be discovered". The ruling set a legal precedent and led to many more such prosecutions over the centuries. To impose the death penalty, however, English courts required proof of penetration; if incomplete, a lesser sentence was imposed.

Mervyn Touchet, born in 1593, was both an MP and justice of the peace. He maintained that his wife and son had conspired against him.

Motivations for criminalizing sodomy

Papal supremacy
By persecuting "sodomites",
the Catholic Church stamped
its moral authority in Europe
and strengthened its power.

Pretext for plunder
Henry VIII used his Buggery
Act to charge Catholic monks
with sodomy, seize their assets,
and crush their authority.

Religious fear
The New England Puritans,
fearing divine retribution
for "unnatural" sins, made
sodomy a capital offence.

Wilful ignorance
Catholic European conquerors
in the Americas misconstrued
and demonized Indigenous
customs and practices.

as hostile crowds were brutal. The last two British executions for sodomy were those of James Pratt and John Smith in London in 1835. The Elizabethan statute remained unchanged until 1861, when the maximum punishment of death was reduced to life imprisonment. Finally, in 1967, same-sex acts were decriminalized in England and Wales, following recommendations from the Wolfenden Committee 10 years earlier.

Continental inquisitions
From the Middle Ages onwards, convictions and executions for sodomy were much more common in mainland Europe than in England. The charge of sodomy was one of many tools used by religious leaders and monarchs to establish their authority and persecute minorities. After the Black Death had swept through Europe in the mid-14th century, "sodomites" were among those blamed, as priests preached that God punished sins with pestilence.

Following the lead of the Papal Inquisition in 1451, the Spanish and Portuguese Inquisitions prosecuted sodomy as a sin connected with heresies that contravened Christian faith. The Spanish Inquisition

prosecuted more than 800 males between 1570 and 1630, with at least 150 burnt at the stake. The Portuguese Inquisition prosecuted some 500 cases in the same period.

France's "liberté"
In France and elsewhere, as Protestantism spread during the 16th century, both Catholics and Protestants used accusations of sodomy and other sexual "crimes" to discredit their religious rivals. In the city of Ghent in newly Calvinist Flanders, five Catholic monks accused of sodomy were burned at the stake in 1578 and three more

The very Mention of this detestable Vice is shocking to human Nature, and shakes the Soul of even great Sinners …
**Argus Centoculi
(pseudonym)**
*Old England, or The Broadbottom
Journal, 2 June 1750*

were flogged. In France, sodomy had been a capital offence, prosecuted by the monarchy since the late Middle Ages, but aristocrats were often spared execution rather than exposed and were instead exiled or denied royal support. Commoners accused of sodomy were often denied a trial and frequently burned to death. Jean Diot and Bruno Lenoir were the last French victims, executed in Paris in 1750.

In 1789, at the start of the French Revolution that overthrew the monarchy, Article 4 of the Declaration of the Rights of Man defined liberty as the freedom "to do anything that doesn't hurt anyone else". Two years later, all French sodomy laws were repealed, but the public remained critical of same-sex desire, associating it with criminality, and the police often pursued men who favoured same-sex relationships.

"Civilizing" the natives
From the 16th century onwards, Spain, Portugal, England, and France were exploring and conquering nations in the Americas, Africa, and the Pacific. Colonies were established and Indigenous peoples were forcibly

LGBTQ+ rights protesters in Mumbai in 2008 call for Article 377 of the Indian Penal Code to be removed. The article criminalizing sexual acts "against the order of nature" was reformed in 2018.

brought under Western rule. As Catholic missionaries arrived, the "natives" had European morality thrust upon them. In Central and South America, Spanish invaders encountered Indigenous peoples whose cultural traditions celebrated what the Spanish perceived as gender reversal; they labelled these individuals *bardajes* ("passive sodomites"), and persecuted them. French explorers in North America later used the term *bardaches* or *berdaches* for these Indigenous people; in 1990, Indigenous peoples would adopt the term "Two-Spirit".

The Caribs of the Caribbean and Mayans of Mexico and Central America – the first groups the invading Spanish encountered – appeared to accept and approve of same-sex relations. European invaders and their Christian priests, however, had no desire to understand native institutions or the spiritual element of traditions that used same-sex sexuality and cross-dressing. They viewed such practices as "devilish" and cruelly repressed them.

Controlling the settlers
Emigrants to North America, such as the Puritan Pilgrims who settled in New England, imposed a rigid moral code on their own Christian communities that emphasized opposite-sex relations – but only within marriage – in a bid to further procreation and create stable families. The crimes of buggery and bestiality carried the death penalty, although this was difficult to apply as two witnesses were required.

One notable rebel was English colonist lawyer Thomas Morton, who fraternized with the local Indigenous peoples and established a liberal community called Merrymount near what is now Boston, Massachusetts. In 1627, his decision to erect a 24 m- (80 ft-) maypole – seen as a blatant phallic symbol – and to stage a festival enraged some Puritans. They accused the community of holding drunken pagan orgies, attacked and occupied the town, and had Morton deported to London. By 1776, when

American colonies declared independence from Britain, sodomy was a capital crime in much of North America and remained so until the 19th century, although the death penalty was rarely carried out.

Enduring impact
By the late 16th century, Spain's strict Catholic precepts, including the demonization of sodomy, were rigidly enforced throughout its huge New World empire. They had significant consequences in Mexico, the Caribbean, and Central and South America, where same-sex relations are still often stigmatized.

France's early decriminalization of sodomy brought a relaxation of laws in many of its colonies, but some West African nations, such as Cameroon and Senegal, retain versions of French sodomy laws. England's Buggery Act and its successors also proved a lasting means of persecution. In 1860, the Indian Penal Code, devised "to inculcate European morality into resistant masses", as Human Rights Watch explains, set a pattern of legislation on British colonies in Asia and Africa that many independent nations still retain. ∎

Female same-sex relationships

The English Buggery Act of 1533 did not explicitly target men, but sodomy was widely perceived as a male penetrative act involving the emission of semen. In the early 17th century, English barrister and judge Edward Coke wrote that women could only be guilty of sodomy if they had sexual relations with a "brute beast". In 1655–65, however, the Puritans of New Haven, North America, briefly made sex between women punishable by death. On the European continent, countries including France, Spain, Italy, Germany, and Switzerland at various times equated female same-sex acts with male sodomy and made them capital offences.

In 16th-century Spain, jurist and priest Antonio Gómez declared that if female same-sex relations occurred using a penetrative instrument, both women should be burned. Yet despite such laws, there is little historical evidence of prosecutions against women.

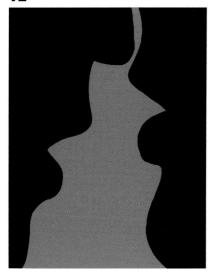

YOU HAVE ME ALL ON FIRE

PORNOGRAPHY (1534)

IN CONTEXT

FOCUS
Same-sex erotic content

BEFORE
11th century French bishop
Marbodius of Rennes pens
erotic lyric poetry about
his female and male
love interests.

AFTER
1748 *Memoirs of a Woman
of Pleasure* (or *Fanny Hill*) by
British author John Cleland
is considered the first English
pornographic novel.

1769 French author Rétif de La
Bretonne's study of sex work,
Le Pornographe, popularizes
the term "pornography".

1860s Excavations at Pompeii,
Italy, reveal erotic paintings in
Pompeian homes, including
images of young men.

1872 Irish author Sheridan
Le Fanu publishes the Gothic
novella *Carmilla,* about a
young woman who is preyed
on by a female vampire.

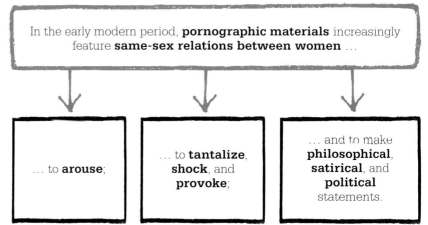

In the early modern period, **pornographic materials** increasingly feature **same-sex relations between women** …

… to **arouse**;

… to **tantalize**, **shock**, and **provoke**;

… and to make **philosophical**, **satirical**, and **political** statements.

Following the invention of the printing press around 1440, sexually explicit material, once strictly private, could be produced in quantities for a growing European audience. Initially only for the wealthy and literate, by the 18th century, pornography was circulated to all classes, often illustrated by explicit images. For those who were illiterate, such images were also circulated on their own. Aimed at a male readership, the material ranged from prose, plays, and poetry to satirical pamphlets with lewd illustrations that poked fun at the establishment, especially the Church.

Italian libertine Pietro Aretino wrote many bold letters and satirical pieces, including his *Ragionamenti* (*Dialogues*) of 1534 – one of the first known examples of pornographic texts in early modern Europe. The *Ragionamenti* feature frank discussions between two sex workers about masturbation, dildos, vaginal and anal sex, group sex, and male–male and female–female sex.

Sex between women
A number of French writers in the late 18th century depicted female–female sex, sometimes for satirical or political reasons. Anti-royalist pamphlets, for instance, featured

See also: Homoeroticism and the French Renaissance 60–61 ▪ The criminalization of sodomy 68–71 ▪ Early modern lesbianism 74–79 ▪ Erotic friendship in America and Europe 92–95 ▪ Revolutionary France 100–01

Ah Lud! How you squeeze me in your Arms; don't you see I am naked to my Smock?
Venus in the Cloister
Sister Agnès in response to Sister Angélique's attempts to seduce her

Queen Marie Antoinette in pornographic poses with other women. Rumours of her sapphic relationships were rife during the revolutionary turmoil that led to her execution in 1793.

Pornographic tales of female–female sex often employed the trope of an experienced older women teaching an "innocent" younger woman about sex, usually by engaging in physical acts with her. French writer Nicolas Chorier's *Aloisiae Sigeae Toletanae Satyra Sotadica de Arcanis Amoris et Veneris* was written in Latin and published under a pseudonym in 1660. Translated into French, and later into English as *The School of Women*, the erotic novel features lessons from Tullia (aged 26) to her young cousin Octavia (15), whom she instructs in sexual practices.

Erotic fiction of this kind was often set in nunneries, mocking the Church. *Venus in the Cloister or The Nun in her Smock,* published in 1683 under the pseudonym Abbé du Prat but attributed to French writer Jean Barrin, features Sister Angélique (19) and Sister Agnès (16). In a series of dialogues, the elder instructs the younger on topics like sex between women, voyeurism, fellatio, orgies, sex between men, and incest.

Enlightenment philosopher Denis Diderot's *La Religieuse* (*The Nun*), an anti-clerical work criticizing religious institutions, was published in France in 1796. Its focus is a young nun's bid to escape convent life and the Mother Superior who seeks a lesbian relationship with her.

The erotic use of female same-sex relationships for a male gaze has endured as a pornographic trope. However, in *Passions Between Women* (1994), Irish–Canadian writer Emma Donoghue asserts that in many of these early texts women were actually accorded clear agency and their erotic pleasure affirmed. ▪

Diderot's *La Religieuse* details the young Sister Suzanne's relationships with three Mother Superiors – one who befriends her, another who persecutes her, and a third who fails to seduce her.

Pietro Aretino

Born in 1492 in Arezzo, Italy, Pietro Aretino was the son of a humble shoemaker. Claiming to be the son of a nobleman, he set himself up as a painter to the elite in Perugia before moving to Rome in 1517.

Aretino was a skilled writer of poetry, plays, and satirical prose. He used his literary talents to pen scathing attacks on his powerful contemporaries, lampooning the rich and famous. Aretino's biting satire was highly effective, and he became wealthy when the nobility sent him gifts to persuade him not to criticize them.

In 1524, however, Aretino published *Sonetti lussuriosi* (*Lewd Sonnets*) to accompany some graphic illustrations, and these, together with his lascivious reputation as a prolific lover of men as well as women, proved to be a step too far. Forced to leave Rome, he moved to Venice, where he spent the rest of his life.

One of Aretino's friends was the artist Titian (1488/90–1576), who painted several portraits of him. Aretino died in 1556, supposedly suffocating when he could not stop laughing.

MY JOY, MY CROWN, MY FRIEND!

EARLY MODERN LESBIANISM (1586–1688)

IN CONTEXT

FOCUS
**Female–female desire
in literature**

BEFORE
***c.*1440** In Mainz, Germany,
Johannes Gutenberg sets up
Europe's first printing press.

1516 Italian Ludovico Ariosto's
epic poem *Orlando furioso* tells
of love between a princess and
a cross-dressing woman.

1534–36 *Ragionamenti* –
pornographic dialogues by
Pietro Aretino – portray
explicit female–female sex.

AFTER
18th century The Greek
poet Sappho of Lesbos is held
up increasingly as a paragon
of lesbianism.

1878 "Love Stronger than
Death" by British poet Mary F.
Robinson describes the poet's
separation from her female
lover in death.

All the Olympic torches,
Illuminated in their course,
Are not lovelier ornaments
Than the eyes of my beautiful
Beloved.
Anne de Rohan

In the late 16th and 17th centuries, **printed works are circulated
in growing numbers**.

Anatomical treatises, travel
writing, poetry, plays, and
pornography all address the
subject of **erotic love
between women**.

**Classical ideas of
sexuality**, including
female–female sex and
love, are **increasingly
shared**.

The expression of female–female sex **reaches a wider audience**.

From the mid-16th century in Europe, the availability of printed works began to increase dramatically, as their sale and distribution moved from printers to commercial booksellers and publishers. This fledgling industry gathered pace through the 17th century as Latin and Greek texts gave way to the vernacular, literacy rates rose, and accessible collections of scientific, medical, and other information – such as almanacs and encyclopedias – emerged.

Among the expanding volume of printed works were new accounts of women's erotic love and desire for other women. While these works embraced the classical Greek and Roman understandings of female–female sex rediscovered during the Renaissance, they also added contemporary views and more specific definitions that began to separate female–female sex from other "sins against nature".

Literature and art that dealt with female desires continued to be produced by men for men, but some women found a way, mostly through poetry, to express their own experiences of female–female intimacy. The discovery of a poem written in 1586 by Mary Maitland, a Scottish collector of poetry, makes her the first named lesbian poet since Sappho. Over the next century, she was joined by other writers, such as Anne de Rohan in France, Katherine Philips in Wales, and Aphra Behn in England.

The male viewpoint

That women might "unnaturally" desire erotic intimacy with other women posed a conundrum for men. According to theological and medical views at the time, women were more governed by their passions than men, whose phallus-centred notions about what constituted "sex" led them to view female–female erotic acts as either impossible or an imitation of male behaviours. In the 1615 *A Discourse of Marriage and Wiving*, English clergyman Alexander Niccholes sarcastically asked: "What Female Comfort can one woman finde, Within the bed with other woman-kinde?" The implicit answer was "nothing", so men tried to find a cause for such desires within the female body.

See also: Sappho of Lesbos 24–27 ▪ Gender and sexuality in ancient Rome 30–35 ▪ Renaissance Italy 58–59 ▪ Erotic friendship in America and Europe 92–95 ▪ Sapphism 98 ▪ The diaries of Anne Lister 102–03

Medical writers and jurists focused on the clitoris, which, when deemed to be over-large, was thought to spur women on to "abuse" their genitals through rubbing or penetration. In both popular culture and official circles, it was debated whether such women were "hermaphrodites" (people who would be known today as intersex), had miraculously experienced a change in sex, or were dressing and living "fraudulently" as men (today's trans). Women with anatomical differences who came to the attention of authorities underwent intrusive examinations by doctors and midwives to find their "true" sex.

In 1671, midwife Jane Sharp published *The Midwives Book* – the first midwifery manual written by an Englishwoman. She too sees female–female sex as an imitation of male–female sex and claims it is rife in foreign parts: "… some lewd women have endeavoured to use it [the clitoris} as men do theirs [the penis]. In the Indies and Egypt, they are frequent, but I never heard but of one in this country."

Tales of the reputed behaviours of non-European women figured large in the popular imagination, fed by the accounts of male travellers. Describing the efforts of North African "witches" to entice other women with their caresses, Andalusian diplomat and scholar Leo Africanus (*c.*1485–*c.*1554) called them an "abominable vice" and the result of demonic possession. French geographer Nicolas de Nicolay (1517–83) related how in the Ottoman *hamman*, or public baths, women "sometimes become so fervently in love the one of the other… [that they] handle and grope them everywhere at their pleasures". French merchant Jean-Baptiste Tavernier (1605–89) likewise invoked the "unvoluntary restraint" of the Ottoman sultan's *seraglio*, or harem, which encouraged Turkish women to follow "the wicked example of the men" who engage in sodomy.

Labelling and naming
Various terms were used – by men – to signify women who engaged in sex with other women. As well as

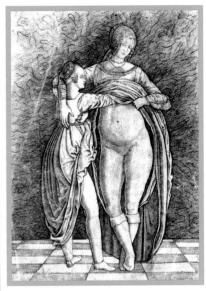

Printed erotic engravings, such as this Italian work of a young girl undressing an older woman, became widely shared in the 16th century.

"sodomitess" and "hermaphrodite", vague condemnations such as "unlawful sin or vice", "abuses her body", or "plays the part of a man" were used by disapproving writers. A less judgemental phrase – *donna* »

In *As You Like It* (1599), English playwright William Shakespeare lightheartedly depicted the desire of Celia for her friend Rosalind, who has cross-dressed as a shepherd.

The theatre of cross-dressing

From the 1580s onwards, many plays – although less explicit than other written sources – portrayed female–female love, largely through female cross-dressing. This had become a convention of Italian Renaissance theatre, following the traditions of cross-dressing in ancient Greek and Roman dramas. Plays on public stages in England, France, and Spain would often depict a female character expressing erotic desire for a woman who, passing as male, often encourages such attention.

Although the plays mostly end with the revelation of "true" sex and heterosexual marriage, they catered to an audience keen to watch homoerotic scenes.

Also popular were the many adaptations of the Roman poet Ovid's tales of the nymph Callisto – impregnated by Jove while disguised as Diana – and of Iphis and Ianthe – where Iphis, a girl raised as a boy, has her sex changed by the goddess Isis so she can wed Ianthe, the girl she loves.

> Thy body is a natural paradise,
> In whose self, unmanur'd,
> all pleasure lies,
> Nor needs perfection; why
> should'st thou then
> Admit the tillage of a harsh
> rough man?
> **John Donne**

con donna (meaning "woman with woman") – appeared in *Lives of Fair and Gallant Ladies*, written in 1665–66 by French soldier, historian, and traveller Pierre de Bourdeille, seigneur de Brantôme. His description of the alleged sexual experiences of "illustrious ladies" at the French court – the fullest, most gossipy account of lesbianism during this period – employs all the male explanations of the day.

Proposing that an Italian noblewoman imported *donna con donna* to France, Brantôme argues that a woman's practice of *frigarelle* (a term for rubbing) may be caused by simple inclination, her anatomy, or circumstances – such as being segregated in a convent or *seraglio*. Ultimately, he maintains that such sex is counterfeit and "merely the apprenticeship to the great business with men". His tolerant yet dismissive attitude echoed that

Nymphs embrace in a "kissing war" in Flemish artist Anthony van Dyck's painting *Mirtillo Crowning Amarillis* (1632). Pastoral scenes of all-female societies in the classical past engaged in erotic acts were a popular motif.

of 17th-century Italian and French pornography, which depicted explicit sexual encounters among women as titillating but insignificant.

When writers labelled women who love women, they largely used derogatory words. The most common was "tribade" – from *tribas*, Latin for someone who rubbed someone. In 1566, French scholar and printer Henri Estienne distinguished between a woman who had "simulated" a husband's role with a dildo – for which she was burned alive – and the "sordid" acts of "tribades in ancient times". By 1600, the term "tribade" was associated with both classical and contemporary women across Europe.

Leo Africanus used the term "fricatrice" (from the Latin *fricare*, to rub) to describe the "witches" of North Africa. In the "clitoris" entry of his mid-17th-century anatomy, Danish surgeon Thomas Bartholin called women-loving-women "confricatrices" or "rubsters", with the activities of rubsters understood to involve "frigging" one another.

The influence of Sappho

When Nicolas de Nicolay sought a point of comparison for Turkish women in the *hamman*, he invoked the name of the ancient Greek poet Sappho of Lesbos. By this time, Sappho's poetic fragments, including lyrics of love to women as well as men, had begun to appear in printed works, where she was held up as an exemplar of Greek lyric poetry.

English poet John Donne appropriated the figure of Sappho in "Sappho to Philaenis" (1633). In this haunting lament, Sappho complains that her poetic fire has been quenched because her desire for poetry has been replaced by her desire for Philaenis – a woman. Obsessed with Philaenis's body and its resemblance to her own, she claims that her beloved is nature's

> Would mighty Jove grant me
> the fortune
> With you to have your
> Brutus' part
> And metamorphosing
> our shape,
> My sex into his will convert...
> **Mary Maitland**

"best work", with which her poetry could never compare. The poem explicitly denies the attractions of sex with men and celebrates the pleasures of two female bodies.

The female gaze

Beyond the unusually sympathetic male voice of Donne were women writers who addressed female–female love seemingly from personal experience. In Mary Maitland's untitled "Poem 49", the female poet-speaker contemplates her beloved's perfection and proclaims herself ravished by their mutual affection. She compares their love with famous male–female couples such as Brutus and Portia; with male pairs such as Achilles and Patroclus, following the classical ideal of male intimacy; and with the biblical figures of Ruth and her mother-in-law Naomi.

Anne de Rohan, a member of a noble family from Brittany, wrote poems and letters that addressed women in passionate terms. Written in 1617, her poem *"Sur une dame nommée Aimée"* ("On A Lady Named Beloved") left no doubt that the object of her love was a woman. Writing in mid-17th century Britain,

Katherine Philips addressed numerous love poems to female "friends". Several convey her feelings of jealousy, anger, or sorrow towards women who have betrayed or abandoned her. More often, though, Philips celebrates passionate female "amity". Repeatedly emphasizing that women's affection is based on their similarities – the qualities of mutuality, reciprocity, sympathy, and equality – she claims that love for women is a spiritual experience, a "sacred union" of one soul in two bodies, raising women above the "factious world" of men and politics.

Although well known in literary circles, Philips, like Maitland and de Rohan, wrote of her desires privately, and in veiled terms. But in 1688, England's first professional woman writer and some-time spy Aphra Behn published an overtly lesbian poem, "To the Fair Clorinda", which set the tone for the next century's more forthright exploration of intimacy between women. Religion continued to condemn female–female sex, and the law and society generally ignored it, but the printed word had given lesbians a new freedom to express their desires and identity. ∎

> No bridegroom's nor crown-
> conqueror's mirth
> To mine compared can be:
> They have but pieces
> of this earth,
> I've all the world in thee.
> **Katherine Philips**

Katherine Philips

Born in London in 1632, Katherine Philips was the daughter of an English cloth merchant. When her father died, she moved to Wales and at 16 married James Philips, a Welsh Parliamentarian and prominent citizen of Cardigan, where Katherine spent most of her remaining life. As part of a close-knit literary circle known as the "society of friendship", Philips assumed the name "Orinda", sharing love poems with her two closest friends, Anne Owen and Mary Aubrey, "Lucasia" and "Rosania". Struggling to maintain her intimacy with them after they married, she wrote that "we may generally conclude the Marriage of a Friend to be the Funeral of a Friendship".

Although Philips intended her work to be circulated only privately, an unauthorized edition of her poetry was published in January 1664. She died three months later of smallpox.

Key works

1664 "Friendship's Mystery"
1664 "To My Excellent Lucasia, on Our Friendship"

O THOU, MY LOVELY BOY

MALE–MALE LOVE POETRY (LATE 16TH–17TH CENTURIES)

In late 16th-century England, during the reign of Elizabeth I, the rediscovery of classical literature that swept from Renaissance Italy across Europe prompted a surge of poetry describing male–male love. English writers drew on classical precedents such as romances between gods and mortals, Greek and Roman idealizations of male friendship, and the Roman poet Virgil's *Eclogues* (37 BCE). In 1594, poet Richard Barnfield published *The Affectionate Shepherd*, imitating Virgil's second eclogue to depict the longing of the speaker, Daphnis, for a "fair boy that had my heart entangled". He was the first Elizabethan to explore such themes in published verse. Its homoerotic frankness was unprecedented in England: "If it be sinne to love a lovely lad, Oh then sinne I".

Barnfield named the boy Ganymede – the beautiful youth abducted by a lustful Zeus in Greek mythology – highlighting the male desire implied. The explicit imagery, though couched in pastoral symbolism, would not have been lost on an audience that was classically educated. In early modern Europe, "Ganymede" was also used as a term for "a man who is penetrated by other men".

Marlowe and Shakespeare

In the play *Edward II*, published in 1594, dramatist, poet, and spy Christopher Marlowe explored the king's passion for Piers Gaveston, which cost the monarch his throne and life. Marlowe also wrote homoerotic verse; his narrative poem *Hero and Leander* (1598) dwells on the appeal of "Amorous Leander, beautiful and young", whom the

O would to God, so I might have my fee,
My lips were honey, and thy mouth a bee!
Then shouldst thou sucke my sweete and my faire flower,
That now is ripe and full of honey-berries …
Richard Barnfield
The Affectionate Shepherd, 1594

See also: Gender and sexuality in ancient Greece 20–23 ▪ Sappho of Lesbos 24–27 ▪ Renaissance Italy 58–59 ▪ The criminalization of sodomy 68–71 ▪ Male love in Edo Japan 84–85 ▪ Same-sex narratives in Urdu poetry 96–97

Christopher Marlowe led an erratic life, cut short when he was stabbed to death at the age of 29. His enemies accused him of blasphemy and sodomy.

"lusty god" Neptune attempts to seduce, mistaking him for Ganymede. The poem's narrator appears enamoured with Leander's physical form: "in his looks were all that men desire".

First published as a series in 1609, poet and playwright William Shakespeare's 154 sonnets elevate male friendship, acclaim male beauty, and dissect the pain of love's vicissitudes, among other themes.

The first 126 sonnets are addressed to a young man, described as a "fair youth", with whom Shakespeare appeared to have a passionate relationship. He asserted that his poetry in praise of his beloved friend would make his love immortal: "My love shall in my verse ever live young". While there is no evidence that these so-called "fair youth" sonnets offended the public when they first appeared, publisher John Benson retitled some of them and, in others, altered the pronouns from "him" to "her" in a 1640 anthology.

On the emotional evidence of Shakespeare's sonnets, he would today be considered bisexual. In Sonnet 42, for example, his beloved male friend has apparently had sex with the poet's mistress. The poet consoles himself with the specious logic, drawn from Classical ideals, that since "my friend and I are one", she therefore "loves me alone".

Rochester's explicit style

In the late 17th century, during the bawdy Restoration years that followed Cromwell's Puritanical rule, John Wilmot, Earl of Rochester wrote frank and sometimes crude verse depicting sexual encounters with men and women. "Missing my whore, I bugger my page" runs one line of his poem "Song. The Debauchee". The talented satirist and wit died of syphilis in 1680, aged 33. In the following decades, with the spread of molly houses, male–male relationships became more widespread and overt, and public censure of these relationships became increasingly severe. ▪

A woman's face with nature's own hand painted
Hast thou, the master-mistress of my passion …
William Shakespeare
Sonnet 20

George Villiers was painted by Flemish artist Paul Rubens in 1625. The portrait captures the elegance and bravado that attracted James I.

Close relations

In the Elizabethan and Jacobean eras, the gentry and nobility sometimes used kinship terms when writing of close, possibly sexual relationships with other men. Shakespeare takes a paternal interest in his "fair youth" in Sonnet 37: "As a decrepit father takes delight / To see his active child do deeds of youth, / So I … take all my comfort of thy worth and truth".

James I was infatuated with his favourite George Villiers and made him first Viscount, then Marquis, and finally 1st Duke of Buckingham. His many letters to Villiers are full of affection, humour, and coded allusions to their sexual contact. A letter from the king to Villiers in 1623 ends with "God bless you, my sweet child and wife, and grant that ye may ever be a comfort to your dear dad and husband." Villiers was evidently so secure in the king's affections that he reciprocated with similar intimacy, calling the king his "dad", "master", and "maker", and himself the king's "child", "servant", "slave", and "dog".

MY CLERK JUDGED THEY WERE BOTH WOMEN

AFAB CROSS-DRESSERS AND "FEMALE HUSBANDS" (17TH–18TH CENTURIES)

IN CONTEXT

FOCUS
Transing

BEFORE
***c.* 8th century CE** Lebanese Christian St Marinos the Monk is assigned female at birth but decides to live their life as a man.

1431 In France, Joan of Arc's refusal to forego soldier's clothing gives a court grounds to execute her for heresy.

AFTER
1838 Ann Hants, the wife of bricklayer Henry Stoake, sues for divorce and reveals that her husband was AFAB.

1865 When retired British Army surgeon James Barry dies in London, UK, it is discovered that they were assigned female at birth.

1877 Samuel M. Pollard, who is AFAB, marries Marancy Hughes in Nevada, US, and later claims to have dressed as a man to earn a better living.

Instances of cross-dressing and "female husbands" can be found in numerous court records, newspapers, texts, pamphlets, and plays of the 17th and 18th centuries in Britain, North America, and Europe. They record individuals assigned female at birth (AFAB) who chose to dress and act as men (sometimes permanently) to gain access to the legal, social, and economic benefits often reserved for men. Some of these individuals also chose to have sexual relations with and/or marry women.

American non-binary social and cultural historian Jen Manion uses the term "transing" to indicate these behaviours, which transcended gender binaries at the time. They cannot be so easily understood using today's identity labels but are still recognizable as a socially transgressive part of LGBTQ+ history.

The power of wives
Cases of "female husbands" sometimes came to light when a wife denounced her husband on the grounds of deception or "hermaphroditism". This could be because she had been unaware of her husband's sex and so felt duped,

Long before people identified as transgender or lesbian, there were female husbands and the women who loved them. Female husbands … were true queer pioneers.
Jen Manion
Female Husbands: A Trans History, 2020

or because the relationship had soured and she wanted a favourable divorce. Many more such marriages than those exposed may well have thrived out of the public glare.

Most reported cases of "female husbands" were among the working classes, but there are some reports from the upper classes, such as that of James Howard and Arabella Hunt, in which both partners were gentry. Howard took a male name when courting Hunt two or three months before the couple married in London in 1680. At that point,

See also: Drag 112–17 ▪ Boston marriages 118–19 ▪ Gender nonconformity and colonial constraints in Africa 120–21 ▪ Male impersonators 126

Howard was still legally married to a man. Six months later, by which time Howard's husband had died, Hunt asked for an annulment, citing Howard's "double gender". A jury of midwives examined Howard, declaring them "a perfect woman in all her parts", and the marriage was pronounced void in December 1682. Howard died soon after the case, while Hunt went on to become an acclaimed lutenist.

Multiple marriages

In 1746, Charles Hamilton married Mary Price. Assigned female at birth, Hamilton had begun cross-dressing aged 14 and secured apprenticeships with doctors in order to become an itinerant vendor of medicines and advice. Price was the niece of Hamilton's

"Female husband" Charles Hamilton is flogged in this cartoon, which appeared in 1813 when Henry Fielding's sensationalized account of the 1746 court case was published.

landlady in southwest England. Almost two months after the marriage, Price denounced her husband as a woman to authorities in Glastonbury.

When the case was tried, the court was unsure how to prosecute Hamilton, who was finally charged with fraud but prosecuted under the 1744 Vagrancy Act and publicly flogged. Newspaper reports later revealed that Price was the 14th of Hamilton's "wives". Shortly after the court case, British novelist Henry Fielding's fictionalized account – *The Female Husband* – popularized the use of the term.

Case dismissed

While courts often ruled that wives were deceived, this was not always the case. When Mary Parlour took her husband Samuel Bundy to court in London in 1759, under pressure from her neighbours, it was revealed that she had known her husband was AFAB; she did not appear at the trial, and Bundy was acquitted. ▪

Catalina/Antonio de Erauso

Born in 1585 or 1592 in San Sebastian, Spain, Catalina de Erauso entered the novitiate but left the convent at age 15. Dressed as a man and taking the name Antonio, Erauso travelled in Spain, then sailed to the New World, pursuing a chequered career around South America.

Erauso's memoirs employ female pronouns for their life as a woman and male pronouns for their life as a man. They describe many relationships with women, often calculated to obtain gifts and dowries. Serving as a soldier in Peru, Chile, and Bolivia, Erauso also committed multiple crimes and killed many people. In Bolivia, Erauso escaped a death sentence by confessing to a bishop that they were a "woman", a virgin, and a nun, brought up in a convent.

Sent back to Spain, Erauso was awarded a pension by Philip IV for years of military service. A dispensation from Pope Urban VIII permitted Erauso to continue to dress in men's clothing. Returning to the New World in 1630, they worked as a mule-driver in Mexico and died in 1650.

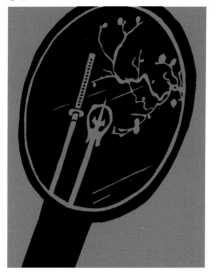

THE GREAT MIRROR OF MALE LOVE
MALE LOVE IN EDO JAPAN (1687)

IN CONTEXT

FOCUS
Male love freely expressed in literature and life

BEFORE
794–1185 The first substantial documented evidence of male–male desire in Buddhist monasteries emerges during Japan's Heian period.

1192 The Kamakura period begins, and samurai warriors replace court governments as rulers. Male love may always have been commonplace in the warriors' male-dominated lives.

AFTER
1872 Sodomy is criminalized in Japan in the early Meiji era; this is repealed in 1880 under a version of the Napoleonic Code of 1804 allowing same-sex relations in private.

2010 Tokyo's Metropolitan Assembly approves a bill forbidding the sale of sexually stimulating publications to those aged under 18.

No era in the history of Japan is more closely associated with male–male relationships – specifically the practice of "boy love" between an older man and an adolescent – than the Edo, or Tokugawa, era. Extending from 1603 until 1867, this was a time of peace, prosperity, and cultural expression under the feudal system of the Tokugawa shogunate. It was preceded by the near-constant civil wars of the Sengoku period and succeeded by far greater restrictions of same-sex relations during Japan's modernization and Westernization in the years of the Meiji Restoration.

I have attempted to reflect in this great mirror all of the varied manifestations of male love.
The Great Mirror of Male Love
Introduction

During the Edo era, Japan's urban centres, particularly the capital Edo (now Tokyo), became known for their vibrant entertainment districts that catered to an expanding, pleasure-seeking middle class.

In literature and life
The emerging lifestyle, described as *Ukiyo* or "floating world", was well documented in literature and art. Stories and depictions of love and sexual acts between older men and those known as *wakashū* ("youth") were widely distributed. One of the most prominent authors of this genre was Ihara Saikaku, who published *Nanshoku Okagami* (*The Great Mirror of Male Love*) in 1687. Not only did this collection of homoerotic love stories elevate love between older and younger men, it even went so far as to denigrate the love of women as "foolishness" and a source of danger.

In another story of the era, *Denbu Monogatari* (*A Boor's Tale*), anonymously authored between 1636 and 1643, the characters debate the relative merits of boy-love and woman-love. While woman-love wins, they concede that boy-love is "well suited" to the aristocracy.

See also: Favourites in Han China 28–29 ▪ Male–male love poetry 80–81 ▪ Gender transgression in modern China 134–35 ▪ Kathoey in Thailand 220–21 ▪ LGBTQ+ activism in Asia 254–55 ▪ Chinese *lala* communities 276–77

Contemporary sources used two principal terms to describe romantic relationships among men. These were *nanshoku*, meaning "male colours" (as the Japanese character for colour can also mean "lust"), and *wakashudō* ("way of youth"), which is sometimes shortened to *shudō*. *Nanshoku*, a word of Chinese origin, is thought to have been introduced to Japan by Buddhist monks who studied in China. In these communities, pederasty between older monks and younger acolytes was common practice and often theologically justified as both educational and romantic.

In the ruling class

The ruling samurai class, who often trained as Buddhists, assimilated the concept of male love. Following the practice of *wakashudō*, an experienced warrior would take a younger boy as an apprentice and lover, formalized by a "brotherhood contract" that lasted until the boy's coming of age ceremony (*genpuku*). Until the Meiji restoration, the perception of age was not strictly

Hairstyle of a younger *wakashū* (adolescent boy)

Hairstyle of an older *wakashū* with forelocks (*maegami*) cut into "corners" (*kado*)

Hairstyle of a young man (*yaro*)

Hairstyle of an adult man

Hairstyle of a woman

Wakashū in Edo Japan had the crown of their heads shaved and wore forelocks styled in different ways to indicate their status. Adult men also had the crown of their head shaved, but women did not.

defined, and there is evidence of *wakashū* ranging from seven to 30 years old.

While widespread depictions of *shudō* suggest a celebration of same-sex desire, male–male love, like many aspects of Edo society, followed a strict social code and was not perceived as a sexual identity. Whereas homosexuality is understood as an attraction between individuals of the same gender, much of the appeal of *wakashū* stemmed from their difference from older men. They were sometimes interpreted as a distinct third gender.

A young male kabuki actor (left) pulls away from an older suitor in this early 18th-century painting by Japanese artist Miyagawa Isshō.

In wider Edo society

Shudō soon spread from the upper classes to wider Edo urban society, particularly to its nightlife, via sex workers and the dance dramas of kabuki theatre. The distinctive dress and hairstyle of a *wakashū* – a kimono with flowing sleeves and a partially shaved head with side forelocks – were considered highly erotic and were sometimes adopted by female sex workers to better attract clientele.

All changed from 1868 under the rule of Emperor Meiji. As Japan opened itself to the West, its legal structures and views of sexuality, gender, and relationships changed dramatically. The practice of "boy love" was not instantly erased but increasingly became the subject of contempt and condemnation. ▪

SUBCUL AND PUB

1700–1899

TURES
LICITY

Molly houses – private clubs where men can socialize – are in their heyday in the city of London.

1720s

Dutch soldier **Maggiel van Handtwerpen** is outed as AFAB and sentenced to 12 years' hard labour.

1769

British landowner **Anne Lister** begins a diary; she writes about her romantic and sexual relationships with women.

1806

AMAB dancers called *köçekler*, who present as female, are banned in the Ottoman Empire.

1857

1723–1810

In India, Urdu poet **Mir Taqi Mir**, master of the *ghazal*, frequently writes of erotic love between men.

1789

The French Revolution sparks pamphlets celebrating same-sex acts and decrying sodomy laws.

1820s

In southern Africa, **Shaka Zulu** permits same-sex acts between men in his large and well-run army.

While the 18th and 19th centuries are often considered eras of progress – containing, as they do, the Age of Enlightenment and the Industrial Revolution – the story told by LGBTQ+ historians is more complex. Authorities continued to prosecute same-sex behaviour in this period, and some consider the Victorian era of the 19th century to be when homophobia as we understand it today was invented. There undoubtedly was progress in understanding the existence of gender and sexual variance – which captured the attention of 19th-century doctors who were creating the field of sexology – but in both the West and the East, there were also reversals. In the Ottoman Empire, the Tanzimat ("Reordering") of the 19th century

saw the Ottomans embrace Western values – including Western distaste for anything that did not conform to heterosexual, cisgender norms. In those parts of Africa colonized by the British, centuries-old practices and beliefs were suppressed in favour of teaching British concepts of sexual deviance and intolerance. In India, British laws outlawed same-sex sexual acts and expressions of gender variance.

Developing community
The period was particularly notable for the development of communities of like-minded people, whether they were women gathering to celebrate (and emulate) the ancient poet Sappho or cross-dressers meeting at London's molly houses. Such meetings could and did incur the wrath of authorities, as seen by the

storming of William Dorsey Swann's drag balls in the 1880s in the US, but the communities survived, even when forced into the shadows.

The nascent LGBTQ+ scenes represented by such communities were not simply places to meet, but fundamental to LGBTQ+ subcultures. Such subcultures had their own trends and their own secret codes – as evidenced by the creation of the language of Polari, developed in the late 19th century as a way for gay men to communicate under the radar. Drag balls, molly houses, and women's salons are clearly precursors to the forms of community experienced in the modern gay or lesbian club. They are also precursors to the modern activist groups who rallied for LGBTQ+ rights. This is the case with the Anandrynes, a group of

Karl Maria Kertbeny publicly uses the terms "homosexual" and "heterosexual" in a letter to a Prussian minister.

William Dorsey Swann, the Black American "Queen of Drag", hosts drag balls in Washington, DC.

Emma Trosse uses the term *Sinnlichkeitslose* ("without sensuality") to describe those we would now call asexual.

1868   **1880s**   **1890**

1860   **1871–1914**   **1886**   **1895**

The British Penal Code in India outlaws same-sex acts and punishes hijras for their gender nonconformity.

During the "Belle Époque" ("beautiful epoch") in France, Paris is renowned for its flourishing bohemian queer cultural scene.

The Bostonians, a novel by American Henry James, describes a "Boston marriage" – a relationship between two financially independent women living together.

Oscar Wilde is convicted of "gross indecency" and gaoled for two years' hard labour for sexual acts with men.

same-sex-loving women who met in France in the 18th century and put their name to revolutionary political pamphlets that called for tolerance.

Love on the page

Although the meeting places of LGBTQ+ people were often in the shadows, texts from this period often brought LGBTQ+ experiences into the light. Some of these writings were strictly private and would not be discovered until many years later – including Anne Lister's diaries, considered by many to be the "Dead Sea Scrolls" of discoveries in lesbian history – but others existed in the open. Many of the LGBTQ+ pamphlets written during the French Revolution were explicit in their descriptions of the joys of same-sex liaisons, as were the

Indian authors of *chaptinamas*, erotic poems about love between women – albeit written by men.

Less bawdy representations of same-sex interactions were also published by sexologists such as Karl Heinrich Ulrichs, Karl Maria Kertbeny, and Emma Trosse, whose scientific literature sought for the first time to categorize and explain "homosexuality" – and in Trosse's case, asexuality – as a natural phenomenon. The scientific label of "homosexual" carried little of the stigma of terms such as "sodomite", but many records of LGBTQ+ life at the time took a more negative stance. The highly publicized, sensationalistic trial of writer Oscar Wilde in the UK in 1895, for example, prompted a moral panic about homosexuality, forcing many men to keep their sexuality secret.

Transing gender

The 18th and 19th centuries provide wide-ranging examples of people transing gender. Some of these people are known to us because they were observed in societies where imperial rule aimed to suppress them, as with the *yan dauda* of the Hausa people in Nigeria. Others – such as the many AFAB people who fought as men in armed conflicts in this period for a number of reasons, but were discovered and punished – are known because of criminal proceedings. The case of Dutch soldier Maggiel van Handtwerpen is just one such example. While people who historically transed gender did so for multiple reasons, some see their legacy as both trans communities and the drag scene, which would become so important to modern LGBTQ+ culture. ∎

MAKING WHAT USE I PLEASE OF MY OWN BODY
MOLLY HOUSES (18TH CENTURY)

I n 1690, the Society for the Reformation of Manners was formed in Tower Hamlets in London, UK. This campaigning group was set up with the goal of suppressing brothels, street sex work, profanity, and other behaviours that it considered immoral. Among the Society's targets were "mollies" – men and gender-diverse people who took part in LGBTQ+ subcultures of the time.

Safe spaces
Mollies met in "molly houses", the early equivalent of modern gay bars and sex clubs. These were generally found in taverns, coffee houses, or private houses, and were often run by women, some of whom were known as "mothers". Legal records document around 30 locations in London, but there is also some evidence of molly houses in other major cities around the country.

At this time, sex between men was illegal and being caught in the act of sodomy was punishable by death. Molly houses provided privacy and a place where people could socialize, find same-sex partners, or act out gendered fantasies by cross-dressing. Molly houses existed in

Molly houses were safe places for engaging in cross-dressing and role-play, here satirized in *A Morning Frolic, or the Transmutation of the Sexes*, a British print from *c*. 1780.

London from around 1700 until about 1830, though their heyday was the 1720s.

Determined to stamp them out, the Society for the Reformation of Manners gathered information on their activities, often undercover, employed officers (then known as "thief takers") to raid premises, and raised money to prosecute mollies in court. Official records

See also: The criminalization of sodomy 68–71 ▪ Drag 112–17 ▪ The trial of Oscar Wilde 124–25 ▪ The first gay village 146–47 ▪ The spread of ball culture 214–15

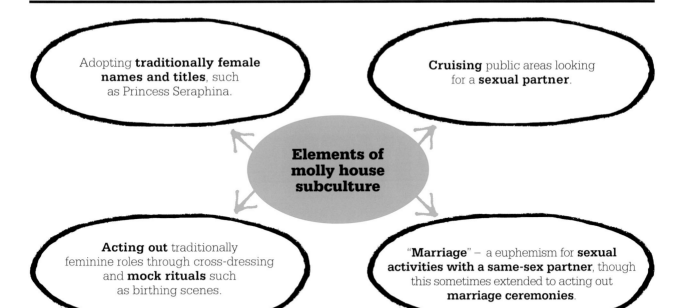

Adopting **traditionally female names and titles**, such as Princess Seraphina.

Cruising public areas looking for a **sexual partner**.

Elements of molly house subculture

Acting out traditionally feminine roles through cross-dressing and **mock rituals** such as birthing scenes.

"**Marriage**" – a euphemism for **sexual activities with a same-sex partner**, though this sometimes extended to acting out **marriage ceremonies**.

and newspaper reports provide detailed evidence of an otherwise hidden subculture.

Developing culture

The thriving subculture of molly houses is one of the earliest examples of how commerce shaped LGBTQ+ communities, with venues created for individuals to meet, spend money, and socialize. Many of the behaviours in molly houses have parallels with modern LGBTQ+ culture. Some visitors used female names and pronouns, wore women's clothing, or imitated what were perceived as female activities, anticipating the cross-dressing masquerades that emerged in the 19th century – and that themselves helped shape the modern drag ball.

Police raids eventually forced people who identified as mollies underground, with prosecutions against same-sex activities in the 19th century mainly involving individual encounters or extortion. ▪

[The mollies] imitated all the little vanities that custom has reconcil'd to the female sex.
Edward Ward
The London Clubs, 1709

The case of Princess Seraphina

In 1732, "Princess Seraphina", a cross-dresser in London's Covent Garden, prosecuted a man named Tom Gordon for assaulting them and stealing clothes and money. Seraphina, a gentlemen's servant, butcher, and messenger for mollies, had to prosecute Gordon under their birth name John Cooper.

During the trial, it emerged that the plaintiff was known to all their neighbours as Princess Seraphina; some neighbours had never known them by any other name. Seraphina often borrowed clothes from their female neighbours, attended balls, and had relationships with men. There is also evidence that they worked as a nurse.

The trial ended with Gordon being acquitted. There is no evidence that Seraphina was ever prosecuted for the behaviour revealed at their trial.

CONVERSING WITH MY BELOVED

EROTIC FRIENDSHIP IN AMERICA AND EUROPE (18TH–19TH CENTURIES)

IN CONTEXT

FOCUS
Women's intimate relationships

BEFORE
c. **630–570 BCE** The poet Sappho, born on the Greek island of Lesbos, writes about love and longing between women. The words "sapphic" and "lesbian" are derived from her name and place of birth.

AFTER
1897 Henry Havelock Ellis uses the term "invert" to describe women who desire other women.

1921 The UK parliament votes down a bill to make lesbianism illegal, to avoid bringing attention to the practice.

1970s–80s Political lesbians urge all women, regardless of their sexual orientation, to exclude men from their lives.

E vidence of erotic and romantic friendship between women before the 20th century is strongest in Europe and America, where middle- and upper-class women not only spent days and weeks at a time in each other's company but also had the leisure time and education to write letters and keep diaries. In spite of the need for discretion, material revealing intimate and profound bonds between women survives.

The gender divide

As trade expanded and countries industrialized from the 18th century, middle- and upper-class men and women in America and Europe

See also: Sappho of Lesbos 24–27 ▪ AFAB cross-dressers and "female husbands" 82–83 ▪ ▪ Sapphism 98 ▪ The diaries of Anne Lister 102–03 ▪ Boston marriages 118–19 ▪ Female writers' rejection of labels 168 ▪ Political lesbianism 206–07

> Industrialization and the growth of trade lead to middle- and upper-class **social roles sharply divided by gender**.

⬇

> Men occupy the **public sphere of work and politics**; women are confined to the **private sphere** centred on the **home**.

⬇

> Reliant on one another, women become **soul mates**, sharing **interests**, **support**, **companionship**, and often a **sense of oppression by men**.

⬇

> **Women form romantic attachments with each other.**

---

began to live very separate lives. Men were often away fighting, trading, or nation-building while women stayed at home, raising the family. Even when men were at home, men and women rarely socialized and spent little time together. For many men and women, marriage was not entered into out of love or for intellectual stimulation but for monetary gain, security, and procreation.

The Enlightenment, an 18th-century intellectual movement that promoted principles of equality and individualism, ultimately widened the gap between the sexes. Egalitarian ideals were generally applied mainly to men, who were seen as more independent and rational than women. Despite better access to education, women were typically viewed as emotionally and intellectually inferior.

Close bonds

Encouraged to socialize among themselves, women often formed close bonds. They would shop and take tea together, support family and friends who were unwell, offer one another aid during pregnancy and childbirth, and stay with one another for extended periods, often sleeping in the same bed.

When they were apart, women would write to each other, often sharing their most intimate thoughts and feelings. They showed their affection by making presents for one another and naming their daughters after particular friends. In boarding schools, it was common for older girls to "adopt" younger girls, who would call them "mother" – often forming lifelong connections.

Few women could afford to live independently, and their family and social circle placed immense pressure on them to marry. Once married, it was very difficult for a woman to leave her husband. Any money or property that a woman owned became her husband's on marriage, and any children remained in the custody of her husband if she left him.

This does not mean that women never established homes together. Working-class women sometimes formed mutually supportive relationships with other women, but low pay generally made this unfeasible in the long run. There are also examples of individuals assigned female at birth who cross-dressed and married women, but this would have been a difficult »

Do you know sir, that until you came along I believe that she loved me almost as girls love their lovers. I know I loved her so. Don't you wonder that I can stand the sight of you.
Mary Hallock
American author (1847–1938)

The Ladies of Llangollen

Lady Eleanor Butler and Sarah Ponsonby formed such an intense connection that they decided to elope together. The two upper-class Irishwomen met in 1768, when Eleanor, then 29, became teacher to the 13-year-old Sarah. In 1778, their first elopement was foiled by their families, but a second attempt succeeded.

Living on modest pensions and small stipends from their families, who had eventually resigned themselves to the relationship, the couple bought a cottage in Llangollen Vale, Wales. The many visitors to the cottage included the Duke of Wellington, poet William Wordsworth, and – in 1822 – diarist Anne Lister.

The women's union was widely accepted, perhaps because it was not viewed as sexual. Some women admired the pair for avoiding the sexual duties of marriage, and some men viewed them as spiritually pure on account of their "virginity". Eleanor died in 1829 and Sarah in 1831.

Lady Eleanor Butler (left) and Sarah Ponsonby considered suing a magazine in 1791 when it implied that their relationship was sexual.

path to pursue. It was much easier to lead a sexually independent life for women who had class privilege, an income, and education, such as Lady Eleanor Butler and Sarah Ponsonby, known as The Ladies of Llangollen, who lived together for more than 50 years.

Letters and diaries

It was common for women to engage in close physical contact, usually in the form of hand holding, cuddling, hugging, kissing, and sometimes breast fondling, but there is little surviving mention in their writings of genital contact. Women's letters, diaries, poetry, and fiction mainly show a strong emotional connection, expressed in exhortations of "desire" and heartfelt wishes to be in another woman's presence.

Nineteenth-century American poet Emily Dickinson had a number of close relationships with women, including with her sister-in-law and former schoolmate Susan Huntington Gilbert and fellow poet Catherine Scott Turner (also known as Kate Anthon). These three women stated that they loved each other greatly and that they wanted to live and die together. They claimed they could truly be themselves around one another and be regarded as whole human beings in ways that men would never understand.

Men rarely felt threatened by close female friendship, because they had unshakeable confidence in their sexual superiority and in the bond between a man and a woman. Same-sex physical intimacy was typically seen as something that happened in the non-Western world or only among sex workers.

Women were guarded when it came to revealing sexual desires towards one another, and often wrote in code and metaphors,

Poet Emily Dickinson (possibly shown here, left) never married yet wrote astonishing love poems, inspired by her intense female relationships, including with Catherine Scott Turner (right).

warning each another to hide or burn letters. In the early 19th century, British landowner Anne Lister recorded her relationships with women, which included genital sex, in coded diaries. But most women writing about a relationship with another woman spoke about the joining of two souls and building a life together.

Most of the written records of romantic or erotic friendships come from white, educated, upper-class women, but there is some evidence

I don't want anyone to kiss me now. I turn Mr. Games away this morning. No kisses is like youres.
Addie Brown
Letter to Rebecca Primus, 1859

A **satirical print** from *c.* 1820 depicts Englishwomen Lady Strachan and Lady Warwick being spied on by their husbands. The women's relationship was seen as more than friendship.

previously frowned upon, was suddenly encouraged in order to counter female–female desire, and the popular fiction engendered by pashes dwindled away.

Direct challenge

As women became more independent, particularly after World War I (1914–18), close relationships between women came to be feared as a direct challenge to heterosexuality and patriarchal power. Suffragists campaigning for women's right to vote drew strength from close female friendships, just as many feminists would in the 1970s. Political lesbians took this one step further when they advocated lesbianism as a political choice rather than a sexual identity – a refocusing on female–female relationships as opposed to unequal male–female relationships. ∎

for romantic or erotic friendships between women of colour, such as that between Black American women Addie Brown and Rebecca Primus, in Hartford, Connecticut, whose relationship lasted from 1859 until 1869. Rebecca kept a large number of letters, now in the possession of Connecticut Historical Society, that demonstrate deep feelings between her and Addie as well as the many difficulties of their relationship, which would have been highly visible in Hartford's Black community. Although the relationship seems to have had the support of the women's families – Addie was brought to live with Rebecca's family for a while – both women eventually married men and their intimacy faded.

Pashes and smashes

In the second half of the 19th century, same-sex connections between women were more likely to be labelled as lesbianism, and treated as an illness or as sinful. In the US, students at the women-only colleges of New England, who were known to form "pashes", "smashes", or "crushes" on one another, began to cause concern by the 1880s. Such attachments had long been tolerated, and had spawned a whole genre of popular fiction, because educated young women were not generally viewed as sexual, but in 1882, members of the Associates of Collegiate Alumnae decried the damage caused by pashes. They called the "extraordinary habit which [girls] have of falling violently in love with each other, suffering all the pangs of unrequited attachment" as "vices of body and imagination".

British physician and sexologist Henry Havelock Ellis's *Studies in the Psychology of Sex, Volume 2, Sexual Inversion* (1900) has a long section on the school friendships of girls, including an appendix detailing his evidence. As the authorities increasingly questioned the innocence of pashes, schools began to police such relationships. Interaction with men's colleges,

At one end of the continuum lies committed heterosexuality, at the other uncompromising homosexuality; between, a wide latitude of emotions and sexual feelings.
Carroll Smith-Rosenberg
American academic (1936–)

MAKING LOVE WITH ONE'S OWN LIKENESS

SAME-SEX NARRATIVES IN URDU POETRY (18TH CENTURY–1858)

IN CONTEXT

FOCUS
Same-sex erotic love

BEFORE
c. **1253–1325** Indian poet Amir Khusro writes Hindavi mystical love poetry for his Sufi teacher.

c. **1590** Jewish poet Sarmad writes Persian love poetry about his beloved, a Hindu man named Abhai Chand.

AFTER
1861 British rulers institute anti-sodomy laws in India.

1927 *Chocolate*, a collection of Hindi short stories about male–male desire by Indian writer Pandey Bechan Sharma, is denounced, sparking the first public debate on homosexuality.

1942 Urdu writer Ismat Chughtai pens a story about lesbianism, called "Lihaaf". She is sued for obscenity.

2018 Anti-sodomy law is overturned by the Indian Supreme Court.

Urdu poetry employs a convention, drawn from Persian poetry, of gendering both lover-speaker and beloved as male. In mystical poetry, the beloved is interpreted either as God or as a witness of love for God. In 18th- and 19th-century poetry, however, the beloved is often a human male, who wears a cap, flies kites, and kisses the male lover-speaker.

Major northern Indian poets, such as Mir Taqi Mir, and minor ones, such as Najmuddin Shah Mubarak (pen-name Abru), routinely wrote about erotic love between men. While the genre known as the *ghazal* often consists of self-contained couplets, many *ghazals* also tell a story. One example is by famous Indian poet Qalandar Bakhsh Jur'at (pen-name Jur'at), in which a man laments the departure of his lover, a soldier.

Narrative romances, known as *masnavi*, recount love stories between men and women as well as between two men, often with a mystical dimension. One man is usually (but not always) older than his partner, whether male or female. Abru's short narrative poem "Advice to a Beloved" is unique because the male speaker advises a youth on

This 1750 Indian miniature, *Two Ladies Embracing at a Jharoka* (a stone window or balcony), portrays erotic love between two women.

how to fashion himself into a beloved whom many men will desire, and explains how to find a long-term male partner. The poem, set in Delhi, is realistic, not mystical, and ends with a prayer that readers also may find love.

Love between women

A remarkable development, which began in the city of Lucknow, northern India, from about 1780 onwards, is a variation of the poetry called *rekhti*, in which the speaker is female. These poems talk about women's lives and everyday

See also: Sappho of Lesbos 24–27 ▪ The *Kama Sutra* 36–37 ▪ Male–male love poetry 80–81 ▪ Ismat Chughtai's obscenity trial 162

> Girlfriend, how delightfully we spent last night.
> My hands devoted themselves to you last night.
> **Ahmed Ali Nisbat**
> **Court poet of Nawab of Awadh (r. 1814–27)**

pursuits, such as shopping, picnicking, and meeting friends and neighbours. This type of poetry was written in the 17th century, in the Urdu language, but it was in the 18th century that it began to focus not on wifehood, motherhood, or male lovers but almost entirely on female friends and lovers.

The poets, mostly Muslim men, wrote in the same registers (romantic, humorous, melancholy) about male–female love, male–male love (with a male speaker), and female–female love (with a female speaker). Female–female sex was termed *chapti* (clinging) and a narrative poem about it is called a *chaptinama*. Famous and popular *rekhti* poets, including Jur'at, Rangin Saadat Yaar Khan (pen-name Rangin), Insha Allah Khan (pen-name Insha), and Nazir Akbarabadi wrote *chaptinamas*. Insha and Rangin also wrote many

Courtesans, such as the woman depicted in this 18th-century Indian watercolour, *Courtesan in a Window*, are said to have been the inspiration for the poetry of Rangin.

ghazals about female–female love. A woman's intimate companion or lover was called her *dogana* (double).

Rangin describes rituals that women conducted to form couples and even to "marry among their female companions". Such couples were known as each other's *ilaichi* (cardamom) or *zanakhi* (breast-bone), based on the rituals they performed.

Suppression of poetry

Following the defeat of the First War of Indian Independence, which had begun in 1857, fully fledged British rule was established in 1858. Urdu literary scholars, influenced by puritanical Victorian norms, dubbed non-mystical erotic poetry and poetry about same-sex desire obscene and it went out of circulation. Urdu poetry in translation was excised and bowdlerized to focus on male–female love. ▪

Languages and poetry

The Urdu language developed in northwest India in the 12th century, and was a linguistic compromise following the Muslim conquest. It was first termed Hindi, the language of India, as distinct from Persian, the language of Muslim-ruled kingdoms. Urdu is closely related to Hindi, which evolved in the 7th century, and both have the same grammatical structure. Colloquial Urdu is no different from colloquial Hindi, and is easily understood today.

Love poetry in Sanskrit, Tamil, and most other Indian languages usually has a female speaker in love with either a God, or a human male with mystical dimensions. Written mostly by men, *rekhti* derive the female speaker from these traditions but replace her male lover with a female one.

Following British rulers' criminalization of same-sex relations in 1861, poetry about male–male love was lost.

Rekhti largely disappeared, but examples by famous poets, preserved in the archives, have, since 2001, been rediscovered, printed, and translated.

> Come, let's play at doubled clinging, why sit around, better labour free.
> **Jur'at**
> **Part of a *chaptinama***

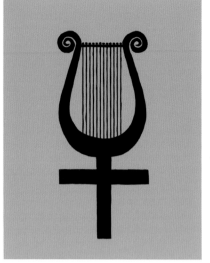

FINDING YOURSELF IN THE BOSOM OF YOUR KIND
SAPPHISM (18TH–19TH CENTURIES)

apphism, a term used for same-sex relationships between women, became more culturally visible, particularly in literary texts, in the 18th and 19th centuries. France was the centre of sapphic discourse, although it also appeared across Western Europe and North America.

Depicting intimacy between women was an overt challenge to male-dominated societies where heterosexuality was the approved "norm". Authors who described erotic female friendships were boldly articulating a reality that was publicly obscured and vilified.

Progressive writings

Such texts were mostly written by wealthy women like British poet Mary F. Robinson, whose *A Handful of Honeysuckle* (1878) and *An Italian Garden* (1886) include sapphic verse. She also wrote copious letters to fellow poet Vernon Lee (Violet Page), "whose love is even my air of life". But aristocratic sapphists were also the target of political propaganda – French queen Marie Antoinette,

Two actresses perform a play by American writer Natalie Barney in *c.*1906. Inspired by earlier sapphists, Barney lived and wrote openly as a lesbian and had many romantic affairs.

executed by revolutionaries in 1793, was often depicted as a lesbian in satirical tracts and pamphlets.

There is also evidence of sapphic relationships between lower-class women, particularly in same-sex spaces such as factories, brothels, prisons, and servants' quarters. ∎

See also: Sappho of Lesbos 24–27 ▪ Erotic friendship 92–95 ▪ The diaries of Anne Lister 102–03 ▪ Boston marriages 118–19 ▪ Female writers' rejection of labels 168

WEARING THE MAN'S ATTIRE AND PUTTING ON THE SWORD
AFAB PEOPLE IN COMBAT (1769)

IN CONTEXT

FOCUS
Gender transgression in the army

BEFORE
1623 Spanish "Lieutenant Nun" Antonio de Erauso reveals that he is AFAB to avoid execution after being arrested in Peru.

AFTER
1816–59 Irish-born military surgeon James Barry serves in the British Army. Only when he dies in 1865 does it become apparent that he was AFAB.

1862 Albert D.J. Cashier, one of at least 250 AFAB people to fight as men in the American Civil War, joins the Union Army at 18, and lives the rest of his life as a man.

1911 After Ottoman forces kill her brothers, Tringe Smajli, the daughter of an Albanian clan leader, lives as a man for safety reasons, and fights as one in the Battle of Deçiq.

There are countless historical examples of AFAB (assigned female at birth) individuals who joined the army presenting as men. These people have been variously referred to as women in disguise, or female cross-dressers. But the fact that many individuals continued to live as men after wartime means that for some, joining the army as a man was also a narrative of transition, and a way to begin again as what we would now call a transgender man.

Men on trial
We will never know the true number of AFAB people who fought wars as men. But some individuals did have their status revealed and recorded, and Dutch soldier Maggiel van Handtwerpen is one of the best-documented examples.

Van Handtwerpen first enlisted in 1746 under the name Johannes van Ant, and two years later married Johanna Martina Kramers, a sergeant's daughter. After his AFAB identity was revealed in 1751, van Ant was exiled from garrison cities for entering into an illegal marriage. In 1762, he married Cornelia Swartsenberg, a pregnant woman who later listed him as the father on the child's birth certificate. He served in the army again, this time as Maggiel van Handtwerpen, until a former colleague recognized him in 1769. He was tried before being flogged, sentenced to 12 years' hard labour, and exiled from the Netherlands. ∎

[I am] by nature and character, a man, but in appearance, a woman … Mother Nature treated me with so little compassion.
Maggiel van Handtwerpen, 1769

See also: AFAB cross-dressers and "female husbands" 82–83 ▪ Male impersonators 126 ▪ Transgender rights 196–203 ▪ Don't Ask, Don't Tell 272–75

FAR FROM OUTRAGING NATURE, WE SERVE HER

REVOLUTIONARY FRANCE (1780s–1790s)

IN CONTEXT

FOCUS
Revolutionary laws

BEFORE
1750 Parisian pair Jean Diot and Bruno Lenoir are executed after a city watchman catches them having sex; they are the last people in France executed for same-sex intercourse.

1770s The Chevalier d'Éon, a French soldier, spy, and writer, becomes the subject of debates in both England and France; they dress alternately as a woman and a man.

AFTER
1940 The Nazis invade France; French homosexuals are persecuted and sent to concentration camps.

1942 France's Vichy government changes the age of consent of 21 for same-sex sexual relations, compared to 15 for different-sex couples. The ages of consent are not equalized until 1982.

The French Penal Code of 1791 is often celebrated for legalizing same-sex acts in what appears on the surface to be a move ahead of its time. The new code was implemented by the National Constituent Assembly, a revolutionary body that held power between July 1789 and September 1791. However, the code did not explicitly mention same-sex

intercourse; it simply did not include any laws that prohibited it between consenting adults.

This change, while very important legally and culturally, was not a result of any particular public support for homosexuality, or any conviction among lawmakers that it was now acceptable. Rather, laws against same-sex acts were removed because they were rooted in religion and its doctrines of sin. The Assembly was influenced by the thinkers of the Enlightenment, who were deeply critical of religion, believing it stood in opposition to science and reason. Many Enlightenment thinkers openly abhorred homosexuality: the French writer Voltaire wrote in 1764 that it was an abomination, though he later argued for same-sex acts to be decriminalized.

Lewd literature

The outbreak of revolution in 1789 – which led to the overthrow of the monarchy three years later –

Françoise Raucourt was head of the Anandrynes. In 1789, she was arrested as a royalist and sentenced to six months in prison, where she met her life partner, Henriette Simonnot-Ponty.

See also: Sodomy and the medieval Catholic Church 42–45 ▪ Homoeroticism and the French Renaissance 60–61 ▪ The criminalization of sodomy 68–71 ▪ The decriminalization of same-sex acts 184–85

An illustration from "Les Petits Bougres au Manège" ("The Little Bugger-go-Round"), which defended same-sex intercourse on the grounds of individual liberty.

coincided with an outbreak of proud and often explicit pamphlets about same-sex relations, with provocative descriptions of same-sex acts. One of the first notable pamphlets of its kind was the "Confession de Mademoiselle Sapho" (1784). Published by writer Mathieu-François Pidansat de Mairober, it contains a story about a young lady who is taught by an older woman how to have intercourse with her. Typically of the time, the teacher is called a "tribade" (from the ancient Greek *tribo*, "to rub") and is described as having what we would now call intersex genitals, with which she can penetrate her young protégé.

There were similar pamphlets celebrating relationships between men, including "Les Petits Bougres au Manège" ("The Little Bugger-go-Round", 1793–94), in which the anonymous author derides the unappealing genitals of the women of Paris, and claims that he and his peers are driven to have sex with

each other by the disease-ridden state of the city's female sex workers. The author also notably declares men's bodies to be their own property – a revolutionary idea – suggesting that if a man's body is his own property, he should be free to do what he wants with it.

The political ideology behind such pamphlets is even more evident in "Les enfants de Sodome à l'Assemblée Nationale" ("The Children of Sodom at the National Assembly", 1790), written by the Marquis de Villette. This pamphlet takes the form of a plea to the National Assembly to get rid of laws against sodomy. Historians, however, have largely concluded that such pamphlets – which were frowned upon by the authorities – played little to no role in the legalization of 1791.

Police and the penal code
The removal of laws against sodomy did not change public perceptions of homosexuality; it also did not stop the police from persecuting France's LGBTQ+

community. British historian Julian Jackson's work on the diaries of three Parisian police chiefs has shown that they simply turned to other laws, such as those against public indecency, to continue to prosecute same-sex behaviour. Police chief Louis Canler described the lack of anti-sodomy laws in the new code as a "lacuna to fill". Still, the new code did mean that same-sex couples could be together, with less fear of legal persecution, as long as they did so in private. ▪

Pleasure is the only reality; to acquire as much as I can is my sole aim.
"Les Petits Bougres au Manège"

The Anandrynes

The "Confession de Mlle Sapho" contains a supposed address by Françoise Raucourt, an actress, to the "Anandrynes", which was repeated in several other pamphlets such as "Anandria ou Confessions de Mlle Sapho" ("Anandrynes or Confessions of Mlle Sappho", 1789). Another speech of Raucourt's is supposedly contained in "La Liberté ou Mlle Raucourt à toute la secte anandrine assemblée au foyer de la Comédie-Française" ("Liberty, or Mlle Raucourt to

the whole Anandryne sect assembled in the foyer of the Comédie-Française"), 1791.

The Anandrynes – whose name means "women without men" – were a real sapphic society, founded in 1770 and led by Raucourt in the 1780s and '90s. The group's membership was so exclusive that new recruits were stripped naked before members decided whether they could join. Raucourt was often described by her contemporaries – in tabloids and gossip rags – as a priestess of the Temple of Lesbos.

I LOVE, AND ONLY LOVE, THE FAIRER SEX

THE DIARIES OF ANNE LISTER (1806–40)

IN CONTEXT

FOCUS
Same-sex relationships

BEFORE
1680 Arabella Hunt and AFAB cross-dresser James Howard are married in London, with Howard signing the register as their male persona.

1746 British novelist Henry Fielding publishes *The Female Husband* – a sensationalized account of Charles Hamilton, who married Mary Price in the same year.

AFTER
1885 The Criminal Law Amendment Act strengthens British legislation against sex between men. An effort in 1921 to ensure this act covers sex "between female persons" fails.

1928 *The Well of Loneliness*, a lesbian novel by Radclyffe Hall, is published. British courts judge it as obscene, and the book is not published again in the UK until 1959.

nne Lister was a wealthy, independent woman whose family owned Shibden Hall in Yorkshire, UK. From the age of 15 until her death, Lister wrote diaries that describe in detail her intimate relationships with women. Her diaries were revealed in full in the 1980s, and have had a profound impact on women's history and the history of sexuality.

Lister's writings ran to almost four million words. The content included everyday topics, such as current events and business life,

which provide an insight into the life of a 19th-century woman of the gentry. But one-sixth of the diaries was devoted to Lister's private life. Her first diary entry, on 11 August 1806, began to document her relationship with her first love, fellow school pupil Eliza Raine.

That Lister's intimate diaries survived is unusual, as they contain detailed accounts of her sexual relationships and could very easily have been destroyed by her or at various points after her death. In 1808, Lister began to use a secret

A	=	2	U	=	6	Mr.	=	x
B	=	c	V	=	9	Mrs.	=	$\dot{x}$
C	=	ɔ	W	=	8	Miss	=	$\divideontimes$
D	=	o	X	=	W			
E	=	3	Y	=	7			
F	=	u	Z	=	9	bb	=	€
G	=	n				cc	=	ɜ
H	=	Q	ll	=	đ	dd	=	φ
I	=	4	mm	=	⊣	ee	=	;
J	=	4	nn	=	⅄	ff	=	ψ
K	=	ↆ	oo	=	!	gg	=	ⱨ
L	=	d	pp	=	‡	th	=	√
M	=	—	rr	=	f	sh	=	∧
N	=	\	ss	=	=?	ch	=	∇
O	=	5	tt	=	Ⅳ	and	=	x
P	=	†						
Q	=	‖						
R	=	P						
S	=	P=						
T	=	Ⅳ						

Lister devised a secret code in order to write explicitly about her most private thoughts. Her "crypthand" uses a mixture of numbers, mathematical symbols, and Greek letters.

See also: Erotic friendship in America and Europe 92–95 ▪ AFAB cross-dressers and "female husbands" 82–83 ▪ Boston marriages 118–19 ▪ Butch and femme 152–55 ▪ Female writers' rejection of labels 168

> I know my own heart and understand my fellow man. But I am made unlike anyone I have ever met. I dare to say I am like no one in the whole world.
> **Anne Lister**
> **20 August 1823**

code – her "crypthand" – for writing about her private thoughts and experiences. Most of this encoded text is about love and sex.

Half a century after Lister's death, her diaries, secreted behind panels in Shibden Hall, were discovered by her relative John Lister. One night, John and his friend Arthur Burrell started to decipher Anne's crypthand and discovered the sexual content it

revealed. Burrell urged John to burn the diaries, but instead John returned them to their hiding place.

After John's death in 1933, the building passed into the ownership of Halifax Borough Council and the journals were found and archived, with access to the coded sections strictly controlled. Then, in 1983, Halifax historian Helena Whitbread asked to see Lister's letters and was told about the diaries and entrusted with the code. She spent five years decoding the material, and published it as *I Know My Own Heart* (1988) and *No Priest But Love* (1993); republished in two volumes as *The Secret Diaries of Miss Anne Lister* (2010 and 2020).

Love and commitment

Anne Lister's status as a member of the landed gentry gave her a considerable social advantage, making it easier – despite gossip and mockery – for her to pursue relationships with women. After her affair with Eliza Raine, Lister cultivated a relationship with Isabella Norcliffe, who in 1814

introduced Lister to Mariana Belcombe. The two began a love affair that continued during Mariana's later marriage to Charles Lawton. Lister's final partner was Ann Walker – an heiress and thus her social equal, who lived with her from 1834. That year, the two women exchanged rings in a blessing at Holy Trinity Church in York. ▪

"Gentleman Jack" was how Lister was known to locals in her lifetime. The British TV series by that name depicts the relationship between Lister (right, played by Suranne Jones) and Ann Walker (left, played by Sophie Rundle).

Anne Lister

Born in Halifax, Yorkshire, in 1791, Anne Lister attended boarding schools in her youth, and at the age of 24 moved to live with her aunt and uncle at Shibden Hall. Proud of her family and its ancestral home, which dates from about 1420, she became the sole owner of Shibden Hall after the death of her aunt in 1836.

Lister was highly educated, with a love of ancient Greek history and Classical literature. As a member of the landed elite, she held conservative social views, though she rejected the idea of heterosexual marriage.

Lister's extensive estate included town properties and interests in various industries, such as railways and mining. Among other advantages, her wealth enabled her to indulge her passion for travel. She journeyed often within Britain, Ireland, and Europe, and had a passion for walking and mountain climbing.

In 1839, Lister and Ann Walker set out on a journey to Russia. In 1840, in the foothills of the Caucasus Mountains, Lister became feverish from an insect bite. She died six weeks later, aged 49.

THIS SCANDALOUS TUMULT

CHANGING OTTOMAN SOCIETY (19TH CENTURY)

IN CONTEXT

FOCUS
Influence of Western heteronormativity

BEFORE
1599 In *Table of Delicacies*, a tract on etiquette, Ottoman historian Mustafa Ali talks of lower-class "vipers of lust" corrupting palace servants.

1627 One tale in Ottoman poet Nev'izade Atayí's *Heft nan* (*Seven Stories*) highlights love between two young Ottoman Muslims and the two Christian men who enslave them.

AFTER
1923 Mustafa Kemal Atatürk becomes president of the new Turkish Republic, after World War I shatters Ottoman rule.

1991 Turkish pop star Zeki Müren, who plays with gender norms, is named State Artist.

2003 The first Gay Pride Parade is held in Istanbul. It attracts 100,000 people in 2013 but is banned in 2015.

As **its power wanes**, the Ottoman Empire becomes known as "the **sick man of Europe**".

→

Its rulers strive to **reform and control** all aspects of society, including **public morality**.

↓

Although same-sex activity **technically remains legal**, Ottoman society gradually becomes more **conservative and heteronormative**.

The 19th century was a period of immense change in the Ottoman Empire. It had a profound effect on the expression and acceptance of same-sex desire and gender in Ottoman communities, opening new divides that remain to the present day.

Shaken by sustained military defeats and territorial losses, the 19th-century Ottoman elite sought to preserve the Empire's power and prestige by emulating their European rivals. The result was a period known as the Tanzimat ("Reordering") in the middle of the century. It was marked by a new ethos stressing the equality of citizens regardless of race, religion, language, gender, or social class. It also reimagined the earlier gender landscape, composed of women, beardless young men, and adult males, as one of binaries – men and women, adults and children.

Concealing older norms
Ottoman elites looked to Western European political, economic, legal, and artistic models for inspiration. With some evident embarrassment, they attempted to conceal the traditional acceptance of same-sex desire and gender fluidity that had earlier characterized their society.

See also: Ottoman gender and sexuality 62–63 ▪ Defining "homosexual" and "heterosexual" 106–07 ▪ Hijras and British colonialism 108–09 ▪ Drag 112–17 ▪ LGBTQ+ Muslims 278–79

British, French, and other travellers had often expressed disgust or disbelief when writing about the homoeroticism and gender nonconformity they had observed in Ottoman society and among the Empire's non-Turkic peoples. As such practices moved underground, Ottoman intellectuals occasionally expressed their approval of the disappearance of such behaviours from public life, perceiving this as evidence of the increasing modernity of their nation.

Western European literary works were increasingly translated into Ottoman Turkish while the Indigenous tradition of literature that described same-sex desire between men gradually dwindled. Similarly, French, German, and English manuals of medicine in Ottoman Turkish introduced heteronormative European medical theories into the Empire's scientific communities. Such theories created a supposedly objective basis for the gradual elimination of same-sex desire and gender diversity from public life.

Sultan Abdülmecit, here in an image from *Hadikatü'l-müluk* (*Garden of Kings*), a history of the Ottoman dynasty, began to apply the Tanzimat reforms from the start of his reign (1839–61).

In the mid-19th century, the government imposed two legal changes of profound importance. One was the 1857 banning of köçekler, young male dancers who performed in female dress, which led to their gradual disappearance from public spaces. The other, finalized in 1859, was a new legal code, valid alongside Islamic law, which established age, consent, and public morality as the cornerstones of state intervention into citizens' sexual activities. Same-sex acts were not explicitly banned and were therefore technically legal, but the law was vague enough to provide ample room for oppressive measures at the state's discretion.

Creeping conservatism

Rather than fast or decisive changes, the 19th century brought a period of flux and transition in the history of same-sex desire and gender diversity in the Ottoman Empire. Whatever their impact when they first appeared, the era's new laws created a firm foundation for the seismic shifts of the following century. As the conservatism of the late-19th century gave way to the nationalism of the 20th, more rigid approaches to sexuality and gender rapidly took hold. ▪

Köçekler perform for an Ottoman sultan and his court in a 16th-century image, evidence of their acceptance and popularity at the time.

Köçekler

A key feature of Ottoman city life were dancers assigned male at birth who wore female attire and adopted feminine behaviours when on stage. Known as köçekler (plural of köçek), they performed for both male or mixed-gender audiences in Istanbul and beyond.

Köçekler came from the vast Empire's Greek, Jewish, Roma, Armenian, or other non-Muslim communities, reflecting the intersection of ethnicity, religion, and gender in this singular, often celebrated social group.

Youths were recruited as köçekler (sometimes forcibly) before they grew beards, and many continued to perform well beyond puberty. Some engaged in sex work with male audience members, and some married women and started families.

Several male admirers wrote biographies of famous köçekler that also describe their impact on Ottoman society. Despite various bans – allegedly because of fighting when spectators vied for köçekler's attentions – the popular shows continued until the end of the 19th century.

AN ENTIRELY DIFFERENT LAW OF NATURE

DEFINING "HOMOSEXUAL" AND "HETEROSEXUAL" (1869)

Early Church laws **prohibit same-sex activity**. Henry VIII's Buggery Act of 1533 then writes this prohibition into **secular law**.

The **language** commonly used to describe **same-sex behaviour** is derogatory, **framing it as a sin**.

Karl Maria Kertbeny argues that consensual sexual acts **should not be subject to criminal law**, and that same-sex desires are **psychologically and emotionally innate**.

Kertbeny coins the term "homosexual" to create neutral, unjudgmental language to describe same-sex behaviour.

The background to the creation of the terms "homosexual" and "heterosexual" is a complex one. The Austro-Prussian War of 1866 played a part, with the Prussian victory resulting in the exclusion of Austria from Germany. Major political changes followed, with both Austria-Hungary and the North German Confederation revisiting and revising their legal codes.

In 1859, former Prussian lieutenant Karl Ernst von Zastrow was arrested on suspicion of raping and murdering two young boys. This was damaging for the discussion of same-sex adult relationships in Germany. Although an 1869 report

See also: The criminalization of sodomy 68–71 ▪ Sexology and psychoanalysis 132–33 ▪ Kinsey's research on sexology 164–65 ▪ The decriminalization of same-sex acts 184–85 ▪ Removal of homosexuality from the DSM 219

by the Prussian Medical Affairs Board argued against the inclusion of an anti-sodomy statute, Paragraph 175 criminalizing sex between men was brought into German law in 1871. Many other countries had such secular versions of former religious law. In 1969, sex between men was decriminalized in Germany, with Paragraph 175 repealed in 1994.

Arguing for emancipation

Hungarian writer Karl Maria Kertbeny is the first person to have used the terms "homosexual" and "heterosexual", in an 1868 letter to German lawyer Karl Heinrich Ulrichs. "Homosexual" was used to refer to erotic acts performed by individuals of the same sex, and "heterosexual" to erotic acts between men and women. Kertbeny then used the term "homosexual" publicly in 1869 in two open letters to the Prussian Minister of Justice, where he requested that sodomy be decriminalized in the penal code for the North German Confederation.

A political cartoon from 1907 by German artist Willibald Krain pokes fun at Paragraph 175 by suggesting that many of the great writers in Germany are breaking it.

This portrait of Karl Maria Kertbeny dates from around 1865. In his early years, Kertbeny witnessed two homosexual suicides, which may have been why he became an activist, but he chose to write anonymously.

Kertbeny's work, alongside that of Ulrichs and others, added to the medicalization of same-sex attraction. He claimed that homosexuality was natural and innate and thus required protection under law and religion. His argument unfortunately gave rise to the targeting of this identity as an illness or defect. This can be seen today with conversion therapy, which views sexual orientation and gender identity as "conditions" that can be "cured" or "suppressed".

Ulrichs' theory of "urning"

According to Ulrichs, someone with a feminine nature trapped in the body of a man was an "urning"

He cannot act differently. He did not give himself this love direction. And he cannot eliminate it, either.
Karl Heinrich Ulrichs

(derived from the word Uranus, a Greek god who was portrayed as both a father and a mother) and so represented a third sex. This theory was unpopular in Ulrichs' lifetime. He was forced to resign from his legal post in 1857 over rumours about his sexuality, and was jailed twice in 1867 before being banished from his homeland. ▪

THEY SAY IT'S THE SOUL WHICH IS HIJRA

HIJRAS AND BRITISH COLONIALISM (1871)

IN CONTEXT

FOCUS
Colonial laws against LGBTQ+ communities

BEFORE
c. 400 BCE–c. 200 BCE Hijra communities are first mentioned in the *Kama Sutra*.

1858 The British government takes over direct rule of India from the East India Company and begins to introduce new legislation.

AFTER
1947 India wins independence, but retains colonial laws governing gender and sexuality.

2010 Indian writer and activist A. Revathi publishes *The Truth About Me*. It is thought to be the first published autobiography of a hijra person.

2013 India's Aadhaar Card – a form of ID required for almost all essential services – introduces a "transgender" option to its registration form.

Hijra is a name for a community of gender nonconforming people, mostly concentrated in Northern India, but also in other parts of India, Pakistan, and Bangladesh. Other similar, regional terms include *kinnar* in North India, *khwaja sira* in Pakistan, and *aravani* in the South Indian state of Tamil Nadu.

Some hijras are born intersex, and many undergo a castration ritual called *nirvaan*, although others do not. The term itself is sometimes controversial, as it has been used as a derogatory name that focuses gender identity on the genitals, but today many hijras claim the term for themselves.

Criminalization

There is evidence in art and literature that hijra communities have existed in South Asia for well over 2,000 years. During the Mughal era of the 16th–19th centuries, they often held key roles within the Imperial court, working as spiritual leaders and protectors of harems. However, when the British colonized India in the 19th century, new laws were brought in to control many minority communities. Hijras were first criminalized under Section 377 of the 1860 Indian Penal Code, which also prohibited oral and anal sex, and any same-sex activity. The law associated hijras and other LGBTQ+ people with paedophilia and bestiality.

In 1871, the new Criminal Tribes Act further targeted "eunuchs", preventing them from wearing female clothing, dancing in public, or living with children. This was due to claims that hijras enslaved and castrated children,

This etching of a hijra person is from 1808. It was not until the 1850s that hijras were seen as a danger to British colonial rule.

Hijras are aften invited to give blessings to newborn babies and to couples at weddings. They are believed by some to have special powers, offering fertility and long life to those they bless.

despite no evidence that this was a widespread practice. These laws were based on the dominant moral values of Victorian Britain, declaring hijras to be "against the order of nature", and with the explicit aim of eradicating the community entirely.

Legacies of colonial law

Part of the Criminal Tribes Act was repealed in 1911, but it has nonetheless had long-lasting consequences on the governance and social stigmatization of hijra people. India has been independent from colonial rule since 1947, but there still remain colonial legacies for the legal status of hijra communities today.

In 2014, a case in India's Supreme Court followed Pakistan and Bangladesh in legally recognizing hijras as a third gender, ruling that they should be granted all the fundamental rights afforded by the Indian constitution. It was a landmark ruling offering hope

Hindu scriptures always speak of the third gender.
Devdutt Pattanaik
Indian mythologist (1970–)

to hijra communities, and was followed in 2018 by the Supreme Court's ruling of Section 377 as unconstitutional, decriminalizing same-sex activity.

While these rulings lay important groundwork, the impetus behind them is yet to materialize as policy. A Transgender Persons (Protection of Rights) Bill, first introduced in 2016, planned to include quotas for hijras in education and public appointments. The bill was controversial, and when it was passed in 2019 quotas for hijras were absent, as was any substantive legal change regarding their access to essential services. The final bill has been criticized by activists for echoing the colonial-era criminalization of LGBTQ+ people in India through strict legal categorization based on genitalia, rather than self-identification.

The community's future

There are thought to be up to two million hijra people living in India today, although there are no official statistics. Parallels have been drawn between hijras and trans women, non-binary people, and other LGBTQ+ identities. Some hijras embrace this comparison, while others prefer to think of themselves as a distinct third gender. They remain a stigmatized community, associated with sex work and begging, as well as dancing and performance. In recent years, though, there have been more positive representations and opportunities for hijras to tell their own stories in literature and the media. ▪

We are not hypocrites. We live our sexuality openly, being true to our souls and our bodies.
Laxmi Narayan Tripathi
Hijra rights activist and Bollywood actress (1979–)

NOT SEEKING MEN, BUT SEEKING EACH OTHER

BELLE ÉPOQUE PARIS (1871–1914)

IN CONTEXT

FOCUS
Bohemian queer culture

BEFORE
1791 The new French Penal Code includes no infringement of "personal" matters, and thus decriminalizes same-sex acts.

1800 A ban on women wearing trousers comes into effect in Paris. The law is rescinded formally in 2013.

AFTER
1928 English writer Radclyffe Hall's *The Well of Loneliness* is published; the character of Valérie Seymour is based on Paris salon hostess Natalie Clifford Barney.

1937 Chez Moune, now Paris's longest-running lesbian bar and nightclub, opens its doors.

1971 French lesbian feminists split off from the Homosexual Front for Revolutionary Action to establish the activist group *Gouines rouges* (*Red Dykes*).

The period in French history from the end of the Franco-Prussian war in 1871 to the outbreak of World War I in 1914 is known as the "Belle Époque" – the "beautiful epoch". This was a time of economic prosperity, technological innovation, and flourishing art and culture. It was also an age of decadence, in which Paris became a hotspot for artists, philosophers, and anyone else attracted to its bohemian scene. LGBTQ+ people in particular saw France as a haven from the stricter laws of their own nations. The *demimonde* – a group that encompassed women on the fringes of society, often sex workers, and their elite male patrons – included many women who preferred female company.

Sapphist subcultures
The new cultural freedoms did not mean that Paris was free of social restrictions. For example, women in the capital were not allowed to wear trousers without a licence unless they were cycling or riding a horse. This patriarchal law, intended to keep women from "men's professions", made the choice to wear masculine clothes an especially transgressive move for Parisian sapphists – women who loved other women.

The law did not prevent Parisian women from embracing butch fashions. Bohemian painter Louise Abbéma – known for her 50-year relationship with her muse, actress Sarah Bernhardt – famously wore men's suits and smoked cigars. Such an open display of gender nonconformity and sexual

French writer Colette captured the mood of Belle Époque society with her sensuously provocative novels, which cast an intense spotlight on traditional female roles.

See also: Sappho of Lesbos 24–27 ▪ Molly houses 90–91 ▪ Sapphism 98 ▪ Revolutionary France 100–01 ▪ The first gay village 146–47 ▪ Butch and femme 152–55

preference among the rich and celebrated was simply seen as another form of eccentricity.

By the time of the Belle Époque, Paris already had a reputation for sapphism. In 1880, French historian Nicole G. Albert described Paris as a "Mecca of sapphism", and by 1914 the city had earned the nickname "Paris-Lesbos". Businesses and venues sprang up to meet the

Belle Époque women meet for romantic liaisons in a tearoom in this 1911 illustration from French magazine *L'Assiette au Beurre*. Some wear the dapper butch fashion of the period.

needs of this developing population. Montmartre and Les Halles were known for their bars, cafés, and bathhouses, while the Carrousel du Louvre was a popular outdoor rendezvous spot. Members of the exclusive society *Les Rieuses* (*The Merry Women*) met monthly for candlelit dinners and other pleasures. The neighbourhood of Pigalle had two well-known cafés – Mme Armande's La Brasserie du Hanneton and Mme Palmyre's La Souris – where rich and poor women alike could meet.

Evidence for a sapphic subculture can be seen in the art and literature of the time. Toulouse Lautrec, for example, famously painted women at the Moulin Rouge, including the clown and dancer Cha-U-Kao, who had a relationship with a woman known to us as Gabrielle the Dancer.

Women also met in private homes for "salons" – gatherings of writers, artists, and intellectuals. A feature of French culture since the 17th century, salons now served as social events for women seeking like-minded partners. American heiress Natalie Clifford Barney, for example, created an informal "Women's Academy" for female writers. Her salon included many great LGBTQ+ writers of the time, from fellow expatriates Gertrude Stein and Alice B. Toklas to French writer Colette. ▪

My queerness is not a vice, not deliberate, and harms no one.
Natalie Clifford Barney
Aventures de l'Esprit, 1929

Natalie Clifford Barney (right) with her lover, British poet Renée Vivien. Barney is dressed as Sappho, as she often was for her sapphic salons.

The salon of Natalie Clifford Barney

Perhaps the most famous women's salon of Belle Époque Paris was the *Académie des Femmes* hosted by American writer Natalie Clifford Barney (1876–1972), known to her guests as "The Amazon".

Many of Barney's Friday salons were held in her garden, where a Greek-style "temple of friendship" set the scene for Barney and her circle to perform plays and dances in tribute to Sappho of Lesbos. These salons were extravagant gatherings, fortified with gourmet food, punch, and whisky. On one

occasion, the guests were treated to a dance by a naked "Lady Godiva" arriving on horseback.

Described by some today as the "Queen of the Lesbians" of Paris, Barney was famed for her romantic relationships. She was the inspiration for a number of literary works, including Liane de Pougy's *Idylle Saphique* (1901), which describes the young Barney coming to proposition a beautiful French courtesan, boldly dressed as a "page sent by Sappho".

WE'RE ALL BORN NAKED AND THE REST IS DRAG

DRAG (1880s)

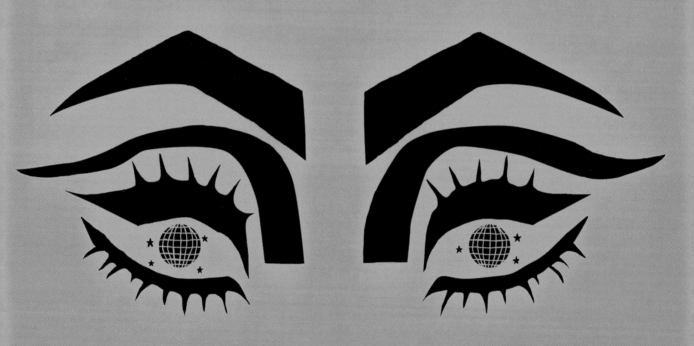

IN CONTEXT

FOCUS
Gender-subversive performance

BEFORE
1870 AMAB cross-dressers known as Fanny and Stella are arrested after wearing women's clothes in public. Their trial includes the first known use of the term "drag".

1880 In Manchester, UK, police raid a "fancy dress ball" and arrest 47 men, many dressed in female clothes.

AFTER
2017 Lebanon's first drag ball, "The Shade Starts Now", takes place in Beirut, a city with an active drag scene, despite limited LGBTQ+ rights in most of the Middle East.

2022 *Time* magazine names the 2016 season of *RuPaul's Drag Race* as one of "the 50 most influential reality TV seasons of all time".

... attired in handsome silks and satins, each in complete feminine costume, they indulged in a "drag".
The Washington Critic
Reporting on one of William Dorsey Swann's drag balls, 1888

Drag is the act of dressing in a gender-subversive way for performance. The practice has existed since at least the 6th century BCE, when Greek playwrights cast men in every female role. Women were seen as unsuited and inferior for such performances of high art. Likewise, from the 1590s in England, men portrayed female characters in the plays of William Shakespeare. In Chinese opera of the Tang dynasty (618–907 CE), both women and men would play the opposite gender. Italian opera of the 18th and early 19th centuries cast castrated men (castrati) in women's roles, and then women in men's clothes (travesti) in male roles.

Cross-dressing – which is simply the act of wearing clothes that society dictates belong to another gender – may overlap with drag, but one does not rely on the other. Today, drag culture can involve both cis and trans people of any gender and has moved away from explicitly gendered presentations.

Parties and balls
In 18th-century Britain, dressing-up parties known as "masquerades" were held at molly houses, mostly in

Two Black performers pose as dancing partners on stage in this photograph from around 1903. Black Americans played a key role in the origins of modern drag culture.

London. These secret gatherings were attended by a range of people, including men dressed as women, who mixed with other men and used names such as Primrose Mary, Lady

William Dorsey Swann

Born into slavery in 1858, William Dorsey Swann grew up in Maryland, USA. Following emancipation, he worked as a hotel waiter and a college janitor.

By the early 1880s, Swann had moved to Washington, DC, where he began to organize parties, or "drags". At these events, a group, including previously enslaved men, would dress in "handsome silks and satins". The people who attended the drags became known as the House of Swann.

Swann called himself the "Queen of Drag" – the first recorded use of the phrase that later became "drag queen".

Swann was arrested several times, including for female impersonation. During a raid on a ball for his 30th birthday, he fought with the police – one of the first recorded acts in the US of resistance to the arrest of LGBTQ+ people. Publicly shamed, eventually Swann gave up running the balls, though his brother Daniel continued making costumes for drag balls up to the 1950s. Swann died in 1925.

See also: AFAB cross-dressers and "female husbands" 82–83 ▪ Molly houses 90–91 ▪ Male impersonators 126 ▪ The Harlem Renaissance and the Jazz Age 148–51 ▪ Camp 180–81 ▪ The spread of ball culture 214–15

Godiva, and Black-eyed Leonora. One masquerade regular – John Cooper, a gentleman's valet, who was also known as Princess Seraphina – gained particular notoriety in 1732 following a court case at London's Old Bailey.

After the American Civil War (1861–65), private drag parties, or balls, began to develop among newly emancipated Black communities. In the 1880s and 1890s, William Dorsey Swann organized a number of balls in Washington, DC, where men – mostly formerly enslaved Black men, like Swann himself – would arrive in women's clothes and dance with other men.

To attend one of Swann's balls was risky, and a number of events ended in police raids and arrests. Following a raid in 1896, Swann was jailed for 10 months for running a "disorderly house" – or brothel. He applied to the US president, Grover Cleveland, for a pardon. This was denied, but it was the first example in the US of a legal appeal to uphold the rights of gay people to gather without threat of arrest. Swann

referred to himself as "the queen of drag" and was the first to organize his ball performers into a "house" – a safe space where they could gather. This concept was picked up in the 1970s by Black and Latine drag queens in New York City, who drove the creation of a ballroom culture of drag performance built around family-like "houses".

Popular entertainment

William Dorsey Swann's drag balls were secret, ticket-only events, but drag – in the form of female and male impersonators – was popular in the late 19th and early 20th centuries in American vaudeville theatres and Britain's music halls. These public venues offered entertainment to growing urban populations in the form of "variety shows", including men and women who sang or danced dressed as the opposite gender. Some, such as the British performers Bert Errol and Vesta Tilley, and American Julian Eltinge, found fame on both sides of the Atlantic. In Britain, too, pantomime dames – characters such as Widow Twankey and Mother Goose, played by a man in drag – became familiar to theatregoers. The elaborately costumed dame is a popular part of Britain's Christmas pantos today.

After World War I, music halls and vaudeville theatres declined as people opted for cinema. Performers, including Julian Eltinge, made the transition into film, but from the 1920s drag became a feature of a thriving nightclub scene in European

Coccinelle was a French trans actress, entertainer, and activist who began her career as a drag queen in the Paris clubs Madame Arthur and Le Carousel in the 1950s.

and American cities. Drag also took on more of an overtly LGBTQ+ identity as the clubs provided a relatively safe space for gay people and those who did not conform to the gender assigned to them at birth. Berlin, especially, supported a widespread LGBTQ+ subculture, with around 80 gay clubs by 1925, including Eldorado, famed for its drag acts and dance parties.

In the US, the prohibition laws (1920–33) banning the production and sale of alcohol drove drinking to underground clubs (speakeasies) where LGBTQ+ people could gather, dance, and perform. By 1930, drag performers had become a popular feature of the clubs – especially in Harlem – in what became known as the "Pansy Craze". Some drag queens, such as the openly gay Ray Bourbon and Jean Malin, attained commercial success, with Malin appearing in drag in the 1933 film *Arizona to Broadway*. »

The Rocky Twins were Norwegian drag artists who performed in nightclubs during the 1920s and '30s. They played across Europe and the US as part of the "Pansy Craze".

Drag language

Term	Meaning
Bar queen	A drag queen who has made their living working in bars.
Beat	To apply make up perfectly.
Bio queen	A cis woman performing in feminine drag.
Drag mother	Someone who acts as a mentor for drag daughters, helping them develop their own drag.
Fierce	High praise, meaning someone looks flawless.
Kiki	When two or more drag performers get together for a party, gossip, or catch up.
Reading	Insulting other performers. A group of queens "reading" each other is known as a "library".
Real/realness	Convincingly close to whatever the performer is trying to imitate.
Shade	A subtle, teasing insult – pointing out another queen's faults.
Spilling the tea	Sharing gossip.

Suppression and rebirth

America's repeal of prohibition in 1933 marked the end of the "Pansy Craze" as alcohol licences were issued only to "orderly" venues, forcing many underground clubs to close. In films, the Motion Picture Production Code, also known as the Hays Code (1934) – a strict set of censorship rules drawn up by American politician Will H. Hays – came into force, banning sex, drugs, homosexuality, and the appearance of drag artists in films.

In Berlin, too, 1933 saw the closing of gay clubs and the suppression of drag as the Nazi party took control of Germany and persecuted LGBTQ+ people. Suppression of drag continued during World War II, although in both the US and British armed forces, drag shows became a regular part of troop entertainment. After the war, drag again became part of a vibrant gay club scene in cities such as New York, London, and Berlin. In Paris, Madame Arthur opened in 1946 as "the first transvestite cabaret in Paris". Along with Le Carrousel club, it hosted trans performers such as Bambi and Coccinelle – meaning "ladybird" – throughout the 1950s.

In the UK, the popularity of television in the 1960s and '70s brought drag artists, such as Danny La Rue and Dame Edna Everage, out

Drag king Spikey van Dykey performs at the 2016 Austin International Drag Festival, Texas, US. Spikey, also known as Jamie Kalman, says drag kings do not get the same recognition as drag queens.

of clubs and onto the screen. Adding elaborate costume and film-star glamour to an act steeped in music hall tradition, La Rue became one of the UK's highest-paid artists and in 1969 the first drag queen to appear in a Royal Variety Performance.

Drag and LGBTQ+ identity

In the US, drag became part of the LGBTQ+ assertiveness that emerged in the 1960s – although not necessarily welcomed by all in the gay community. Drag queen Flawless Sabrina organized drag beauty pageants across the US throughout the 1960s, culminating in an annual national event – the Miss All-America Camp Beauty Pageant – in New York City. The pageant was captured in the 1968 documentary film *The Queen*, which featured drag queen Crystal LaBeija, who became a founding figure of New York Black and Latine ball culture in the 1970s and the mother of the house of LaBeija.

In 1979, The Sisters of Perpetual Indulgence – a drag nun and activist group – was formed in San Francisco. Since then, the Sisters have continued to present in a drag style called "genderf***", where they

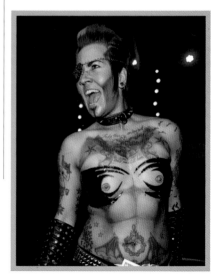

openly display their masculine features and wear extravagant make up and costumes based on nuns' habits. The group has chapters in cities worldwide, where they function primarily as a charity and protest organization raising money and awareness for people living "on the edges", including AIDS victims and LGBTQ+ drug users.

Worldwide exposure

In 1985, American drag queen Lady Bunny organized Wigstock, an outdoor drag festival that became an annual event in New York City. One regular participant was RuPaul, who over the next two decades achieved commercial success as a drag artist. In 2009, he starred – as host and judge – in a new TV reality series, *RuPaul's Drag Race*. Hugely popular with many worldwide spinoffs, including in the UK, Australia, France, and Thailand, the show has changed the way drag is viewed in mainstream culture and introduced millions of people to the language of drag. But it has been criticized for having an outdated and limited viewpoint on drag, presenting mainly "pretty" and feminine drag.

Some TV shows have broken away from the format set by *Drag Race*, notably the American series *The Boulet Brothers' Dragula*, which began in 2016. It includes all types of drag performers with a strong focus on horror-style drag in a competition to crown the next drag "Monster".

Drag is also branching out into experimental forms. Ideas of gender are disrupted by performers such as Cheddar Gorgeous and the

A drag queen performs at the 2020 Pride Parade in Taipei, Taiwan, one of the largest in East Asia. The city has a thriving drag scene, centred around the LGBTQ+ bars in Ximending.

alien-inspired Juno Birch in the UK; Berlin-based, avant-garde performer Hungry; and the performance art movement Tranimal, which began in Los Angeles in the mid-2000s. All are challenging the dominant feminine aesthetics of drag. ∎

RuPaul

Born in 1960 in California, RuPaul Andre Charles moved to New York where he became a well-known dancer and drag performer on the LGBTQ+ scene. Music success came in 1993 with the release of his first album *Supermodel of the World*, which produced the surprise hit "Supermodel (You Better Work)". Reaching number two on the US Dance Club Songs chart and selling 500,000 copies, it boosted RuPaul's growing career.

Throughout the 1990s, RuPaul was getting noticed, landing parts in several films and working as a model for MAC cosmetics. In 1996,

he began hosting his own TV talk show, *The RuPaul Show* – he was one of the first openly gay men to do this – and also a radio show with his long-time friend and collaborator, the singer, DJ, and media personality Michelle Visage.

Since 2009, RuPaul has been the host – and an executive producer – of the wildly successful, Emmy and Tony-award-winning TV series *RuPaul's Drag Race*. Through the show, he has helped people around the world accept and admire drag performers.

TWO LADIES, LIVING SWEETLY AND DEVOTEDLY TOGETHER

BOSTON MARRIAGES (1886)

IN CONTEXT

FOCUS
Female–female love

BEFORE
1849 American poet Henry Wadsworth Longfellow publishes his novella *Kavanagh*, which is about a couple based on Charlotte Cushman and Matilda Hays.

AFTER
1985 Lillian Faderman details Boston marriages in her book *Surpassing the Love of Men*.

1993 In the US, Women's Studies scholars Esther D. Rothblum and Kathleen A. Brehony argue that the term "Boston marriage" should be revived to describe modern romantic and non-sexual relationships between women.

2004 The first same-sex marriage in the US takes place between Tanya McCloskey and Marcia Kadish in Cambridge, Massachusetts.

Henry James's 1886 novel *The Bostonians* revolves around the "women question" – the tension at that time between traditional gender roles and the ideas of the growing women's suffrage movement. At the novel's heart is a relationship between two suffragists, the wealthy Olive Chancellor and the young orator Verena Tarrant. Olive pays Verena's father off, allowing Verena to move into Olive's home as her protégée. The two live there

Charlotte Cushman (left) and Matilda Hays (right), an American actor and an English-Creole writer, lived in a Boston marriage for 10 years.

alone together, until Olive's position in Verena's life is threatened by the appearance of Basil Ransom, a Southerner with traditional views on a woman's place, who begins to court Verena. The novel ends with Verena leaving both Olive and her life as a suffragist to marry Basil.

The novel captured a particular kind of relationship between women in the late 19th century, and after its publication, such relationships between American women – living together without the financial support of men – were referred to as "Boston marriages".

Privileged partners

Many of the best known examples of Boston marriages come from New England's white upper classes, including financially independent women involved in the arts or in the suffrage movement. The great actor Charlotte Cushman lived in Boston marriages with several women over her lifetime – although she died in 1876, before the term was invented. Henry James's own sister, Alice, a diarist, lived in a Boston marriage with Katharine Peabody Loring. As lesbian historian Lillian Faderman has

See also: Early modern lesbianism 74–79 ▪ Erotic friendship in America and Europe 92–95 ▪ The diaries of Anne Lister 102–03 ▪ Marriage equality 288–93

noted, these relationships were especially prevalent between academics. Faderman has estimated that at Wellesley College, Massachusetts, only 1 of the 53 female faculty members in the late 19th century was married to a man; the rest lived with other women. One of the most notable marriages was between poet Katharine Lee Bates (author of the patriotic anthem "America the Beautiful") and economist Katharine Ellis Coman.

A sanitized legacy

Discussions of Boston marriages have often chosen to portray these relationships as close platonic friendships, or at most as romantic relationships without a sexual component. These portrayals may stem from a Victorian desire to categorize Boston marriages as merely romantic friendships, wherein women might share beds, kiss, and show chaste affection to each other before going on to marry men. Even now, some historians

The Bostonians was made into a 1984 film starring Vanessa Redgrave. It was an international success, with Redgrave nominated for several awards.

portray Boston marriages as sexless. Other scholars, such as American historian Blanche Cook, argue that such sexual criteria are not applied to heterosexual relationships; they assume that at least some of the women in Boston marriages were erotically motivated and note, as well, the historical impossibility of knowing "for sure".

What is certain is that the friends and neighbours of these loving pairs typically did not condemn them, but treated them on a par with heterosexual married couples. The diaries and letters of women in Boston marriages also make clear that these relationships, motivated by a mix of love and passion, were the primary and most important in these women's lives. ▪

Do you remember, darling
A year ago today
When we gave ourselves
to each other
Before you went away
At the end of that pleasant
summer weather
Which we had spent by
the sea together?
Sarah Orne Jewett
**Anniversary poem
for Annie Fields**

Sarah Orne Jewett and Annie Adams Fields

One of the most famous Boston marriages of the 19th century was between Sarah Orne Jewett and Annie Adams Fields. Fields, born in 1834, was a social reformer, philanthropist, and writer, known for the literary salon that she and her husband – James T. Fields, editor of *The Atlantic* – established at their home on Boston's Charles Street. After James's death in 1881, Jewett, a writer, paid a condolence visit to Charles Street and, by all accounts, was Fields's partner from that point on. Jewett, 15 years her junior, wintered at Charles Street, summered in their holiday home in Manchester-by-the Sea, and otherwise lived in Fields's home in South Berwick, Maine. The pair also travelled together to Europe and the Caribbean.

Fields and Jewett socialized with a group of other women in Boston marriages. While many couples' correspondence remained strictly private – or was destroyed – Fields's and Jewett's writings survive, leaving us with a clear picture of their deep love for each other. Jewett also described their relationship in her 1877 novel *Deephaven*, and after Jewett's death from a stroke in 1909, Fields published her correspondence in the *Letters of Sarah Orne Jewett* (1911). These letters were heavily edited, however, to remove more personal information, leading some biographers to miscategorize their relationship as a deep friendship. When Fields died in 1915, she was buried beside her husband.

SIMULTANEOUSLY A BEAUTIFUL WOMAN AND A POTENT MAN

GENDER NONCONFORMITY AND COLONIAL CONSTRAINTS IN AFRICA (LATE 19TH CENTURY)

IN CONTEXT

FOCUS
Traditional gender fluidity

BEFORE
1624–63 Njinga Mbande rules the Mbundu people of southwest Africa. Europeans report that Njinga dresses as a man and has a harem of men dressed as women.

***c.* 1820s** Shaka, leader of southern Africa's Zulu empire, permits male-to-male sex in his powerful army but forbids sexual relations with women.

AFTER
1970s Igbo genderqueer crossdresser Area Scatter sings and plays the thumb piano across eastern Nigeria.

1980s Nigerian-born Rotimi Fani-Kayode explores Yoruba sexuality and spirituality in acclaimed photographic portraits of Black gay bodies.

2006 Same-sex marriage becomes legal under South Africa's Civil Union Act.

The European colonization of Africa advanced rapidly in the late 19th and early 20th centuries, increasing from around 10 per cent in 1870 to almost 90 per cent by 1914. With it came Western Christianity and the enforcement of new moral codes to exclude and criminalize anything that diverged from heterosexuality.

Western nations generally viewed Africans whose behaviours differed from their own as deviant and primitive. Making no effort to preserve African cultural practices, most colonial powers introduced penal codes that reinforced European ideas of "moral" and "civilized" modernity. The new laws frequently disrupted local patterns of gender, sex, and sexuality.

Blurring of gender

In different areas of Nigeria, Oyo, Yoruba, Nnobi, and Igbo women frequently engaged in same-sex marriages that were not necessarily

Same-sex relations were common among African warriors such as the Zande here, who battled colonial powers in Central Africa in the 1800s.

See also: The earliest evidence for LGBTQ+ people 18–19 ▪ AFAB cross-dressers and "female husbands" 82–83 ▪ The LGBTQ+ struggle in modern Africa 306–07

> One who is physically male can vibrate female energy, and vice versa. That is where the real gender is.
> **Malidoma Somé**
> **Shaman of the Dagaaba people of Ghana**

sexual. If one partner owned land and gave their name to the children, they were sometimes culturally understood as male. Such liaisons still exist, traditionally between women who cannot bear children and those who can, enabling a childless woman to have access to children. Colonial powers wholly misunderstood such relationships.

In Lesotho, traditional *motsoalle* relationships are close, sometimes sexual, long-term friendships between women that have long existed alongside opposite-sex marriage but became rarer as a result of 20th-century homophobia. In Nigeria, Hausa *yan dauda* are self-identified men who have long dressed, acted, and lived in ways often ascribed to women but now are often forced to live secretly.

Alien labels
Introduced by Western colonialism, terms such as gay, lesbian, and homosexual were largely alien to precolonial African culture. The Dagaaba people of Ghana traditionally believe that female or

male energy, rather than simply sexual anatomy, is what determines gender. Among the Mbuti of Central Africa, gender is not assigned until after puberty.

Beliefs in androgynous, intersex deities have been recorded among more than 20 peoples across Africa, indicating widespread acceptance of historical transgender behaviour. Trans men (*okule*) and trans women (*agule*) of the Lugbara people still conduct spiritual ceremonies in parts of Uganda and the Democratic Republic of Congo. The Zulu of Southern Africa term their transgender shamans *insangoma*.

By imposing its concept of gender and sexuality, Europe stigmatized much that was natural and fluid. European languages still struggle to capture the meanings of some traditional relationships, resulting in oxymoronic qualifiers, such as "boy wives", "female husbands", and "male daughters."

Cultural amnesia
One devastating effect of colonization is that European laws introduced to criminalize "deviant" sexual identities still exist in many African countries. The Western demonization of traditional African practices appears to have provoked a cultural amnesia, so that nations ignore their own history and perpetuate the punishment of queer people, claiming that LGTBQ+ concepts emanate from Europe.

Yet many Africans have now begun re-presenting their sexual identities in transgressive ways that reflect their traditions and precolonial times. Decentring Western concepts of gender, sex, and sexuality, they are now reclaiming their own unique past. ▪

Èṣù

A complex *òrìṣà* (deity) of the Ifa religion of the Nigerian Yoruba people, Èṣù (or Eshu), is the god of the crossroads and is reputedly able to switch genitals at will to appear as a man or a woman. Because of this fluid sexuality, the deity has become an icon of queerness, existing at the intersection of genders and playing a mediating role. Although Western Christianity and 19th-century colonial powers identified Èṣù as a devil, the trickster god is essentially protective and enforces natural and divine laws, maintaining a balance between good and bad. Èṣù also serves as an emissary between the divine and earthly realms.

Èṣù is among the most widespread and worshipped of all deities, also featuring in the Afro-Caribbean Santería religion, Haitian voodoo, and Candomblé, an African diasporic religion that developed in Brazil during the 19th century.

An Èṣù dance staff (*ogo elegba*) from the 19th century depicts the spirit as a male–female pair. The male figure carries a ritual flute.

THAT WHICH APPEARS IN NATURE IS NATURAL
FIRST RECOGNITION OF ASEXUALITY (1890s)

IN CONTEXT

FOCUS
Scientific recognition of asexuality

BEFORE
1886 In Germany, Richard von Krafft-Ebing uses the term "sexual anaesthesia" to refer to asexual people in his *Psychopathia Sexualis*; the same term is used by Magnus Hirschfeld in his 1896 *Sappho und Sokrates*.

AFTER
1994 Canadian psychologist Anthony F. Bogaert suggests that one per cent of the population is asexual.

2002 The world's first explicit legal protection for asexuality is passed in New York state's Sexual Orientation Non-Discrimination Act.

2004 The magazine *New Scientist* devotes an issue to the subject of asexuality.

Often considered the first work to recognize asexuality as a sexual orientation, German teacher Emma Trosse's *Ein Weib? Psychologisch-biographische Studie über eine Konträrsexuelle* (*A Woman? Psychological-biographical study of a contrary-sexual*) was banned in Leipzig when she published it there anonymously in 1897. Due to its

The dandy, a 19th-century man known for his theatricality and fashion, was once associated with celibacy and an aversion to sex, though this later became an aversion to sex with women.

discussion of sexuality, the essay violated the German penal code as an "obscene document".

Ein Weib addressed the phenomenon of *Sinnlichkeitslose*, those without sensuality. This term can be seen as a precursor to the modern identity term "asexual" and, unlike earlier references, did not seek to medicalize it. Trosse saw a lack of sensuality as natural, rather than as a condition in need of either medical intervention or criminal persecution. The *Sinnlichkeitslose* included people who had no sexual or erotic interests – and also no desire for any kind of intimacy with others. Because of this, a person without sensuality might instead find that their work became their life's passion; in Trosse's case, a life dedicated to science provided the fulfilment usually ascribed to sexual partnership. Trosse herself identified as *sinnlichkeitslos*.

Uranian urges

Trosse positioned her work as a continuation of a tradition of writings on countersexuality – an umbrella term for anything that was not heterosexuality. She took up Karl Heinrich Ulrichs's use of the term "urning", or "Uranian", and

See also: Defining "homosexual" and "heterosexual" 106–07 ▪ Sexology and psychoanalysis 132–33 ▪ Kinsey's research on sexology 164–65 ▪ *The Asexual Manifesto* 218 ▪ The aromantic and asexual spectrum 280–83

Timeline of terms to describe asexuality

1869 Karl-Maria Kertbeny, a Hungarian campaigner, uses the term **monosexual** to describe people who do not have sex, only masturbate.

1886 German sexologist Richard von Krafft-Ebing classifies the "condition" of experiencing no sexual desire as **sexual anaesthesia**.

1922 "Androgyne" American writer Jennie June is scornful of **"anaphrodites"**, who neither sexually desire nor "adore" women.

1948 Alfred Kinsey, the American sexologist, includes **category X** on his famous Kinsey Scale for those who experience no sexual desire.

broadened its meaning to apply not only to "outwardly male persons" but also to women and people without sensuality. Ulrichs used the term to describe homosexual men – who he said had the sensual feelings of a woman, linking sexuality to some innate gender. Trosse suggests that *Sinnlichkeitslose* represent a third sex, as they have the sensuality of neither a man nor a woman.

Trosse spoke of a general lack of sensuality (what we now might call asexuality) in the same terms in which she described a Uranian's lack of sensual attraction towards their heterosexual partner, and described the feelings of shame and revulsion that might be felt towards sex. She also claimed that women were not sensual by nature and that sensuality could not cause love, but that love created sensual feeling – a description that fits the modern concept of demisexuality.

From asensual to asexual
While it is unclear exactly when or how the language of the 1890s, and Trosse's "without sensuality", shifted to the use of "asexual", the latter undoubtedly has its roots in the work of Trosse and her fellow German sexologists. In 1920, the Presbytery of New Orleans, in the United States, charged Reverend Carl Schlegel with disseminating immoral doctrines. The records of their investigation quote Schlegel as advocating for the same laws for "homosexuals, heterosexuals, bisexuals, asexuals" – proof that by the early 20th century, "asexual" had become a known term in public discourse. ▪

Emma Trosse

Born in Gransee, Prussia (now in Germany) in 1863, Emma Trosse would become the first woman to write a scientific monograph on lesbianism. She became a teacher, living and working for many years with boarding school mistress Hermine Dulsmann, in what some have considered to be a romantic relationship. In the 1880s and 1890s, she was perhaps the only woman allowed to attend psychology lectures at Friedrich Wilhelm University in Berlin, and made a name for herself with her writings on countersexuality. After Trosse married Georg Külz, a doctor, in 1900, she had to give up teaching due to rules surrounding teacher celibacy, and instead worked in the sanatorium her husband owned, writing about and researching diabetes. Trosse died in 1949.

Key works

1895 *Homosexuality in relation to marriage and the question of women's rights*
1897 *A Woman? Psychological-biographical study of a contrary-sexual*
1897 *Is free love immoral?*

THE LOVE THAT DARE NOT SPEAK ITS NAME

THE TRIAL OF OSCAR WILDE (1895)

IN CONTEXT

FOCUS
Same-sex acts as a crime

BEFORE
1835 James Pratt and John Smith are hanged – the last men in England executed for sodomy.

1885 In Nottingham, UK, 19-year-old Thomas Swift is the first person to be convicted of "gross indecency with another male", under Section 11 of the 1885 Criminal Law Amendment Act.

AFTER
1957 In Britain, after a three-year enquiry, the Wolfenden Committee recommends that "homosexual behaviour between consenting adults in private should no longer be considered a criminal offence".

2017 Oscar Wilde and around 50,000 other men are pardoned posthumously for same-sex acts.

In 1861, the death penalty for buggery was abolished in England and Wales, although it remained a serious offence. Beyond this, the law and the public took little interest in homosexuality. By the end of the 19th century, however, all aspects of intimacy between men had become potentially criminalized.

In 1870, the trial of Fanny and Stella – assigned male at birth and charged under their birth names Frederick William Park and Ernest Boulton – brought wide publicity to a homosexual London subculture. Fanny and Stella were part of a theatrical troupe, dressing in women's clothes on and off stage. They were charged with corrupting public decency and committing "the abominable crime of buggery".

Fanny and Stella were found not guilty, but the trial fuelled the fire of homophobic opinion, stoked by the press. In 1885, British MP Henry Labouchere added a clause – known as the "Labouchere Amendment" – to the Criminal Law Amendment Act, which went beyond the established terms of buggery and sodomy to introduce the ambiguous charge of "gross indecency" for any sexual activity between men. This change in law was used to convict Oscar Wilde and thousands of other men over the next 70 years.

Fame and notoriety

In early 1895, Anglo-Irish writer Oscar Wilde – already established on the London literary scene – was riding a wave of popularity, with two successful plays in London's

Oscar Wilde and Alfred Douglas, pictured here in 1893, began their affair in 1891, when Douglas was a student at the University of Oxford.

See also: The criminalization of sodomy 68–71 ▪ Male–male love poetry 80–81 ▪
The decriminalization of same-sex acts 184–85

In his poem "Two Loves", Oscar Wilde's lover Alfred Douglas writes of "**the Love that dare not speak its name**".

At his trial, Wilde is asked whether Douglas's poem refers to love that is "**improper**" or "**unnatural**".

Wilde describes this love as a **pure, noble form of affection** that exists between **an elder and a younger man**.

Oscar Wilde

Born in Dublin in 1854, Oscar O'Flahertie Wills Wilde studied at Trinity College Dublin and at Oxford, where he won the Newdigate Prize for the poem *Ravenna*. His first poetry collection was published in 1881, and the next year he travelled to the United States on a 150-city lecture tour, promoting himself as a leading light of the Aesthetic art movement, following its mantra of "Art for art's sake".

In 1884, Wilde settled in London and married Constance Lloyd, with whom he had two sons. Over the next 10 years, Wilde wrote prolifically, including poetry, journalism, short stories, plays, and his only novel, *The Picture of Dorian Gray*.

After his release from Reading Gaol in 1897, Wilde left the UK – estranged from Constance and unable to see his children. He finally settled in Paris, where he died in 1900.

Key works

1891 *The Picture of Dorian Gray*
1895 *The Importance of Being Earnest*
1898 "The Ballad of Reading Gaol"

West End – *The Importance of Being Earnest* and *An Ideal Husband*. As part of the Aesthetic movement that promoted cultural and personal freedoms, Wilde also embraced "dandyism", appearing in flamboyant clothes, such as knee breeches, velvet jackets, and ruffled blouse. Branded as unmasculine, this ran contrary to late Victorian ideals of manhood based on religious piety, duty, and sobriety.

The artist crushed

Wilde, who engaged in same-sex relationships from his thirties, was passionately involved with Lord Alfred Douglas, a poet and journalist 16 years his junior. Douglas's father, the Marquis of Queensberry, left a calling card at London's Albemarle Club on 18 February 1895, on which he called Wilde a "posing somdomite [sic]". Wilde decided to sue Queensbury for libel.

The defence brought in a number of male sex workers with whom Wilde had engaged in various sexual activities. The fact that the men were young and working class were damning for Wilde and the case was dropped. He was prosecuted instead, convicted on 25 May at the Central Criminal Court (the "Old Bailey") of gross indecency, and sentenced to two years' hard labour. The trial was a sensation, feeding public fears about homosexuality as a moral and physical threat, and forcing gay men to act with even greater caution. ▪

If prison and dishonour be my destiny, think that my love for you and this idea, this still more divine belief, that you love me in return will sustain me …
Oscar Wilde
Letter to Lord Alfred Douglas

I COULD EXPRESS MYSELF BETTER DRESSED AS A BOY
MALE IMPERSONATORS (1890s–1920)

During the late 19th and early 20th century, male impersonation was a popular form of entertainment in British music halls, and popularity of this art form spread to the US. Many impersonators were assigned female at birth; some identified as genders that we would recognize as trans and non-binary today.

Charles (Annie) Hindle, one of the first famous male impersonators, performed in the US from 1868 after emigrating from the UK as a child. Assigned female at birth, they lived a large part of their life as a man, and had relationships with women.

The most famous of all was British impersonator Vesta Tilley, the stage name of Matilda Alice Powles, who started acting at the age of three and soon supported her entire family with her income from touring Britain and the US. The UK's highest earning woman throughout the 1890s, she ran military drives for World War I in character.

Male impersonation often involved singing and dancing, with comedy to the fore in music halls renowned for their raucous and bawdy humour. Hugely popular, these performers paved the way for many modern-day drag kings. ∎

Sheet music for In the Pale Moonlight, performed by Vesta Tilley. Creating characters such as "Burlington Bertie", she would dress as, and mock, young men.

BONA TO VADA YOUR DOLLY OLD EEK!
THE SECRET LANGUAGE OF POLARI
(LATE 19TH CENTURY–1960s)

IN CONTEXT

FOCUS
LGBTQ+ subcultures and languages

BEFORE
1887 British lesbian Anne Lister's diaries are discovered to have been written in a form of crypthand, using Greek letters, numbers, and symbols.

1915 British journalist Alfred Barrett founds *The Link*, a lonely hearts newsletter using coded phrases such as "broad-minded" and "bohemian" to signal homosexuality.

AFTER
2010 The World Oral Literature Project at the University of Cambridge includes Polari on a list of endangered languages since it has barely been used for 30 years.

2016 On his final album, British musician David Bowie incorporates terms from Polari into the song *Girl Loves Me*.

Polari (from the Italian *parlare*, "to talk") was a form of cant or cryptolect – a language used to deceive. In the early 20th century, when sex between men was still illegal, Polari was used in Britain and Ireland, mainly by gay men, to signal their sexuality to one another and to communicate without fear of being discovered or persecuted.

Polari originates from the 19th century, drawing on Mediterranean Lingua Franca – a pidgin language used by sailors – and Parlyaree, a cant used by Travellers based heavily on Romani. It was prevalent in port cities, reaching London through its use by criminals, traders, sex workers, and those in the theatre.

Constantly developing, Polari added words from Yiddish, such as "schnozzle" for nose, and Cockney rhyming slang such as "hampsteads" (Hampstead Heath) for teeth. It also made heavy use of irony.

Decline in usage

The partial decriminalization of sex between men in the UK in 1967 lessened the need for a cryptolect among gay communities. Prior to this, Polari's increasing exposure in mainstream media in the 1950s and 1960s had already begun to undermine its value, with British comedian Kenneth Williams well known for his use of simplified Polari in radio and television shows. Drag queens also began to incorporate the slang into their acts. In the context of gay pride, some gay men also viewed the existence of a secret language as a by-product of an era of repression. ∎

Those things are forced upon you. They're not just a camp joke. They're practical.
Bette Bourne
British actor (1939–)

See also: Molly houses 90–91 ▪ The diaries of Anne Lister 102–03 ▪ Drag 112–17 ▪ Brazilian Pajubá 169 ▪ Camp 180–81

SEXOLO
AND SE
IDENTIT
1900–69

GY
XUAL
IES

Germany's post-war Weimar Republic is an era of tolerance; Berlin becomes an LGBTQ+ epicentre.

1918–33

Anders als die Andern (*Different from the Others*), a German silent film, is the first sympathetic on-screen portrayal of gay characters.

1919

American singer Gertrude "Ma" Rainey's "Prove It On Me Blues" becomes an anthem for lesbianism with its lyrics about female–female desire.

1928

In a letter to a woman who has asked him to treat her son, **Austrian physician Sigmund Freud** argues that people should not be ashamed of homosexuality.

1935

1919

Magnus Hirschfeld founds the Institute for Sexual Science in Berlin, known for its pioneering transgender surgeries.

1928

British author Radclyffe Hall's *The Well of Loneliness* is published. Its protagonist is interpreted as both butch lesbian and trans.

1933

The Nazis begin to persecute men who have sex with men; up to 15,000 are sent to concentration camps by 1945.

The first half of the 20th century was a tumultuous period of massive social and political upheaval; it was characterized by two world wars, widespread decolonization movements, struggles for suffrage, and the rise of communism by way of revolutions. LGBTQ+ people were swept up in these changes, but until recently their roles within these events were rarely explored by historians. LGBTQ+ histories of the early 20th century show a burgeoning community coming out into the open, facing reactionary oppression, and fighting back against it.

Brutality and oppression

General Eisenhower discovered, after trying to "ferret out" the homosexuals in the US Army during World War II, that the Women's Army Corps ran on the labour of lesbians at even the highest levels. While Eisenhower let the lesbians stay, his impulse to root out LGBTQ+ people was typical of the period. The Lavender Scare of 1950, for example, would see LGBTQ+ people identified and fired from roles in the US civil service. Convictions continued in the many nations with laws against sodomy – often using evidence from the accused's neighbours or colleagues – until it was decriminalized. Sodomy laws were struck down in many Western nations in the 1960s and 1970s, though their legacies have lingered longer in former colonies.

Where police forces were employed to identify LGBTQ+ people, officers took to the task with violent zeal. In Nazi Germany, the Gestapo sought out men who had sex with men and sent them to concentration camps. From 1964, Brazilian police forces targeted the transgender community during the country's military dictatorship. In the 1960s, the US police regularly raided LGBTQ+ meeting places such as Compton's Cafeteria in San Francisco and New York gay bar The Stonewall Inn.

Queer knowledge

Despite such oppressive measures, LGBTQ+ people would not be silenced. Different facets of LGBTQ+ identity were explored and developed during this period. The figure of the butch lesbian, for example, was popularized and shaped by the progressive atmosphere of the 1920s. From 1919, German physician Magnus

The Kinsey Scale is first introduced in American biologist Alfred Kinsey's *Sexual Behavior in the Human Male*.

1948

Christine Jorgensen's medical transition is covered in newspapers in the US, making her an instant celebrity.

1952

American writer **Susan Sontag's *Notes on Camp*** explores the performative nature of campness and its ties to the gay community.

1964

Sodomy is decriminalized in England and Wales; the rest of the UK follows suit by 1982.

1967

1946

The Centre for Culture and Leisure, one of the world's first homophile groups, forms in the Netherlands.

1950

The "Lavender Scare" sees LGBTQ+ civil servants in the US fired due to government fears of links to communism.

1964

A secret language called Pajubá develops in Brazil's trans community to help people avoid police raids.

1966

At Compton's Cafeteria in San Francisco, trans people and drag queens resist police harassment.

Hirschfeld's institute in Berlin advanced sexological research and pioneered major transgender surgeries. Patients travelled from other countries for the promise of transformation. Not only a research centre but also a place for LGBTQ+ people to meet and find support, the institute was a tragic casualty of Nazi persecution.

Many of the figures who went through the early transgender surgeries became important icons for the trans community – former US Army GI Christine Jorgensen being a prime example after her transition made the newspapers in 1952. Jorgensen was so famous that when Taiwanese trans woman Xie Jianshun made the news following her own transition, she was dubbed the "Chinese Christine". The celebrity status of these women reflected a public fascination with medical research and procedures. However, other early recipients of surgery, who did not want their trans status to be out in the open, often struggled with exposure and harassment from wider society, who did not approve of transition.

Fighting back

The mid-20th century saw LGBTQ+ people mobilize to secure their human rights. The most obvious of these rights was freedom from persecution. Striving for acceptance by cisgender, heterosexual society, "homophile" liberation activists pursued assimilationist policies. Homophile campaigns desexualized LGBTQ+ life by focusing on romance over eroticism, and stressed the need for LGBTQ+ people to be discreet and "respectable". Groups formed across the US and Europe, advocating for the end of sodomy laws and for same-sex marriage.

In the 1960s, however, activist organizations began to take more radical approaches. Inspired by the Black American activists of the Civil Rights movement, gay liberation groups turned to direct action, such as political campaigns and protest marches. Frank Kameny, an activist who had been dismissed from the US Army Map Service for his sexuality, coined the simple slogan "gay is good". This represented a major shift, calling for LGBTQ+ identity to be not merely tolerated but celebrated – and it was, in the new community bookstores, bars, and social clubs that began to spring up. LGBTQ+ communities around the world were developing a strong public presence. ■

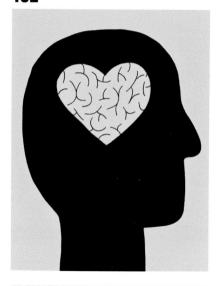

HOMOSEXUALITY IS NO VICE, NO DEGRADATION

SEXOLOGY AND PSYCHOANALYSIS (LATE 19TH–EARLY 20TH CENTURIES)

IN CONTEXT

FOCUS
Science and psychology

BEFORE
1869 Karl Maria Kertbeny coins the terms "heterosexual" and "homosexual".

AFTER
1948 American biologist Alfred Kinsey's *Sexual Behavior in the Human Male* is published, arguing for a spectrum of sexual activity from exclusive heterosexuality to exclusive homosexuality.

1953 Kinsey follows his first report with *Sexual Behavior in the Human Female*.

1973 In the US, homosexuality is removed as a mental illness from the Diagnostic and Statistical Manual of Mental Disorders (DSM).

2019 The American Psychoanalytic Association (APsaA) apologizes for having classified homosexuality as a mental disorder.

Sex outside marriage was subject to varied legal and medical treatment in the 19th century. While the courts focused on the sexual act, doctors and psychologists focused on the individual and the cause of their desires. Same-sex desires would receive particular attention.

The science of sexology was most advanced in German-speaking Europe. Austro-German professor of

psychiatry Richard von Krafft-Ebing rejected the widespread belief that sexual abnormalities resulted from cultural degeneration. He based his work on the testimony of individual cases and regarded them as sexual variations rather than exceptions from a sexual norm, which was how they were seen by the general public and by doctors specializing in sexual behaviour.

Krafft-Ebing's *Psychopathia Sexualis* (*Sexual Psychopathy*) of 1886 introduced such terms for alleged sexual perversions as "sadism" and "homosexuality" to wider audiences. These ideas also gained traction in the English-speaking world after the 1897 publication of *Sexual Inversion* by British sexologist Havelock Ellis and co-author John Addington Symonds.

In 1905, Austrian physician Sigmund Freud described homosexuality as repellent. Over the next three decades, however, the founder of psychoanalysis changed his views dramatically.

This photo is from the collection of Richard von Krafft-Ebing, whose famous book, aimed at physicians, was written partly in Latin to discourage the general public from reading it.

See also: Defining "homosexual" and "heterosexual" 106–07 ▪ Persecution during the Holocaust 156–61 ▪ Kinsey's research on sexology 164–65 ▪ Removal of homosexuality from the DSM 219 ▪ Bisexuality 262–65

Freud's theory of sexuality

According to **Freud**, sexual "perversity" is a **normal phase of development** in infancy and childhood.

⬇

Everyone is, at least latently, **bisexual**, and both **same-sex and different-sex desires** stem from this innate bisexuality.

⬇

Sexual "perversity" can **persist into adult life** if a child encounters **developmental problems**.

⬇

Neurosis in heterosexual people is often caused by a **fear of unconscious same-sex desire**.

In 1935, writing to an American woman who had asked him to treat her son, he stated that "homosexuality is … nothing to be ashamed of". Five years earlier, he had signed a petition calling for the decriminalization of sex between men. Freud's stance was all the more remarkable given that his work was being condemned by the Nazis in Germany.

A universal feature

Although radical, Freud did not approach sexual diversity from the point of view of later 20th-century liberationist campaigners. He believed that what he called "polymorphous perversity" was a universal feature of human life, and an expected phase of development in infancy and childhood that could, as a result of certain developmental problems, persist into adult life. Freud asserted that everyone was, at least latently, bisexual. While he did not think that people could be "cured" of homosexuality, he did think that therapy might enable them to reconnect with heterosexual desires that were repressed.

Freud also believed that unconscious same-sex desire was a major factor behind the development of neuroses among heterosexuals. A range of behaviours could, he thought, be explained by traumatic experiences in the past and sexual fantasies that had been repressed.

Medical sexology

Building on, but diverging from, earlier medical sexology, Freud's ideas established sexuality at the core of the identity of the modern individual. Sexual imagery – including phallic imagery, such as his beloved cigars – was seen as a key element of the interpretation of dreams, something that became an important psychoanalytic tool. His followers became enormously influential, but in the US they increasingly focused on seeing sexual complexity as evidence of mental illness rather than of human diversity.

That view was challenged by the Kinsey reports in 1948 and 1953 and by lesbian and gay rights activists rejecting the medicalization of homosexuality. Psychoanalysis, however, was slower than many other areas of psychology to end its view that LGBTQ+ people were in need of treatment. ▪

[Homosexuality] cannot be classified as an illness; we consider it to be a variation of the sexual function caused by a certain arrest of sexual development.
Sigmund Freud
"Letter to an American Mother", 1935

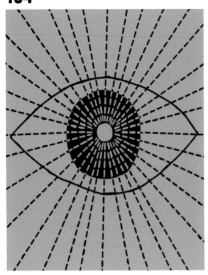

VISIONS OF TRANSFORMATION
GENDER TRANSGRESSION IN MODERN CHINA (1912–1950s)

IN CONTEXT

FOCUS
Gender nonconformity

BEFORE
1598 Chinese physician
Li Shizhen publishes the
*Compendium of Materia
Medica*, cataloguing five types
of non-males and five types of
non-females.

1740 Pu Songling's *Strange
Stories from a Chinese Studio*
is published posthumously. It
includes a story titled *Renyao*
(*The Human Prodigy*) in which
a woman is found to be a man.

1768 Chinese poet Chen
Duansheng begins writing the
20-volume *Tale of the After
Life*, which features the theme
of male impersonation.

AFTER
2004 Taiwan introduces the
Gender Equity Education Act
to promote gender equality.

2022 China lowers the age
limit for gender affirmation
surgery from 20 to 18.

Gender transgression in China is evident in **traditional theatre**, the role of **eunuchs**, and a fascination with **gender-nonconforming people**.

Scientific developments lead to new insights into gender transgression, fuelling popular fiction and newspaper reports on the subject.

Chinese people begin to see gender affirmation surgery as a **feasible medical option** for gender-nonconforming people.

The transgression of gender boundaries has a long history in Chinese culture. In imperial China, AMAB actors had played female roles since the Han dynasty (206 BCE–219 CE), and in the 17th and 18th centuries, during the Qing dynasty, female writers had incorporated tales of AFAB gender nonconformity in *tanci* (plucking songs). The Chinese court employed eunuchs (castrated AMAB people) to serve the emperor and his relatives. Over time, some eunuchs, such as Wei Zhongxian (1568–1627) and Li Lianying (1848–1911), became powerful, even achieving offices of state in the case of Wei Zhongxian. Among ordinary people, however, individuals who assumed a different gender role from the one assigned at birth were known as *renyao* – "human-monsters".

Stories of sex metamorphosis and infants that would today be called intersex had long circulated among Chinese physicians, but it was not until the 19th century that medicine began to offer explanations for gender nonconformity. After the Opium Wars of 1839–42 and 1856–60, Western influence in

See also: Favourites in Han China 28–29 ▪ Male impersonators 126 ▪ The first gender affirmation surgeries 136–41 ▪ Transgender rights 196–203 ▪ LGBTQ+ activism in Asia 254–55

China expanded and knowledge of Western biomedicine became more widespread.

Changing perceptions

After China became a republic in 1912, scientific understandings of sex and gender accelerated with the emergence of endocrinology – the study of hormones. Chinese writers reported on sex-reversal experiments on animals taking place in Europe that located the seat of sexual development in endocrine secretions. In the 1920s and '30s, scientists began to understand that maleness and femaleness were malleable constructs that could be altered through the levels of sex hormones in the body. It therefore followed that everyone was "bisexually" constituted, and sex became scalar rather than discrete or absolute.

Palace eunuchs carry the Empress Dowager Cixi, the de facto ruler of China from 1861 – when her six-year-old son became emperor – to her death in 1908.

These insights transformed the way writers described the old phenomena of Chinese eunuchs, hermaphrodites, and *renyao*. Although eunuchs had traditionally retained a distinct masculine identity, in the light of modern science they were recast as feminized bodies.

This led to a new fascination with gender transgression. In 1934, the Chinese public was enthralled by media reports of Yao Jinping, an AFAB person from Tianjin who claimed to have turned into a man overnight. After examining Yao, doctors in Shanghai discovered that their self-proclaimed "sex reassignment" was actually a hoax. Even so, the press often compared Yao with Lili Elbe, an early recipient of gender affirmation surgery in Europe. Before Yao, most people in China saw "sex change" (as it was understood in Chinese society at the time) as a possibility only in the context of animals or intersex people. After Yao, the Chinese

> Right now I very much accept being called … transgender … I hope to accept this identity of mine such that I could affirm myself with self-respect and confidence. This is called transgender pride.
> **Joanne Leung**
> **Transgender activist, Hong Kong**

public started to entertain the idea that people who were not intersex might also want to "change their sex". Discussions of sex mutability were incorporated into fiction, such as Gu Junzhen's short story "Sex Change" (1940).

New acceptance

By the 1950s, "sex change" had become a possibility, however remote, for individuals hoping to alter their "bodily sex". The case of Xie Jianshun, who underwent "sex change" surgery in Taiwan in the early 1950s, particularly increased awareness of surgical intervention. Xie's name made headlines, and commentators often called her the "Chinese Christine", a reference to Christine Jorgensen, an American trans woman who underwent gender affirmation surgery in Europe and the US in 1951–52. The case of Xie Jianshun signalled the beginning of trans visibility in Sinophone communities, in line with the rest of the world. ▪

NATURE MADE A MISTAKE, WHICH I HAVE CORRECTED

THE FIRST GENDER AFFIRMATION SURGERIES (1917–31)

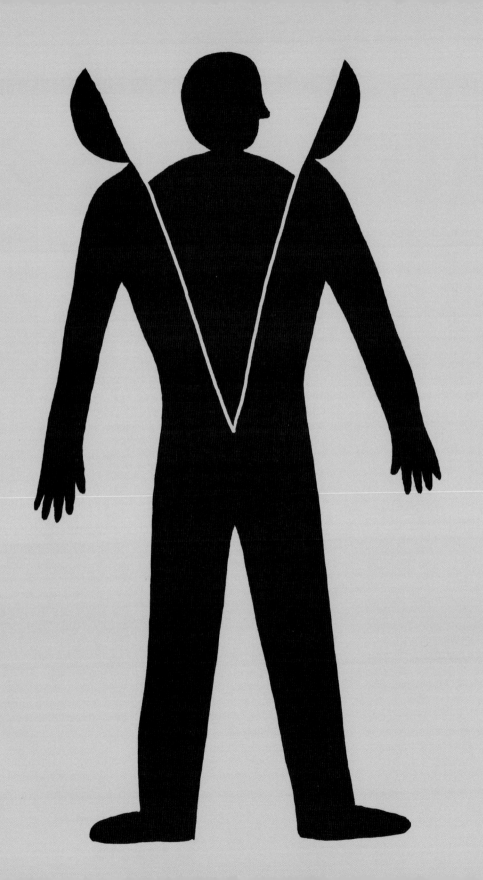

IN CONTEXT

FOCUS
Pioneering transgender surgeries

BEFORE
1906 Karl M. Baer, an intersex man, receives "masculinization" surgery in Berlin, Germany.

AFTER
1935 The male growth hormone testosterone is chemically synthesized.

1936 Russian surgeon Nikolaj Bogoraz introduces a primitive form of phalloplasty.

1938 British biochemist Edward Charles Dodds creates the first synthetic oestrogen.

1946 In Britain, plastic surgeon Harold Gillies performs the first gender affirmation phalloplasty.

1972 Sweden becomes the first country in the world to provide free gender affirmation treatment, in the form of hormone therapy.

Main types of gender affirmation surgery

"Feminization" surgeries		"Masculinization" surgeries	
Penectomy	Removal of the penis	**Hysterectomy**	Removal of the uterus
Orchiectomy	Removal of the testicles	**Oophorectomy**	Removal of the ovaries
Vaginoplasty	Creation of a vagina	**Phalloplasty**	Creation of a penis
Mammoplasty	Chest enlargement	**Mastectomy**	Removal of breasts
Facial surgery	Surgery to make the face more "feminine"	**Facial surgery**	Surgery to make the face more "masculine"

Gender affirmation surgeries are surgical procedures – first developed in the early 20th century – that alter a person's physical characteristics to resemble more closely those associated with their identified gender. The surgeries are broadly split into two categories: "feminization" surgeries, which result in anatomy that is typically considered female by a given society; and "masculinization" surgeries, which result in anatomy that is typically considered male by a given society. Before gender affirmation surgeries were available, transgender people who sought medical help were subjected to sometimes forceful conversion therapies, aimed to suppress affirmed gender. They were also often assumed to be involved with sex work or other criminalized activity. As a result, some trans people attempted to perform their own surgery, while others lived secretive lives, hiding the gender they were assigned at birth.

Early surgery

Some historians claim that Alan L. Hart, an American physician, was the first transgender person to receive "masculinization" surgery. Assigned female at birth in 1890, Hart had displayed "masculine" tendencies from childhood, playing games that society expected boys to play, preferring farm work to more traditionally "feminine" tasks, and writing essays at school under the name "Robert". Hart studied medicine at university, graduating in 1917. In the same year, he persuaded a fellow physician, Joshua Allen Gilbert, to carry out a full hysterectomy on him, arguing that as an "abnormal inversion" he needed to be sterilized. After the operation, Hart started using he/him pronouns and changed his legal name. He went on to have a successful medical career as a radiologist, pioneering X-ray techniques to detect tuberculosis.

Hart's surgery is understood by most historians as affirmation of a male identity, but some have challenged this, suggesting that Hart was a lesbian who adopted a male identity to pursue love affairs with women. They point to a historical context in which sexual relationships were understood within a framework of traditional heterosexual marriage, suggesting that it was more viable for Hart to present as a man than as a lesbian. Others, however, have insisted that Hart experienced life as a male from childhood and that to suggest otherwise disregards the existence of transgender identities.

The arguments over Hart have resulted in tensions within the LGBTQ+ community, with different

See also: Intersex rights 48–53 ▪ Transgender rights 196–203 ▪ Conversion therapy is banned 286–87 ▪ Transgender pregnancy and reproductive healthcare 304–05

groups each claiming Hart as an early activist. How Hart truly identified is unlikely to ever be known. This lack of personal affirmation from the past highlights a difficulty in categorizing historical figures as a given LGBTQ+ identity.

Trans recognition

While Hart was undergoing surgery, German physician and sexologist Magnus Hirschfeld was advocating for gay, trans, and intersex rights. In Berlin, in 1919, he founded the Institute for Sexual Science – the world's first sexology institute – providing psychological and medical services, counselling, sex education, and contraception. It became a haven for thousands of LGBTQ+ people, offering them legal support, health treatment, and shelter from abuse.

At the institute, Hirschfeld applied his theory of "sexual intermediacy", which asserted that people do not fit neatly into the rigid categories of "man" and "woman", either physically or psychologically. He proposed a system of many different types of gender and sexuality, falling between "fully male" and "fully female" – effectively

Hysterectomy was performed, her hair was cut, a complete male outfit was secured.
Joshua Allen Gilbert
on Alan L. Hart's gender affirmation

Soon the day will come when science will win victory over error, justice a victory over injustice, and human love a victory over human hatred and ignorance.
Magnus Hirschfeld

suggesting a wide natural spectrum. He eventually calculated that there were more than 40 million variations in human sexuality.

Hirschfeld coined the term "transvestite" as a category for those who habitually and voluntarily wore the clothes of the opposite sex. Cross-dressing had previously been thought of simply as a form of homosexuality, but Hirschfeld realized that it could apply to others who were not homosexual. He highlighted how clothing was central to the physical and psychological wellbeing of those who cross-dressed. With this premise, he challenged the German police, who would sometimes arrest transvestites, fine them, and even imprison them for up to six weeks. Hirschfeld convinced the police to recognize "transvestite passes" – doctors' notes that officially identified a person as a transvestite, allowing them to avoid harassment.

However, Hirschfeld became unhappy with the "transvestite" term, as he increasingly understood the complex internal psychology »

Magnus Hirschfeld

Born to a Jewish family in Prussia in 1868, Magnus Hirschfeld earned his medical degree in 1892, later setting up a medical practice in Berlin. He founded the Scientific Humanitarian Committee in 1897, which aimed to defend the rights of homosexual people and repeal laws that criminalized same-sex acts. With the motto "through science to justice", the organization had around 700 members at its peak, across 25 cities in Germany, Austria, and the Netherlands.

In 1899, Hirschfeld published the *Yearbook of Intermediate Sexual Types*, the world's first research journal dedicated to sexuality. The publication continued until 1923, by which time Hirschfeld – a public figure who was both Jewish and homosexual – had become the target of right-wing attacks. He left Germany in 1932 and died in Nice, France, in 1935.

Key works

1904 *Berlin's Third Sex*
1910 *The Transvestites*
1914 *Homosexuality of Men and Women*

Lili Elbe often modelled for her wife, artist Gerda Wegener, as in this 1925 portrait. A Danish court dissolved their marriage in 1930 after Elbe's gender affirmation surgery.

that lay behind the outward appearance of many patients. At first, he described what he observed as "total transvestism", but finally he coined the term "transsexual" in 1923 for those who desired to live as a different gender from the one they were assigned at birth. This distinguished cross-dressing people from those who today would be considered transgender.

Pioneering transformations

In the 1920s, aware of the dangerous self-surgery that some of his patients contemplated, Hirschfeld began to offer surgical interventions at his institute. Arguably the most remarkable of Hirschfeld's patients was Dora Richter, one of the first known transgender women to receive "feminization" surgery. Richter was assigned male at birth, in 1891, and grew up on a farm in the Ore Mountains on what is now the Germany–Czechia border. After she displayed "feminine"

tendencies and reportedly tried to remove her penis with a tourniquet at the age of six, Richter's family let her live as a girl.

As an adult, Richter travelled to Berlin, where she took up seasonal work as a "male" waiter at hotels, living as herself for the rest of the year. How Richter made her way to the institute is unclear, but some sources claim that she was released into Hirschfeld's care by a sympathetic judge following an arrest for cross-dressing. She later lived and worked at the institute as a domestic servant and began to undergo a series of surgeries.

The first surgery, in 1922, was an orchiectomy – the removal of her testicles. The resulting hormonal change reduced Richter's beard growth, and her body shape altered, becoming fuller with noticeable breast tissue. In 1931, Richter underwent a penectomy – the removal of her penis – and a vaginoplasty – the surgical construction of a vagina. Although these techniques were rudimentary, the success of Richter's surgery attracted other trans women to Hirschfeld's institute.

One such woman was Lili Elbe, a painter, who later became the subject of the heavily fictionalized 2000 book *The Danish Girl* and 2015 feature film of the same name. Having lived openly as a woman for at least 20 years, but also as a man within a marriage, Lili was desperate to affirm herself as female. She underwent an orchiectomy at the institute in 1930 and had three further surgeries at Dresden Women's Clinic over a period of 16 months. The first of these was to transplant an ovary into her abdomen, the second to remove her penis and scrotum, and the third to transplant a uterus and construct

Christine Jorgensen

Assigned male at birth in New York City in 1926, Christine Jorgensen grew up feeling "lost between the sexes". She was drafted into the US Army aged 19 and studied photography after her discharge in 1946. Having read about gender affirmation treatments in Europe, Jorgensen travelled to Denmark in 1950 and met Dr Christian Hamburger, a physician who specialized in the study of hormones. She received extensive hormone therapy and was granted permission in 1951 by Danish officials to undergo a series of surgeries.

In December 1952, the New York *Daily News* ran a front-page story about Jorgensen under the headline "Ex-GI Becomes Blonde Beauty: Operations Transform Bronx Youth". On her return to the US in 1953, Jorgensen became an instant celebrity. Her poise and charm won the hearts of the public and she launched a nightclub act, appeared on television, radio, and the stage, and wrote an autobiography that sold almost 450,000 copies. Jorgensen died in 1989 but remains a role model for many trans people today.

I think we (the doctors and I) are fighting this the right way – make the body fit the soul, rather than vice versa.
Christine Jorgensen
A Personal Autobiography, **1967**

a vagina. These surgeries allowed Elbe to legally change her name and sex; she received a passport that listed her as a woman under the name Lili Ilse Elvenes.

Facing the consequences
The recipients of the first gender affirmation surgeries mostly spoke positively of their experiences. Alan L. Hart asserted that he was the happiest he had ever been after his transition and associated surgery, stating his intention to live as a man for the remainder of his life and declaring that he was "ashamed of nothing". However, stigma surrounding the identity of early recipients – and a general lack of understanding of variations in sexuality – meant they also endured frequent harassment. Hart was publicly exposed by a former classmate who had known him pre-transition, which triggered a pattern of moving from place to place to avoid being revealed as he advanced his medical career.

A maker of chest binders fits a specially designed example for a client in Taipei, Taiwan, in 2018. Chest binders often act as the start of the "masculinization" process.

The surgeries were also not without physical risk. Shortly after Lili Elbe's final surgery, her body rejected her transplanted uterus, which became infected. She died from cardiac arrest associated with the infection in September 1931.

The rise of Nazism in 1930s Germany led to the persecution and exile of many of Hirschfeld's patients. When Hitler became German chancellor in 1933, the Nazi party purged LGBTQ+ organizations and publications that it saw as "unGerman". Students and Nazi troopers attacked Hirschfeld's institute and publicly burnt its archives.

Affirmation, not cure
The impact of the first gender affirmation surgeries extended beyond the lives of those who underwent surgery to other transgender people. Most notably, the surgeries marked the start of a shift from medicine as a "cure" for transgender people to a way of affirming gender.

Further surgeries brought further developments in surgical techniques, with rapid advances in plastic surgery during and after World War II. This included phalloplasty, a surgery that uses grafted tissue to create a penis. There were also advances in non-surgical care for transgender people, such as sex-hormone

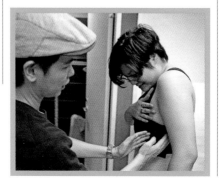

I can't begin to express how remarkable it feels to finally love who I am enough to pursue my authentic self.
Elliot Page
American actor, on coming out as transgender, 2020

therapies following breakthroughs in the isolation and synthesizing of testosterone and oestrogen for commercial use. Such advances paved the way for people across the globe to receive treatments, including – in the 1950s – Christine Jorgensen, the first in the United States to become widely known for their gender affirmation surgery.

For many transgender people, the availability of gender affirmation surgeries granted them the power to live in bodies that felt right for them. Today, a growing number of trans people – including some non-binary people – undergo extensive surgery, and continued advances in surgical techniques allow improved function, sensation, and appearance. For some people, however, gender affirmation surgeries reinforce the idea that gender is determined by physical characteristics. This may be problematic for those who do not neatly fit into the gender binary, and is particularly problematic for trans people who do not want to change their body. Trans people may experience social pressure to undergo surgery, and as of 2022 more than 30 nations still ban gender change without surgery. ■

TO SHOW WHAT IT MEANS TO BE GAY

LGBTQ+ FILMS (1919)

IN CONTEXT

FOCUS
Queer cinema

BEFORE
1894 A short film made in the laboratory of American inventor Thomas Edison shows two men in a close dancing embrace.

1895 In the UK, media coverage of famous writer Oscar Wilde's trial puts same-sex relationships in the public spotlight.

AFTER
2017 *Moonlight* is the first LGBTQ+ film to win the Best Picture Oscar.

2018 Chilean actress Daniela Vega becomes the first trans person to present an award at the Oscars ceremony.

2021 The children's animated film *The Mitchells vs the Machines* features an LGBTQ+ main character, Kate.

By 1910, millions of people were watching moving pictures – first as single-reel films (shorts) and then as longer features. At first, European film studios, such as Gaumont and Pathé in France, dominated the new industry, until filmmakers were drawn to the favourable climate and open spaces of California, in the US, making a base in the village of Hollywood, which opened its first studio in 1911.

LGBTQ+ people were shown on screen from the outset, but how they were represented varied according to levels of censorship and existing stereotypes and prejudices. Drag – a cross-dressing

See also: Drag 112–17 ▪ The trial of Oscar Wilde 124–25 ▪ The first gender affirmation surgeries 136–41 ▪ The first gay village 146–47 ▪ Ball culture 214–15

Manuela and her teacher Fräulein von Bernburg kiss in a 1958 remake of *Mädchen in Uniform*. The original 1931 film, directed by Hungarian Leontine Sagan, had the first ever all-female cast.

American silent film *Salomé* – based on the 1891 play of the same name by Oscar Wilde – was rumoured to have an all-LGBTQ+ cast, including the bisexual lead actress Alla Nazimova. Four years later, *Wings* – winner of the first Academy Award for Best Picture – showed what is considered to be the first on-screen male gay kiss, as a World War I pilot bids farewell to a dying compatriot.

It was in Germany, though, that films started to examine LGBTQ+ themes most openly. Relaxation of censorship in the Weimar Republic (1919–33) and a demand for cheap entertainment gave German filmmakers freedom to experiment. In 1919, *Anders aus die Andern* (*Different from the Others*) was the first film with openly homosexual characters. An artist's passion for his male model was the subject of *Mikaël* in 1924, while probably the first clearly drawn lesbian character appeared in *Die Büchse der Pandora* (*Pandora's Box*) in »

act performed in musical halls and theatres in cities such as London, Paris, and New York – soon transferred into film. A 1914 silent feature, *A Florida Enchantment*, involved not only cross-dressing but also the transformation of both leading characters into the opposite sex. Cross-dressing male characters were used for comic effect, as was the portrayal of some men as "sissies" – dressing and behaving in an effeminate way, though not explicitly gay. In the 1912 silent Western short, *Algie, the Miner*, for instance, the extravagantly clothed but notionally heterosexual Algie kisses two miners on the cheek.

Beyond the laughter

As feature films became more popular in the 1920s, filmmakers had more scope to explore LGBTQ+ subjects. An orgy scene in the 1922 silent film *Manslaughter*, directed by American Cecil B. DeMille, included the first intimate on-screen kiss between women. In 1923, the

What you call sin,
I call the great
spirit of love.
Mädchen in Uniform, 1931

Anders als die Andern

Released in 1919, the German silent film *Anders als die Andern* (*Different from the Others*) was the first positive portrayal of homosexuality in cinema. Austrian director Richard Oswald also wrote the film, in conjunction with Magnus Hirschfeld, a German physician and sexologist who founded Berlin's Institute for Sexual Science and played a doctor in the film.

The lead character, violinist Paul Körner, falls in love with a pupil, Kurt Sivers. Körner is blackmailed by a former lover, who threatens to expose him as a homosexual. The musician resists his accuser and the two appear in court. Körner is jailed and – his reputation ruined – dies by suicide.

The film was originally titled *Paragraph 175*, which referred to a German law of 1871 that criminalized sex between men. After some initial success, the film was attacked by religious and right-wing groups. The Nazis believed they had destroyed all copies in 1933, but one, discovered in 1976, survived.

Pupil and teacher, played by Fritz Schülz (left) and Conrad Veidt (right), embrace in a scene from *Anders als die Andern*.

> They're here, they're queer, get hip to them.
> **B. Ruby Rich**
> **On "new queer" films**

1929. An early German sound feature, *Mädchen in Uniform* (*Girls in Uniform*), released in 1931, was cinema's first overtly lesbian film.

Censors and the hidden gay

By the early 1930s, American films were still portraying gay men as effeminate, or "pansy" – a word first recorded in 1929. At the same time, two bisexual actresses – Marlene Dietrich from Germany and Greta Garbo from Sweden – brought female–female desire to Hollywood. In *Morocco* (1930), Dietrich plays a

cabaret singer who, dressed in a man's tuxedo, kisses a female fan on the lips. In *Queen Christina* (1933), Garbo, playing the titular lesbian Swedish monarch, does the same to a lady-in-waiting.

Such LGBTQ+ depictions were brought to an abrupt end in 1934 by the enforcement in the US of the Motion Picture Production Code – the Hays Code – which banned "perverse" subjects such as cross-dressing and homosexuality. The sexuality of homosexual characters could be hinted at only through dress and mannerisms. Often these characters were played as villains, such as Joel Cairo in *The Maltese Falcon* (1941), and the murderers Brandon and Phillip – played by two gay actors, John Dall and Farley Granger – in British director Alfred Hitchcock's *Rope* (1948).

Pushing the boundaries

Despite the Hays Code, an avant-garde movement of filmmakers emerged in the US in the 1940s and '50s, creating short experimental works on LGBTQ+ subjects. Gay

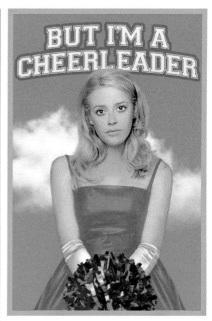

In the 1999 American comedy *But I'm a Cheerleader,* Natasha Lyonne plays Megan Bloomfield, a 17-year-old lesbian whose parents send her to a conversion therapy camp.

filmmaker Kenneth Anger produced a series of homoerotic shorts, beginning with *Fireworks* in 1947. Another gay American, Gregory Markopoulos, also dealt with same-sex desire in the 1949 dream-like short *Christmas U.S.A.* In the 1960s, he was assisted by German filmmaker Rosa von Praunheim.

The Hays Code was officially withdrawn in 1968, but by that time American and European mainstream cinema had already begun to address gay and lesbian issues. In the UK – six years before the legalization of "homosexual acts" – *Victim* (1961) starred gay British actor Dirk Bogarde as a man blackmailed for a homosexual

Hedwig and the Angry Inch (2001) stars American John Cameron Mitchell as Hedwig, a gender-nonconforming rock singer. The film won the Audience Award at the 2001 Sundance Festival.

The 2018 film *Rafiki*, directed by Wanuri Kahiu, follows the love affair between two Kenyan girls, Kena and Ziki. It was Kenya's first lesbian film.

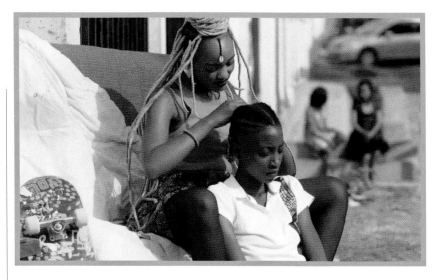

affair. In the US in the same year, *The Children's Hour* included a sympathetic portrayal of Martha, a lesbian teacher. However, Martha dies by suicide at the end of the film, one of the many instances of the killing-off of queer characters in these early films – a trope that has become known as "bury your gays".

Into the open
The 1970s saw a widening of LGBTQ+ expression in film. In the US, *The Boys in the Band* (1970) focused entirely on a group of gay characters, while queer camp cinema was championed by gay director John Waters in films such as *Pink Flamingos* (1972) and *Female Trouble* (1974), both starring the drag queen Divine.

In the 1980s and early '90s, an increasing number of LGBTQ+ films entered the mainstream, delivering more rounded queer characters. In Hollywood, *Making Love* (1982) was a sympathetic portrayal of a gay man, followed in 1985 by *Desert Hearts* – a rare lesbian film with a happy ending. British directors also sought out LGBTQ+ themes in history and literature: Derek Jarman depicted a 14th-century king who had male lovers in *Edward II* (1991) and Sally Potter's *Orlando* (1992) brought British writer Virginia Woolf's gender-bending novel to life.

In 1992, American film scholar B. Ruby Rich coined the term "new queer cinema" to describe the flowering of LGBTQ+ themes in film and a new wave of independent gay filmmakers, such as Liberian American Cheryl Dunye, whose first feature *The Watermelon Woman* (1996) explores the experiences of a young Black lesbian. Hollywood has continued the queer cinema trend noted by Rich into the 21st century, with releases such as *Brokeback Mountain* (2005) – about the love between two cowboys – and the coming-of-age drama *Moonlight* (2016). In India, Bollywood films – such as *Aligarh* (2015), the story of a gay university professor who is suspended from his job – have also explored LGBTQ+ themes. ∎

Rosa von Praunheim

Born Holger Radtke in 1942 in German-occupied Latvia, avant-garde film director Rosa von Praunheim was adopted and moved to East Berlin and then Frankfurt. After studying art, he embraced filmmaking and created a new name – a combination of the German for "pink" (*rosa*), referring to the pink triangle worn by homosexuals in concentration camps, and the area of Frankfurt (Praunheim) where he grew up.

Von Praunheim directed his first film in 1967. His 1971 feature *It Is Not the Homosexual Who Is Perverse, But the Society in Which He Lives* made him an LGBTQ+ figurehead and prompted the formation of more than 50 gay rights groups in West Germany. The 1986 feature *A Virus Knows No Morals* was one of the first to address the AIDS crisis, and he followed this in 1990 with three documentaries – *The AIDS Trilogy*, shot in New York City and Berlin, which attacked what he saw as the hypocrisy and apathy surrounding the AIDS epidemic. Von Praunheim has continued to make films on gay, lesbian, and trans subjects into the 21st century.

A POWERFULLY QUEER PLACE

THE FIRST GAY VILLAGE (1920s)

Just as Paris had become a hub for LGBTQ+ life during the late 19th century, the Weimar Republic era of post-war Germany in 1918–33 saw people flocking to Berlin as a new centre of tolerance and LGBTQ+ culture. The intense concentration of LGBTQ+ people and businesses in Schöneberg, around a square called Nollenbergplatz, have led some to consider this district the world's first gay village.

LGBTQ+ people who made Schöneberg their home included Anglo–American writer Christopher Isherwood and German movie star Marlene Dietrich, who was a visitor at the exclusive lesbian club Monbijou des Westens. Its owner, Elsa Conrad, was a Jewish woman sent to a concentration camp in 1937 and recorded as having a "lesbian disposition" by the Gestapo. Conrad was able to leave the camp and the country in 1938.

Guests at Eldorado in Berlin pose in their lipstick and dresses in this photograph from the early 1930s. Eldorado hosted drag shows and welcomed gender transgression.

See also: Molly houses 90–91 ▪ Belle Époque Paris 110–11 ▪ The trial of Oscar Wilde 124–25 ▪ The Harlem Renaissance and the Jazz Age 148–51 ▪ Persecution during the Holocaust 156–61 ▪ The spread of ball culture 214–15

Elsa Conrad's club was one of around 40 LGBTQ+ venues in the area in the 1920s. Among the most famous clubs were Eldorado, Toppkeller, Monokel, and Dorian Gray, so named for Oscar Wilde's novel. When sexologist and Berlin resident Magnus Hirschfeld coined the term "transvestite" in 1907, he may have been describing the female-presenting guests who frequented Eldorado. The rise of Adolf Hitler's Nazi party and his election as Germany's chancellor in 1933 ended the Weimar Republic and brought Berlin's glittering bastions of LGBTQ+ life to a halt. Nazi crackdowns forced many LGBTQ+ establishments to close.

Marginalized districts
Today there are gay villages – or "gaybourhoods" – in cities around the world. Among the most famous are Soho (London, UK); Zona Rosa (Mexico City, Mexico); Chueca (Madrid, Spain); Darlinghurst (Sydney, Australia); and Greenwich Village (New York City, US). Their development into celebrated

Rainbow flags hang from balconies in Chueca, the gay village in Madrid. Previously a poorer neighbourhood, Chueca is now one of the biggest LGBTQ+ districts in Europe.

LGBTQ+ districts has been a gradual and varying process. In many cases, less desirable areas were likely to have a higher concentration of LGBTQ+ people. Canal Street in Manchester, UK, was a decaying area hit by industrial decline as the Rochdale Canal began to fall out of use in the 1950s. Gay men in particular began to meet in its dark alleyways, and by the 1980s police would scour the area by boat and on foot to crack down on cruising. It was not until LGBTQ+ developers rejuvenated the area in the 1990s that it became

a lively, welcoming home for the community. This has, however, brought new investors to the area, threatening LGBTQ+ spaces as the area becomes more desirable to big development companies – and subsequently more expensive.

Negative consequences
While the LGBTQ+ community itself has been accused of taking part in gentrifying urban areas – pricing out other marginalized groups – gentrification now also threatens to erase gaybourhoods around the world. In the district of Midtown in Atlanta, Georgia, for example, urban planner Petra Doan has suggested that the area has been "degayed" by the city through rent increases and refused permits for LGBTQ+ events. ▪

LGBTQ+ people **move to cities** in search of **community and acceptance**.

⬇

As a marginalized demographic with **many young people** and **little financial support**, and facing **discrimination** in employment, they move into **less affluent areas**.

⬇

LGBTQ+ businesses spring up to cater for LGBTQ+ inhabitants – **neighbourhoods become "gaybourhoods"**.

⬇

Gaybourhoods become **targets for gentrification** and the **popularity of the area** drives up rental prices, **pricing out** the original tenants.

SURELY AS GAY AS IT WAS BLACK

THE HARLEM RENAISSANCE AND THE JAZZ AGE (1920s–1930s)

IN CONTEXT

FOCUS
**Queer performance and
Black artistic culture**

BEFORE
1899 In *The Future of the
American Negro*, author and
reformer Booker T. Washington
advocates education as the key
to social advancement for
fellow Black Americans.

1910 W.E.B. Du Bois founds
The Crisis magazine, which
later publishes the work of
Black gay writers like Alain
Locke and Countée Cullen.

AFTER
1956 Harlem-born writer and
civil rights activist James
Baldwin's *Giovanni's Room*
describes a bisexual man's life
in Paris.

1989 The British film *Looking
for Langston* is inspired by
Richard Bruce Nugent's story
Smoke, Lilies, and Jade (1926).

The vibrant Black literary
movement known as the
Harlem Renaissance was
centred on Upper Manhattan, New
York City, where it co-existed with
Black visual art, jazz, and blues in
the 1920s and 1930s. While few of
the movement's writers were overtly
gay, some Black musical performers
paraded their sexuality and found
more tolerance in communities like
Harlem than elsewhere. The area
had a few colourful venues, such
as the Clam House, where figures
like cross-dressing singer Gladys
Bentley could thrive, and similar
circles flourished in Washington,
DC, Chicago, and in Paris, France,
as Jazz Age music spread.

See also: Belle Époque Paris 110–11 ▪ Drag 112–17 ▪ The first gay village 146–47 ▪
Black lesbian feminism 210–13 ▪ Ball culture 214–15 ▪ Queer of colour theory 297

In Harlem, I found courage
and joy and tolerance …
I don't have to lie.
Mark Thornton
Gay protagonist in Blair Niles'
novel *Strange Brother*, 1931

Black Americans (referred to at the
time as "Negroes") had gathered in
city areas like Harlem to find work in
the decades after the 1865 abolition
of slavery, often moving to the North
from the impoverished South. Many
had fought in World War I but, in the
South especially, were shut out of
politics by discriminatory policies
that curtailed their right to vote. The
Harlem Renaissance linked artistic
production to activism in a bid to
enact political and social change.
Its promoters and writers challenged
the racist images and stereotypes
about Black Americans that
proliferated at the time.

A dandy "New Negro"
Educated and essentially middle-
class, Harlem Renaissance writers
largely accepted the dominant
heterosexual values of their age.
Few were openly gay, but clues have
emerged in the stories, verses, or
love letters of figures such as Alain
Locke and Countée Cullen. Writer
and activist James Mercer Langston
Hughes never came out, but enjoyed
gay male company and penned
unpublished love poems about men.
    One of the era's most important
ideologues, Locke was known to be
homosexual and was described as a
"dandy", an "effeminate, gay man", »

Harlem's nightclubs, here on a 1933
map, attracted hedonists of all classes to
enjoy music, dance, and social fluidity.
"Gladys" is here part of the Clam House
name, such was Bentley's fame.

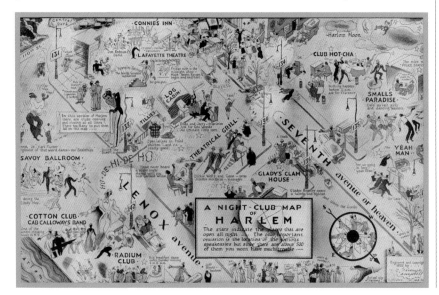

Gladys Bentley

Born in Philadelphia in 1907,
Gladys Bentley would later
write that as a child she felt
rejected because her mother
had wanted a boy – the spur
perhaps that drove her to
invent a life on her own terms.
Aged 16, she ran away and
found refuge in Harlem and,
hearing that the gay-friendly
Clam House needed a pianist,
she applied. Her considerable
musical talent as a pianist and
singer won her the job, and
she began to perform there
dressed in smart male evening
attire and later played at the
exotic Ubangi Club.
    Bentley recorded several
blues songs but achieved her
most lasting fame in cabarets
and speakeasies. A towering
figure often in top hat and
tails, she would perform at the
centre of a retinue of adoring
male sailors. While some
thought her overt lesbianism
was a publicity stunt, it was a
daring, transgressive, and
radical affirmation of who she
was. She later performed at
Mona's 440, one of San
Francisco's first lesbian bars
but, in a less tolerant post-war
America, she claimed to be
heterosexual. Bentley died in
near poverty in 1960.

Ma Rainey performs with her jazz band in Chicago in 1924. In Harlem, she played with a band drawn from members of the Fletcher Henderson Orchestra, including Louis Armstrong.

with just a "hint of a swagger", but was guarded about his intimate life. The title of his 1925 anthology *The New Negro*, which included essays, poetry, and fiction by gay writers such as Countée Cullen and Claude McKay, signalled the educated, artistic, liberated Harlem Renaissance community's rejection of the enslavement, segregation, and suppression associated with the "Old Negro" of Southern plantations. Yet life in the South provided fertile subject matter for writers such as Alabama-born novelist Zora Neale Hurston, one of the era's most revered authors.

Scandal and secret lives

Much of the most influential writing of the period appeared in Black periodicals such as *The Crisis*, edited by writer W.E.B. Du Bois, one of the founders of the National Association for the Advancement of

Colored People (NAACP). But it was the magazine *Fire!!* in 1926 that caused a furore for content touching on sex work and homosexuality. Designed to challenge respectable older Black values, it scandalized some who deemed it "vulgar". Only one issue ever appeared before the venture collapsed, deep in debt, and its headquarters burned down.

The single issue of *Fire!!* included "Smoke, Lilies, and Jade", a tale of bisexuality and male desire by overtly gay writer and artist Richard Bruce Nugent, who is said to have painted homoerotic images on the walls of the apartment he shared for a few years with writer Wallace Thurman. Though once arrested for sex with a man, Thurman denied his homosexuality and married Harlem social activist Louise Thompson. Even Nugent married, as did Cullen; both unions soon ended in divorce.

Harlem writer Dorothy West, who published her second novel *The Wedding* (1995) at the age of 87, had a lesbian relationship with Marian Minus, the co-editor of her literary journal *Challenge*, founded in 1934. West's fiction expressed a deep

scepticism of the transactional nature of heteronormative marriage; her female characters chafed under traditional gender roles and sought to create matriarchal communities.

Blues and poetry

Jazz and its precursor, soulful blues, were African American styles of music and dance that had spread from New Orleans to other urban centres – especially New York City in the 1920s Jazz Age – becoming an integral part of Harlem's artistic scene and a global phenomenon. Most Harlem Renaissance writers, however, found the music vulgar and too Southern, as did many of Harlem's Black newspapers, which condemned the "immorality" of certain performers who displayed daringly subversive sexualities.

Metaphor and innuendo were hallmarks of the blues, while singer Gertrude "Ma" Rainey's "Prove It On Me Blues" (1928) became a veritable anthem for Black lesbianism. Its overtly transgressive lyrics left little room for misinterpretation. The poster advertising the song's release also featured a blues woman in drag seducing two women beneath the watchful eyes of a police officer.

You just did what you wanted to do. Nobody was in the closet. There wasn't any closet.
Richard Bruce Nugent
Gay writer and artist (1906–1987)

> Went out last night with
> a crowd of my friends,
> They must've been women
> 'cause I don't like no men.
> **Ma Rainey**
> **"Prove It On Me Blues"**

Ma Rainey, Bessie Smith – heralded as the Empress of the Blues and notorious for her hard-drinking, bisexual lifestyle – and lesbian but closeted singer Alberta Hunter were pioneers of an early Black feminist art that focused on working class issues including domestic violence.

Black American women's poetry at this time often confronted the struggle of trying to live up to the idealized image of the "New Negro" woman, devoted to raising the next generation while keeping private lesbian passions in check. Verses by Philadelphia-based poet Mae Cowdery, who was part of the wider Harlem artistic community, express an undercurrent of erotic same-sex desire. A line from one poem reads: "The feel of your hand, On my breast, Like the silver path of the Moon".

The poems of Boston-born writer Angelina Weld Grimké, who lived in Harlem from 1930, were often about female friendship – both erotic and platonic. Aged 16, in a letter to her friend Mary P. Burrill, she had expressed the hope that "in a few years you will come to me and be my love, my wife". Later in life, she wrote love poems to women while twice married to men.

Harlem freedoms

In Harlem's varied cultural scenes, men and women sang songs and wrote poetry that expressed same-sex love for each other. Same-sex acts in the 1920s were as illegal in Harlem as elsewhere, and like their white counterparts, Black men were often arrested if caught soliciting for sex with other men. But Harlem society was more accepting. Its gay subculture had a distinctive African American character and irresistible vibrancy. In the 1920s and 1930s, the Rockland Palace on W155th Street was home to the extravagant annual Hamilton Lodge balls, which attracted thousands of spectators. Visitors to these and Harlem's other costume balls included "slumming" white people with little empathy for the Black community but there for the thrill of observing and dressing as they pleased and dancing with whom they liked. Speakeasies, such as the Clam House where the larger-than-life Gladys Bentley performed, were both exciting and tolerant of different sexualities.

Private parties were also safe havens and varied from rent parties that raised funds to help the needy pay for lodgings to opulent events hosted by A'Lelia Walker, daughter of a self-made Black millionaire mother, held on her Hudson River estate or at her lavish townhouse on West 136th Street. Such parties' guest lists included Harlem's artists, writers, and activists – many of them gay – and scores of white celebrities, too.

Ultimately, Harlem in the 1920s and 1930s offered queer people a space to gather without overt persecution and, through its exuberant art, literature, and music, fuelled the Black community's goal of progressive social change. ∎

Josephine Baker

Born in 1906 to an impoverished mother in St Louis, Missouri, Josephine Baker joined a Black American theatre troupe in New York City aged 15. Playing bit parts, she also worked as a dresser under the tutelage of blues singer Clara Smith, her first "lady lover", then joined the cast of Eubie Blake and Noble Sissle's *Shuffle Along* (1921), Broadway's first Black hit show. Baker's success in *Chocolate Dandies* (1924) took her to Paris, France, in 1925 to star in *La Revue Nègre,* a show born of the city's fascination with emerging Black American culture. Baker's overtly sexual *danse sauvage* in a banana skirt created a sensation and lasting fame in Europe – not equalled in the US, despite a brief return to Broadway in 1936.

Baker worked for the French Resistance during World War II, and was awarded the *Croix de Guerre* and *Légion d'honneur*. She later campaigned against racism and was one of two female speakers at the 1963 March on Washington in the US. Her colourful life also included four marriages, male and female lovers, and 12 adopted children. She died in Paris in 1975.

YOU'RE MORE THAN JUST NEITHER, HONEY

BUTCH AND FEMME (1920s–1970s)

IN CONTEXT

FOCUS
Lesbian identities

BEFORE
1834 British landowner Anne Lister, nicknamed Gentleman Jack, exchanges rings with her lover Ann Walker in an English country church.

1886 German psychologist Richard von Krafft-Ebing's *Psychopathia Sexualis* identifies four types of lesbianism, from mild to intense depending on the degree of masculinity.

AFTER
1992 In the US, self-identified femme Joan Nestle publishes *Persistent Desire: A Femme-Butch Reader*, an anthology of femme-butch writing.

1993 Butch singer k.d. lang appears on the cover of *Vanity Fair* in the US with cisgender model Cindy Crawford.

As lesbianism emerged from the shadows during the 1920s many lesbians in European and US cultures identified and behaved as either "butch" or "femme". Butch women presented masculinely through their clothes and mannerisms, while femme women adopted hyper-feminine characteristics and dress. They often formed butch–femme pairs.

Female autonomy
Several factors contributed to the growing confidence of the masculine lesbian. In the West, the campaign for women's suffrage, improving education for girls, freedom from

See also: Early modern lesbianism 74–79 ▪ AFAB cross-dressers and "female husbands" 82–83 ▪ Sapphism 98 ▪ The diaries of Anne Lister 102–03 ▪ The Harlem Renaissance and the Jazz Age 148–51 ▪ Butler's *Gender Trouble* 266–67

A great many women can feel and behave like men. Very few of them can behave like gentlemen.
Radclyffe Hall
The Well of Loneliness, 1928

restrictive clothing from the 1890s, and the availability of birth control for women in some countries from the 1920s made it easier for women to diverge from the traditional roles and appearance expected of them.

The two world wars (1914–18 and 1939–45) also accelerated female autonomy. The return of mutilated and shell-shocked soldiers after World War I undermined the image of strength and stoicism that defined Victorian masculinity, blurring the supposed psychological differences between the sexes. And while the men had been away fighting, women had done jobs traditionally performed by men. These women sometimes wore trousers, which were made fashionable by film stars such as Greta Garbo. In *The Single Standard* (1929), Garbo plays a debutante who wears the jackets and trousers of her on-screen lover, arguing that women and men should be judged by the same standards.

The emergence of rebellious masculine women in the early 20th century was accompanied by new theories in psychoanalysis and sexology. British psychologist Havelock Ellis, author of the seven-volume *Studies in the Psychology of Sex* (1897–1928), theorized that women who desired other women were "inverts", who had a male soul. Ellis claimed that a true invert was neither male nor female, but a third gender.

Class protection

Greater freedoms enabled lesbians possessing wealth and status to conduct their relationships openly.

Several high-profile couples embraced masculine–feminine roles. In the UK, writer Radclyffe Hall, known as "John" to her friends, lived with Una Troubridge from 1917 until Hall's death in 1943. In Paris, masculine-presenting »

A butch–femme couple embrace in "Le Feu" ("The Fire"), a 1924 illustration from French poet Paul Verlaine's *Fêtes galantes*. The couple appropriate male–female gender roles.

Radclyffe Hall

Born in in Bournemouth, UK, in 1882, Radclyffe Hall grew up with her mother and stepfather. Her own father left home when Hall was just two, albeit providing a large fortune for the child. Hall never had to work or marry to support herself.

Hall considered herself an "invert", a term coined by her friend Havelock Ellis, author of *Sexual Inversion* (1897). Ellis wrote the preface for the first edition of Hall's landmark lesbian novel *The Well of Loneliness* about a masculine lesbian called Stephen Gordon.

Hall met femme-presenting British sculptor and translator Una Troubridge in 1915 and fell in love. The couple lived a full life together, raising dogs and pursuing their own careers. They usually dressed to reflect male–female gender roles, with Hall wearing male suits and Una appearing more feminine. They remained together until Hall's death in 1943.

Key works

1924 *The Unlit Lamp*
1928 *The Well of Loneliness*

American writer Gertrude Stein began a relationship with fellow American Alice B. Toklas that lasted from 1910 until 1946, when Stein died; while Stein was a leading figure in 20th-century literature, Toklas, a notable cook, performed a "wifely" role, organizing their literary and artistic salons.

Greater opportunities

Unprotected by wealth or status, working-class lesbians were more exposed to censure, but the increased presence of women outside the home in the early 20th century made it easier for lesbians to meet each other, form communities, and instigate relationships, often taking on butch–femme roles.

In the US, lesbians in New York City were drawn to Harlem, where a lively Black nightlife had taken root, and to Greenwich Village. Lesbians formed communities around drag balls, house parties, speakeasies, and clubs, where lesbians and gay men could express themselves without fear of condemnation. In addition, some Black lesbians, such as blues singers Ma Rainey and Gladys Bentley, had developed a butch style that exuded panache and

The elements of butch/femme lie in oppression, but we do not languish there.
Sally R. Munt
British scholar in gender/sexuality studies

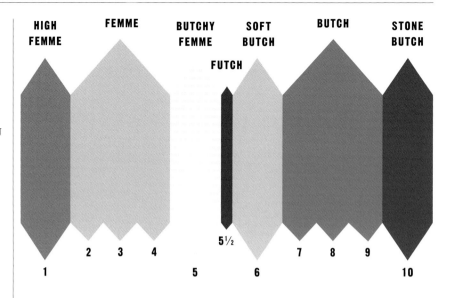

The femme–butch scale, or "futch" scale, is used by some women in the LGBTQ+ community to identify where they sit between femme and butch. High femme is someone who presents in a traditionally feminine way, while stone butch is someone who is very masculine.

confidence, defying the oppression they faced in everyday life. Such women were powerful examples to working-class white lesbians as well as to Black lesbians.

Identity rather than style

By the 1940s and '50s, butch had become an identity in the US and UK, not just a style. It was not inherently tied to sexuality, but as gay and lesbian communities began to organize, butch became a way to describe masculine lesbians looking for feminine partners.

Butch women sought to create a tough exterior as a response to the sexism, homophobia, and racism they experienced. Modelling themselves on rebellious white working-class men, whose own oppression was rooted in class, they favoured cropped hair, leather jackets, white T-shirts, denim, work boots, and chains. This appropriation of a white male persona was a way of claiming

masculinity for themselves. Some butches also used the pronouns "he/him", long before public transgender movements had developed.

While butch lesbians had a clear identity, femmes found it more difficult to mark themselves out as queer, and sometimes doubted their own queerness since it did not align with masculinity. Even though a femme partner was highly sought after by butches, "true lesbianism" was often thought to be rooted in masculinity.

Femme lesbians were often associated with bisexuality, as they were presumed to be more likely to enter into relationships with men – a fear that led to the trope of "femme-as-eventual-betrayer". In fact, many femmes reinforced butches' masculinity through what has come to be called "gender labour" – emotional and physical care-giving. The fact that femmes could pass as heterosexual or bisexual provided them with useful access to mainstream culture at a time when butch lesbians were being shut out of public debate.

Attack and renewal

As butches became more visible through the 1950s and '60s, spawning a lively butch–femme bar scene, especially in the US, the discrimination they faced increased, particularly from the police and heterosexual men, who regarded butches as a threat and femmes as victims in need of heterosexual rehabilitation.

During the Vietnam War (1955–75), the term butch was used to remove lesbians from the US military through dishonourable "blue" discharges, a banning that had been introduced towards the end of World War II to weed out individuals, mainly gay men and lesbians, deemed to have "undesirable habits".

As gay men and lesbians left the armed forces, they often gravitated to urban centres such as New York City and San Francisco, where they formed communities. In these new neighbourhoods "butch" and "femme" were far more acceptable. In 1955, however, the Daughters of Bilitis, the first lesbian organization in the US, dismissed butch and

A butch–femme couple embrace in Cape Town, South Africa. The Black lesbian counterparts of butch and femme identities are "stud" and "fish".

Who was I now – woman or man? That question could never be answered as long as those were the only choices; it could never be answered if it had to be asked.
Leslie Feinberg
Stone Butch Blues, 1993

femme identities as "role-playing". They urged lesbians to integrate with wider society.

By the 1970s, some lesbian feminists were questioning the butch–femme model on other grounds, maintaining that its replication of heterosexual roles reinforced the patriarchy and supported hierarchies in women's relationships with each other. Other lesbians responded that the butch–femme dynamic disrupted and challenged traditional gender roles. They also pointed out that the lesbian feminist critique makes sweeping generalizations about butch–femme relationships and adds to the perceptions that butches are not womanly enough to be women. Today, identity labels of butch and femme are still used, but many gradations of "butchness" have been added, breaking down the strict binary between the two and capturing the nuances of a range of possible queer identities, including bisexual and trans identities. ∎

Feinberg's *Stone Butch Blues*

Stone Butch Blues (1993), by American transgender butch lesbian Leslie Feinberg, is a novel that reflects the difficulties and discrimination faced by butches and femmes in 1970s America. It explores themes of gender, sexuality, and intersectionality, showing how butch–femme bar culture developed and then collapsed when it came under attack from both heterosexual men and feminists.

Stone Butch Blues is a key text for queer community organizing. It popularized the term "stone butch", which refers to a lesbian who does not want to be touched sexually, only do the touching. Feinberg received the 1993 Lambda Literary Award and the 1994 American Library Association Gay and Lesbian Book Award. Feinberg died in 2014, the year the 20th anniversary edition of the book was released.

WE WHO WORE THE PINK TRIANGLE

PERSECUTION DURING THE HOLOCAUST (1933–45)

IN CONTEXT

FOCUS
LGBTQ+ persecution

BEFORE
1871 Paragraph 175 of Germany's penal code is adopted, making sexual acts between men a crime.

1919–33 The Institute for Sexual Science operates in Berlin, until it is looted by Nazi paramilitaries.

AFTER
1988 East Germany repeals Paragraph 175.

1994 After the unification of East and West Germany, Paragraph 175 is fully repealed.

1995 The US Holocaust Memorial Museum campaigns to locate homosexual survivors and document their stories.

2017 Germany's parliament votes to quash all convictions under Paragraph 175 and compensate the victims.

From 1933 to 1945, in what is known as the Holocaust, the Nazi German regime systematically murdered six million Jewish people. Other population groups, including Roma, Jehovah's Witnesses, and LGBTQ+ people, were also targeted in this state-sponsored persecution. It is thought that thousands of LGBTQ+ people may have been killed.

As with other groups who were targeted, for years afterwards, LGBTQ+ victims and survivors were discredited in historical accounts. Not until the 1970s did the stories of this group begin to be heard.

Moreover, historians today need to be cautious when talking about sexual or gender identity and the Holocaust. While some LGBTQ+ people were open about their identity prior to being arrested, some only discovered their identities from being in a single-sex environment in concentration camps. Some prisoners were forced to exchange sex for food or protection, which is not an indicator of identity.

Weimar Germany

To understand the persecution of LGBTQ+ people in the Holocaust, we need to look at it in the context of the Weimar period of 1919–33, after Germany's defeat in World War I. Although sex between men had been criminalized in 1871, with the introduction of Paragraph 175 of the German Imperial Penal Code, Germany in the early 20th century largely recognized, and in some places celebrated, LGBTQ+ people.

In the febrile atmosphere of the Weimar years, many social and cultural norms were challenged. Berlin, Germany's capital, was

Ernst Röhm (right), commander of the SA from 1931, described himself as "same-sex oriented". This became a public scandal. Hitler defended Röhm at first, but had him murdered in 1934.

Berlin in the Weimar years hosted numerous LGBTQ+ venues. Published in 1928, the city guide "Berlin's Lesbian Women" featured 13 lesbian meeting places, all in the borough of Schöneberg.

home to around 100 gay bars, clubs, and meeting places, and was nicknamed the "gay capital of the world". Same-sex attraction featured with increasing frequency in German films, press, and literature. In 1919, German Jewish physician Magnus Hirschfeld opened the Institute for Sexual Science in Berlin. The world's first institute of its kind, it contained thousands of resources on gender, sexuality, and eroticism. It also offered counselling, sex education, and medical services, including treatment for gender dysphoria.

Prejudice against same-sex attraction still existed in Weimar Germany. Many citizens disliked the increased visibility of sexuality in media and daily life. Generally, however, LGBTQ+ people were not persecuted; indeed, there were campaigns to abolish Paragraph 175. Then, in January 1933, Nazi leader Adolf Hitler came to power.

See also: The criminalization of sodomy 68–71 ▪ Defining "homosexual" and "heterosexual" 106–07 ▪ The first gender affirmation surgeries 136–41 ▪ LGBTQ+ people on films 142–45 ▪ The first gay village 146–47

These people will naturally be publicly degraded [and] expelled … they will be shot in the concentration camp, while attempting to escape.
Heinrich Himmler
On LGBTQ+ people, 1937

Persecution by the Nazis

Homosexuality was condemned by the Nazis. The party's ideology included perpetuation of the "Aryan race" (a racist concept of a Germanic superior people) – a view that was incompatible with non-heterosexual relationships. Some Nazis, including Heinrich Himmler, commander of the SS (Hitler's paramilitary force), believed that LGBTQ+ people, like Jews, were inferior humans.

Three months after Hitler became chancellor, students from the National Socialist Student League stormed the Institute for Sexual Science, attacking staff and smashing equipment. Later that day, the SA (the Nazi paramilitary wing before the SS) continued the destruction. Hirschfeld was abroad at the time, and immediately went into exile. This watershed event was followed by the raiding of LGBTQ+ meeting points and the shutting down of gay journals, such as *Die Freundschaft* (*Friendship*).

For the persecutors, identifying LGBTQ+ people was harder than with many other stigmatized social groups. Jews stated their religion on birth certificates, census forms, and governmental records; communists often had a party membership. Gender nonconformity and non-heterosexuality were less visible.

In 1934, the Berlin Gestapo (secret police) instructed the city police to send them lists of suspected homosexual men. The Gestapo used the term "homosexual", but the targeted group included anyone who was not heterosexual. Then, in 1935, Paragraph 175 was made stricter, outlawing contact between men of any type that could be construed as sexual. During interrogations, the accused were forced to name their sexual partners, thus implicating more men. Approximately 53,400 men were convicted under Paragraph 175 during the Nazi period. Of these, 5,000–15,000 were sent to concentration camps.

The Nazi persecution of LGBTQ+ people was in many ways limited. It barely extended beyond Germany, Austria, and the Netherlands – in contrast to that of Jews, who were persecuted across Europe. Moreover, Paragraph 175 did not extend to women. Nazi jurists considered criminalizing lesbian acts, but some argued that intimate relationships between women were more difficult to distinguish from friendships than those between men. Some people also believed that female homosexuality did not pose the same threat to society as male homosexuality. Female same-sex behaviour was never outlawed, but was nevertheless stigmatized. Even prior to the Nazi regime, for many people it went against social norms and gender ideals, such as motherhood.

Men with the pink triangle

In the concentration camps, homosexual men were identified by a pink triangle sewn onto their »

On 6 May 1933, Nazis raided the Institute of Sexual Science in Berlin. Its unique library of over 20,000 books and journals on LGBTQ+ subjects was pulled out and burned in the streets.

Triangles for prisoners in concentration camps

Concentration-camp inmates were labelled with an inverted coloured triangle. Jews wore two yellow triangles that formed a Star of David. Different categories of Jews wore a yellow triangle combined with one of another colour.

Political prisoners

Criminal prisoners

German emigrants

Jehovah's Witnesses

Homosexual prisoners

"Asocial prisoners"

Jewish prisoners

Jewish homosexual prisoners

uniform. Multiple accounts from survivors recall that men with the pink triangle were treated worse, both by guards and other inmates, than any other prisoner group except Jews. The "175ers", or "filthy queers", had to sleep with their hands outside their covers. In some camps, they were isolated from other prisoner groups. In Auschwitz, Buchenwald, Sachsenhausen, and Mauthausen, they were given the worst and physically harshest jobs.

One person who experienced these conditions was Josef Kohout, whose story was one of the few first-hand accounts from this prisoner group, and was published under the pseudonym Heinz Heger in 1972. Kohout came from a well-to-do Catholic Austrian family. In 1939, he was convicted under Paragraph 175 and sentenced to 6 months in prison, and in January 1940 he was transported to Sachsenhausen and assigned hard labour in a clay pit. He recalled how gay men and Jews were targeted by the SS, *kapos* (prisoners who were made to serve as supervisors), and other inmates. Subjected to systematic violence, they were verbally and physically abused and tortured daily. In mid-1940, Kohout was transferred to Flossenbürg, where he remained in inhumane conditions until mid-1945, when he was liberated and reunited with his mother in Austria.

Institutional torture

The Nazis wanted to "reeducate" homosexual men, and believed that labour-intensive work, in cement plants, brickworks, and gravel pits, would turn them into "real men". Nazi scientists and doctors also conducted medical experiments on homosexual men to find a "cure" for their sexuality. These measures included the use of psychotropic drugs, or injections of hormones or vaccines. From 1942, concentration-camp commandants had the power to order the castration of pink-triangle prisoners.

The pink triangle is associated with one of the highest mortality rates in Nazi concentration camps. An estimated 55–65 per cent of these men died. The mortality rate for political prisoners – who were also imprisoned for "reeducational purposes" – was 40 per cent.

Sachsenhausen concentration camp at Orienberg, near Berlin, was used initially for political prisoners but later also for "inferior" groups, including an estimated 1,200 homosexual men.

A memorial to the "pink triangle" prisoners at Buchenwald concentration camp. One of those held here was Rudolf Brazda, who in 2008 broke his silence and spoke publicly about his experience.

Persecution of gay women

Although Paragraph 175 did not apply to women, a number of gay women were still convicted and incarcerated in Nazi prisons and concentration camps. Some were persecuted on the basis of their multiple identities – for example, Jewish gay women. Others were arrested on the grounds of other sex laws, such as the age of consent law, which was gender neutral. However, most "Aryan" gay women were not targeted unless they were also criminal and/or communist. Being Jewish was a key factor.

One well-known case is that of Elsa Conrad, a businesswoman and owner of multiple lesbian bars in Berlin. Arrested in 1935, she was sent to Moringen concentration camp in 1937. Some scholars argue that her Jewish identity was central to her persecution, because she could not be convicted on the basis of Paragraph 175 alone. In 1938, she was released when she agreed that she would go into exile, and she moved to Nairobi, Kenya.

The pink triangle was reserved for men. Most of the known gay women in concentration camps wore a black triangle, which identified "asocial" people. "Asocial" was a very vague term, but was primarily used for the unemployed, the homeless, sex workers, and gay women. These women experienced a similar stigma to gay men; often

met with prejudice, they were described as strange, abhorrent, revolting, perverted, and corrupt.

After World War II

Despite the Nazi defeat in 1945 and the liberation of most prisoners from concentration camps, numerous "pink triangle" men were transferred to other prisons. Sex between men remained criminalized until 1967 in East Germany and 1969 in West Germany. It was not until 1994 that Paragraph 175 was fully removed from the German penal code. In 2002, convictions for homosexuality during the Nazi era were annulled but, unlike other prisoner groups, gay victims did not receive compensation for another 15 years.

Due to the stigma and shame attached to same-sex attraction, many survivors could not return to their homes and families. Many did not speak about their experiences. These accounts are crucial to history, and they must be told. ∎

If I finally speak, it's for people to know what we, homosexuals, had to endure in Hitler's days … it shouldn't happen again.
Rudolf Brazda
Czech–German concentration camp survivor (1913–2011)

Friedrich-Paul von Groszheim

One of thousands of Germans imprisoned and abused for his homosexuality, Friedrich-Paul von Groszheim was born in Lübeck, Germany, in 1906. In 1937, along with 230 other men from Lübeck, he was arrested by the Nazis under Paragraph 175. Sentenced to 10 months in prison, he was made to wear the letter "A" on his uniform, meaning *Arschficker* ("arse-f***er"). In 1938, he was rearrested and tortured. Given an ultimatum between being sent to a concentration camp or being castrated, he chose castration. As a result, he was declared "unfit" for military service when World War II broke out.

In 1943, von Groszheim was again arrested and was sent to Neuengamme concentration camp. This time he was classed as a political prisoner and wore a red triangle.

After World War II, von Groszheim settled in Hamburg. He did not talk about his Holocaust experiences until 1991, when he featured in the film *We Were Marked with a Big A*, screened in 1993. He died 10 years later.

I AM A REALIST AND NOT AN OBSCENE WRITER

ISMAT CHUGHTAI'S OBSCENITY TRIAL (1944)

IN CONTEXT

FOCUS
Censorship of LGBTQ+ literature

BEFORE
1933 *Angarey*, a collection of Urdu short stories and a play, is banned for its radical themes.

1935 The Progressive Writers Association is established with an anti-imperialistic and reforming focus.

AFTER
1976 Chughtai's contribution to literature is recognized with the award of the Padma Shri, an Indian medal of honour.

1994 Chughtai's memoir *Kaghazi hai Pairahan* (*The Paper Attire*), which includes an account of her obscenity trial, is published.

1998 In Delhi, right-wing groups vandalize cinemas screening Indian–Canadian director Deepa Mehta's film *Fire* because of its lesbian content.

I n 1944, Indian novelist Ismat Chughtai was summoned to appear in Lahore High Court for a charge of obscenity against her short story "Lihaaf" ("The Quilt"). In "Lihaaf", a woman looks back on her childhood, in which she discovers a sexual relationship between a wealthy Muslim woman, Begum Jan, and her female domestic worker, Rabbo. The story also explores the psychological trauma the narrator suffers as a child when Begum Jan makes sexual advances towards her.

The trial and its aftermath

Pre-Independence India was a deeply patriarchal society, with the Indian elite joining British colonizers to censure and control. It was controversial for a woman, let alone an upper-class Muslim such as Chughtai, to write about sexuality in general and lesbianism in particular. The trial hinged on the story's language, with one witness suggesting that a story in which a respectable women had "ashiqs" (lovers) must be obscene. Chughtai's lawyer dismissed this

In my stories, I've put down everything with objectivity. Now, if some people find them obscene, let them go to hell.
Ismat Chughtai

on the basis that "Lihaaf" could be about a non-respectable woman. Chughtai was eventually acquitted, but the trial came at a huge personal cost: she faced criticism from her family and received hate mail, though she became acclaimed in later years.

Homophobic attitudes still lead to censorship in India. Demands for bans on art with LGBTQ+ themes continue, with lesbianism attracting particular ire thanks to its challenge to straight, male orthodoxy. ∎

See also: The *Kama Sutra* 36–37 ▪ Same-sex narratives in Urdu poetry 96–97 ▪ Hijras and British colonialism 100–00 ▪ The trial of Oscar Wilde 124–25

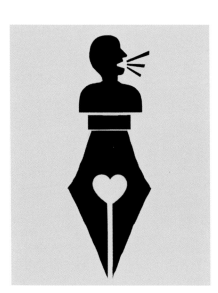

WE DO NOT SPEAK OF LOVE. OUR FACES SCREAM OF IT
THE BEAT GENERATION (1940s–1950s)

Around the time American gay rights activists were coming together to form the Mattachine Society, a literary movement was brewing in New York City, where writers Allen Ginsberg, Jack Kerouac, William S. Burroughs, and Herbert Huncke had met at Columbia University in 1944.

The Beat Generation, as Kerouac named them in 1948, were known for their avant-garde work and bohemian lifestyles. Their poetry and prose was influenced by the rhythms of jazz and techniques such as free verse and stream-of-consciousness. Breaking boundaries, they wrote openly about alcohol and drugs – and about their same-sex desires. Letters, memoirs, and their creative works reveal that gay sex was common among the inner circle. Ginsberg, for example, had experiences with both Burroughs and Kerouac, and both Ginsberg and Burroughs identified as gay.

A mixed legacy
The Beat Generation inspired readers with their openness about their sexual exploits, and laid the groundwork for the free love and nonconformist movements of the 1960s. However, the group was also overwhelmingly white and male, and readers have since criticized the racism and misogyny that is prevalent in many of their works. ∎

Allen Ginsberg is best known for the poem "Howl" (1956), which sparked an obscenity trial for publisher Lawrence Ferlinghetti in 1957 due largely to its ecstatic descriptions of gay sex.

NOT AN ALL-OR-NONE PROPOSITION

KINSEY'S RESEARCH ON SEXOLOGY (1948, 1953)

IN CONTEXT

FOCUS
Sexual behaviour

BEFORE
1897 British physician Havelock Ellis publishes his research on homosexuality in *Sexual Inversion*. It is one of the first sexological texts that takes a sympathetic view of homosexuality.

1919 German sexologist Magnus Hirschfeld founds the first Institute for Sexology in Berlin.

AFTER
1976 Sex educator Shere Hite publishes *The Hite Report on Female Sexuality* in the US. *The Hite Report on Men and Male Sexuality* follows in 1981.

1998 American psychologist William E. Snell, Jr. creates the Multidimensional Sexual Self-Concept Questionnaire with 100 questions measuring sexual orientation.

American biologist Alfred Kinsey's reports on human sexuality shocked the public in the 1940s and '50s, revealing the prevalence of female masturbation and premarital sex. They also brought out into the open the frequency of homosexual behaviour and attraction.

Sexuality research

Kinsey's research took the form of interviews – first with students in Indiana, and then with participants across the US. He collected detailed sexual histories in person, using a survey with more than 100 questions. He and his team would eventually gather 18,000 histories.

After founding the Institute for Sex Research (ISR) in 1947, Kinsey published his work in two groundbreaking reports: *Sexual Behavior in the Human Male* (1948) and *Sexual Behavior in the Human Female* (1953), both created with collaborators Wardell Pomeroy and Clyde Martin.

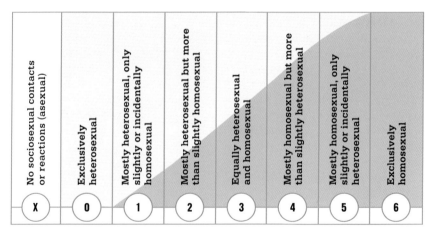

The Kinsey Scale describes a person's sexual behaviour at a given time and ranges from 0 (exclusively heterosexual) to 6 (exclusively homosexual), with varying bisexual responses in between. An additional grade, X, indicates no sociosexual contacts or reactions.

See also: Defining "homosexual" and "heterosexual" 106–07 ▪ Bisexuality 262–65 ▪ The aromantic and asexual spectrum 280–83 ▪ Pansexuality 294–95

> Only the human mind invents categories and tries to force facts into separated pigeon-holes. The living world is a continuum in each and every one of its aspects.
> **Alfred Kinsey**

Together, the reports sold nearly 1 million copies. They provided evidence that same-sex attraction and behaviours were common – in fact, the "major proportion" of the men who answered his questions would have some homosexual experience. Kinsey's team used a seven-point scale to catalogue the sexual histories they collected. A "0" was "exclusively heterosexual", a "1" was "predominantly heterosexual, only incidentally homosexual", with "6" being "exclusively homosexual". This scale was published in *Sexual Behavior in the Human Male* along with research showing that a significant amount of people did not fit into categories of entirely heterosexual or homosexual.

Kinsey's work helped to show that sexual behaviour is fluid, although the Kinsey Scale was later criticized for positioning homosexual and heterosexual attraction as opposites on a single continuum. This means that a high level of homosexual attraction must equate to a low level of heterosexual attraction on the scale, as it can only measure the two in relation to each other.

Scales after Kinsey

Several other scales for measuring human sexuality have since been proposed. In the US, in 1978, the Klein Sexual Orientation Grid (KSOG) asked questions about the past, present, and future to show how sexuality might change. It showed degrees of homosexuality or heterosexuality, with bisexuality as a midpoint; Kinsey had used the term "bisexual" to indicate intersex.

In 1979, American psychologist Michael D. Storms proposed the Storms Scale, which uses a graph with an X axis for heteroeroticism (erotic attraction to the opposite sex) and a Y axis for homoeroticism (erotic attraction to the same sex). While the Storms model has been praised for including asexuals as part of the scale, it has also been criticized for its binary approach to gender. It essentially uses "same sex" and "opposite sex" attractions for its axes. ▪

Kinsey's 1953 report on female sexual behaviour met with sensationalism in the press. The report said only 3–9% of women were predominantly or exclusively homosexual.

Alfred Kinsey

Born in Hoboken, New Jersey, US in 1894, Alfred Kinsey rebelled against his strict Protestant upbringing by choosing to study biology, first at Bowdoin College, Maine, and then at Harvard, in Cambridge, Massachusetts. He joined Indiana University after receiving his doctorate in evolutionary biology in 1919.

From 1920 to 1928, Kinsey studied gall wasps, but in 1928 he was asked to coordinate a new course on "Marriage and Family" for married and senior students. A meticulous and data-driven researcher, Kinsey was soon surprised to discover how little large-scale research had been done on human sexual behaviour, and resolved to fill that gap.

Kinsey's two major reports attracted controversy for covering taboo topics, such as masturbation and adultery, but also for revealing the prevalence of sexual activities enjoyed by men and women. In 1953, Kinsey faced a Congressional investigation of his finances that led him to lose his funding. He died only three years later, in 1956, of heart disease and pneumonia.

IT WAS A WITCH HUNT

THE LAVENDER SCARE (1950)

IN CONTEXT

FOCUS
Homophobia and anticommunism

BEFORE
1946 The US State Department's Appropriations Committee has concerns about security risks. The Secretary of State has discretion to fire people to ensure national security.

1948 Alfred Kinsey's *Sexual Behavior in the Human Male* is published, increasing public awareness of homosexuality.

AFTER
1952 The first *Diagnostic and Statistical Manual of Mental Disorders* (DSM) lists homosexuality as a "sociopathic personality disturbance".

1961 The Mattachine Society of Washington, D.C. is founded by civil servant Franklin Kameny. It works to fight anti-gay discrimination and federal exclusionary policies.

During the 1950s, the US becomes **increasingly fearful of threats from within**, including communism.

LGBTQ+ people, especially those serving in government or the military, are **seen as "subversives"** – **morally corrupt** and prone to **communist influence or blackmail**.

Suspected homosexuals are **interrogated and fired**, with a few subsequently **becoming radicalized**, while public discomfort grows.

F rom the late 1940s to the 1960s, there was a mass removal, by sacking or resignation, of lesbian and gay civil servants in the United States. It was nicknamed the "Lavender Scare", after the term "lavender lads", used by Senator Everett Dirksen to refer to homosexual men, and the "Red Scare", used for the US government's fear of communist infiltration.

In the 1940s, public awareness of homosexuality was growing, and gay people were forming communities. In 1947, the U.S. Park

Police targeted gay men through a "Sex Perversion Elimination Program". In 1948, Congress passed, and President Truman signed, Public Law 615, which sought treatment for "sexual psychopaths" in Washington, D.C. This law enabled the arrest and punishment of gay people while also labelling homosexuality a mental illness.

The Red Scare
During the 1950s, the Red Scare gripped the US government. Between 1950 and 1954, Senator

See also: Kinsey's research on sexology 164–65 ▪ Towards gay liberation 170–77 ▪ The decriminalization of same-sex acts 184–85 ▪ The Stonewall Uprising 190–95 ▪ Removal of homosexuality from the DSM 219

Joseph McCarthy was involved in campaigns to seek out communists, resulting in many of those accused losing their jobs or being refused employment, despite often not belonging to the Communist Party. In a speech in February 1950, McCarthy said he had a list of 205 known Communists working in the State Department. He later claimed that in two cases, communism was directly linked to homosexuality.

Those suspected of communism and homosexuality became further associated as both were portrayed as morally weak or psychologically unwell, godless, and a threat to traditional family structures. Both were also believed to recruit new members into their underworlds. In

Two senators, Kenneth Wherry (left), a Republican, and J. Lister Hill (not pictured), a Democrat, conducted the first congressional investigation into homosexuality in the federal workforce.

this febrile atmosphere, John Emil Peurifoy, Deputy Under Secretary of State, went on to claim that there was a "homosexual underground" in the State Department, leading to 91 employees being outed and let go.

Further interrogations

Between March and May 1950, the Wherry–Hill Investigation, led by Senators Kenneth Wherry and J. Lister Hill, represented the first major investigation in what was later to be called the Lavender Scare. They questioned government officials to determine how many of Peurifoy's 91 employees had been rehired and found that 13 had been. Wherry and Hill were concerned that there was no central record of the reasons for employees being let go.

The Senate felt that more needed to be done to investigate the employment of homosexuals. This was to be achieved through the

Hoey Committee Investigation. Chaired by Senator Clyde Hoey, this subcommittee investigated a wider range of departments, such as federal agencies, law enforcement, the judiciary, and medical authorities. The Hoey Committee produced the *Employment of Homosexuals and Other Sex Perverts in Government* report, which stated that nearly 5,000 homosexuals had been found. The report influenced government security manuals and offered a basis for President Eisenhower's 1953 Executive Order #10450, which allowed a candidate's sexuality to determine their suitability for federal government.

Researchers have concluded that thousands of government employees lost their jobs during this period. Many more may have left before they were outed. As well as hardship, careers were curtailed, and tragically some people even died by suicide. ▪

A government document shows civil servant Andrew Ference, who was interrogated in 1954 and forced to resign after telling them he was gay. He died by suicide four days later.

I freely admitted that I was gay. And then they said, "We also want five names of other people you know."
Bob Cantillion
Former US Navy serviceman

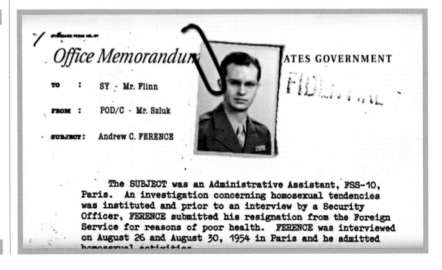

Office Memorandum ... ATES GOVERNMENT

TO : SY - Mr. Flinn

FROM : POD/C - Mr. Szluk

SUBJECT : Andrew C. FERENCE

The SUBJECT was an Administrative Assistant, FSS-10, Paris. An investigation concerning homosexual tendencies was instituted and prior to an interview by a Security Officer, FERENCE submitted his resignation from the Foreign Service for reasons of poor health. FERENCE was interviewed on August 26 and August 30, 1954 in Paris and he admitted homosexual activities.

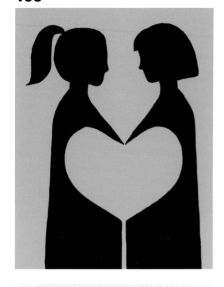

A LOVE OF OUR OWN KIND

FEMALE WRITERS' REJECTION OF LABELS (1951–1979)

IN CONTEXT

FOCUS
Female creative writers

BEFORE
1852 In a letter, American poet Emily Dickinson expresses her desire for her sister-in-law, Susan Gilbert.

1884 Under the name Michael Field, British writers and lovers Katherine Bradley and Edith Cooper begin to publish work that speaks openly of female same-sex love and sexuality.

1928 American author Djuna Barnes bases *The Ladies Almanack* on her Paris lesbian circle. She later declares, "I am not a lesbian. I just loved Thelma [Wood, an artist]".

AFTER
1985 British author Jeanette Winterson writes about teenage lesbianism in *Oranges Are Not the Only Fruit*, a semi-autobiographical novel.

B etween the 1920s and 1950s, women in the US and Europe began to assert more strongly their attachments to women, often associating with other "sapphists" in literary salons and private clubs. However, it was rare for female writers in same-sex relationships to identify as lesbians until the sexual revolution of the late 1960s. They may have feared prejudice, and its impact on their work, but for some women it was also a philosophical objection to gender stereotyping.

Keeping quiet
British writer Ivy Compton-Burnett revealed nothing in public of her sexuality and deep attachment to decorative arts expert Margaret Jourdain, yet after Jourdain's death in 1951, she wrote to a friend, "I wish you had met her, and so met more of me". She was similarly circumspect about the close relationship she went on to have with Madge Garland, the editor of British *Vogue*.

Irish-British novelist Iris Murdoch had multiple relationships with men and women, but also refused labels.

You move me deeply, as you know. But I cannot offer you more than I ever could, and even for that time and space divide us.
Iris Murdoch
Letter to Brigid Brophy, 1960

"Too great exactitude would come amiss," she wrote in verses to writer Brigid Brophy, with whom she corresponded in hundreds of intimate letters from 1954 to 1967.

In the US, Pulitzer Prize-winning poet Elizabeth Bishop, also resisted gender stereotyping, even refusing to allow her work to be included in female anthologies. Her celebration of female love that begins "It is marvellous to wake up together" was found only after her death in 1979. ■

See also: AFAB cross-dressers and "female husbands" 82–83 ▪ Erotic friendship in America and Europe 92–95 ▪ Sapphism 98 ▪ Butch and femme 152–55

I AM WITH YOU, I AM LIKE YOU

BRAZILIAN PAJUBÁ (1964–84)

The secret language *Pajubá* or *Bajubá* ("gossip") was first adopted by the trans community to minimize police harassment during Brazil's military dictatorship from 1964 to 1984. It is largely rooted in West African languages such as Yoruba and the dialects of Candomblé, Umbanda, and other religions combining Catholic and African elements. These religions spread in Brazil as some 4.9 million enslaved Africans arrived between 1501 and 1866. Broadly supportive of LGBTQ+ members, they became safe spaces for some trans people, and their words, combined with Brazilian Portuguese, formed the new slang.

Initially, transgender and *travesti* communities used Pajubá to pass secret warnings and escape police violence, as their clubs were often raided. Sex workers also used it to alert each other to undercover police or violent clients, and it is credited with saving many lives.

A long road
Pajubá was formally set down and translated in the 1990s. It is now used more widely in the LGBTQ+ community and often heard in Brazilian soap operas. Yet, while Pajubá is now more mainstream, trans and gender nonconforming Brazilians stress the importance of remembering its origins in the struggles and violence they still encounter in a country that reports more murders of trans people than anywhere else in the world. ∎

Samba dancers perform in 2022 at Rio de Janeiro's carnival, an annual event famed for the extravagant costumes with which participants freely express their gender and sexuality.

See also: The secret language of Polari 127 ▪ Transgender rights 196–203 ▪ Indigenous American Two-Spirit people 258–61

GAY IS GOOD

TOWARDS GAY LIBERATION (1950s–1980s)

IN CONTEXT

FOCUS
LGBTQ+ rights

BEFORE
1791 Same-sex acts
between two consenting
adults are legalized in the
French Penal Code.

AFTER
1990 The first South African
Pride parade is held in
Johannesburg.

1992 Online LGBTQ+ activist
group Digital Queers is
established in the US.

1992 The first Argentinian
Pride is held in Buenos Aires.
Many of the 250 marchers
wear masks to avoid being
recognised.

1994 Asia's first Pride march
takes place in Manila, the
Philippines.

2000 The Netherlands
becomes the first nation to
legalize same-sex marriage.

World War II had a
transformative effect
on LGBTQ+ culture,
especially in the US. People from
different backgrounds were thrown
into the military and vital services,
and same-sex relationships
flourished despite persecution. After
the war ended, however, there was
backlash, with social conformity
and traditional families increasingly
valued, and many LGBTQ+ people
faced homophobic laws and feelings
of shame. This in turn shaped the
homophile movement, which
supported and represented LGBTQ+
people in the 1950s and '60s.

Homophile groups were more
conservative than later gay liberation
groups, partly out of caution. In
Germany and the UK, male–male
sex acts were against the law.
Thousands were arrested, and many
British men were imprisoned after
being solicited by undercover officers
posing as gay men. In France, same-
sex relations were legal, but police
sought to entrap homosexuals by
using laws against public indecency.
In the US, sodomy was illegal in
almost every state, and the Lavender
Scare saw many LGBTQ+ people
forced out of US government jobs.
The Netherlands and Scandinavian
countries had more liberal laws, but
same-sex relations in which an
adult had sex with an individual
under 21 were still illegal.

As a result, to publicly identify
as homosexual was a brave stance.
Most activists used pseudonyms
to protect their identity, and many,
especially in Europe, preferred
"homophile" to "homosexual", feeling
that the latter term emphasized sex
more than love. Their assimilationist
politics focused on integration rather
than liberation, and some argued
that homosexuals were treated
badly because of their "over the
top" and "promiscuous" behaviour.
Homophiles were mostly middle
class, and wanted to be seen as
discreet and respectable, and to
be heard. They organized meetings,
campaigned for legal change, and
published periodicals.

Daughters of Bilitis was a
good coming out place,
where women could get their
act together and find out
who they were.
Del Martin
Co-founder of Daughters of Bilitis
(1921–2008)

Early homophile groups
One of the first homophile groups
was the Dutch Cultuur en
Ontspannings Centrum (COC;
Centre for Culture and Leisure).
Founded in 1946, this was a place
where members could meet, build a
social network, find partners, and
learn more about homosexuality.
Swedish and Norwegian branches
formed in 1949 and 1950, with
the Swedish branch becoming
independent under the name
Riksförbundet För Sexuellt
Likaberättigande (RFSL; Federation
for Sexual Equality) in the early
1950s. RFSL also offered social
meeting places and campaigned
for same-sex marriage.

In the US, the Mattachine
Society was formed in 1950, its
offshoot ONE in 1952, and the
Daughters of Bilitis in 1955. Los
Angeles-based ONE also published
an influential magazine, which the
US Postal Service Office declared

Del Martin (left) and Phyllis Lyon
(right) founded the Daughters of Bilitis
in 1955. The San Francisco-based
group was the first lesbian civil rights
organization in the US.

See also: The Compton's Cafeteria Riot 182–83 ▪ The Stonewall Uprising 190–95 ▪ Transgender rights 196–203 ▪ CAMP Australia 204–05 ▪ The creation of the Pride flag 224–25 ▪ The AIDS epidemic 238–41 ▪ Section 28 248–49

obscene in 1954 and refused to deliver; ONE won the resulting lawsuit in 1958. In the UK, the Homosexual Law Reform Society formed in 1958 and campaigned for the legalization of same-sex relationships. Its first meeting, in London, was attended by more than 1,000 people.

In France, Arcadie (also known as Club Littéraire et Scientifique des Pays Latins) was founded in 1954, combining a literary review that emphasized the homophile message of dignity and respectability in gay and lesbian communities with a social group that held dances and sponsored lectures. A number of other publications associated with the homophile movement also emerged, including the Danish magazine *Vennen* (*The Friend*, 1949) and American publications the *Mattachine Review* (1955) and *The Ladder* (1956).

A global community

Led by COC, the largest activist group in the 1950s, the global homophile community came together in its first joint meeting,

The Mattachine Society

In 1950, a group of gay men in Los Angeles who had been inspired by communism formed the Mattachine Society. It received a boost when founding member Dale Jennings was arrested for "lewd behaviour" in a park in 1952. Jennings and the society contested the charge and the case was dismissed. Membership swelled to more than a thousand after the incident, chapters appeared in

---

Early LGBTQ+ activism in the US

Society for Human Rights
• Produced America's first gay periodical, *Friendship and Freedom*
• Raided by police within months of its set-up and subsequently disbanded
• An inspiration for later groups

Daughters of Bilitis
• Aimed to educate the public and help lesbians "understand themselves"
• Followed the Mattachine model, stressing assimilation
• Folded in 1970, though local chapters continued to operate until the 1990s

Chicago		San Francisco	
1924	**1950**	**1955**	**1969**
	Los Angeles		New York City

Mattachine Society
• Goals include "Unify homosexuals isolated from their own kind"
• Despite radical origins, largely non-confrontational in tactics
• Splintered into different groups by the early 1960s

Gay Liberation Front
• Formed in the aftermath of the Stonewall Uprising
• Favoured direct action and organized the first Pride marches
• Evolved into other groups, including Canadian and British wings

---

the International Congress for Sexual Equality, in 1951. Representatives from Denmark, West Germany, the UK, Italy, Switzerland, and the Netherlands met in Amsterdam, and sent a telegram to the United Nations demanding equal rights. From this

San Francisco, New York City, Chicago, and Washington, DC, and a newsletter and several periodicals were published.

The society was hugely influential but was torn between radical and non-confrontational politics. In 1952, many original members left and the group became more conservative. Several chapters disbanded in the 1960s, while the Washington, DC, and Philadelphia chapters moved in a more radicalized direction.

congress, a new organization was born. The International Committee for Sexual Equality (ICSE) was a collaboration between Denmark's League of 1948, RFSL, Swiss gay magazine *Der Kreis* (*The Circle*, 1932–1967), and later ONE, as well as other groups. It sponsored »

I knew that I was gay in every bone of my body. So I did the only thing I could do. I started the movement.
Harry Hay
Co-founder of the Mattachine Society
(1912–2002)

> We reject society's attempt to impose sexual roles and definitions of our nature.
> **New York City Gay Liberation Front**
> **Mission statement**

congresses, organized meetings, dinners, dances, and cabarets, and worked to change discriminatory laws and attitudes around the world. Although the ICSE wound down in the early 1960s, it played a vital role in creating a transnational homophile identity.

Activism in the 1960s

While homophile organizations' respectable politics and community building were considered radical for their time, as the 1960s wore on some LGBTQ+ people began to demand more direct action. In the US, groups in Washington, DC, New York City, and Philadelphia joined together to form the East Coast Homophile Organizations (ECHO) in 1963. From 1965 to 1969, this group organized "Annual Reminder" pickets in which representatives from several Mattachine Societies gathered outside the White House, bearing placards and formally dressed in suits, ties, and dresses. The San Franciscan Society for Individual Rights (SIR) formed in 1964, and worked to build a community with drag shows, dinners, bridge clubs, softball games, art classes, and meditation groups. The group opened the nation's first gay and lesbian community centre in 1966, and by 1968 SIR was the largest homophile organization in the country.

By 1965, the New York Mattachine Society had changed tactics. They took inspiration from Frank Kameny, the founder of the Mattachine Society of Washington, who had been an astronomer for the US Army Map Service before being dismissed for his sexuality. He

Protesters including Frank Kameny (second in line) demonstrate on Armed Forces Day 1965 against the exclusion of LGBTQ+ people from the military.

broke from the reserved traditions of the homophile movement, saying that homosexuality was "good and desirable", and took inspiration from Black civil rights campaigns to organize more militant action, such as public demonstrations. In 1966, groups came together in the North American Conference of Homophile Organizations (NACHO), which held conferences, started gay groups, coordinated a legal defence fund to challenge anti-LGBTQ+ laws and regulations, and organized national demonstrations. In an indication of the further change to come, the group disbanded after a 1970 conference in which older members clashed with more radicalized activists.

Activism was not limited to North America and Europe. In 1967, Latin America's first known LGBTQ+ rights organization, Nuestro Mundo (Our World), was formed in Buenos Aires by Héctor

---

Early homophile movements are **non-confrontational** as persecution necessitates **slow, careful steps** to progress.

After the Stonewall Uprising, groups such as the Gay Liberation Front are **increasingly eager to assert themselves** in the public sphere.

The **battle for civil rights** becomes more vocal, as the seeds planted by early groups flower into **global marches and campaigns** in the 1970s and '80s.

Alongside campaigning, the growth of **gay cafés, publications, and bookstores** helps propel gay culture **into the mainstream** in many nations in the 1990s and beyond.

Anabitarte, a trade unionist who had been expelled from the Communist Party of Argentina because he was gay. In South Africa, the Law Reform Movement emerged in 1968, and successfully challenged a proposed change to the apartheid regime's Immorality Act that would have criminalized same-sex acts.

Gay liberation

By the late 1960s, the conservative post-war consensus was falling apart as younger people pushed against more traditional views. Student protests in France, anti-Vietnam demonstrations in the US, and the rise of feminism and radical movements such as Black Power challenged the political and social status quo. Many of these movements rejected consumerism and sexual taboos, and gay liberation gained momentum and became associated with wider left-wing causes.

In June 1969, a police raid on the Stonewall Inn, a gay bar in New York City, was resisted by patrons and passers-by. It was not the first LGBTQ+ uprising against the police: Los Angeles' Cooper Do-nuts Riot (1959), San Francisco's Compton's Cafeteria Riot (1966), and protests at Los Angeles' Black Cat Tavern (1967) all predated it. Nor was it the beginnings of gay liberation, which arguably started with the more militant actions of the New York Mattachine Society. But Stonewall made the headlines, and was the spark that sent gay liberation global.

In the weeks after the Uprising, the Gay Liberation Front (GLF) was formed in New York City, consciously taking its name from the National Liberation Fronts of Vietnam and Algeria. Protest marches – held in June to commemorate Stonewall – took place through the 1970s, and by the 1980s were commonly referred to as Gay Pride parades.

In contrast to homophiles' desire to fit in, gay liberationists saw direct action and societal change as the answer, and "coming out" as gay to friends, family, and co-workers was considered a form of activism. »

The 1993 March on Washington for Lesbian, Gay, and Bi Equal Rights and Liberation saw around one million people gather together to call for equality for LGBTQ+ people.

The Purple Pamphlet

Homosexuality and Citizenship in Florida, colloquially known as the Purple Pamphlet, was an anti-LGBTQ+ propaganda pamphlet published by the Florida Legislative Investigation Committee (FLIC) in the US in January 1964. Led by Senator Charley Johns, the committee had been conducting a witch hunt of homosexuals for several years in schools, universities, and government agencies, claiming they were connected to communist indoctrination.

The booklet featured pornographic images and a list of terminology used by the gay community, and sold for 25 cents a copy. It was designed to stir up homophobia and provoke stricter LGBTQ+ legislation, but instead it was criticized for its explicit imagery. Dade County, Florida, threatened legal action, while a gay book club in Washington, DC, sold copies. The backlash hit the committee's funding, and it was disbanded in 1965.

We were sexual liberationists and social revolutionaries, out to turn the world upside down.
Peter Tatchell
LGBTQ+ activist and member of the UK Gay Liberation Front

Gay liberationists wished to remove or transform institutions such as gender and the nuclear family that were seen as conservative and limiting.

The new liberation groups consciously defined themselves against traditional homophile organizations, but the movements interacted through the 1960s and '70s. Publications in the US that helped bridge the gap included *Vector* (San Francisco), *Drum* (Philadelphia), *Homosexual Citizen* (Washington, DC), and *The Advocate* (Los Angeles).

From national to global

The GLF was short-lived but opened the door for a number of different groups. The Gay Activists Alliance (the GAA, founded in 1969), Street Transvestite Action Revolutionaries (STAR, 1970), and the National Gay Task Force (later the National LGBTQ Taskforce, 1973) all formed in New York City. In 1977, lesbian activist Jean O'Leary led the first delegation of LGBTQ+ activists to the White House. In 1988, she and psychologist Robert Eichberg co-founded National Coming Out Day, an annual awareness event.

Stonewall and the GLF had a global impact. From 1969, Australian organizations formed in Sydney and Melbourne, while Canada (1970–72) and the UK (1971–74) had their own Gay Liberation Fronts, with the UK's GLF splintering into the Lesbian and Gay Switchboard helpline and newspaper *Gay News*. One effect of this growth was the Americanization of gay culture and movements – seen in the global spread of the Pride parades and flag – which may have hampered local movements in fully expressing their own identities.

In Sweden, RFSL became more active in the 1970s and '80s with parades and school information activities. In France, activists disrupted a 1971 live radio broadcast called "Homosexuality, This Painful Problem", and Front Homosexuel d'Action Révolutionnaire (FHAR) was formed not long after. In Argentina, Frente de Liberación Homosexual (FLH) was formed in 1971, taking an anti-imperialist and anti-capitalist stance. A Brazilian activist group called SOMOS was created in 1978 by students and staff at the University of São Paulo. In South Africa, a gay subculture

blossomed in the '70s and '80s with supper clubs, bars, gay-owned businesses, and a newspaper, *EXIT*. The Gay Association of South Africa (GASA) was formed in 1982, but, like the earlier Law Reform Movement, it was headed by white middle-class gay men. Activism continued to be divided along racial lines: GASA supported a pro-Apartheid candidate in the 1987 elections, and was expelled from the International Lesbian and Gay Alliance (ILGA), an umbrella organization focusing on legal issues, later that year. In 1988, Gays and Lesbians of Witwatersrand (GLOW) was formed under Simon Tseko Nkoli, with predominantly Black people involved.

Diversity and inclusiveness

While women were involved in many homophile and gay liberation groups, some groups – including ICSE, FHAR, and COC – have been criticized for being male-centric and not dealing with lesbian concerns. LGBTQ+ women also struggled for recognition within many women's liberation movements, and a number

> … LGBTQ people should have the same rights, opportunities, and obligations as everybody else in society.
> **RFSL, 2016**

> This rainbow capitalist culture is distressing, especially when you consider how many companies fail to support the LGBTQ community when it counts.
> **Ianne Fields Stewart**
> American actor and activist

of groups formed as a result. In 1953, activist Suzanne de Pues formed Centre Culturel Belge / Cultuurcentrum België (CCB; Culture Centre Belgium), an inclusive group for gays and lesbians, after being heckled and humiliated at an ICSE meeting. In the US, the Daughters of Bilitis, founded in 1955, were followed by other prominent groups. The Lavender Menace formed in New York City in 1970 after the National Organization for Women

A 2021 protest against rainbow capitalism. The commodification of events such as Pride, and the "pinkwashing" of corporate brands, is a source of frustration for many activists.

(NOW) distanced itself from LGBTQ+ causes. New York also gave birth to the Lesbian Avengers, who formed in 1992 and mixed humour with activism.

As activism became more diverse and more widespread, representation also grew. In the 1970s, gay characters such as Jodie Dallas, played by Billy Crystal in the American sitcom *Soap*, became more prominent on TV. Music acts such as Boy George, Frankie Goes To Hollywood, and k.d. lang enjoyed global success, and in video games, 1988's *Caper in the Castro* featured a lesbian detective on the hunt for a kidnapped drag queen. Gay bars, cafés, and bookshops became an increasing feature of city streets.

Modern activism
In the 1980s, the HIV/AIDS epidemic hit LGBTQ+ communities hard. Some volunteers, particularly those directly affected by the epidemic,

were no longer able or no longer wished to participate in activism. Other groups, such as ACT UP, founded in New York City in 1987, focused on HIV/AIDS activism and awareness. These campaigns helped politicize a new wave of lesbians and gay men.

From the '90s onwards, gay liberation's radical protests have largely been eclipsed by movements that foreground pro-assimilation thinking and political responsibility. While many gay liberationists challenged political and social institutions such as marriage, contemporary movements are more likely to seek political support for civil rights such as marriage equality and trans inclusion. Significant issues remain around LGBTQ+ rights around the world, but progress has been very real, something that was highlighted when the United Nations enshrined LGBTQ+ rights as human rights in 2011. ∎

The Australian bank ANZ rebranded several ATMs as "GAYTMs" from 2014 in support of Sydney Gay and Lesbian Mardi Gras. As LGBTQ+ culture has become mainstream, many brands have associated themselves with it.

DEMOCRACY WITH REPRESSION IS NOT DEMOCRACY
LATIN AMERICAN LGBTQ+ MOVEMENTS (1960s–1970s)

IN CONTEXT

FOCUS
Campaigns for LGBTQ+ rights

BEFORE
1591 The first known *travesti* (a trans femme identity unique to Latin America) arrives in Brazil as an enslaved person.

1830s The decriminalization of same-sex acts in Brazil and mass immigration from Europe leads to a thriving male homosexual subculture in Buenos Aires.

AFTER
1980 The brutal arrest of a group of lesbians in São Paulo, Brazil, launches a repressive campaign of gender policing.

1983 At the end of the military dictatorship in Argentina, an archaic law allows for the arrest of hundreds of gay people.

1992 The Association of Travestis and Liberated people (ASTRAL) is founded in Rio de Janeiro, Brazil.

In the 1960s and 1970s, **dictatorships and repressive governments** hold sway in many Latin American countries.

⬇

LGBTQ+ rights and the rights of many other groups – including **women and people of colour** – are **crushed**.

⬇

The fall of these regimes brings **greater freedom** and galvanizes LGBTQ+ groups to **fight for their rights**.

⬇

Today, many Latin American countries **recognize LGBTQ+ rights** and are among **the most progressive in the Global South**.

Each of the 33 nations of Latin America has its own political and social context, but in the 1960s and 1970s, much of Latin America experienced similar political upheaval. This period included revolutions, military dictatorships, and guerrilla movements, alongside the birth of social movements for women's rights, racial equality, and LGBTQ+ rights. LGBTQ+ people fought for greater visibility, an end to discrimination, and equality.

New movements
Latin America's first documented LGBTQ+ movement was the Argentinian group Nuestro Mundo (Our World). Founded in 1967 by trade unionist Héctor Anabitarte, the group aimed to raise awareness

See also: Colonial Latin America 66–67 ▪ Brazilian Pajubá 169 ▪ Towards gay liberation 170–77 ▪ Transgender rights 196–203 ▪ The AIDS epidemic 238–41

Drag queen Mary Gambiarra speaks at a protest during the annual Pride celebration of LGBTQ+ rights in Brasilia, Brazil, in July 2022.

of the oppression of LGBTQ+ people in Argentinian society. Nuestro Mundo protested against police brutality towards LGBTQ+ people, which the authorities claimed was necessary to protect family values in Argentina.

From 1976 to 1983, a military dictatorship ruled Argentina and up to 30,000 people, including LGBTQ+ people, disappeared or were killed. At this time, the Homosexual Liberation Front was founded and they created the first gay magazine of Latin America: *Somos* (*We Are*).

In Mexico, the Frente de Liberación Homosexual (FLH) was founded in 1971 by Nancy Cárdenas and Luis González de Alba to raise awareness of LGBTQ+ populations in Mexican society. The meetings took place in secret because of the repressive government of President Luis Echeverría and the homophobia common in Mexican society.

In 1978, Brazil's first gay newspaper was published. Named *O Lampião da Esquina* (after Brazilian bandit and folk hero Lampião), it reported on all fights for social justice, including LGBTQ+ groups. In 1979, the first openly gay Brazilian organization, Somos, was founded, inspiring the formation of other gay and lesbian groups in cities such as Rio de Janeiro, Curitiba, and Salvador.

Chile's first lesbian organization, known as the Feminist Lesbian Collective Ayuquelen, was founded in 1984, after the 1980 constitution made transgressions against the state, family, and the Catholic Church illegal. Ayuquelen challenged compulsory heteronormativity in Chile, and was the voice of resistance for LGBTQ+ people during the dictatorship of Augusto Pinochet (1973–1990). Pinochet defended conservative values and persecuted and imprisoned his political opponents, including LGBTQ+ writers and activists.

In the 1980s, the HIV/AIDS crisis hit LGBTQ+ communities across the Americas. The Church framed the epidemic as a divine intervention, while hundreds died. The 1990s, however, were marked by growing LGBTQ+ visibility and the first Brazilian Pride Parade was held in Rio de Janeiro in 1995. In 2010, Brazil legalized same-sex adoption and Argentina legalized same-sex marriage. Chile, Uruguay, Mexico, Colombia, and Ecuador have also made same-sex marriage legal.

However, the region still suffers from homophobic and transphobic violence. Research shows that there were 387 murders and 58 suicides of LGBTQ+ people in Brazil in 2017. ▪

Rosely Roth

Born in 1959 to Jewish parents in São Paulo, Brazil, Rosely Roth studied philosophy and anthropology, worked as an anthropologist, and dedicated her life to researching lesbian experiences in Brazil.

In 1981, Roth founded Grupo de Articulação Lésbica, through which she created the *Chana Com Chana* newsletter for lesbians and feminists. When *Chana Com Chana* (*Pussy On Pussy*) was banned from a local bar in São Paulo because of its lesbian and feminist content, Roth helped organize a protest in the bar on 19 August 1983 – an event that is widely referred to as the Brazilian Stonewall.

Eventually, the owners of the bar apologized and allowed the publication, in a victory for Brazil's first lesbian protest. After the matter was resolved, 19 August became Lesbian Visibility Day in São Paulo state. Roth is considered a pioneer in the Brazilian LGBTQ+ movement. After several years of living with depression, she died by suicide in 1990.

QUEER PARODY

CAMP (1964)

Camp sensibilities have long been tied to queer communities, particularly gay male communities. The word "camp" in an LGBTQ+ context was first listed in the *Oxford English Dictionary* in 1909. It was defined as "ostentatious, exaggerated, affected, theatrical; effeminate or homosexual; pertaining to, characteristic of, homosexuals".

Artifice

+

Excessiveness

+

Challenging norms

+

Ironic detachment

=

Camp

The dictionary did not give the origin of the word, only saying that it was obscure.

The most influential work on camp is American writer Susan Sontag's *Notes on Camp* (1964). In describing camp, Sontag focused on artifice, aestheticism, and "the spirit of extravagance". For Sontag, "Camp sees everything in quotation marks", and viewing things camply suggests seeing the performative role in everything in society.

Sontag cited work that embraces this extravagant superficiality, such as the plays of Anglo-Irish writer Oscar Wilde (1854–1900) and the drawings of British illustrator Aubrey Beardsley (1872–98). Sontag also highlighted how gender fluidity is integral to camp. She described camp as the "triumph of the epicene style" – a style with characteristics of more than one gender.

Pure or deliberate?

Sontag's essay differentiates between "pure" camp and "deliberate" camp. She maintained that pure camp is rooted in genuine passion. It is always "naïve" and the result of "seriousness that fails" because it is "too much" – so bad that it's good. Examples include

The ultimate Camp statement: it's good *because* it's awful.
Susan Sontag
Notes on Camp, 1964

Faye Dunaway's explosive depiction of Joan Crawford in the 1981 film *Mommy Dearest*, which was derided by critics at the time but has since achieved cult status. Deliberate camp, on the other hand, is the attempt to replicate the camp aesthetic, but the intentional nature of this undermines its impact.

American artist and writer Philip Core added to Sontag's idea of camp in his work *Camp: The Lie That Tells The Truth* (1984), defining camp as excessiveness that challenges social

Kenyan–Mexican actor Lupita Nyong'o attends the 2019 Met Gala in New York City. Her outfit encapsulated that year's theme – "celebrating camp".

and political norms. Australian-born writer Moe Meyer went further, challenging Sontag's interpretation of camp. In *Reclaiming the Discourse of Camp* (1994), he tied it explicitly to queer culture, defining it as political, critical, and "queer parody" of others and a solely queer discourse that cannot be appropriated by others as mere style. Meyer maintained that Sontag's definition of camp was "dead".

Influential aesthetic

Camp has been connected to queer culture since its earliest use and was linked to the language of Polari, which was common among gay men in Britain until the 1960s. Today, campness is still culturally associated with femininity and gay men through exaggerated behaviour and mannerisms. This can be seen in performers from Liberace and Elton

John to Madonna and Lady Gaga. Other examples include pantomime dames and drag queens, the Eurovision Song Contest, and the extravagant fashion shows of the late Alexander McQueen. Camp remains an influential aesthetic and cultural movement well into the 21st century. ▪

British actor James Doherty playing Widow Twankey in 2016 in the pantomime *Aladdin*, at the Lyric Hammersmith Theatre, London.

Pantomime dames

The British pantomime dame epitomizes many of the qualities of camp. The dame is always a female character played by a male actor, and while extravagantly feminine in terms of costumes, make-up, and wigs, does not hide typically masculine traits, often heightening them for the audience's amusement. This comic character interacts with the audience, specializing in innuendos and double entendres, and treads the line between being overtly sexual and family-friendly.

A staple of pantomime, the dame first appeared in the show *Harlequin and Mother Goose* in the Theatre Royal, London, in 1806. Widow Twankey, the archetypal dame character that embodies camp sensibilities, was introduced to the pantomime *Aladdin* in 1861. She pretends to be highly cultured and refined despite being named after Twankey Tea, a cheap brand of tea that was sold at the time. Today, many queer comedians play this and other dame roles in British theatres at Christmas time.

SCREAMING QUEENS

THE COMPTON'S CAFETERIA RIOT (1966)

In August 1966, one of the first LGBTQ+ uprisings in the United States took place in San Francisco's Tenderloin district. The riot broke out at Compton's Cafeteria, in response to police harassment of the city's trans and drag communities. Due to the lack of media coverage and an absence of contemporary police records, the specific date is unknown, and for decades the event was lost to history. It was rediscovered and brought to popular attention by trans historian Susan Stryker in her 2005 documentary *Screaming Queens*. At the time the film was made, Compton's was thought to be the earliest known act of collective militant queer resistance to police harassment, although earlier events, such as the Cooper Do-nuts Riot of 1959, have been noted since then.

Tensions erupt
Compton's Cafeteria was at the heart of the Tenderloin district, a relatively impoverished area with a growing LGBTQ+ population in the 1960s. Open all day and night, it became known as a safe place – compared with other spaces – for members of this community to congregate, especially drag queens and trans women, many of whom were sex workers. However, such customers were not welcomed by the staff, who claimed that they deterred gender-conforming people from coming into the cafeteria. Staff frequently called in the police, who would arrest customers for the crime of "female impersonation".

Tensions finally erupted into violence when a trans woman responded to an attempted arrest by throwing coffee in a police officer's face. Items from the cafeteria were thrown, windows were broken, and the police were forced to retreat to

Transgender women and gay men stood up for their rights and fought against police brutality, poverty, oppression, and discrimination.
Plaque at the site of Compton's Cafeteria

See also: Towards gay liberation 170–77 ▪ The Stonewall Uprising 190–95 ▪ Transgender rights 196–203 ▪
The Pulse shooting 308–09

Causes of the Compton's Cafeteria Riot

Trans women and drag queens seek safety in numbers at Compton's Cafeteria.	Management and staff frequently call the police to disperse these customers.	Police harass trans and drag customers, arresting them for female impersonation.	Trans and drag customers retaliate, sparking wider fightback and resistance.

the streets, where they called for reinforcements. The riot continued outside the premises, with a police car damaged and a newsstand set alight. Over the following days, protesters picketed the cafeteria, smashing the windows when the glass was replaced. After the riot, the cafeteria began closing at midnight; it shut down in 1972.

The Compton's Cafeteria Riot ignited a tinderbox of unrest in the LGBTQ+ community in San Francisco. The frustrations of trans women in particular had reached a tipping point. In addition to being routinely harassed by police, many of these people, especially those who were sex workers, lived with the everyday threat of violence – on the streets or from clients. Such issues were systematically ignored by the city's law enforcers.

The events at Compton's spurred the LGBTQ+ community to mobilize. Shortly after the riot, the queer political group Vanguard, which had formed a year earlier, organized a symbolic street "sweep". Walking with brooms, they drew attention to attempts by the police to "sweep the streets clean" of the LGBTQ+ community. Over time, a network of transgender support services was established. In 1968, this led to the founding of the National Transsexual Counseling Unit (NTCU), the first peer-run trans support and advocacy organization in the world.

A key player in the work to improve police–community relations was Sergeant Elliot Blackstone, a long-time LGBTQ+ advocate. He had been appointed in 1962 as the San Francisco Police Liaison Officer to the "homophile community", and after the Compton's Cafeteria Riot he was assigned to mediate the grievances that led to it. In 1973, Blackstone was targeted as part of a backlash against trans acceptance, when members of the Police Department raided the NTCU offices and also tried to frame him with narcotics. ▪

Felicia Elizondo

Born in San Angelo, Texas, US, in 1946, Latina trans activist Felicia Elizondo left home at the age of 14 and moved to San Jose, California. She was a sex worker there and in San Francisco.

Elizondo volunteered to serve in the Vietnam War in 1965, but was dishonourably discharged from the US Navy six months later after confessing that she was gay. Returning to San Francisco, she became a drag performer under the name Felicia Flames. A patron of Compton's Cafeteria, she was interviewed extensively in the documentary *Screaming Queens*.

Elizondo worked for non-profit organizations including the San Francisco AIDS Foundation, and campaigned to combat racism in the trans community. In 2016, as part of events to commemorate the 50th anniversary of the Compton's Cafeteria Riot, she succeeded in getting the section of Taylor Street where the cafeteria had stood renamed to honour the uprising. City officials resisted changing it to "Compton's Cafeteria Riot", so it became "Gene Compton's Cafeteria Way". Elizondo died in San Francisco in 2021.

NOT THE LAW'S BUSINESS

THE DECRIMINALIZATION OF SAME-SEX ACTS (1967)

IN CONTEXT

FOCUS
LGBTQ+ rights

BEFORE
1250–1300 Sodomy becomes criminalized in most of Europe and prosecuted under Catholic ecclesiastical law – in some cases punishable by death.

1533 England's Buggery Act, passed by Henry VIII, makes sodomy a civil offence, with hanging the ultimate penalty.

1791 France's Penal Code omits any explicit reference to same-sex acts or any laws that prohibit same-sex activity between consenting adults.

AFTER
2018 The Supreme Court of India rules that consensual same-sex acts should no longer be criminalized.

2011 The United Nations issues its first-ever report on the human rights of LGBTQ+ people.

In the 1930s and during World War II, men who had sex with men (MSM) had been increasingly imprisoned, exiled, and killed in Germany, Italy, Spain, Portugal, and the Soviet Union. After the war, many nations – including the UK and the US – still targeted MSM. In both countries, prosecutions of MSM soared.

The change begins

By 1954, more than 1,000 MSM were imprisoned annually in the UK. That year, they included aristocrat Lord Montagu of Beaulieu. In September, the UK government established the Wolfenden Committee, led by educationalist John Wolfenden. Its brief was to investigate the legality of same-sex acts and sex work.

The 15 committee members – four women and 11 men – took evidence from psychiatrists, police and probation officers, religious leaders, and three prominent gay men – art historian Carl Winter, Anglo-Canadian journalist Peter Wildeblood, and eye-surgeon and author Patrick Trevor-Roper, who highlighted the blackmail and suicides that had resulted from laws

---

Dudgeon v. United Kingdom

In 1976, Belfast shipping clerk and gay activist Jeffrey Dudgeon lodged a complaint with the European Commission of Human Rights regarding the criminalization of same-sex acts in Northern Ireland. He had been interrogated by the Ulster Constabulary, who regularly raided the homes of gay men. Dudgeon charged that the law had a "restraining effect on the free expression of his sexuality". His complaint was judged admissible, and a hearing was set for 1981 in the European Court of Human Rights in Strasbourg, France. The court upheld Dudgeon's case, ruling that criminalizing same-sex acts represented an unjustified interference with his private life.

It was a landmark case for LGBTQ+ human rights – the first in the community's favour. It led the UK Parliament to extend its Sexual Offences Act to Northern Ireland and set in motion the decriminalization of same-sex acts in all EU member nations.

See also: Sodomy and the medieval Catholic Church 42–45 ▪ The criminalization of sodomy 68–71 ▪ Revolutionary France 100–01 ▪ Persecution during the Holocaust 156–61 ▪ Towards gay liberation 170–77

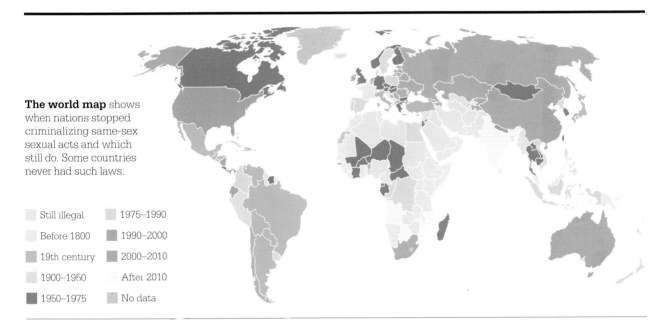

The world map shows when nations stopped criminalizing same-sex sexual acts and which still do. Some countries never had such laws.

- Still illegal
- Before 1800
- 19th century
- 1900–1950
- 1950–1975
- 1975–1990
- 1990–2000
- 2000–2010
- After 2010
- No data

criminalizing same-sex acts. The men's names were concealed in the final report, which appeared in 1957.

Between consenting adults
The bestselling document concluded that private same-sex acts between consenting men over the age of 21 should no longer be criminalized and that it was "not the law's

> It is not, in our view, the function of law to intervene in private lives of citizens, or to seek to enforce any particular pattern of behaviour.
> **Wolfenden Committee**

business" to adjudicate private morals. The report also rejected the classification of homosexuality as a disease, but suggested that male sex work should be illegal. The report's recommendations on sex work became law in 1959, but Conservative prime minister Harold Macmillan would not pursue decriminalizing same-sex acts – a decision supported by the press, religious leaders, and politicians.

The Homosexual Law Reform Society, founded in 1958, lobbied tirelessly for the reforms. In 1967, the Sexual Offences Act decriminalizing sex between adult consenting males was finally approved for England and Wales. It became law in Scotland in 1980 and in Northern Ireland in 1982.

A long struggle in the US
Canada decriminalized same-sex sexual activity in 1969. It took the US much longer, although the American Law Institute had voted to repeal consensual sodomy in 1955. Illinois was the first state to overturn its

sodomy laws in 1961. Spurred by LGBTQ+ activism, from the 1970s onwards, 36 states followed suit. In 2003, the Supreme Court's ruling that private sexual conduct is protected by constitutional rights effectively struck down all remaining sodomy laws across the US.

Since then, LGBTQ+ rights have advanced globally, although in 2022, 69 nations – many in Africa – still criminalized same-sex sexual acts. ▪

LGBTQ+ activists in Port of Spain, Trinidad and Tobago's capital city, protest in 2018 against the nation's colonial-era ban on same-sex acts. The ban was overturned the same year.

PROTES
PRIDE,
COALIT
1969–89

TS,
AND
ION

In the Stonewall Uprising in New York City, LGBTQ+ people resist police raids at a local gay bar.

The Campaign Against Moral Persecution (CAMP) first meets in Sydney, Australia, led by Christabel Poll and John Ware.

The first kathoey cabaret opens in Thailand, with AMAB gender-nonconforming performers.

The Combahee River Collective, a Black lesbian feminist group in the US, release their statement on oppression.

1969　　**1971**　　**1974**　　**1977**

1970　　**1972**　　**1976**　　**1978**

Street Transvestite Action Revolutionaries, a radical collective of gender-nonconforming people in New York City, is formed.

The House of LaBeija is founded in the US. It is the first "house", or community, in Black and Latine LGBTQ+ ball culture.

Michel Foucault's History of Sexuality (Volume 1) explores the relationship between sex, sexuality, and power.

The first Pride flag is designed in San Francisco by Gilbert Baker; it has eight coloured stripes.

The 1969 Stonewall Uprising in New York City, US, sparked LGBTQ+ activism around the world. Existing groups were inspired to increase their efforts and new organizations sprung up. Many of these movements, consciously or otherwise, emulated their counterparts in the US, leading to an Americanization of LGBTQ+ culture. Stonewall itself became an LGBTQ+ touchstone, later celebrated annually around the world in Pride marches. The rainbow flag, designed by San Francisco drag queen and activist Gilbert Baker in 1978, is now the best-known symbol of LGBTQ+ culture in the world.

Theory and identity

LGBTQ+ people were not the only activists at work in the 1970s. Environmentalism, feminism, civil rights, and anti-war protests all saw people take to the streets to demand change. LGBTQ+ people were present in many of these causes, sometimes forming dedicated submovements that addressed LGBTQ+ issues. The groups were often formed as a response to homophobia within wider movements or communities.

Important theoretical work emerged from many such groups. The Black lesbians of Boston's Combahee River Collective, for example, made waves with their Collective Statement, a 1977 document that defined their work as an interlocking struggle against racism, sexism, heterosexism, class oppression, and imperialism. American scholar Gloria Anzaldúa explored the tensions she felt as a Chicana feminist lesbian in her semi-autobiographical 1987 book *Borderlands/La Frontera*. At the same time, white feminists were writing pamphlets advocating for political lesbianism, which encouraged women to prioritize relationships with each other, ceasing relationships with men.

The 1970s and '80s saw the publication of many foundational works of queer theory. French philosopher Michel Foucault's *The History of Sexuality* was published in 1976, and would be expanded on by major queer theorists in the coming decades. Novelists and scholars employed gender-neutral pronouns, and *The Asexual Manifesto*, which was issued in 1972 by the New York Radical Feminists' Asexual Caucus, called for political asexuality as the only escape from sexual oppression.

Harvey Milk, an openly gay politician and advocate for LGBTQ+ rights, is assassinated in San Francisco.

1978

Monique Wittig's provocative essay "The Straight Mind" famously argues that "lesbians are not women".

1980

The AIDS epidemic begins, initially called "gay-related immune deficiency" by the US Centers for Disease Control.

1981

Lesbians and Gays Support the Miners raises money for and marches alongside striking mine workers in the UK.

1984–85

1979

The Gay Fathers Coalition is created in the US. It later becomes the Family Equality Council.

1980s

The term "*takatāpui*", a traditional Māori term meaning "intimate companion of the same sex", is reclaimed by increasing numbers of LGBTQ+ Māori.

1982

Olympic decathlete and gay activist Tom Waddell organizes the first Gay Games in San Francisco and 1,350 athletes compete.

1988

Section 28 in the UK bans local authorities from anything that "promotes" homosexuality or its acceptance.

Minds, bodies, and souls

In 1973, the American Psychiatric Association (APA) voted to remove homosexuality from its Diagnostic and Statistical Manual of Mental Disorders (DSM), no longer classing it as a mental disorder. The move was a result of lobbying from LGBTQ+ activists and support from researchers, but not all members of the APA approved. In an apparent compromise, several new disorders relating to LGBTQ+ people appeared in the new edition of the DSM, treating their identities as mental illnesses in need of treatment. These classifications propped up damaging (and profitable) conversion therapy programmes that claimed to offer heterosexuality as their "cure".

While the DSM painted homosexuality as an illness, an actual disease brought the issue of LGBTQ+ healthcare to the forefront of the community's concerns. From around 1981, the AIDS crisis had a catastrophic – and preventable – effect on the LGBTQ+ community. Misled, maligned, and ignored by governments, thousands of men who had sex with men were left to die from what playwright Larry Kramer called "a plague that was allowed to happen". AIDS organizations such as ACT UP refused to allow these deaths to go unnoticed, organizing public events such as "die-ins" that demanded that the US government take notice.

In the UK, governmental neglect became governmental oppression in 1988. On the back of the AIDS crisis, capitalizing on stigmas that they had allowed to fester, the British government passed Section 28, a series of laws that banned the "promotion" of homosexuality in local authorities – and, by extension, in their schools.

Beyond the West

By the end of the 1980s, the key battles of the LGBTQ+ rights movement in the West had largely moved beyond sodomy laws to other issues: healthcare, same-sex marriage, adoption, and freedom from discrimination. But elsewhere in the world, the basic right of LGBTQ+ people to exist remained in jeopardy. Some Asian nations were more accepting – including Japan, Vietnam, and Thailand, where LGBTQ+ communities were growing – but in China and India, as in much of Central Asia and Africa, decriminalization was a dream yet to be realized. ∎

I'M GAY AND I'M PROUD

THE STONEWALL UPRISING (1969)

IN CONTEXT

FOCUS
LGBTQ+ protests

BEFORE
1959 In the US, LGBTQ+ people clash with law enforcement at the Cooper Do-nuts Riot in Los Angeles.

1966 The Compton's Cafeteria Riot takes place in San Francisco after police harass LGBTQ+ people.

1967 An LGBTQ+ protest is held at Los Angeles' Black Cat Tavern after a police raid.

AFTER
1969 The Gay Liberation Front is formed in New York City.

1970 The first Pride parades take place across the US.

2019 Five million people attend "Stonewall 50 – WorldPride NYC 2019", which commemorates the 50th anniversary of Stonewall.

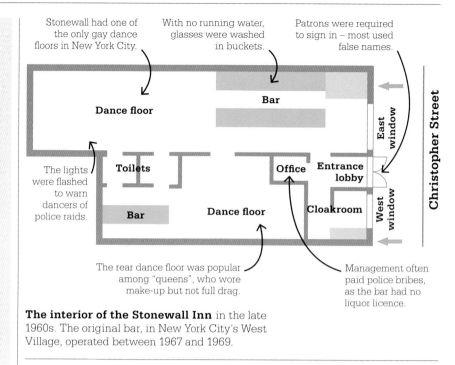

Stonewall had one of the only gay dance floors in New York City.

With no running water, glasses were washed in buckets.

Patrons were required to sign in – most used false names.

The lights were flashed to warn dancers of police raids.

The rear dance floor was popular among "queens", who wore make-up but not full drag.

Management often paid police bribes, as the bar had no liquor licence.

The interior of the Stonewall Inn in the late 1960s. The original bar, in New York City's West Village, operated between 1967 and 1969.

The Stonewall Inn in New York City, US, was the site of one of the most important events in modern LGBTQ+ history. The Stonewall was a mob-run Greenwich Village bar, primarily serving a gay, male clientele as well as some drag queens.

During the 1960s, the LGBTQ+ community was especially vulnerable. Sex between men was criminalized across the US, there were very few places to gather and meet other LGBTQ+ people, and the police often ignored crimes committed against the community. Organized criminals saw an opportunity: LGBTQ+ customers were easier to exploit, could be forced to pay "protection" fees, and were unlikely to make official complaints if they were served watered-down alcohol.

Police raided the Stonewall Inn and other mob-run LGBTQ+ bars frequently to check IDs and look out for "immoral" behaviour. They also received bribes to look the other way, with bar management generally tipped off in advance when a raid was planned. But the raid on Stonewall on 28 June 1969 came without warning – and was met with an uprising.

Stonewall was not the first mass act of resistance by LGBTQ+ people against discriminatory laws and police violence. The years running up to it had seen other uprisings including the Compton's Cafeteria Riot in San Francisco and the Cooper Do-nuts Riot, in which protestors threw food and rubbish at police arresting LGBTQ+ people in a Los Angeles café. By 1969, pressure was building. Conservative beliefs about race, gender, and society were being challenged by young radicals, and LGBTQ+ people had grown increasingly frustrated by oppression and the slow pace of change. Stonewall was a visible act of protest from a community that was no longer prepared to be silenced, and the uprising became a symbol that would resonate around the world – and be retold so many times that its events have grown legendary.

The raid and the legend

That night, it's clear that the usual pattern of a raid ending after an ID check and a handful of arrests did not take place. But beyond that, the reality of the Stonewall Uprising is harder to pin down.

According to the popular account, the uprising began when a regular either threw a shot glass that smashed the mirror behind the bar, or lobbed a piece of brick at police officers. This sparked

See also: Towards gay liberation 170–77 ▪ The Compton's Cafeteria
Riot 182–83 ▪ Transgender rights 196–203 ▪ The creation of the Pride flag 224–25

Everyone in the crowd felt that
we were never going to go
back. It was like the last
straw. It was time to reclaim
something that had always
been taken from us.
Michael Fader
Patron of Stonewall Inn

collective rebellion, as inn-goers
and members of the local
community gathered to protest
on Christopher Street, just outside
the venue, and resisted arrest.
As the crowd grew, the story goes,
some began to throw more bricks
and stones at the police. Drag
queens formed a dancing can-can
kick line in the street and chanted
and mocked their assailants.

However, the level of violence
during the event, like many other
details, changes depending on who
is telling the story, from full-blown
riot and arson to more jovial
chanting and singing, with
minimal violence. The number of
protesters varies from around 100
to 600 or more, despite the fact the
Stonewall's capacity was only
around 200. The diversity of those
present also changes – from a
primarily white, gay male clientele
to a racially diverse gender
nonconforming community.

Who threw the first stone?
Three well-known patrons, Marsha P.
Johnson, Sylvia Rivera, and Stormé
DeLarverie, are often identified as
having started the uprising. But
Johnson stated that she didn't arrive
until around 2am, when the »

**Police attempt to push past
protesters** outside the Stonewall in
one of the few surviving photos of the
night. The resistance that met the
police raid has shaped LGBTQ+ culture.

Marsha P. Johnson

When asked what the "P"
stood for in her name, Marsha
P. Johnson (she/her) would
often quip "pay it no mind".
Johnson was a self-described
drag queen and a fixture of the
New York City LGBTQ+ scene.
Born in 1945 in New Jersey,
she moved to New York City at
the age of 17, where she
adopted her name. She
struggled with her mental
health, but became a popular
figure, and was often referred
to as the "Mayor" (or "Queen")
of Christopher Street.
　　Following the Stonewall
Uprising, she became a
founding member of the
Gay Liberation Front, before
leaving to co-found Street
Transvestite Action
Revolutionaries (STAR), an
LGBTQ+ youth support
organization, in 1970. She
posed for Andy Warhol's
1975 collection Ladies and
Gentlemen, but while the
silk-screen prints sold for
thousands of dollars, Johnson
received very little income
from them. She was found
dead in the Hudson River in
1992, with her death quickly
ruled a suicide – a verdict that
was challenged and later
changed to "undetermined".

Before Stonewall, LGBTQ+ rights campaigns tend to be **diplomatic** and **wary of causing offence**.

After Stonewall, the Gay Liberation Front becomes the **first LGBTQ+ organization** to use the word **"gay" in its name**.

The next year, the **first Gay Pride marches** take place in in Chicago, New York City, San Francisco, and Los Angeles.

Within two years, every major American city has a gay rights group.

uprising was already well underway. Sylvia Rivera was also not present for the raid itself. According to multiple accounts of events that night, a gender nonconforming woman was being detained, and when she shouted out for help, the crowd was galvanized into action. Some claim the woman was Stormé DeLarverie, but she both confirmed and denied this account at different times.

Rioting or dancing?

Many facts remain disputed, but others are now accepted. There is no evidence bricks – or, as Rivera once claimed, Molotov cocktails – were used as missiles, although some projectiles were thrown. Rather than a single can-can kick line, there were several, and a number of participants remember the chants being sung, to the tune of the contemporary American children's show *Howdy Doody*: "We are the Stonewall girls / We wear our hair in curls / We don't wear underwear / To show our pubic hair." The popular name "Stonewall Riots" has also been contested. Many

people who were present reject the term entirely and say they were dancing in the street and cheering instead of rioting – their preferred terms for the event being "uprising" or "rebellion".

Storytelling and oral histories are an important part of LGBTQ+ history, and there has been a great deal of mythologizing of that summer night. There is no doubt that the story of Stonewall is powerful, and for many people the exact details are less important than what it symbolized: that the LGBTQ+ community had mobilized against its oppressors.

Stonewall and Pride

Over the next few days, hundreds of people gathered outside the inn to protest. Anger and a desire for change grew, and was channelled into the establishment of several

The 30th NYC Pride March in New York City in 1999. By the '90s, Pride was as much a celebration as a call to action, with younger marchers joining veterans of the Uprising.

pioneering LGBTQ+ rights movements in the months that followed. LGBTQ+ people felt spurred to protest visibly and in public, in a stark contrast to the more conservative and reserved forms of campaigning that had previously dominated, organized by homophile groups such as the Mattachine Society.

Within a month, a community of activists formed the Gay Liberation Front (GLF). GLF were the main instigators of the first Christopher Street marches in 1970, on the anniversary of the uprising, in New York City, Chicago, San Francisco, and Los Angeles. The movement quickly became more organized, and branches of GLF formed across the world and set up their own marches, notably in the UK. The events, which increasingly became known as Gay Pride or simply Pride, are generally held towards the end of June – often the last weekend of the month – in recognition of the date of the Stonewall Uprising. In cities across Germany and Switzerland, Christopher Street Day parades celebrate LGBTQ+ culture and the uprising's legacy.

GLF, however, was short-lived. By 1970, former members had formed the Gay Activists Alliance (GAA), and the radical Street Transvestite Action Revolutionaries (STAR) was founded by Sylvia

Rivera and Marsha P. Johnson, who part-funded the group's provision of housing and support for LGBTQ+ youth, particularly trans individuals, with their own sex work. STAR dissolved in 1973, but its impact remains noteworthy. It was the first LGBTQ+ youth shelter in the US, and had an important focus on those more marginalized within the community, such as trans youth of colour.

Stonewall and Pride today

Stonewall has remained a touchstone for many LGBTQ+ people. It has been memorialized in film, music, art, and literature. However, given the plethora of different accounts of the uprising, there is yet to be a universally accepted version. In 2015, a film directed by Roland Emmerich, *Stonewall*, was criticized as being inaccurate and was accused of "white-washing" history for inventing a small-town hero. More recent attempts to separate facts from folklore include the *New York Times* video *The Stonewall You Know is a Myth. And That's OK*, made for the 50th anniversary of the uprising.

It was a rebellion, it was an uprising, it was a civil rights disobedience – it wasn't no damn riot.
Stormé DeLarverie
American singer and LGBTQ+ activist
(1920–2014)

The original Stonewall closed in 1969, but a new LGBTQ+ bar celebrating its legacy opened on the site in 2006. Today, the venue is part of the Stonewall National Monument.

Banners at Pride marches claiming "the first Pride was a riot" remain relatively common to this day. They touch on an important debate regarding the role both of Pride parades and of Stonewall itself. Some claim that parades should be protests for rights yet to be attained and events that speak for people who do not have a voice, such as those in countries where same-sex acts are still illegal. For others, the jovial atmosphere of Pride parades is crucial, providing a party environment that acts as a counterpoint to the shame that many feel growing up LGBTQ+.

The debate continues, but neither the importance of Pride parades in the LGBTQ+ movement nor the importance of Stonewall as a catalyst for Pride are in question. In 2016, the Stonewall Inn and the streets around it were designated a US National Monument, the first of its kind recognizing LGBTQ+ rights and history. ∎

No police at Pride

The relationship between LGBTQ+ communities and the police has often been troubled. Where laws have criminalized LGBTQ+ people, the police have led their enforcement. They have also sometimes gone beyond the law in their use of oppression and violence.

Given these historic and ongoing abuses of power, many LGBTQ+ people feel unsafe around police and law enforcement agencies. This has led to demands that there should be "No police at Pride" to ensure the parade is a "safe space" for people attending. Others, however, have argued that Pride festivals are a useful place to rebuild connections with law enforcement and move forward together. The topic remains controversial, and attempts at compromise that are made – such as groups of LGBTQ+ police being allowed to join the march as long as they are not uniformed – remain unsatisfactory for many LGBTQ+ people.

Parade-goers at Brighton Pride acknowledge the events of Stonewall. Brighton's parade is one of the UK's largest and best known, bringing 500,000 people to the city.

EQUALLY VALID, EQUALLY JUSTIFIED, EQUALLY BEAUTIFUL

TRANSGENDER RIGHTS (1970)

IN CONTEXT

FOCUS
Gender and LGBTQ+ rights

BEFORE
1944 British trans man Michael Dillon secures a doctor's letter to say that he is intersex, the only legal grounds in the UK for accessing gender affirmation surgery.

AFTER
2004 The British parliament passes the Gender Recognition Act, enabling trans people to apply for a Gender Recognition Certificate (GRC).

2010 In the US, the Affordable Care Act prevents insurance companies from denying transgender-related care.

2015 The European Court of Human Rights rules to protect all trans people against discrimination on grounds of gender identity.

It is clear that many transgender persons do not fully enjoy their fundamental rights both at the level of legal guarantees and that of everyday life.
Thomas Hammarberg
Council of Europe Commissioner for Human Rights

Many countries avow **equal rights for their citizens** without distinctions of any kind.

But across the world, **transgender people face discriminatory laws**, even after other marginalized groups have gained their civil rights.

To avoid being **persecuted**, **marginalized**, and **criminalized**, many transgender people **hide from society**.

Emboldened by the rise of the LGBTQ+ movement, transgender people become **more visible** and **assert their rights**.

Transgender rights refer to the equal treatment of transgender people. The transgender rights movement calls for full legal gender recognition, equal access to healthcare, and the eradication of discrimination, stigma, and violence against transgender people. It includes everyone who does not identify with the sex and gender assigned to them at birth, including trans women and trans men, as well as non-binary gender identities.

Excluded and persecuted

Like any civil rights struggle, the campaign for transgender rights was born out of the experience of bigotry and hate. Subjects of intrigue, confusion, and stigma, transgender people have long suffered discrimination in almost every area of life – at home, at work, on the street, and within society in general – leading many to hide their true identity.

Research across the world shows that transgender people are still more likely than other people to suffer from mental health issues and homelessness due to prejudice and rejection. A 2021 government report in the UK, for example, found that transphobic hate crimes had increased by 16 per cent on the previous year, alongside a rise in hate crimes against the wider LGBTQ+ community. It also found that 88 per cent of transgender people did not report hate crimes.

Transgender people are also more likely to suffer sexual and domestic violence, as well as higher rates of self-harm and suicide compared to the general population. According to the Trans Murder Monitoring Project, which has been collecting data since 2009, a record 375 transgender people were murdered across the world in 2021. The report found that trans women of colour formed the majority of trans people murdered in the US.

See also: Intersex rights 48–53 ▪ The first gender affirmation surgeries 136–41 ▪ Pronouns and neopronouns 216–17 ▪ Conversion therapy is banned 286–87

The persecution of transgender people was not always universal. Across the world, there are examples of gender nonconforming people who were once respected by their communities. The hijra, gender nonconforming people in South Asia, were accepted for centuries, as were the gender nonconforming Indigenous American people now known by the term Two-Spirit. This changed during colonial times. Gender as a binary structure was closely tied to Christian teachings, and missionaries vilified transgender people, instilling a legacy of stigma, discrimination, and violence towards them that still exists today.

Enough is enough
The Western transgender rights movement dates back to the Compton's Cafeteria Riot of 1966, which broke out at Gene Compton's Cafeteria in San Francisco, US, when trans and drag queens retaliated against police harassment. Three

Many transgender people lived in accordance with their gender identity secretly. American musician Billy Tipton (1914–89), shown here on piano, was not discovered to be trans until he died.

years later, in 1969, a police raid of Stonewall Inn in New York City triggered a hugely influential uprising by LGBTQ+ people.

The following year, LGBTQ+ communities across the world marched in memory of the Stonewall Uprising, initiating the annual Pride parades and many of today's LGBTQ+ organizations. These included Street Transvestite Action Revolutionaries (STAR), a radical collective of gender nonconforming people in New York City, founded by American trans women Marsha P. Johnson and Sylvia Rivera. At the time, the term "transvestite" was used to describe a wide range of different identities, including cross-dressers, drag queens, and trans women. STAR campaigned and »

The murder of Brandon Teena

In 1993, a young American trans man called Brandon Teena was murdered with his friends Philip DeVine and Lisa Lambert, in Humboldt, Nebraska. Teena had been targeted by two of his peers after starting to present as a boy. They had forced him to undress and later raped him. After Teena reported the rape to the police, the perpetrators murdered him and his friends.

Despite testimonies of Teena being transgender, he was routinely misgendered by the authorities and media following his murder. The headstone on his grave is inscribed with his previous name and describes him as "daughter, sister, & friend". Teena's story, however, led to increased awareness about hate crimes against trans people in the US, especially after it was made into the film *Boys Don't Cry* (1999).

Brandon Teena died aged just 21. In 2018, journalist Donna Minkowitz apologized for ignorance about trans people in her report on his murder.

STAR demonstrate outside a women's prison in New York City in 1970. The group's founders hold the corners of the banner: Sylvia Rivera (left) and Marsha P. Johnson (right).

Day of Remembrance (TDoR) was held in San Francisco, California, to remember transgender people who had been murdered. The following year, the transgender flag – pink, light blue, and white horizontal stripes – made by American trans woman Monica Helms was flown for the first time at a Pride parade in Phoenix, Arizona.

fundraised in the early 1970s to support LGBTQ+ people who were homeless or sex workers. Also active in the political fight for gay and queer rights, it criticized the New York City-based Gay Activists Alliance (GAA) for deliberately sidelining transgender people in order to achieve their own political goals more quickly. Rivera claimed that gender nonconforming people, trans people, drag queens, and other members of STAR were being told to stay at the back of the protest marches, causing deep conflict among the LGBTQ+ community.

Action steps up

In the 1990s, academics and writers emerged to champion transgender rights specifically, and the visibility of transgender issues slowly grew. In 1992, lesbian and transgender activist Leslie Feinberg published the pamphlets "Transgender Liberation: A Movement Whose Time Has Come" and "Transgender Warriors". In Washington, D.C., American genderqueer and intersex activist Riki Anne Wilchins founded GenderPac – the first national organization to represent the transgender community – in 1995. American gender theorist Kate

Bornstein's book *Gender Outlaw* (1994), comparing her former life as a perceived heterosexual man and Scientologist with the lesbian writer, performer, and non-binary person that she now is, also proved to be important. Writing about her gender affirming surgeries and gender fluidity, topics that had never been covered so openly or poignantly, Bornstein helped change the public's perception of trans people.

By the turn of the century, trans people started to receive more recognition both socially and legally, and countries began to adopt anti-discrimination legislation to protect them. In 1999, the first Transgender

We have to be visible. We should not be ashamed of who we are.
Sylvia Rivera
"Queens in Exile: The Forgotten Ones", 2002

ID documents

A key demand of transgender people is the right to change their gender marker on ID documents. Without this right, they may be refused healthcare, education, employment, and even their right to vote. Having to show ID documents that do not match their gender identity can also expose them to abuse and violence.

By the early 21st century, many countries had introduced laws to enable people to change their gender identity officially. However, a medical diagnosis of gender dysphoria (a sense of mismatch between biological sex and gender identity) was generally necessary. This requirement is slowly being dropped. In 2022, more than 15 countries – including Argentina, Brazil, Uruguay, France, Denmark, Portugal, Iceland, Luxembourg, Ireland, and Greece – permit gender recognition through a legal process based on self-declaration. In the US, federal law allows gender markers on passports to be based on self-declaration, but requirements for other forms of ID are determined by individual states, which vary in their practice. As of July 2021, 21 US states allow people to change their gender marker on their driver's licence using self-declaration, and as of April 2020, 10 states permit changes to birth certificates based on self-declaration.

There have also been calls for non-binary legal gender recognition, often marked X on passports and other forms of ID. Several countries now recognize non-binary gender identities officially by law, including Australia, Canada, Argentina, Brazil, Chile, Denmark, Germany, Malta, Iceland, Pakistan, and India. The US began issuing passports with a third gender marker in 2021, and a number of US states allow for some form of non-binary legal recognition on driving licences, birth certificates, and state IDs.

In some countries, there is pressure to dispense with gender markers entirely, in the same way that race, religion, and marital status are often no longer recorded. In 2020, the Dutch government stated its intention to remove them.

Access to healthcare
Healthcare – specifically access to transition-related treatments such as hormone replacement therapy and gender-affirming surgeries – is one of the most important issues facing transgender people. In the early 20th

Activists in Pakistan observe Transgender Day of Remembrance, held across the world on 20 November to commemorate trans people who have been lost to violence and suicide.

Riki Anne Wilchins

Born in 1952, Riki Anne Wilchins (they, theirs, them) founded GenderPAC, the first national transgender advocacy group in the US. The group produced "The First National Study on Transviolence", a project based on surveys from over 500 respondents. Instrumental in raising awareness of the discrimination faced by transgender and intersex people, Wilchins also helped lay the foundations for Intersex Awareness Day.

Wilchins' work includes the newsletter "In Your Face" and the 2002 anthology *GenderQueer: Voices From Beyond The Sexual Binary*. German film director Rosa von Praunheim's 1996 documentary *Transexual Menace*, about the lives of transgender people, was inspired by Wilchins' activism.

Key works

1995 "The First National Study on Transviolence"
2002 *GenderQueer: Voices From Beyond The Sexual Binary*

---

century, a few transgender people were able to access surgeries and interventions, but these did not become recognized and more widely accessible until decades later. In the UK, for example, gender affirmation surgery for trans women was not legalized until 1967, because of an ancient law forbidding the mutilation of the penis – the same did not apply to the vulva.

Until the late 20th century, only a handful of doctors around the world performed gender-affirming surgeries, making it extremely difficult for trans people to access them. If they could afford it, some trans people travelled abroad to access the treatment they needed at specialist centres such as the world-renowned clinic for gender-affirming surgery set up in Casablanca, Morocco, by French gynaecologist and surgeon Georges Burou.

Even when gender-affirming surgery was obtained, it did not necessarily bring equality. When British trans model and socialite April Ashley, who underwent surgery at Burou's clinic in 1960, tried to claim maintenance payments from her former husband

Arthur Corbett, a British aristocrat, Corbett succeeded in filing for annulment on the basis that Ashley was male. The case set a precedent that remained in place in the UK until the Gender Recognition Act of 2004.

Being transgender was classified as a medical disorder in manuals used to diagnose psychiatric illnesses in the US. These included the Diagnostic and Statistical Manual of Mental Health Disorders (DSM) and the International Classification of Diseases (ICD), »

Transgender woman April Ashley leaves court in February 1970. The judge ruled that her marriage to Arthur Corbett had been invalid because she "was at all times male".

which were maintained by the World Health Organization (WHO) until 2013 and 2019, respectively.

People can now seek gender-affirming healthcare in many countries. For people under 18, gender-affirmative care refers to social support from family and professionals – such as using correct pronouns and names and supporting their aims – alongside access to puberty blockers that temporarily pause puberty. Fully reversible and only given to young people who have already entered puberty, puberty blockers can protect them from non-reversible physical changes, which often cause deep distress. In many countries, young people can now access cross-sex hormones between 16 and 18 years of age and have gender-affirming surgeries later if they require them. Provision for young people has caused controversy, and more than a dozen US states have either banned or are considering banning any kind of gender-affirming care for young people (generally defined as under 18, but in Alabama, 19 or younger).

Anti-gender forces

The increased visibility of trans people and increased recognition of their rights have produced a significant backlash in politics and public debate. Trans-exclusionary radical feminists (TERFs), or "gender critical" people, who fight for "sex-based rights", have been particularly vocal. They claim that transgender rights infringe upon those of cisgender women and wider society. These views are shared by the "anti-gender movement"; believed by the United Nations (UN) to be funded by far-right and religious forces, it also opposes reproductive rights, LGBTQ+ rights, and sex education.

The main points of contention for both these anti-trans groups are access to gendered spaces – such as bathrooms, domestic violence refuges, prisons, and women's

The fight for trans equality is a feminist cause.
Fox Fisher
British visual artist and trans campaigner (1980–)

hospital wards – and access to legal gender recognition without a medical diagnosis of gender dysphoria. Despite there being no substantial evidence that trans women pose risks to other women in gendered spaces, trans women's access to them has triggered a polarizing debate, often linked to wider cultural conflict. More than 200 anti-trans bills have been introduced in the US, mainly in relation to bathroom access, participation in women's sport, and support for trans youth.

In Britain, pressure to strip back legal rights for transgender people has even been supported by the country's Equalities and Human Rights Commission (EHRC). In 2022, the EHRC issued guidance that permits organizations to exclude trans people from gendered spaces. Such guidance relies on an exemption in the country's 2010 Equality Act, which says that trans people can be lawfully excluded from single-sex services to achieve a "legitimate aim" and if all other options have been exhausted.

Such caveats are sometimes used to prevent transgender women from participating in cisgender women's sport. Opponents to trans women's inclusion claim that

Gains and reversals for transgender people

GAINS
- More visible, audible, and assertive
- Growth in support organizations in many countries
- Greater entitlement to gender recognition
- Better access to gender affirmation surgery and hormone therapy

REVERSALS
- Increasing hate crimes and violence against trans people across the world
- Opposition from right-wing religious and political forces and trans-exclusionary radical feminists

A demonstrator holds a Black Trans Lives Matter sign at a rally in New York City in 2020. The event was part of a nationwide protest at the murder of two Black trans women in Philadelphia.

women who have transitioned post puberty have an unfair advantage due to potential differences in strength and muscle mass, while supporters argue that all transgender and cisgender bodies vary in athletic ability.

At international level, decisions concerning trans women's inclusion are made by the sporting bodies concerned. The International Olympic Committee has allowed trans women to compete with other women since 2004, provided they have been in hormone therapy for at least a year prior to the competition. However, other international sports bodies have an outright ban on transgender women competing at elite levels. In 2020, World Rugby banned trans women who had transitioned post-puberty, as did the Fédération internationale de natation (International Swimming Federation) in 2022.

Still fighting

Transgender rights have progressed in the past few decades, yet across the world trans people are still routinely discriminated against. In the Middle East, Asia, and Africa, 14 countries specifically criminalize transgender people, often under cross-dressing laws dating from colonial times. In Europe, the parliament in Hungary passed legislation in 2020 that makes it impossible for transgender or intersex people to legally change their gender, cancelling rights they had previously held and violating the European Convention on Human Rights.

The need not only to gain equal rights but to then protect them against erosion and abolition means that trans activism is as necessary today as it was in 1970, when Marsha P. Johnson and Sylvia Rivera founded STAR. Until the world finally casts aside oppressive gender norms based upon the sex assigned at birth, and allows all people to express themselves without fear of criminalization, violence, or humiliation, the fight for transgender rights goes on. ∎

Sometimes people try to destroy you, precisely because they recognize your power – not because they don't see it, but because they see it and they don't want it to exist.
Janet Mock
American writer and transgender rights activist (1983–)

Travesti

In Latin America, the *travesti* – a term that encompasses transvestite/cross-dressing, non-binary, transgender, and in some cultures, intersex people – have long endured social exclusion, violence, and stigma. Vulnerable and marginalized, in spite of laws to include and recognize them, *travesti* accounted for more than two-thirds of transgender murders in the world in 2021.

Such persistent persecution has led some *travesti* activists to reject state interventions, which they claim have simply mobilized right-wing opposition against them. Activists Suzy Shock in Argentina, among the first countries to officially recognize self-declared gender identity, and Claudia Rodríguez in Chile urge *travesti* to embrace their differences and desires and rely only on themselves. They have claimed the term "to monster" to describe their rejection of normalization and their exaltation of the *travesti* body and power.

Aleika Barros of Brazil prepares to compete in Miss International Queen, the world's biggest beauty pageant for transgender women, in Pattaya, Thailand, 2007.

YOU HAVE NOTHING TO LOSE BUT YOUR HANGUPS

CAMP AUSTRALIA AND THE SYDNEY MARDI GRAS (1970s)

IN CONTEXT

FOCUS
Gay liberation in Australia

BEFORE
1770 Explorer James Cook proclaims British sovereignty over Australia.

1788 Britain's sodomy laws are implemented in Australia, making male–male sex a capital offence (female–female sex is not covered by the laws).

AFTER
1985 After public fear about HIV/AIDS puts Mardi Gras in doubt, it continues under the theme "Fighting for Our Lives".

1987 Attendance at Mardi Gras tops 100,000; events include a car rally and flower arranging.

1988 Sydney Mardi Gras is renamed Sydney Gay and Lesbian Mardi Gras.

2017 Same-sex marriage is legalized in Australia after a national poll in which 62% voted in favour of change.

L GBTQ+ identities have been present throughout Australia's history. While evidence of LGBTQ+ culture among Indigenous Australians on the mainland is scarce, the Tiwi Islands, to the north of Darwin, have a tradition of "sistergirl" and "brotherboy" identities, which might be described today as non-binary.

During the colonial period, convicts and political prisoners from Britain and Ireland were relocated in a policy known as transportation. Sex between men was punished, albeit unevenly: in 1796, labourer Francis Wilkinson was tried for

An unheard-of event. Homosexuals demonstrating in the streets as homosexuals, and unashamedly so.
Brian Woodward
CAMP member, 1972

buggery but acquitted, while whaling officer Alexander Brown was executed for the offence in 1828.

A force for change

Australia gained its independence in 1942. But while Britain began to liberalize its anti-LGBTQ+ laws in the 1950s and '60s, Australia was slower to act, and police continued to arrest men for same-sex acts. Frustrated by the lack of progress, activists began to organize.

In July 1969 – weeks after New York City's Stonewall Uprising – the Australian Capital Territory (ACT) Law Reform Society formed in Canberra. A few months later, the Australian arm of America's Daughters of Bilitis, a lesbian campaigning and support group, was founded in Melbourne.

Sydney's Campaign Against Moral Persecution (CAMP) would become the best-known early group – "camp" was a label used in Australia before "gay" became widespread. The group's launch was announced in a feature in the *Australian* newspaper in 1970 by co-founders Christabel Poll and John Ware. The pair, along with Ware's boyfriend Michael Cass, were photographed and spoke

See also: Towards gay liberation 170–77 ▪ The decriminalization of same-sex acts 184–85 ▪ The Stonewall Uprising 190–95 ▪ The AIDS epidemic 238–41 ▪ Marriage equality 288–93

A protester is arrested at the 1978 Sydney march that was the forerunner of Mardi Gras. The *Sydney Morning Herald* named many of those involved, and some lost their jobs as a result.

openly about their sexuality. This move underlined the group's initial focus on the importance of coming out. By encouraging LGBTQ+ people to come out into the open, CAMP aimed to counter harmful stereotypes in the media and show that LGBTQ+ people were normal people who deserved respect and privacy. In 1971, the group had its first official meeting, and within a few months CAMP had 1,500 members – some, but not all, of whom were LGBTQ+ – across Australia, with branches in big cities and university campuses. It set up a telephone helpline and published a magazine, *Camp Ink*.

Public opinion in Australia was shifting, but oppression continued. In 1972, law lecturer George Duncan, who was gay, died after being thrown into Adelaide's River Torrens. His assailants were widely believed to have been vice squad officers. Public outrage led to reform, and in

1975 South Australia decriminalized same-sex acts, with other states following – Tasmania was the last to do so, in 1997.

Sydney Mardi Gras

CAMP inspired other organizations, including Melbourne's Society Five and Sydney's Gay Solidarity Group (GSG). On 24 June 1978, the GSG staged a street festival in Sydney to commemorate the Stonewall Uprising and protest against discrimination. At 11pm, a group began to march towards Hyde Park, while a sound system played gay liberation anthems. Despite the event having a permit, New South Wales police confiscated the sound system, blocked the crowd, and pulled protesters into nearby police vans, arresting 53 of them.

Only a handful of people were charged, but the police response further galvanized activists. Multiple protests took place in July and August, with further arrests made. Dubbed the Mardi Gras Parade, the event went ahead again in 1979 and 1980, and in 1981 was moved

to February so it could take place in the summer. By the mid-1980s, it was attracting over 100,000 people despite criticism that it excluded some LGBTQ+ groups. Debate continues over its present name, the Sydney Gay and Lesbian Mardi Gras, but its attendance reached an estimated 500,000 in 2019, and events now spread over three weeks. Once met with violence, Mardi Gras is now the biggest LGBTQ+ celebration in Oceania. ▪

A participant in the 1978 protest attends the Mardi Gras celebrations 40 years on, in 2018. Veterans of the original march are known as "78ers".

Lex Watson

One of the giants of Australian LGBTQ+ activism, Lex Watson was born in Perth in 1943. But it was in Sydney that he made his mark, after moving there to teach politics in 1964. He became a founder member of CAMP in 1970, organizing a protest outside the Liberal Party Headquarters that is regarded as Australia's first public LGBTQ+ demonstration.

In 1972, Watson became co-president with Sue Willis. He left the group in the mid-1970s,

but his activism continued: he wrote for the gay press, argued against the idea of a "cure" for homosexuality, and defended LGBTQ+ rights on TV – keeping his composure even when an angry audience member poured sewage on him.

In the 1980s, Watson raised awareness about HIV/AIDS and was instrumental in the founding of the Gay Rights Lobby, which fought for legal reform. He was made a Member of the Order of Australia in 2014, a few months after his death from cancer.

FEMINISM IS THE THEORY; LESBIANISM IS THE PRACTICE

POLITICAL LESBIANISM (1970s)

Feminism is the theory; lesbianism is the practice.

IN CONTEXT

FOCUS
Lesbian feminism

BEFORE
1870s A group of Christian women, known as the Sisters of Sanctification, create a women-only commune in Belton, Texas, US; the residents practise celibacy and are advocates of women's equality.

AFTER
1993 British lesbian feminist Nicki Hastie is one of many to criticize definitions of lesbianism as a political choice; she argues for a greater focus on "the sexual and erotic side of being a lesbian".

2008 The first use of the word "TERF" ("trans-exclusionary radical feminist") is recorded online. Building on the radical separatist ideas of the 1980s, they campaign for women-only spaces without trans women.

While a number of the lesbian feminists in the 1970s and 1980s were lesbians in terms of sexuality, the period also gave rise to new political concepts of lesbianism. The political lesbian might never experience attraction to other women, or form romantic or sexual relationships with them, but used the term "lesbian" to describe their cessation of relationships with men. Rather than centring a heterosexual relationship with a man in their lives, these women devoted themselves to forming profound friendships with other women, and dedicated their time to the feminist cause. This was being "woman identified" – as described in the American feminist group Radicalesbians' 1970 manifesto, "Woman Identified Woman".

Politics and pamphlets

1970 was an important year for the lesbian feminist movement. The year before, American feminist Betty Friedan had condemned lesbian feminists at a meeting of the National Organization for Women (NOW), of which she was

See also: The Lavender Scare 166–67 ▪ Black lesbian feminism 210–13 ▪ *The Asexual Manifesto* 218 ▪ "The Straight Mind" 232 ▪ Compulsory heterosexuality 233

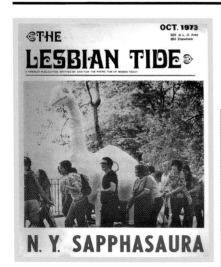

N. Y. SAPPHASAURA

president. Friedan described lesbian feminists as a "lavender menace" – the colour being long associated with lesbianism as well as gay men – who made feminism less palatable by reinforcing stereotypes about feminists being masculine and anti-men. Her comments led lesbian feminists to leave NOW and form their own groups. In 1970, one such group famously interrupted the Second Congress to Unite Women in New York City, where they gave out

Sapphasaura, a giant, papier-mâché lavender dinosaur, was built by the Lesbian Feminist Liberation group in 1973 for a protest at New York's American Museum of Natural History.

copies of "The Woman Identified Woman" while wearing T-shirts that proudly bore their new name – Lavender Menace.

The schism developing between heterosexual and lesbian feminists reached across the Atlantic. In 1979, the Leeds Revolutionary Feminist Group in the UK put out their pamphlet "The Case against Heterosexuality"; a year later, they published "Love Your Enemy? The Debate Between Heterosexual Feminism and Political Lesbianism", largely written by Anglo-Australian feminist Sheila Jeffreys.

"Love Your Enemy" became a key text of political lesbianism. All feminists, it argued, could and should be lesbians. This meant that they should not have sex with men – but they were under no obligation to have sex with women. Heterosexuality was characterized as a central force maintaining the

A lesbian is the rage of all women condensed to the point of explosion.
"The Woman Identified Woman"

oppression of women by men. "Love Your Enemy" also stressed the difference between other lesbian feminists and political lesbians – it claims that many of the former are not "woman identified" because they choose to work alongside men for liberation. Many lesbians, on the other hand, took issue with the co-opting of their sexuality and the idea that lesbianism was a choice, arguing that political lesbians were not truly lesbians. Some political lesbians, however, did discover their attraction to women as a result of the movement.

Separatism spreads

A significant number of lesbian feminist groups post-1970 were separatists: they refused to live or work alongside men (or heterosexual feminists). Radical lesbian movements with these beliefs spread into Mexico in the 1970s, and further into South America in the 1980s and 1990s. They also flourished during the 1980s in France, and Quebec, Canada, due to the writings of Francophone feminists such as philosopher and theorist Monique Wittig. ▪

The Furies Collective

One of the best known lesbian separatist groups was the Furies Collective – 12 activists who, from 1971, lived in a commune based at 219 11th Street in Washington, DC. The house, first rented as a base for *The Furies* newspaper, became the group's home. The members shared money, held lesbian feminist workshops, and ran the Women's Skills Center, which taught classes on practical skills

that separatists might need, from self-defence to DIY and car repair.

The Furies – Ginny Berson, Joan Biren, Rita Mae Brown, Charlotte Bunch, Sharon Deevey, Helaine Harris, Susan Hathaway, Nancy Myron, Tasha Peterson, Coletta Reid, Lee Schwing, and Jennifer Woodul – were all American, mostly white, and working or middle class. Differing class backgrounds and ideologies would cause the collective to splinter apart in summer 1972.

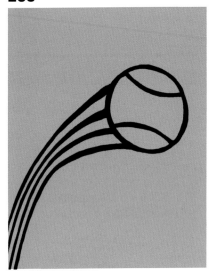

TO BE FREE, TO COME OUT, TO PLAY SPORTS

LGBTQ+ SPORTSPEOPLE COME OUT (1970s–1980s)

IN CONTEXT

FOCUS
LGBTQ+ visibility

BEFORE
1920 Gay tennis player Bill Tilden becomes the first American to win Wimbledon.

AFTER
1999 The International Olympic Committee (IOC) abolishes sex testing for female competitors.

2004 The IOC agrees that anyone assigned male at birth who undergoes reassignment surgery before puberty can compete as a woman.

2013 In the US, basketball player Jason Collins comes out as gay in a first-person account in the magazine *Sports Illustrated*.

2022 British hockey players Kate and Helen Richardson-Walsh become the first same-sex couple to win Olympic gold while playing on the same team.

The 1970s marked a turning point in the visibility of LGBTQ+ participation in professional sport, notably in the US. Until then, almost every LGBTQ+ athlete had hidden their sexuality, fearing that homophobia would limit their opportunities and alienate fans and sponsors. Same-sex sexual relationships were still illegal in many US states, and sporting prowess among men was generally equated with machismo.

Even after the legalization of same-sex acts, most LGBTQ+ athletes did not reveal their sexual identity until after their retirement from sport, as was the case with stellar NFL (National Football League) player David Kopay, who came out as gay in an interview with *The Washington Star* in 1975, three years after he had finished playing. And when people such as MLB (Major League Baseball) player Glenn Burke were open about their sexuality, the press was not necessarily prepared to publicize it, as homosexuality was deemed to be damaging to sport's image. When the press did publish stories of sportspeople – such as British figure skater John Curry – coming out, this briefly caused a scandal.

Out, proud, and winning

By the end of the 1970s, the right of sportspeople to express their sexualities had been taken up by the gay rights movement. In 1982, Olympic decathlete and gay activist

Top British footballer Justin Fashanu, playing for Norwich City Football Club in 1979. In 1990, Fashanu became the first gay footballer to reveal his sexuality while still playing professionally.

American basketball player Layshia Clarendon was the first WNBA (Women's National Basketball Association) player to come out as non-binary, in 2020.

Tom Waddell organized the first Gay Games in San Francisco. Although the International Olympics Committee (IOC) stopped him from calling the games the Gay Olympics, they were a triumph. Some 1,350 athletes from 12 countries competed in 17 sports – a level of participation that has since expanded to 10,000 people, 90 countries, and 30 sports.

In spite of such initiatives, greater visibility of LGBTQ+ athletes at the very top of their sport was slow to emerge. Even in the early 1980s, few female athletes revealed they were gay. Press hysteria about lesbianism generally, and lesbians in sport in particular, culminated in 1981, when American tennis stars Billie Jean King and Martina Navratilova were outed within three months of each other. Fearmongers claimed women's tennis would never recover – and were quickly proved wrong.

New challenges

By the 1990s, greater acceptance had transformed the landscape for LGBTQ+ athletes, but the battle is still not over in large parts of Africa and the Middle East, as controversy over LGBTQ+ fans' representation at the football World Cup in Qatar in 2022 showed. The rights of trans women in sport is also a contentious matter in the West. Opponents of their participation claim they have an advantage over other women in terms of strength, while others argue that there is plenty of scientific evidence to disprove this claim. ▪

Glenn Burke

Born in Berkeley, California, in 1952, Glenn Burke grew up to be a Major League Baseball (MLB) player. Talented at sport from an early age, he entered professional sport after playing college baseball, joining first the Los Angeles Dodgers' minor league in 1971 and then the major league in 1976.

Initially an open secret, Burke's sexuality soon started to affect how he was treated, and in 1978 he was moved to Oakland Athletics, where he faced increasing homophobia. This and an injury led to his retirement from Major League Baseball after only four years. He later told *The New York Times* that prejudice had driven him out.

Burke went on to compete in the Gay Games of 1982 and 1986, first as a sprinter and then in basketball. However, an accident and an addiction to cocaine reduced him to penury, and he died of AIDS-related causes in 1995. In 2015, he was inducted into Baseball Reliquary's Shrine of the Eternals.

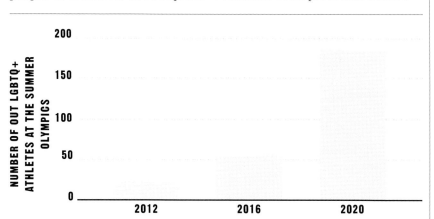

There were at least 186 out Olympians at the Tokyo 2020 Summer Olympics – this is more LGBTQ+ athletes that were out than at all the previous Summer Olympics combined.

I AM STRONGER FOR ALL MY IDENTITIES

BLACK LESBIAN FEMINISM (1970s–1980s)

IN CONTEXT

FOCUS
Intersectionality

BEFORE
1828 In the US, Sojourner Truth wins back her 5-year-old son from an enslaver in the Supreme Court of the State of New York.

1863 Harriet Tubman leads a military raid to rescue 750 enslaved people on the Combahee River, South Carolina, in the Civil War.

1966 America's Black Power movement arises from the civil rights movement, demanding not just racial desegregation but social and political power.

AFTER
1993 The anthology *Lesbians Talk: Making Black Waves*, by Valerie Mason-John and Ann Khambatta, is the first book about British Black lesbians.

I n 1973, Black feminists in the US formed the National Black Feminist Organization (NBFO) to address the "particular and specific needs" of Black women. The founders, many of whom were involved in the Black Panthers (the Black American revolutionary party) and Women's Liberation Movement (WLM), felt these organizations to be lacking because of their focus on a single issue – racism or sexism. The women sought recognition of Black women's specific experience of subjugation. Without cross-referencing racism and sexism, they argued, it was impossible to understand the effect on individuals of inequalities in both areas.

See also: The Harlem Renaissance and the Jazz Age 148–51 ▪ Political lesbianism 206–07 ▪ Anzaldúa's *Borderlands* 246–47 ▪ Queer of colour theory 297

Black lesbians endure **inequality and oppression** because of **race**, **sexuality**, and **gender**.

↓

Anger at these intersecting forms of oppression can be channelled into **protest**, **campaign for change**, and **solidarity with other oppressed groups**.

↓

A Black lesbian is stronger for all her identities.

In 1974, a splinter group of the NBFO in Boston, Massachusetts, who felt that the organization did not acknowledge the importance of sexual identity and was not radical enough to effect the necessary social change, formed the Combahee River Collective (CRC). Founder member Barbara Smith took the group's name from the Combahee River Raid of the American Civil War, which was planned and led by Harriet Tubman, a formerly enslaved woman.

After three years of political activism and discussion, the CRC released its groundbreaking political manifesto – the Combahee River Collective Statement, which defined Black feminism as a struggle against a synthesis of oppressions. It said that Black women, unlike the mainstream WLM, which was white and middle-class, did not have to fight oppression on just one front but on several.

Unique experiences

One of the key points of the CRC Statement was that Black feminists faced additional challenges in organizing because of "the psychological toll of being a Black woman". Black lesbians in particular had no social advantage derived from their race, gender, class, or sexual identity, and minimal access to the resources or power enjoyed by the more socially privileged.

Although the founders of the CRC had split from the NBFO partly because it did not represent lesbian women, the CRC still rejected lesbian separatism – because, the Statement argued, "it so completely denies any but the sexual sources of women's oppression."

Between 1977 and 1980, the Collective held seven Black feminist retreats, for information-sharing, debate, and mutual support. The first were small, hosted in private homes, but the later ones drew »

The Combahee River Collective Statement

In 1977, the Combahee River Collective (CRC) published the Combahee River Collective Statement. This landmark document defined the politics of the CRC as active struggle against oppression based on race, gender, sexuality, and class. It highlighted the reality, for the marginalized in society, of what became known a decade later as intersectionality – how different systems of social inequality "intersect" to create unique conditions of hardship for an individual or group.

The Combahee River Collective Statement was the first publication in history to assert that Black lesbian women were the victims of interlocking oppressions. While identifying racism, sexism, and heterosexism specifically, it also argued that these oppressions are underpinned by the damaging ideologies of capitalism, imperialism, and patriarchy.

No one before has ever examined the multi-layered texture of Black women's lives.
The Combahee River Collective Statement

The Black women's support group at the Berkeley Women's Center, California, US, formed in the mid-1970s, included lesbian poet and activist Pat Parker, editor Margaret Sloan-Hunter, and author April Sinclair.

thousands of women. After the fourth retreat, in 1978, participants were invited to write articles for "The Black Women's Issue" of the feminist literary magazine *Conditions*. Published in 1979 and edited by Barbara Smith and fellow CRC member Lorraine Bethel, the issue set a sales record in feminist publishing. As the fifth CRC retreat noted that year, Black feminism was growing apace, with organizing among Black academic women and Black women in publishing, the emergence of grassroots groups and coalitions with other community activists in various cities, and Black feminist and lesbian culture represented by artists such as the ensemble Sweet Honey in the Rock and poet Audre Lorde.

In 1980, at the suggestion of her friend Audre Lorde, Barbara Smith set up Kitchen Table: Women of Color Press – a publisher with the aim of promoting books by all women of colour. The 1980s was also a prominent time for Black lesbian authors, some of whom shared their stories of same-sex relationships for the first time, such as in the prize-winning novels *The Women of Brewster Place* by Gloria Naylor and *The Color Purple* by Alice Walker (both 1982).

The CRC not only revealed areas in which Black women had lacked visibility, such as publishing, but also fought for them over issues that particularly affected them, such as the risk of physical assault and the lack of reproductive rights. It lent its weight to the campaigns for access to abortion and an end to forced sterilization, and helped set up Black women's shelters for survivors of abuse. In 1979, when 12 Black women and one white woman were murdered in four months in Boston, Smith mobilized support from the wider, white community.

The Collective dissolved in 1980, but had laid the foundations for a new decade of analysis and activism. In 1989, the theory of intersectionality was formalized, and the term coined, by American civil rights scholar Kimberlé Crenshaw, who explained that societies consist of multiple factors of social identity, which intersect to create unique conditions of privilege or oppression.

Black, British, and lesbian
In the UK, the Black Power movement had its own momentum. The British Black Panthers (BBP) formed in 1968, and the Black Liberation Front in 1971. As in the US, a political consciousness also grew among Black British women who realized that gender issues were marginalized within the movement. When the BBP disbanded in 1973, former members Olive Morris, Liz Obi, and Beverley Bryan set up the Black Women's Group in Brixton, London – the first of many Black women's centres in UK cities.

In 1978, the Organisation of Women of African and Asian Descent (OWAAD) was formed as a central hub for these groups, providing practical and political support for Black and Asian women in the issues they faced, including deportations and domestic violence. Some members described themselves as feminist but stressed that they did not identify with the

As a ... Black lesbian feminist socialist mother ... I usually find myself a part of some group defined as other ...
Audre Lorde
Sister Outsider, **1984**

Onyx, published from 1982 to 1984, was the first of three Black lesbian magazines published in the San Francisco Bay Area in the US. *Ache* ran from 1989 to 1993 and *Issues* for a brief time from 2000.

mainstream WLM, and that Black women had different political goals from white women. Others felt that too strong an identification with the Black community risked concealing the patriarchal nature of many of the problems faced by women in general.

Disagreements about the validity of diverse identities – ethnic and sexual – led to the collapse of OWAAD in 1982. Lesbians in the organization had felt relegated to the sidelines, their sexual identity deemed to be a luxury that Black women could not afford. Tensions erupted at the third OWAAD conference, in 1981, when Black lesbians demanded autonomous space for a workshop.

In 1983, the journal *Feminist Review* approached Black women to write and edit a Black lesbian special issue: "Many Voices, One Chant", published in 1984. In one article, four lesbians discussed their experiences of "coming out", arguing that it posed special problems for Black women – who, because of the effects of racism, were more dependent on their families and could less afford to risk rejection from them and from wider society.

Visibility and celebration

Today, in the age of social media, there is more opportunity for Black lesbians to be "seen", albeit not always from a feminist perspective. In 2018, *Diva*, a lifestyle magazine for lesbian women, celebrated women of colour for Black History month in the UK. The issue was guest-edited by Phyllis Opoku-Gymiah, co-founder in 2005 of UK Black Pride, the world's largest annual celebration for LGBTQ+ people of various ethnicities.

The challenge of living at the intersection of multiple minority identities can never be understated, and is highlighted by the global organization Black Lives Matter (BLM). Founded in 2013 to combat violence against Black communities, BLM explicitly supports those who have been marginalized within other Black liberation movements. ∎

… a lot of Black lesbians [in the 1980s] were living double lives and we wanted to make it okay to just be whoever you wanted to be.
Veronica McKenzie
British film director (1965–)

Audre Lorde

Born in 1934 to Caribbean parents in New York City, US, Audre Lorde began writing poetry in her childhood. From 1970 to 1986 she taught at the City University of New York, as professor of English and then as the Thomas Hunter Chair of Literature. From 1984 she was a visiting professor at the Free University of Berlin, where she was part of the inception of the Black movement in Germany.

Lorde embraced her multiple identities, naming herself "Black, lesbian, mother, warrior, poet". She called for women to celebrate their differences, such as race or class. These, she said, were used by society as tools of isolation, but should instead be reasons for growth and liberation.

Lorde dedicated her life to confronting oppression, and urged Black feminists to use the anger they felt about oppression in a constructive way to fight authority. She died in 1992.

Key works

1982 *Zami: A New Spelling of My Name*
1984 *Sister Outsider: Essays and Speeches*

WHATEVER YOU WANT TO BE, YOU BE

THE SPREAD OF BALL CULTURE (1970s–90s)

IN CONTEXT

FOCUS
Black queer expression

BEFORE
1869 Hamilton Lodge, a Black club, holds its first drag ball in Harlem, New York City.

1880s–90s In Washington, DC, formerly enslaved William Dorsey Swann, "the queen of drag", organizes drag balls.

1962 In New York City, artist and writer Marcel Christian holds what is considered the first all-Black drag ball.

1969 Black and Latine drag artists play a key role in the early gay liberation movement.

AFTER
2018 The first series of the TV show *POSE* dramatizes life in the New York ballroom communities of the mid-1980s.

2020 *Legendary*, a TV reality series based on ball culture, features ball houses competing in voguing categories.

Originating in New York City, US, in the 1970s, "ball culture" is a mainly Black and Latine LGBTQ+ subculture in which communities of people, known as "houses", compete for prizes in extravagant pageants, or balls. Contestants "walk" and "pose" – mimicking fashion show catwalks – in different categories, such as "beauty" and "fashion", using a style of dance known as "voguing". They are then judged on

Trans model Octavia St Laurent (1964–2009) strikes a pose at a drag ball in Harlem, New York City, in 1988. The ballroom house of St Laurent was co-founded by Octavia in 1982.

a mix of performance and aesthetic standards, including the ability to "pass" as a different gender.

Ball culture emerged from drag balls, which became popular in the late 19th and early 20th centuries in cities with large Black populations such as New York City, Baltimore, and Chicago. At these interracial balls, men dressed as women and women as men, and same-gender couples danced with each other.

Just as drag balls provided a safer place for Black LGBTQ+ people to gather, so ball culture has allowed Black and Latine LGBTQ+ people to establish family-like networks that provide protection against violence, discrimination, and deprivation.

See also: Molly houses 90–91 ▪ Drag 112–17 ▪ The Harlem Renaissance and the Jazz Age 148–51 ▪ Latin American LGBTQ+ movements 178–79

A still from *Paris is Burning*.
The film's title comes from a ball of the same name, held in 1986 by drag artist Paris Duprée (1950–2011), founder of the House of Duprée in 1981.

Houses are led by house mothers or fathers – or both – offering care and support to their "children". Each mother or father who founds a house chooses a last name that will be taken on by all of the house children.

Taking racism out of drag
In the 1960s, the rise in LGBTQ+ activism led to the spread of drag beauty pageants in cities such as New York City and San Francisco. These commercial events featured some aspects of ball culture but did not always welcome people of colour, who had to whiten their skin with make-up to stand a chance of winning.

Black drag queen Crystal LaBeija publicly railed against the skin-colour bias in the documentary film *The Queen* (1968). Crystal went on to promote racially inclusive balls and in 1972 founded the first house – the House of LaBeija. Houses multiplied in the 1980s, which also saw the development of vogue dancing – based on the poses of fashion models, mixed with movements inspired by martial arts.

Reaching the mainstream
Ball culture was founded on the need for LGBTQ+ Black and Latine people to secure cultural spaces, but it also fascinated outsiders. In 1989, British music impresario Malcolm McLaren released the single "Deep in Vogue", with a video featuring the voguing of New York dancer Willi Ninja. Ninja also starred in American director Jennie Livingston's 1990 documentary *Paris is Burning*, which chronicled New York's ballroom scene. That same year, American singer Madonna's single "Vogue" further popularized voguing.

In the late 1980s and early 1990s, ballrooms started to spread across the US and beyond. In Germany, House of Melody was founded in 2012, while Paris, France, now has more than two dozen official houses.

Ball culture reached a wider audience in 2009, with the highly commercialized TV series *RuPaul's Drag Race*, hosted by Black American performer RuPaul. Such media popularization has attracted criticism; TV, film, and music makers have been accused of appropriating ball culture and profiting from it. ▪

… at a ball, you have the chance to display your elegance, your seductiveness, your beauty, your wit, your charm, your knowledge.
Pepper LaBeija
from *Paris is Burning*

Willi Ninja

Born William Roscoe Leake in 1961, Willi Ninja grew up in Queens, New York City, and started dancing at the age of seven, inspired by Hollywood star Fred Astaire, gymnasts, and martial arts films – hence "Ninja". He joined the Greenwich Village gay scene in the late 1970s, and in the early 1980s formed a dance group. Frequenting Harlem's drag balls, Willi embraced the new style of vogue dancing, adding rapid arm movements, contortions, and angles to become its defining exponent. He took the dance to Europe, where it was picked up by major fashion houses, who used Willi as a model and as a trainer for supermodels Naomi Campbell, Iman, and others.

Willi created the House of Ninja in 1982, serving as its mother and extending membership to all races and sexualities. Diagnosed with HIV in 2003, he continued working, opening his own modelling agency in 2004 and mentoring models and dancers. He died from AIDS-related heart failure in 2006, surrounded by his children from the House of Ninja.

ONE SMALL STEP FOR GENKIND

PRONOUNS AND NEOPRONOUNS (1971)

IN CONTEXT

FOCUS
Inclusive language

BEFORE
1850 The British Parliament passes an act that enables lawmakers to use masculine pronouns (he/him) whatever the gender.

1890 In the US, an article by James Rogers in *The Writer* proposes the gender-neutral pronouns e/em/es.

AFTER
1980 Australian feminist Dale Spender publishes *Man Made Language*, examining how heterosexual men have constructed language in their own interests.

2019 In the US, "they" as the pronoun for a single person who is non-binary is word of the year in the Merriam-Webster dictionary, reflecting a significant rise in the number of times it is looked up.

The use of personal pronouns and neopronouns – words such as "she" and "he" and gender-neutral alternatives – is a much-debated topic in countries that have gendered languages, especially in connection with non-binary people and some feminists.

However, this is by no means a new issue; debates about pronouns long predate the modern LGBTQ+ rights movement.

While "they" has long been used in a singular rather than plural sense both colloquially and to refer to someone whose gender is unknown,

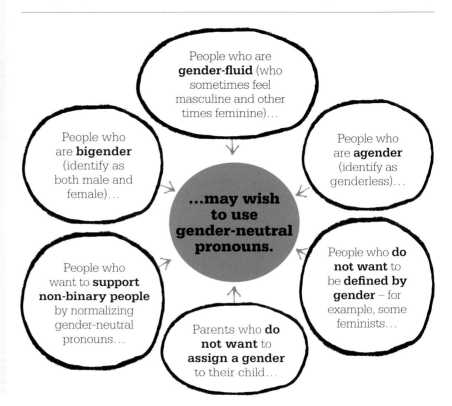

People who are **gender-fluid** (who sometimes feel masculine and other times feminine)…

People who are **bigender** (identify as both male and female)…

People who are **agender** (identify as genderless)…

…may wish to use gender-neutral pronouns.

People who **do not want** to be **defined by gender** – for example, some feminists…

People who want to **support non-binary people** by normalizing gender-neutral pronouns…

Parents who **do not want** to **assign a gender** to their child…

See also: Gender nonconformity and colonial constraints in Africa 120–21 ▪ The first gender affirmation surgeries 136–41 ▪ Transgender rights 196–203 ▪ LGBTQ+ parenting 228–31 ▪ Indigenous American Two-Spirit people 258–61

Gender-neutral pronouns in the English language

Subject pronoun	Object pronoun	Possessive adjective	Possessive pronoun	Reflexive pronoun
they	them	their	theirs	themself
(f)ae	(f)aer	(f)aer	(f)aers	(f)aerself
e/ey	em	eir	eirs	eirself
per	per	pers	pers	perself
ve	ver	vis	vis	verself
xe	xem	xyr	xyrs	xemself
ze/zie	hir	hir	hirs	hirself

unclear, or hidden, it is increasingly being used for people who are non-binary. People who criticize this usage for being grammatically incorrect ignore the complex evolution of pronouns in the English language. The *Oxford English Dictionary* traces singular usage of "they" as far back as the 1375 romance *William and the Werewolf*.

New pronouns
In the 19th century, many countries with gendered language began to pass laws that made male pronouns the default pronouns when gender was unspecified. Although this created ambiguity – for example, did laws that were worded using male pronouns also apply to women? – it remained standard practice until the early 21st century.

In the 1970s, feminists called for more gender-neutral language and attempts were made to create and integrate entirely new pronouns known as neopronouns. In 1971, American feminist writers and editors Casey Miller and Kate Swift created what they called the "human pronouns" tey/ter/tem to help women be recognized "as full-fledged members of the human

race", arguing that the domination of male pronouns relegated women to a lesser role in society. Other attempts by Americans to challenge gendered language included June Arnold's novel *The Cook and the Carpenter* (1973), which uses gender-neutral language throughout, and the Spivak pronouns e/em/eirs, proposed in 1983 by mathematician Michael Spivak.

Most new pronouns in the English language have failed to gain traction, but the singular use of they/them/their is increasing, and general awareness of gender-

If anyone objects, it is certainly ter right – but in that case let tem come up with a better solution.
Casey Miller and Kate Swift

neutral pronouns is spreading. Many other gendered languages – including Spanish, Italian, Portuguese, French, German, and Hebrew – have also tried to incorporate new gender-neutral pronouns. The initiative has been successful in Sweden, where *hen*, officially added to the pronouns *han* (he) and *hon* (she) in 2015, is now used in every day interactions. In Iceland, the gender-neutral *hán* has received similar acceptance.

Change and resistance
People increasingly state their pronouns on business emails and other correspondence, and sometimes declare them when they are introduced to others. New pronouns have met with some resistance. When French dictionary *Petit Robert* included the pronoun *iel*, combining *il* (he) and *elle* (she) in 2021, the move was condemned by the Académie Française, the country's authority on the French language, as pandering to American cultural trends. Nonetheless, it is likely that new pronouns in all languages will continue to emerge as society becomes more accepting of gender diversity and expression. ▪

SELF-CONTAINED SEXUALITY
THE ASEXUAL MANIFESTO (1972)

IN CONTEXT

FOCUS
Political asexuality

BEFORE
1960s Women in the Puerto Rican political group "Young Lords" go on a "sex strike" to protest against sexism.

AFTER
1997 The Asexual Coalition website is created as a home for heterosexuals who have stopped having relationships or sexual relations due to time, effort, or past heartbreak.

2001 David Jay, an American activist, founds the Asexuality Visibility and Education Network (AVEN), which defines asexuality as an intrinsic orientation rather than as a deliberate choice.

2019 American writer and educator Caoimhe Harlock shares a copy of *The Asexual Manifesto* online; it is subsequently archived and transcribed for the first time.

In 1972, the New York Radical Feminists' (NYRF) Asexual Caucus published a statement affirming their commitment to asexuality as a political choice. This caucus was made up of only two women: Lisa Orlando, a lesbian, and Barbara Getz, a heterosexual woman. Orlando established the Asexual Caucus to represent her position that her fellow lesbians were just as bad as men in sexually objectifying each other.

Freedom from patriarchy

The Asexual Manifesto presented an alternative to political lesbianism, but had similar goals. Orlando's final version of the manifesto said that her asexuality was a result of feminist consciousness raising – she had come to feel defined by sexual objectification, both of herself by men and by herself towards other women. She believed that sex was too pervasive in society, and that it had wrongly become synonymous with intimacy. Orlando saw her asexuality not as a natural orientation but as a method of challenging the patriarchy. Although she did not use the term "celibacy", she defined asexuality as a decision to abstain from sex, an alternative lifestyle.

While Orlando did not frame asexuality as an innate identity, the *Manifesto* challenged several societal myths – for example, the idea that a relationship without sex is incomplete – in ways that would become cornerstones of later asexual identity discourse. ∎

Interpersonal sex is no longer important to us, no longer worth the distorted and often destructive role it has played in relationships.
The Asexual Manifesto

See also: First recognition of asexuality 122–23 ▪ Political lesbianism 206–07 ▪ Compulsory heterosexuality 233 ▪ The aromantic and asexual spectrum 280–83

DEPATHOLOGIZING HOMOSEXUALITY
REMOVAL OF HOMOSEXUALITY FROM THE DSM (1973)

IN CONTEXT

FOCUS
Sexuality and medicine

BEFORE
1935 The American Standard Classified Nomenclature of Disease classes homosexuality as a personality disorder.

AFTER
1980 "Gender identity disorder" (GID) is introduced in the DSM-III to describe "transsexualism"; GID was replaced with "gender dysphoria" in the 2013 DSM-V.

2013 After consultation with AVEN, the DSM-V entry on Hypoactive Sexual Desire Disorder clarifies that this diagnosis should not be given to those identifying as asexual.

2019 The 11th edition of the World Health Organization's International Classification of Diseases amends its wording on "gender incongruence" to reflect non-binary experiences.

The Diagnostic and Statistical Manual of Mental Disorders (DSM) was first published in 1952 by the American Psychiatric Association (APA) as a tool for psychiatrists to diagnose mental illnesses in their patients. In its pages on "sociopathic personality disturbance", the DSM included the category of "sexual deviation" – in which homosexuality and "transvestism" were both listed. In the 1968 DSM-II (the second edition), homosexuality and "transvestism" were explicitly defined as mental disorders.

Resistance and removal
The pathologization of homosexuality (classifying it as a disease) caused outrage among newly politicized gay men and lesbians. Psychiatrists, too, lobbied for its removal; studies by American psychologist Evelyn Hooker, for example, proved that gay men were no more mentally disturbed than heterosexual men. After the 1969 Stonewall Uprising, increasing pressure from activists – including protests at the 1970 APA

I think you did it because you knew what love was when you saw it, and you knew that gay love was like all other love.
Letter to Evelyn Hooker
From a gay man thanking her for her work

conference – led to a vote on homosexuality in the DSM. In 1973, after considering competing theories, the APA board voted for its removal, but related disorders (such as ego-dystonic homosexuality – a desire to be heterosexual) took its place in a seeming compromise for advocates of pathologization. Homosexuality – along with other LGBTQ+ diagnoses – was not fully removed from the DSM until 2013. ∎

See also: Sexology and psychoanalysis 132–33 ▪ Transgender rights 196–203 ▪ Don't Ask, Don't Tell 272–75 ▪ Conversion therapy is banned 286–87

THAILAND HAS THREE GENDERS

KATHOEY IN THAILAND (1974)

IN CONTEXT

FOCUS
Gender identity

BEFORE
5th century CE The *Vinaya* – a set of Buddhist monastic rules for monks and nuns – outlines four genders.

AFTER
2016 The Thai constitution is expected to include recognition of a "third gender", but no protections for kathoey or transgender people are given.

2019 Thai filmmaker Tanwarin Sukkhapisit, a kathoey who identifies as non-binary, becomes the first openly transgender member of parliament in Thailand's House of Representatives.

2021 A report by Human Rights Watch and The Foundation of Transgender Alliance for Human Rights in Thailand stresses the continuing and urgent need for legal gender recognition.

In Thailand, kathoey is a gender identity frequently associated with the nightlife and cabaret scenes of the capital, Bangkok, and the tourist-filled seaside resorts of Pattaya and Patong. The first kathoey cabaret show, Tiffany's, opened in Pattaya in 1974.

Kathoey was often translated to mean a trans woman, and was historically applied to intersex people. Since the 20th century, however, the term has broadened its meaning to include any person assigned male at birth (AMAB) who defies conventional gender role expectations. It has also become better known in the West under its common but often derogatory English translation of "ladyboy".

I am not here to entertain, I am here because I got elected.
Tanwarin Sukkhapisit
Thai transgender MP

The presence of more than two genders has long been an aspect of the teachings and creation myths of Buddhism, Thailand's predominant religion. Texts dating back to the 5th century outline four genders: male, female, *ubhatovyañjanaka*, and *pandaka*. *Ubhatovyañjanaka* is believed to mean intersex, while *pandaka* is linked to voyeurism, impotence, and sometimes homosexuality.

The 2000 film *The Iron Ladies* tells the story of Thailand's first LGBTQ+ volleyball team – made up of gay, kathoey, and trans athletes – which won the 1996 national championships.

See also: Drag 112–17 ▪ Hijras and British colonialism 108–09 ▪ The first gender affirmation surgeries 136–41 ▪ Transgender rights 196–203 ▪ LGBTQ+ activism in Asia 254–55

The *Pathamamulamuli*, a Thai creation myth from the 14th century, describes how the makers of the world created male, female, and intersex people. Buddhist teachings on reincarnation and karma fostered the damaging perception that kathoey – the third sex – are those repaying a debt from a previous life, as women trapped in "male" bodies who are doomed to unrequited love. This belief is often reinforced by the depiction of kathoey as tragic characters in popular culture.

Changing ideas

Although it was never colonized by Europeans, Thailand absorbed certain Western ideas on the social control of sexuality in the late 19th and early 20th centuries, including the criminalization of same-sex acts, which entered Thai law in 1908. Yet Thailand's wider acceptance and understanding of gender and sexual difference remained unscathed as the country moved from an absolute to a constitutional monarchy in the 1930s, with same-sex acts decriminalized in 1956.

From the 1980s onwards, kathoey – while long associated with nightlife, performance, and sex work – began to see more mainstream representation in Thai culture. This happened particularly through cabarets, cinema, and beauty pageants, where the ability to "pass" as feminine is both celebrated and presented with unabashed glamour.

Identity and recognition

Kathoey is considered by many to be a distinct gender from male and female, and not all trans women in Thailand identify as kathoey. Some kathoey undergo gender affirming surgery, for which Thailand is seen as a pioneering country, and others present as feminine through dress and make-up.

Although there is an outward perception of gender acceptance and progressiveness in Thailand, there remains a lack of legal recognition for both transgender people and kathoey, who are prohibited from changing their gender on identity documents. This often leads to discrimination

A kathoey dancer getting into costume backstage at the popular Chiang Mai Cabaret Show in 2012. Many kathoey find work performing for tourists at such cabarets.

in employment, housing, and education. Kathoey remain exempt from compulsory military service, and until 2006 this was officially attributed to "mental illness" – a perception that still endures. In 2015, Thailand's Gender Equality Act became the first national legislation in Southeast Asia to protect against discrimination on the grounds of gender expression, although activists question how effectively it is enforced. ▪

The winner of the 2018 Miss Tiffany's Universe pageant, Kanwara Kaewijn, is congratulated by the two runners-up.

Miss Tiffany's Universe

On New Year's Eve, 1974, Tiffany's Cabaret Show – considered to be the first kathoey cabaret show – opened in Pattaya. What began as a three-person performance grew into one of Southeast Asia's biggest cabarets, with more than 100 kathoey performers.

In 1984, Alisa Phanthusak Kunpalin, the managing director of Tiffany's, established the Miss Tiffany's Universe beauty pageant to – in her words – "put transgender women in the spotlight" and promote the rights

and equality of transgender and kathoey people. The following year, she secured national television rights for the pageant, which is growing in popularity since it is now broadcast live on Thai television with an average of 15 million viewers each year.

Kunpalin went on to establish the Miss International Queen pageant in 2004, the largest and most prestigious beauty pageant open to transgender women from around the world. Contestants wear evening gowns and national costumes from their respective countries.

HOMOSEXUALITY BEGAN TO SPEAK ON ITS OWN BEHALF
FOUCAULT'S *HISTORY OF SEXUALITY* (1976)

IN CONTEXT

FOCUS
Sexuality and power

BEFORE
1931 Austrian psychoanalyst Wilhelm Reich argues in his book *Einbruch der Sexualmoral* that sexual repression is enforced in the interests of domination and exploitation, which are, in turn, reinforced by sexual repression.

1968 Students riot in Paris against their government and the Vietnam War. It leads to a general strike of 10 million workers and brings the whole of France to a standstill.

AFTER
1985 In her book *Between Men*, American queer theorist Eve Kosofsky Sedgwick writes that "sexuality" and "desire" are not historical phenomena but social constructs.

1990 American philosopher Judith Butler publishes *Gender Trouble*, which asserts that gender is a social construction.

In 1976, French philosopher, historian, social theorist, and activist Michel Foucault first published *The History of Sexuality: Volume 1* in French. This text is the first of a four-part examination into sexuality in the Western world. The second volume was released in 1984, the third in 1985, and the fourth as a draft version in 2018. The complete work is key for thinking about the relationship between power and sexuality, as well as how sexuality is constructed.

In *Volume 1*, Foucault critiqued the "repressive hypothesis", the idea, especially in the writings of Freud, that from the 19th century onwards,

sexuality was repressed, controlled, and silenced. Foucault believed that psychoanalysis had become the new way to confess, replacing the Catholic confessional, and he refuted the notion that sexuality was repressed, stating that society's control of the discussion around sex led to a "veritable discursive explosion", an increase in discourse around sexuality during this period. This was due to the new science of demographics and interest in birth rates, fertility, and pedagogy.

Unacceptable sex
Foucault described sexuality as a privileged point from which to analyse the workings of power in society. He saw it as a way to examine how power is organized and how human bodies, sex, and sexuality are regulated by the state. His notion of "biopower" defines a form of power that manages the individual and the population, and which emerged in the 18th century. It allows the state to create social

Writing during the 1960s, Michel Foucault expressed a strong dislike for the dominant bourgeois society and a great deal of sympathy for those on the margins of society.

See also: Defining "homosexual" and "heterosexual" 106–07 ▪ Butler's *Gender Trouble* 266–67 ▪ Sedgwick's *Epistemology of the Closet* 268–69 ▪ Heteronormativity 270–71

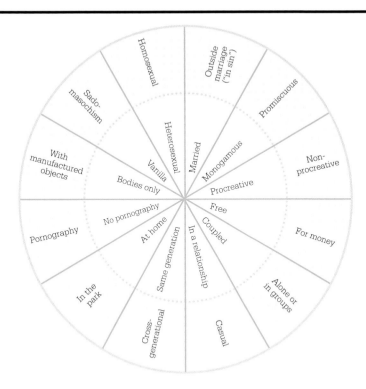

Gayle Rubin expanded on Foucault's ideas by highlighting society's tendency to sort sex into the categories of "good and legitimate" (the "Charmed Circle") and "bad and unacceptable" (the outer limits)

KEY

The "Charmed Circle": "good", "normal", "natural", "blessed" sexuality

The outer limits: "bad", "abnormal", "unnatural", "damned" sexuality

We must conceive of sex without the law, and power without the king.
Michel Foucault
The History of Sexuality, Volume 1

categories that conform to accepted norms, and these communities, in turn, maintain and legitimize the state. Groups that fall outside these norms, however, are not supported and are considered "other".

A counter discourse

Foucault saw sexuality as something that is socially constructed and tied intrinsically to knowledge, power, and discourse. Freud and sexologists of the 19th century categorized sexual activity into that which was "normal" or acceptable and that which was abnormal or pathological.

Psychiatry, the law, and literature of the time provided an analysis of homosexuality and other sexualities, which allowed for more social control of this area, but also made possible a counter approach. This reverse discourse sought to acknowledge that homosexuality was legitimate or natural and it made use of the same language that had been used to disqualify it.

Foucault's influence

In 1969, Foucault became a Professor of the History of Systems of Thought at the Collège de

France, gave lectures around the globe, and was active in leftist political movements – including during the 1968 civil uprisings in Paris – before complications related to AIDS led to his death in 1984.

Foucault's work has been seminal in queer, feminist, and cultural theory. In the United States, his work is drawn on by many thinkers, including cultural anthropologist Gayle Rubin.

Rubin published the highly influential essay "Thinking Sex" in 1982, revising it in 2011. It is a discussion of the feminist sex wars of the late 1970s and early '80s, in which anti-porn and sex-positive feminists clashed over issues including pornography, lesbian sexual practices, BDSM (sex that involves bondage, discipline, sadism, masochism), and sex work. Rubin developed Foucault's idea that sexuality is a human construct rather than a biological entity. She writes that it needs to be understood in its social and historical setting and that notions of what is "acceptable" will inevitably vary. ∎

OUR SEXUALITY IS ALL OF THE COLORS

THE CREATION OF THE PRIDE FLAG (1978)

The Rainbow Pride flag is arguably the LGBTQ+ community's most recognized symbol. Originally conceived in 1978 by Gilbert Baker, a San Francisco drag queen and activist, the symbol made an immediate impact. The flag, first produced by Baker and a team of collaborators, has since evolved into a range of forms that reflect different identities and shifts in LGBTQ+ culture.

Baker began work on designs at the insistence of several friends and city supervisor and gay activist Harvey Milk. The rainbow was chosen as a symbol of diversity and hope, with Baker's design featuring eight colours. Each carried a distinct meaning, from "sex" to "the spirit".

The rainbow flag

The original flags were hand-dyed and sewn by Baker and around 30 volunteers, including artists Lynn Segerbloom (also known as Faerie Argyle Rainbow) and James McNamara. The flags, which were heavy and needed several people to carry them, were first flown for San Francisco Gay Freedom Day Parade on 25 June 1978. While the city's LGBTQ+ community was increasingly accepted, homophobia was a serious issue across the

In Gilbert Baker's original eight-stripe Pride flag, each colour stands for a different aspect of the LGBTQ+ community.

See also: Intersex rights 48–53 ▪ Drag 112–17 ▪ The Stonewall Uprising 190–195 ▪ Transgender rights 196–203 ▪ The assassination of Harvey Milk 226–27

United States, and Milk – who would be assassinated only a few months later – used the occasion to speak to President Jimmy Carter, encouraging him to voice support for the LGBTQ+ community.

Production issues and legibility concerns meant that the colours of the original flag were reduced to red, orange, yellow, green, blue, and purple in mass production, and the six-colour rainbow became the flag recognized today. Gilbert and his co-creators never licensed the design, helping it spread across the globe and move with the times.

Myriad identities

Over the years, LGBTQ+ groups have adapted the flag to represent different identities. Some versions have been controversial. Within the lesbian community, for example, there has been debate over an appropriate design. The "labrys" flag, created by graphic designer Sean Campbell in 1999, featured a two-headed axe and was seen as butch. The "lipstick lesbian" flag, which showed painted lips and was created by designer Natalie McCray in 2010, was seen as only femme-inclusive. While there is no single, widely accepted lesbian flag as yet, there are now myriad flags representing many facets of the LGBTQ+ community, including pup pride, genderqueer pride, non-binary pride, and polyamory pride.

Progress and inclusivity

More recently, many have adopted more inclusive flags. In 2017, queer Black American civil rights activist Amber Hikes added stripes to represent the struggles faced by queer people of colour. Non-binary American artist Daniel Quasar designed the Progress Pride flag in 2018. It incorporated a chevron in pink, blue, and white (to represent trans identities), brown (for people of colour), and black (for those lost to violence or illness such as AIDS). The chevron points to the right to indicate that there is more progress to be made. In 2021, British activist Valentino Vecchietti made a new flag, including Australian campaigner Morgan Carpenter's intersex flag, to create the Intersex-Inclusive Pride flag. The flags continue to evolve to represent everyone under the LGBTIQA+ (see p.325) umbrella. ▪

Timeline of Pride flags

1978 Gilbert Baker's eight-colour Rainbow Pride flag has proved an enduring icon.

1978 With hot-pink fabric in short supply, the seven-colour striped flag emerges.

1979 Turquoise and indigo stripes combine to create a six-stripe flag.

2017 Amber Hikes adds black and brown stripes to represent queer people of colour.

2018 Daniel Quasar's chevron adds groups including trans people and those lost to AIDS.

2021 Valentino Vecchietti adds a purple circle on yellow for intersex people.

Gilbert Baker

American activist, artist, and drag performer Gilbert Baker is recognized as the designer of the original Pride flag. Born in Kansas in 1951, he was stationed as a medic in the army in San Francisco in 1970, before being honourably discharged in 1972. In the 1980s, he was a member of drag activist group the Sisters of Perpetual Indulgence.

After designing the original eight-stripe Pride flag in 1978, Baker went on to create flags for subsequent Pride celebrations, San Francisco mayor Dianne Feinstein, and the 1984 Democratic Convention.

Baker continued to work as a designer and activist in the decades that followed, and celebrated the 25th anniversary of the Pride flag's creation with a version in Key West, Florida, that was 1.6km (1.25 miles) long. In 2017, Baker died in his sleep in New York City, where he had lived for more than two decades.

LET THAT BULLET DESTROY EVERY CLOSET DOOR

THE ASSASSINATION OF HARVEY MILK (1978)

I n 1977, Harvey Milk became one of America's first openly gay elected officials when he took his place on San Francisco's Board of Supervisors, helping to pass laws banning anti-LGBTQ+ discrimination. Less than a year later, in November 1978, he and San Francisco Mayor George Moscone were shot and killed.

Their murderer was Dan White, a former policeman and fellow Supervisor who had resigned just 17 days earlier over a decision – approved by Milk and others – to build a rehabilitation centre for juvenile offenders in his district.

… we will not win our rights by staying quietly in our closets … We are coming out to fight the lies, the myths, the distortions!
Harvey Milk
Gay Freedom Day Speech, 1978

White later regretted his resignation and tried to return but Moscone would not have him back.

As a gay politician advocating for LGBTQ+ rights at a time of national backlash and increased violence in San Francisco, Milk was aware of the danger he was in. With tragic foresight, he made a recording to be played only in the event of his assassination. It recommended his successor and reiterated the plea he made throughout his career for LGBTQ+ people to come out and stand up for their rights. "If a bullet should enter my brain, let that bullet destroy every closet door," he said. Milk recognized the value of visibility and representation, but also the need to use this to enact genuine legislative change. His assassination made him a martyr for not only San Francisco's gay community but LGBTQ+ rights around the world.

Early activism
Milk moved to San Francisco's Castro District in 1972 and quickly became an important figure in local politics. The area was synonymous with the city's burgeoning gay community, who were estimated to

See also: The Lavender Scare 166–67 ▪ Towards gay liberation 170–77 ▪ The Stonewall Uprising 190–95 ▪ The creation of the Pride flag 224–25 ▪ The murder of Matthew Shepard 284–85 ▪ Marriage equality 288–93

make up a third of the district's active voters. Milk helped found the Castro Village Association, an advocacy group established in response to the refusal of permits to gay businesses. He encouraged LGBTQ+ people to buy from gay-owned businesses, including his shop Castro Camera, and increased LGBTQ+ visibility by organizing the 1974 Castro Village Fair.

Milk would later declare, "...we will not win our rights by staying quietly in our closets," but his rise met with some resentment from the existing gay establishment. Despite huge support in his district, Supervisor elections were determined by city-wide ballots, and Milk was defeated in 1973 and 1975. San Francisco replaced city-wide ballots with district representatives and Milk easily qualified in his district and was elected in 1977.

Political achievements

Milk's election made national news, and he went on to demonstrate a knack for garnering public support, with gay rights an integral part of

Flowers and the latest headlines lie on the steps of San Francisco's City Hall, following the tragic assassination of Harvey Milk and George Moscone.

a wider progressive agenda. He supported the creation of day-care centres for working mothers and the conversion of military facilities into affordable housing, and legally challenged large corporations and housing developers who had been forcing local businesses and residents out of the city.

Wider legacy

Milk's greatest political legacy was his involvement in passing the city's anti-discrimination laws, one of the strongest pieces of pro-LGBTQ+ rights legislation seen in the US. The laws banned discrimination in employment and housing based on sexual orientation. Milk played a major role in responding to the anti-gay backlash by working alongside other activists to defeat the Briggs Initiative (California Proposition 6), which would have mandated the firing of gay and lesbian teachers in

public schools. His death shattered much of the optimism that he had nurtured in the Castro community. Milk remains one of the most high-profile LGBTQ+ officials ever elected in the US, celebrated in books, an opera, and films as a symbol of hope and courage in an ongoing fight for LGBTQ+ rights across the world. ▪

Harvey Milk

Harvey Milk was born to Jewish Lithuanian parents on Long Island, New York in 1930. Growing up, he worked in his grandfather's department store, "Milks", with his brother Robert. Milk studied history and mathematics, writing a weekly student column in which he discussed issues of diversity. He enlisted in the US Navy after graduating in 1951 and was posted in San Diego until he was discharged in 1955 because of his homosexuality.

Returning to New York City, Milk spent time as a teacher, stock analyst, and production associate on Broadway musicals, and became politically active in demonstrations against the Vietnam War. Milk moved to San Francisco in 1972, opening a camera shop, Castro Camera, with his boyfriend Scott Smith.

Milk began working to protect and advocate for his fellow gay business owners. His efforts were recognized by mayor George Moscone, and Milk campaigned to be elected a Supervisor, succeeding in 1977. He and Moscone were assassinated less than a year later on 27 November 1978.

WE'RE JUST ANOTHER FAMILY

LGBTQ+ PARENTING (1979)

IN CONTEXT

FOCUS
Equal parental rights

BEFORE
1956 American organization
Daughters of Bilitis holds the
first known discussion groups
on lesbian motherhood.

1968 Bill Jones becomes the
first single father to adopt a
child in California and one
of the first in the US. He is
advised by a social worker not
to mention that he is gay.

AFTER
1999 In California, a court
allows two gay fathers to
appear on their child's birth
certificate for the first time
in the US.

2005 The UK's Adoption
and Children Act is finally
passed into law, allowing
same-sex couples to jointly
adopt children.

L GBTQ+ people have been
raising children for
generations. However, prior
to the rise of the gay liberation
movement in the 1970s, it was
almost impossible to live openly as
a gay or transgender parent, out of
fear of social condemnation and
persecution. Those who did come
out faced losing contact with their
children, as demonstrated by a
surge of custody cases in the 1960s
involving LGBTQ+ parents who
had left heterosexual marriages.

Driven by struggles in the family
courts, LGBTQ+ parents began to
build community networks. In 1955,
Daughters of Bilitis, a social and
support group, was founded in San

See also: Towards gay liberation 170–77 ▪ Transgender rights 196–203 ▪ Section 28 248–49 ▪ Marriage equality 288–93 ▪ Transgender pregnancy and reproductive healthcare 304–05

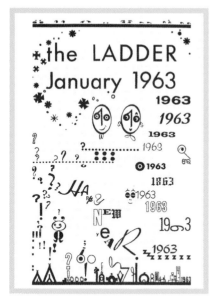

The Ladder **magazine** was published from 1956 to 1972 by Daughters of Bilitis, the first lesbian rights group in the US. The founders also held the first known support groups for lesbian mothers.

Francisco. One of its many aims was to help lesbian mothers and parents caught in custody battles. In 1979, the Gay Fathers Coalition was created in Washington, DC; it later expanded to include lesbian parents and was renamed the Family Equality Council.

The rise of the gay rights movement and a wave of custody cases involving LGBTQ+ parents focused attention on LGBTQ+ parenthood and led to a backlash against same-sex adoption and foster parents. Adoption agencies either rejected applications from LGBTQ+ people or recommended that they stay closeted. In 1968, Bill Jones, a member of San Francisco Bay Area Gay Fathers, became the first single father to adopt in the US and later revealed that he had been advised not to disclose his sexuality.

Out of hiding

In 1978, John Kuiper, a pastor with the Good News Metropolitan Community Church in Albany, New York, adopted a 13-year-old boy from foster care. However, after Kuiper announced in 1979 that he lived with his partner, Roger Hooverman, a court investigation into the adoption was launched.

The inquiry into Kuiper obtained reports from a social worker and his son's school, as well as psychological evaluations. The judge decided that Kuiper was "providing a good home" and granted permanent custody, making him the first openly LGBTQ+ individual to adopt a child in the US. The case was a turning point in establishing that LGBTQ+ individuals were not automatically "unfit" parents and the judge's decision opened doors for more adoptions by gay single parents.

In the 1970s, a new type of family began to emerge when more openly LGBTQ+ people became adoptive parents and lesbian couples began to start families using artificial home insemination. At the end of the decade, New York and California

Frank Martin Gill won a landmark case in 2010 when a Florida appeals court ruled that the state law banning LGBTQ+ individuals from adoption was unconstitutional.

The reverend is providing a good home, the boy loves his adoptive father and wants to be with him. Who knows in this world of ours? You do the best you can and hope it works out.
Judge James Battista
**on granting permanent custody to
John Kuiper of his adopted son**

became the first US states to allow same-sex couples to adopt jointly on a case-by-case basis.

Fighting for equality

In the 1980s and 1990s, LGBTQ+ couples began to explore fertility services, such as artificial insemination, IVF, and surrogacy. Many sperm banks would not serve single mothers or lesbians and excluded same-sex couples by requiring couples to be married to adopt. This discrimination, as well as custody battles between same-sex parents who had split up, emphasized the need for LGBTQ+ families to have legal protection. The fight for rights to equal marriage and parental civil rights became central to LGBTQ+ activism during the 1980s and 1990s.

In 1985, LGBTQ+ activists developed "second-parent adoption". Inspired by step-parent adoptions, second-parent adoptions allowed the applicant to secure parental »

Same-sex adoption worldwide

Joint adoption and second-parent adoption laws exist	Limited laws on joint and second-parent adoption exist	Only second-parent adoption is legal

This map shows countries where LGBTQ+ people can adopt either by joint adoption or second-parent adoption. A joint adoption allows an LGBTQ+ couple to adopt a child together; a second-parent adoption allows the applicant to adopt the biological or adopted child of their partner.

rights with a child that their partner had adopted as a single person or conceived with a sperm donor.

In 2003, the US Supreme Court made a landmark decision in *Lawrence v. Texas*, in which all state sodomy laws across the nation were overturned. The decision led to a growth in public acceptance and normalization of same-sex relationships and the tide began to

turn in the family courts. Judges who were governed by deciding the "best interests of the child" showed an increasing willingness not to automatically rule that LGBTQ+ people were unfit as parents.

Researching outcomes
In 1986, the *New England Journal of Medicine* began a study following the children of lesbian mothers, conceived through donor insemination, from infancy to adulthood. In 2018, the final report indicated that the now 25-year-olds had no significant differences from children of heterosexual, cisgender parents in their scoring on mental health diagnostic scales.

Transgender parent Bianca Bowser stated in 2014 that she had to sign the box for "father" when she registered her children's births. She described the experience as "crushing".

In 2015, the US Supreme Court ruled in favour of marriage equality. Several states used "Religious Freedom" laws to continue to allow discrimination against same-sex adoption. A 2017 ruling by the US Supreme Court made adoption by LGBTQ+ couples or individuals legal in all 50 states, although some religious adoption agencies still use a "religious freedom" argument to exclude LGBTQ+ people.

Parental recognition
In 2001, two lesbian couples in Canada filed a complaint against the Ministry of Health in British Columbia, after they were not allowed to include the names of the non-biological mothers on their children's birth certificates. After the court was informed that heterosexual couples could place the names of non-biological fathers on children's birth certificates when the children had been conceived with sperm donors, the complainants were successful.

By the end of the 20th century, organizations for same-sex parents included transgender and bisexual parents and provided legal advice around custody battles as well as support for new and prospective

We have all the same joy and love – when there's something you need to tell your kid, we figure it out as all families have to figure it out.
Freddy McConnell

Heather Has Two Mommies (1989) by American author Lesléa Newman was one of the first children's books to depict a family with LGBTQ+ parents.

parents. Today, transgender parents still face major barriers in family law, including discrimination in custody battles. Courts can ask for medical tests to confirm gender identity and ex-partners sometimes argue that a trans partner's gender identity may negatively impact their children.

Transgender parents also face challenges in establishing legal relationships and documentation for their children that represents the parent's gender. In 2020, Freddy McConnell, a British trans man who gave birth to his first child in 2019, lost his appeal in the High Court to be recorded as the "parent" or "father" on the birth certificate; he remains listed as the "mother".

In 2015, an American survey found that that nearly a third of trans people had been denied services, experienced harrasment, or been assaulted when presenting an identity document that includes an incorrect name or gender marker. In 2020, a legal victory in the US gave trans parents hope for gaining accurate gender representation on their children's birth certificates.

A new generation
The growth in acceptance and legal recognition for LGBTQ+ parents around much of the world has led to greater representation of LGBTQ+ parents and their children in media, including children's books. LGBTQ+ inclusive curricula have been introduced in schools to help create a safe and comfortable environment for children now being raised by openly LGBTQ+ parents. In 2021, Scotland became the first country to make an LGBTQ+ inclusive curriculum mandatory. LGBTQ+ History Month began in 1994 and recognizes the importance of LGBTQ+ inclusive curricula. It is celebrated in Brazil, Germany, Italy, Finland, Cuba, Hungary, Australia, Canada, the US, and the UK.

The greater visibility of LGBTQ+ parents challenges the argument that heterosexual families are best for the child. Though some legal and family planning services need better training, there is greater awareness and acceptance of LGBTQ+ parents. However, the fight for full parental rights for LGBTQ+ people worldwide goes on. ∎

We're doing this for every LGBT+ couple who had to give up on their hopes and dreams of creating a family. It's time for discrimination to end and for there to be equal treatment with heterosexual couples in the healthcare system.
Megan Bacon-Evans

Whitney and Megan Bacon-Evans won the "Unsung Hero" award at the 2022 DIVA Awards in London for their work promoting LGBTQ+ rights.

The price of parenthood

Many LGBTQ+ couples require egg or sperm donation to start their families and they can experience the same fertility issues as any other member of the population. Fertility treatments can be limited for many LGBTQ+ people and many countries still refuse to offer them at all.

In 2021, British couple Megan and Whitney Bacon-Evans began legal proceedings against the National Health Service (NHS). They alleged that the NHS's

IVF policy discriminates by providing funding for fertility treatment for heterosexual couples after two years of trying to conceive through unprotected sex; whereas LGBTQ+ couples are required to go through fertility treatments that would cost around £30,000 to "prove" their infertility. The couple won their case and in 2022, the UK government announced plans to provide equal access to NHS-funded IVF treatment.

LESBIANS ARE NOT WOMEN
"THE STRAIGHT MIND" (1980)

IN CONTEXT

FOCUS
Lesbian feminism

BEFORE
1949 In *The Second Sex*, French feminist Simone de Beauvoir writes: "One is not born, but rather becomes, a woman."

1969 Monique Wittig's novel *Les Guérillères* imagines an attack on patriarchal society through both physical violence and the use of language.

AFTER
1990 American philosopher Judith Butler's book *Gender Trouble* is published. Its analysis of how sex and gender are societally constructed is influenced by Wittig's work.

2021 French dictionary *Le Robert* is criticized when its online edition includes the pronoun *iel*, a gender-neutral merging of *il* (he) and *elle* (she).

F irst delivered as a lecture in 1978 and published as an essay in 1980, "The Straight Mind", by French philosopher Monique Wittig, was a pivotal moment for critical discussions of feminism, gender, and sexuality. The provocative closing statement, "lesbians are not women", captures its central argument: that the concept of "woman" is so fixed in heterosexual and patriarchal

If we, as lesbians and gay men, continue to speak of ourselves and to conceive of ourselves as women and men, we are instrumental in maintaining heterosexuality.
"The Straight Mind"

systems that it is not only an unsuitable definition for anyone who lives outside those ideas, but also an oppressive one.

The heterosexual contract
Wittig's writing formed part of the radical feminist movement, which focused on the impact of patriarchal political and societal structures on the individual. In "The Straight Mind", her argument is grounded in the theory that society is founded on heterosexual ideas. "Straight society", controlled by the "straight mind", is a political regime that can only conceive of a system ordered by heterosexual relationships. The "heterosexual myths" that reinforce the natural and acceptable status of heterosexual relationships are sustained by the constant oppression of all that is "different/ other" – tied not only to sexuality but also to race and class. For Wittig, this "heterosexual contract" must be broken by refusing the language and signs of straight society and creating new ones to help to combat "straight" societal domination. ■

See also: Political lesbianism 206–07 ▪ *The Asexual Manifesto* 218 ▪ Compulsory heterosexuality 233 ▪ Butler's *Gender Trouble* 266–67

HETEROSEXUALITY IS A POLITICAL INSTITUTION
COMPULSORY HETEROSEXUALITY (1980)

IN CONTEXT

FOCUS
Female freedom from heterosexuality

BEFORE
1970 The phrase "Woman-Identified Woman" is popularized in a pamphlet by the Radicalesbians, an American activist group.

AFTER
1991 American queer theorist Michael Warner uses the term "heteronormativity" to describe the pervasive idea that heterosexuality is the only "normal" or "natural" sexual orientation.

21st century "Compulsory heterosexuality", or "comphet", is widely used to describe how women are taught from an early age to desire men, making it difficult for lesbians to realize their true orientation.

In her 1980 essay "Compulsory Heterosexuality and Lesbian Existence", American lesbian feminist and poet Adrienne Rich suggested an important new idea regarding female sexuality. Her theory sought to explain how women are socialized into participating in heterosexual relationships. They are systematically, if unconsciously, forced through heterosexuality into a position of emotional, economic, and political subordination to men.

Rich argues that heterosexuality is an institution into which women are indoctrinated from a young age, growing up with narratives of sex and romance that reinforce male power. This experience causes women to desire relationships with men, even though, according to Rich, men cannot provide women with the intimacy, love, and understanding that female partners can.

Lesbian orientation
Rich saw the usual definition of lesbianism in terms of erotic bonds as part of the patriarchal dismissal of female experience and proposed a

… women's choice of women as passionate comrades, life partners, co-workers, lovers, tribe, has been crushed …
"Compulsory Heterosexuality and Lesbian Existence"

"lesbian continuum". The affection of mothers, daughters, sisters, and female friends – as well as acts of political solidarity – were motivated by a desire she called "lesbian". Her view of lesbianism as a potential in all women sparked debate between "essentialists", who believe sexuality is innate, and those who see it as socially constructed, as well as among lesbians who claim the label as their hard-won sexual identity. ■

See also: Political lesbianism 206–07 ▪ *The Asexual Manifesto* 218 ▪ "The Straight Mind" 232 ▪ Heteronormativity 270–71

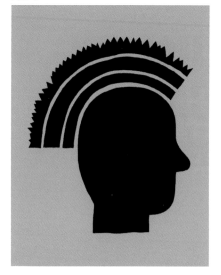

WE DID IT FOR THE UNDERGROUND

THE BIRTH OF QUEER PUNK (1980s)

The term "punk" has a long historical association with homosexuality. In the 17th century, it was used on the streets of London to refer to both sex workers and young men who had sex with older men. In the early-20th-century US, as well as being a general term for degenerates and criminals, it became prison slang

American singer Jayne County, one of the first rock singers to come out as transgender, has influenced musicians such as the Ramones and British singer–songwriter David Bowie.

describing a younger man in sexual relationship with an older inmate, often coerced. The association of "punk" with musical counterculture flourished in the late 1970s, with some tracing the start of this genre to British rock band The Sex Pistols. Wherever it began, punk abhorred conformity, consumerism, and authority. While this new scene was dominated by straight white men – and full of aggressive hypermasculinity – punk's radical appeal soon led to the creation of a distinctively queer submovement.

Homocore to queercore

American writer Liam Warfield attributes the beginnings of the queer punk scene to Toronto, Canada, where a small group of musicians – led by G.B. Jones and Bruce LaBruce – willed it into existence with the creation of their queer punk fanzine *J.D.s* in the mid-1980s. *J.D.s* coined the term "homocore" as a tongue-in-cheek descriptor of the new scene, and the term was rapidly adopted in the US as the name of a Bay Area punk zine created by Tom Jennings and Deke Nihilson. By the 1990s, "homocore" had become "queercore", a movement encompassing not only

> One of the things was not to necessarily make queer culture more acceptable, but to make queer people feel like they could do whatever they wanted.
> **Joshua Ploeg**
> American punk musician and author

music but photography, art, zines, and other media. Other major zines of the era included *Chainsaw* – published by Donna Dresch, who would become the leader of one of queercore's most influential lesbian bands, Team Dresch – and *Fertile La Toyah Jackson*, a Los Angeles-centric zine made by Black American drag queen and artist Vaginal Davis.

The loudest voices in the queercore movement were its bands, who came to prominence playing gigs in small and often unconventional venues, from abandoned buildings to suburban basements. Both the gigs and the records embraced the spirit of DIY: they were community efforts, low in production quality, and made as cheaply as possible. Among the pioneering artists of queercore were lesbian bands such as Team Dresch and Fifth Column (led by *J.D.s'* own G.B. Jones); gay male groups such as Pansy Division and Limp Wrist; the mixed-gender God Is My Co-Pilot; and androgynous,

and gender nonconforming artists such as Jayne County and Phranc, lead singer of Nervous Gender.

Music with a message
Queer punk was just as brash and irreverent as punk itself, with the same tendency towards telling raw and unpolished truths. For many, punk was an expression of anger at society and its institutions, and its songs criticized heterosexual norms. San Francisco band Tribe 8, for example, released "Lezbophobia" in 1995, about straight woman who assumed that lesbians wanted to seduce them, while Seattle band 7 Year Bitch's "Dead Men Don't Rape" was an explosive protest against rape culture. Other songs, however, simply expressed queer desires, like Pansy Division's 1993 "Fem in a Black Leather Jacket", about wanting to take an effeminate man home for the night.

As queercore spread beyond North America, it retained its punk spirit – from Sister George in the UK to the She-Devils in Argentina. The queer punk

The SPEW convention
Queercore was not one, but several movements happening in cities across North America and later the UK, Europe, and South America. The queer punks of these smaller scenes converged on 25 May 1991 for the first SPEW convention at the Randolph Street Gallery in Chicago, Illinois. This queer punk fanzine convention featured queer punk films (including Bruce LaBruce's *No Skin Off My Ass*); drag performances by the likes of

movement has continued to grow in the 21st century. Since 2000, new bands including Hunx and His Punx, PWR BTTM, Dog Park Dissidents, and The Regrettes have continued to challenge the heteronormative status quo through their music. ▪

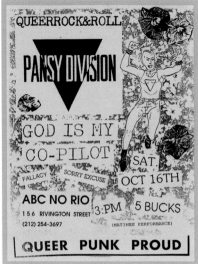

A poster advertising a gig for San Francisco's Pansy Division, who made waves when they toured the US with pop punk stars Green Day in 1994.

Vaginal Davis and female Elvis impersonator Elvis Herselvis; and readings from new queer novels such as Dennis Cooper's *Frisk* (1991). SPEW's afterparty included music by Fifth Column.

The SPEW conference was aware of the political climate of the early 1990s, with booths representing both ACT UP Chicago and Queer Nation. It also ended on a sour note, when organizer Steve LaFreniere was stabbed by homophobes. He survived, and a second SPEW convention took place in Los Angeles in 1992.

TOGETHER I AM EVERYTHING I AM

MĀORI GENDER AND SEXUALITY (1980s)

IN CONTEXT

FOCUS
Takatāpui

BEFORE
1840 The Treaty of Waitangi is signed, cementing a place for British citizens in the newly formed "New Zealand", with acknowledgment of Māori sovereignty over their people and lands.

1972 The US refuses a visa to Māori lesbian activist Ngahuia Te Awekotuku, beginning New Zealand's gay liberation movement.

AFTER
1986 In New Zealand, the Homosexual Law Reform Act makes sex between men legal.

2001 Tīwhanawhana, a *takatāpui* community group, is established by Dr Elizabeth Kerekere in Wellington.

2015 Protests about the treatment of transgender people by the police disrupt the Auckland Pride Parade.

Māori stories include that of **Tūtānekai**, who falls in love with Hinemoa, and who also has a **"*takatāpui*" relationship with his male companion Tiki**.

⌄

The term ***takatāpui*** is used in traditional Māori society to describe **a person in an intimate same-sex relationship**.

⌄

Takatāpui **is reclaimed** by many **LGBTQ+ Māori** and grows increasingly common in the 1980s and beyond.

Māori are the Indigenous people of Aotearoa New Zealand, who trace their ancestry through a series of migrations across the Pacific Ocean. In 1840, British settlers annexed New Zealand, establishing it as a colony a year later. Imposing their idea of Christian values, they violently reshaped or erased many of the things they found distasteful about Māori culture. This included its language, cultural practices, and the diverse expressions of sexuality and gender within the culture.

Precolonial identity

Prior to colonization, Māori viewed sexuality in a less rigid way. Sex was openly discussed in all spheres of daily life. It featured in oral histories, songs, and is depicted in *whakairo* (carving). In the British Museum, London, there is a *papa hou* (treasure box) that depicts a variety of queer sexual acts, carved by an unknown Māori maker in the 18th century.

There are a few accounts of Māori gender diversity in early colonial records. In an 1871 account by a tourist at Whakarewarewa, he writes of his disgust at learning the "Māori belle" he had been flirting with was a "boy". Pre-colonization roles were sometimes defined in a gendered way, but it seems that there was greater flexibility in the construction of gender identity.

Reclamation

The word *takatāpui* is an old Māori word meaning "intimate companion of the same sex". Discovered around the late 1970s in the manuscripts of tribal leader and government official Wiremu Maihi Te Rangikāheke (*c.*1815–96) by academics Ngahuia Te Awekotuku and Lee Smith, it was used to describe the relationship between two male ancestors, Tūtānekai and Tiki. Tūtānekai is known for his pairing with the ancestress Hinemoa, but Te Rangikāheke's story paints a picture of the queerness that may have existed between all three.

The word began to gain popularity from the 1980s onwards to identify anyone of Māori descent with diverse gender identities, sexualities or sexual characteristics. For *takatāpui* and for all Māori, the mid-to-late 20th century was a time of reclamation from colonization. Many *takatāpui* were living vibrant queer lives, even during the period when same-sex acts were illegal. Cities like Auckland and Wellington became beacons for *takatāpui* during the migrations of the 1960s, when Māori began to move into the cities.

In Wellington, trans Māori woman or *whakawahine* Carmen Rupe was an iconic drag queen and activist who defined inner-city queer culture and created welcoming spaces for trans and LGBTQ+ people rejected by straight and cis-gendered communities. In the late 1960s, Rupe founded Carmen's International Coffee Lounge – which sold coffee and facilitated access to sex workers who operated upstairs – and a nightclub called The Balcony.

A contemporary of Rupe's, Georgina Beyer, became the world's first openly transgender mayor in 1995, in Carterton, New Zealand, and in 1999, the world's first openly transgender Member of Parliament.

Takatāpui today

While holding on to ancestral Māori legacies and ideas, *takatāpui* today are frequently involved in the reclamation of the Māori language and the work of decolonizing and re-indigenizing Aotearoa New Zealand. They are also influenced by global queer culture and identities, leading to the establishment of QTBIPOC club nights in recent years to create safe spaces for wide and nuanced identities.

Whether in a nightclub, at a land protection event, or inside a *marae* (traditional Māori communal space), *takatāpui* identity has always been about the legacy of ancestors as well as breaking new ground. ▪

Striking artwork by Māori non-binary artist Huriana Kopeke-Te Aho, who identifies as *takatāpui*, draws on their Māori ancestry and cultural traditions.

A PLAGUE THAT WAS ALLOWED TO HAPPEN

THE AIDS EPIDEMIC (1981)

IN CONTEXT

FOCUS
A medical, social, and political crisis

BEFORE
1959 The first known case of HIV occurs in the Belgian Congo (now Democratic Republic of the Congo).

1964 AZT is developed as a cancer treatment but proves ineffective and is shelved.

Late 1960s HIV travels to the Americas, probably via Haitian people working in the Congo.

AFTER
2007 The first case of someone being cured of HIV is reported.

2012 Truvada is the first drug approved specifically to prevent HIV infection by the US Food and Drug Administration.

2016 United Nations member states commit to ending the AIDS epidemic by 2030.

AIDS, short for acquired immunodeficiency syndrome, is a chronic and potentially life-threatening condition caused by HIV (human immunodeficiency virus). HIV is a viral infection that is most commonly transmitted through unprotected anal or vaginal sex. It can also be transmitted through oral sex, by contact with infected blood, by sharing needles, and from parent to child during pregnancy, childbirth, or chestfeeding. HIV cannot be transmitted via saliva, sweat, or urine.

HIV is a retrovirus, meaning it can enter cells and change their function. It targets immune cells

See also: AIDS activism 244–45 ▪ Section 28 248–49 ▪ The LGBTQ+ struggle in modern Africa 306–07 ▪ Laws lifted against MSM donating blood 310–11

Progression of the HIV virus

Someone is infected with HIV, most commonly through certain kinds of sexual activity.

Two to four weeks later, they develop a flu-like illness, though this isn't always noticeable.

Symptoms may fade for a time. With anti-HIV treatment, this phase can last for years.

Symptoms appear, such as a mild infection, tiredness, fever, and swollen glands in the neck.

Untreated people and a small number of treated people develop AIDS, with more serious infections or cancer.

that fight disease, so it weakens the immune system. Those infected may develop a flu-like illness two to four weeks after being infected, but this can be so mild that it isn't noticed. Most people then have no signs of the virus for several years if they take medicines that target HIV. However, as the virus continues to multiply within the body, people with HIV develop mild infections, excessive tiredness, fever, and swollen glands. If treated, most HIV infections do not progress past this

point. However, if left untreated – and in a small number of treated cases – an HIV infection progresses to AIDS. This typically takes eight to ten years. AIDS develops when HIV has severely damaged the body's immune cells, weakening its capacity to fight off infections and diseases, including some types of cancer. This can be fatal, but improved medical treatments in recent years have substantially improved the life expectancy of people who are living with AIDS.

A global epidemic

HIV is thought to have originated from monkeys or chimpanzees in Central Africa that had a similar virus, SIV. People hunted the animals for meat and came into contact with their infected blood, which spread the virus to humans.

In the 1950s, in equatorial Africa, doctors began finding a rare type of cancer, Kaposi's sarcoma. Presenting as painless red or purple patches on the skin, it usually affects people with a weakened »

Angels in America – performed here in Paris, France in January 2020 – was also made into a TV miniseries in the US in 2003. The series won 11 Emmy Awards the following year.

Angels in America

The AIDS epidemic has inspired several great artistic works. *Angels in America*, a two-part play by Tony Kushner, an American playwright, was commissioned by a theatre in San Francisco in 1991. Since its Broadway debut in 1993, it has been performed in theatres around the world.

The plot centres around two couples, a homosexual male couple and a heterosexual couple, whose stories intertwine. Through their experiences and those of family, friends, ghosts, and angels,

the play explores life, death, love, sex, and community in the context of the AIDS crisis in 1985 in New York City.

Angels in America won many awards, including the Pulitzer Prize for Drama and a Tony Award for Best Play. However, outside literary circles, it was controversial. Productions in some cities sparked protests because of the play's frank depictions of homosexuality and drug use; actors in a production in North Carolina, US, were even threatened with prosecution under indecent exposure laws.

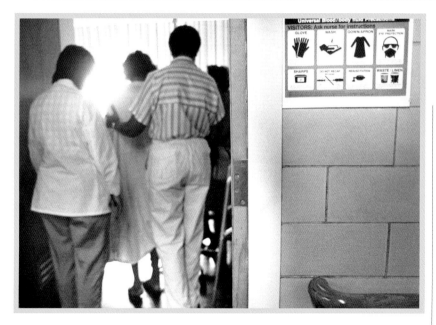

Nurses lead an AIDS patient into his room at Shattuck Hospital, Boston, US in 1988. A sign on the wall advises on how to avoid the exchange of blood and other bodily fluids with patients.

the need for HIV treatment was urgent. The first drug to treat AIDS, AZT, was tested in 1984 and approved for use in the US in 1987. Some heralded this as a breakthrough, but the virus soon developed resistance to AZT. It became apparent that no single drug was the solution to HIV – more research was needed.

A social and political crisis

Alongside the medical crisis, there was also a socio-political crisis due to misunderstandings about HIV and how it is transmitted. There was concern that it could be spread via sweat or saliva, and the public were fearful of people with HIV, leading to discrimination.

Stigma remained even when HIV/AIDS was better understood. The media described it as a "gay plague" and it became stereotyped as a disease of promiscuous homosexual men, with blame for the epidemic placed on gay and

immune system, but the cause of this weakness was unknown. In the US, cases of Kaposi's sarcoma appeared in the 1970s, sometimes with infections that were unusual in healthy people, like fungal lung infections. These cases were rare, and garnered little medical attention.

However, in July 1981, the US Centers for Disease Control (CDC) published a report on 26 gay men with Kaposi's sarcoma, six of whom also had fungal pneumonia. The cases were identified as a single disease, originally called GRID (Gay-related immune deficiency). The numbers grew rapidly and by the year's end, 337 people had been diagnosed with GRID, and 130 had died.

Not all of the people affected were gay. Some had travelled from parts of the world such as Haiti, some were drug users, and some were people with haemophilia (a rare blood clotting disorder) who had received blood transfusions. Consequently, in September 1982, the CDC began using the term AIDS to better describe the illness.

Medical challenges

Though scientists had discovered that viruses could cause cancer, they were less clear about whether retroviruses (like SIV and HIV) could infect humans. Many other possible causes were explored, including chemicals, but research finally shifted to microorganisms. However, by the time an individual was recognized as having the disease, they often had several viral, bacterial, and fungal infections, making it difficult to identify which specific organism was to blame.

Despite these challenges, separate research groups in France and the US declared that they had discovered a new retrovirus that affected AIDS patients in 1983 and 1984. Each group gave their virus a different name and set out to prove that every person with AIDS had the virus. In 1986, a consensus was reached that the viruses discovered by both research groups were the same virus, and it was renamed HIV.

Most drugs at the time were tested for eight to ten years to prove their safety and efficacy but

I have a beautiful address book a friend gave me in 1966. I literally cannot open it again. Ever. It sits on the shelf with over a hundred names crossed out.
Jerry Herman
American composer (1931–2019)

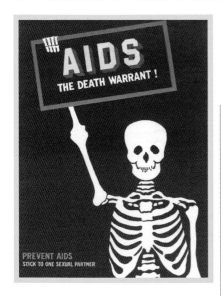

An AIDS prevention poster from the 1990s issued by the Central Health Education Bureau, Delhi, India. It sends a stark message and urges the public to "stick to one sexual partner".

bisexual men and on drug users and sex workers – because of their supposedly "immoral" lifestyles.

This stigma led to the delayed and insufficient response from governments. It took until 1985 for US president Ronald Reagan to make a public statement about HIV/AIDS, despite more than 3,500 related deaths in the US by the end of 1984.

The AIDS epidemic today

AIDS has devastated individuals, families, and communities around the world. Nevertheless, there are reasons for hope. A medical breakthrough in 1996, which involved combining three or more drugs, known as HAART (highly active antiretroviral therapy) became the standard treatment in 1997. It is so effective that AIDS deaths in the US decreased by 47% between 1996 and 1997. More drugs discovered since, that work in different ways, have led to ART (antiretroviral therapy). By 2020, the number of new HIV infections worldwide had halved from their 1996 peak, and AIDS-related deaths have reduced by two-thirds since 2004. Some regions, however, still bear a heavy HIV/AIDS burden, with two-thirds of all cases being in Africa, where access to ART is more limited.

There is more to be done. Although there is greater awareness of HIV/AIDS today, there is still stigma, and people with HIV are barred from some countries. Some people still have poor access to treatments, with cost a common barrier. Work to develop effective vaccines to prevent HIV, and to treat those who have it, continues. ∎

AIDS Memorial Quilt

America's AIDS Memorial Quilt celebrates the lives of people who have died from AIDS-related illnesses. The quilt features individual memorial panels submitted by members of the public, providing family and friends with a way to remember their loved ones.

When the AIDS Memorial Quilt first went on display in 1987 in Washington, DC, half a million people came to see it. At this time, the quilt had 1,920 panels. The resulting publicity carried the movement across the globe and the quilt grew. By 2022, it featured nearly 50,000 panels.

The quilt has become an international symbol of the AIDS epidemic and vividly illustrates the scale of deaths. The project was nominated for the Nobel Peace Prize in 1989 and has inspired similar projects. Today, the quilt is displayed on the US National AIDS Memorial webpage.

The AIDS Memorial Quilt on The Mall, Washington, DC, in 1987. It was conceived in 1985 by activist Cleve Jones in San Francisco, to remember friends who had lost their lives to AIDS.

By 2021, 84.2 million people worldwide had been infected with HIV since the start of the epidemic, and 40.1 million had died from AIDS-related illnesses. As of June 2021, 28.7 million people were accessing antiretroviral therapies (ART).

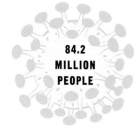

84.2 MILLION PEOPLE

40.1 MILLION PEOPLE

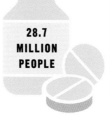

28.7 MILLION PEOPLE

SOLIDARITY IN STRUGGLE
LESBIANS AND GAYS SUPPORT THE MINERS (1984–85)

IN CONTEXT

IN CONTEXT

FOCUS
Solidarity movements

BEFORE
1970 The UK's Gay Liberation Front is formed and exists until 1973, spawning new groups.

1972 British miners seeking higher wages strike for 51 days.

1974 The UK government limits commercial electricity usage to conserve coal stocks, as miners strike for fair pay.

1980 LGBTQ+ activist group Somos joins a rally for workers' rights in São Paulo to oppose discrimination against homosexual workers.

1983 Margaret Thatcher appoints industrialist Ian MacGregor to head the National Coal Board and streamline British mining.

AFTER
2014 The film *Pride* is based on the Lesbians and Gays Support the Miners campaign.

Striking miners are **marginalized** by the UK government and **clash** with the police.

LGBTQ+ communities are marginalized and **discriminated against** by the police.

There is a feeling of solidarity between the two marginalized groups.

They decide to **support each other**, and find that they are **stronger together**.

The 1984–85 British miners' strike was a bitter dispute sparked by the British government's attempt to close at least 20 coal mines, which was opposed by many members of the National Union of Miners (NUM). The strike lasted far longer than earlier miners' strikes and caused immense financial hardship in striking mining communities.

Led by British prime minister Margaret Thatcher, the government used the police, courts, and media in a bid to stop the strike and galvanize public opinion against

the striking miners. Clashes such as that at Orgreave, Yorkshire in June 1984, when police on horseback charged into some 5,000 striking miners, made international headlines. LGBTQ+ people were prominent among those who came to the strikers' support.

Addressing a need
Not all miners were on strike, and there was no national NUM ballot. The High Court ruled the strike illegal and ordered NUM assets to be seized to pay the fines imposed. At this point, fundraising to

See also: Towards gay liberation 170–77 ▪ The Stonewall Uprising 190–95 ▪ Political lesbianism 206–07 ▪ AIDS activism 244–45

support the families of striking miners became critical as, under the 1980 Social Security Act, they could not receive hardship benefits.

During the 1984 London Pride march, gay rights activists Mike Jackson and Mark Ashton publicized the striking miners' cause, and collected funds to support it. They formed the Lesbian and Gays Support the Miners (LGSM) alliance, which soon had groups across the UK and in Dublin, Republic of Ireland. The London group alone collected over £22,000 through street collections, raffles, jumble sales, and events such as the "Pits and Perverts" concert, which raised more than £5,000.

Further support for the miners came from Lesbians Against Pit Closures (LAPC), a splinter group of women who felt intimidated by the gay men at the core of LGSM and sought greater recognition of women's issues and strengths. They raised money at women's venues in London, and donated it to a village women's action group supporting miners in Nottinghamshire.

Mutual support

As the struggle continued into 1985, poverty drove some strikers back to work. In March, the strike ended; the only government concession was the deferment of five pit closures. But new ties had formed. At the 1985 London Pride march, LGSM was joined by the NUM and Welsh miners. For the first time, the 1985 Trades Union Congress and Labour Party Conference passed gay and lesbian rights resolutions. In 1992, as more pit closures were announced, LGSM re-formed as Lesbians and Gays Support the Miners Again (LGSMA), winding down in 2015. ▪

The film *Pride* highlighted the London LGSM group's campaign and its close ties to the Welsh mining village of Onllwyn. *Pride* won the Queer Palm award at the 2014 Cannes Film Festival.

Mark Ashton

Co-founder of LGSM, Mark Ashton was born in 1960 in Oldham, UK, grew up in Northern Ireland, and moved to London in 1978. He was a gay rights activist, supporter of the Campaign for Nuclear Disarmament, and a member of the Communist Party of Great Britain. In 1982, Ashton volunteered for the London Lesbian and Gay Switchboard, providing support to the gay community. When LGSM's work was complete at the end of the miners' strike, Ashton worked as General Secretary at the Young Communist League from 1985 to 1986.

Diagnosed with HIV/AIDS, Ashton was admitted to hospital on 30 January 1987, and died 12 days later. The Mark Ashton Trust was created to raise money for individuals living with HIV and, since 2008, the Terrence Higgins Trust (THT) has also included the Mark Ashton Red Ribbon Fund. His name is featured on the UK's AIDS Memorial Quilt and on a plaque at the entrance of the THT headquarters in London.

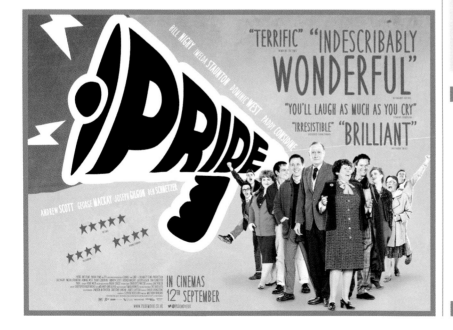

Mining communities are being bullied like we are … One community should give solidarity to another.
Mark Ashton

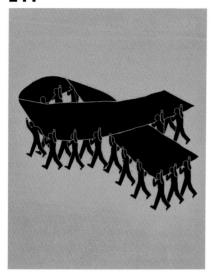

SILENCE = DEATH

AIDS ACTIVISM (1987)

IN CONTEXT

FOCUS
Fighting LGBTQ+ health inequalities

BEFORE
1982 Activists pressure the US Centers for Disease Control (CDC) to change the name GRID (Gay-Related Immune Deficiency) to AIDS.

1983 The first AIDS candlelight memorial is held.

AFTER
1988 The first World AIDS Day takes place on 1 December.

1991 Activists introduce the red ribbon as the international symbol of AIDS awareness.

2003 The US President's Emergency Plan for AIDS Relief (PEPFAR) is launched, committing to spend $15 billion over 5 years.

2005 The number of people dying annually from AIDS peaks at 2.3 million worldwide.

At the start of the **AIDS epidemic**, some **individuals** and **small groups** take action, raising public awareness and lobbying officials.

The scale of the **epidemic grows**. Individual and small group activism is **no longer sufficient**.

As awareness and the scale of the **epidemic increase**, new organizations are founded and others expand to an **international level**.

Larger national AIDS organizations are set up, primarily in the UK and US.

Since its outset in 1981, the AIDS epidemic has affected tens of millions of people worldwide, claiming as many as 42 million lives. It has prompted an array of social and political challenges, including widespread misconceptions about HIV/AIDS, rampant homophobia, discrimination against infected people, insufficient funding for testing, treatment, and research, as well as ineffective management by governments and other organizations. Consequently, public action has been necessary to counter these problems, generating positive change.

At the beginning of the epidemic, small groups and individuals took on the mission. One example is Bobbi Campbell, a nurse in the US. He was one of the first people to be diagnosed with AIDS-related Kaposi's sarcoma, a rare cancer that affects those with weakened immune systems and presents as red or purple patches on the skin. Frustrated by the lack of public health education and press reporting about cases such as his, Campbell put pictures of his cancer lesions in the window of his local pharmacy, urging men with similar lesions to seek medical attention.

See also: Towards gay liberation 170–77 ▪ Latin American LGBTQ+ movements 178–79 ▪ The AIDS epidemic 238–41 ▪ LGBTQ+ activism in Asia 254–55 ▪ Laws lifted against MSM donating blood 310–11

In doing so, Campbell became the first American to publicly come out as having AIDS.

AIDS organizations

As the scale of the epidemic grew in the US and the UK, so did the need for activism. When this need surpassed the capacity of any small group or individual, larger activist organizations were formed. These began on a local level, taking actions such as hosting public memorials and demonstrations, establishing postering or leafleting campaigns, fundraising, and lobbying.

ACT UP (the AIDS Coalition to Unleash Power), formed in 1987 in New York City, is the best known of these organizations. Its first demonstration took place at a busy junction on Wall Street, the heart of the city's financial district. Around 250 demonstrators blocked the road, lying in the street or holding signs, causing major disruption, in which 17 activists were arrested for civil disobedience. Demonstrators made several demands, calling on the US government and pharmaceutical companies to release drugs more quickly and make treatment affordable. More audacious protests, such as depositing the ashes of AIDS victims on the White House lawn, raised public and political awareness and ACT UP's influence spread. Later groups in the US, such as the Black AIDS Institute and the Latino Commission on AIDS, focused on specific sectors.

ACT UP protesters lay siege to the US Food and Drug Administration (FDA) headquarters in 1988 to demand the release of experimental medication for people living with HIV and AIDS.

ACT UP inspired the creation of similar groups in Europe. ACT UP chapters sprang up in many British cities; the London group staged "die-ins" in the late 1980s. Since 1982, the UK's Terrence Higgins Trust, now Europe's largest AIDS charity, has also actively publicized HIV/AIDS and supported sufferers.

A positive impact

The global impact of AIDS activism has been immense, changing the way people view the disease – especially in Africa, where it has been widely misunderstood. While AIDS activism has increased public awareness, reduced stigma, accelerated research, and improved access to treatment, more work is required to counter misconceptions and consequent injustices, and will be until these are eradicated. ▪

Women in AIDS Activism

Women have played a key role in all aspects of AIDS activism, spreading knowledge of how to effectively mobilize to create change. Their intervention was critical in the 1980s to combat the misconception that AIDS did not affect women. This fallacy had prevented women from making informed decisions about risk, excluded them from clinical trials, and disqualified them from government support. In the US in 1988, women called for a boycott of *Cosmopolitan* magazine for spreading false information. They handed out fact sheets, campaigned for medical organizations to accept that women, including lesbians, could get AIDS, and filed lawsuits over gender discrimination. Their acts of civil disobedience calling for change received widespread media attention.

As a result, the CDC's AIDS definition was expanded to include women, as was AIDS research, and affected women received government support.

THE CROSSROADS OF BEING
ANZALDÚA'S *BORDERLANDS* (1987)

IN CONTEXT

FOCUS
Borderlands theory

BEFORE
1903 American sociologist and activist W.E.B. Du Bois uses the term "double-consciousness" to describe the duality of being both Black and American.

AFTER
1991 Gloria Anzaldúa publishes the essay "To(o) Queer the Writer – *Loca, escritora y chicana*". It criticizes the term "lesbian" for being white, English, and middle class and for requiring others to assimilate.

2010 *Borderlands* is banned by the Tucson Unified School System in Arizona for its teaching of "ethnic studies".

2020 Queer theorists publish *Gender, Sexuality and Identities of the Borderlands: Queering the Margins*, a collection of essays that have Anzaldúa's theory at their core.

Anzaldúa uses the term "borderlands" to refer to the area around the US/Mexico border that is considered neither fully Mexican nor fully American. For Anzaldúa, this border is a metaphor for other types of boundary and duality, including queerness.

When *Borderlands/La Frontera: The New Mestiza* was published in 1987, its insights were groundbreaking. The book by Chicana (American Mexican) lesbian feminist Gloria Anzaldúa spans many genres – politics, autobiography, poetry, and multiple Indigenous histories – and deftly switches between the different languages of the US–Mexico border, including various forms of English and Spanish and local dialects.

While *Borderlands* is a feminist and anticolonial work, it is also a foundational piece of queer theory. The physical borderlands of the US and Mexico are a metaphor for the ways in which identities intersect. They are the place where the dominant identity meets the marginalized: white and Latine; male and female; heterosexual and queer. For Anzaldúa, growing up in the borderlands created a hybrid identity – the "mestiza". She, for example, was both Mexican

See also: Colonial Latin America 66–67 ▪ Latin American LGBTQ+ movements 178–79 ▪ Black lesbian feminism 210–13 ▪ Queer of colour theory 297

An altar in San Francisco's Mission district, the centre of LGBTQ+ and Latine culture in the city, displays books and mementos in honour of Anzaldúa's life and work.

and American, both Chicana woman and lesbian, and both male and female.

Chicana lesbianism

Anzaldúa belonged to a wider Chicana lesbian movement that includes writers Cherríe Moraga, Ana Castillo, Naomi Littlebear Moreno, and Carla Trujillo. Much of their work concerns the conflict between their identities as Chicana

As a lesbian I have no race, my own people disclaim me; but I am all races because there is the queer of me in all races.
Gloria Anzaldúa

women – influenced by Catholicism and traditional Aztec/Mexican and American gender roles – and as lesbians. *Borderlands* describes a fear of being disowned by her Chicane culture for her lesbian identity. Similarly, Moraga, in *Loving in the War Years* (1983), describes her "anglicization" as a result of compulsory heterosexuality (the dominance and enforcement of heterosexuality within a patriarchal society) in the Chicane community.

Although these women were active in the Chicana feminist movement, they were ostracized by heterosexual Chicana feminists in what Chicane historian Yvette Saavedra has called the "Chicana schism". Nonetheless, both groups drew on their Aztec and Mexican heritage in their calls for equality. Anzaldúa and Moraga evoke Aztlán (the mytho-historical place the

Gloria Anzaldúa

Born in 1942, Gloria Anzaldúa grew up near Brownsville, Texas. Her parents were migrant farmers until the family moved to Hargill, Texas, so that the children could complete their education.

In 1977, after gaining a master's degree at the University of Texas at Austin, where she had also taught classes on *La Mujer Chicana* (The Chicana Woman), Anzaldúa abandoned a doctorate to move to California. She joined activist circles and

I will have my serpent's tongue – my woman's voice, my sexual voice, my poet's voice. I will overcome the tradition of silence.
Gloria Anzaldúa

Aztecs left to settle in what is now Mexico) as a utopia that could be rebuilt to welcome all sexualities.

Borderlands has inspired queer theorists beyond Central America and been used to understand intersections around the world. Its format, combining multiple genres, is also a blueprint for queer theorists who mix the personal and creative with the political and historical to create accessible and anti-academic texts. ▪

taught and published works on feminism, sexuality, and the experiences of marginalized women. Anzaldúa had relationships with men and women, and considered her lesbianism a conscious choice. She died in 2004.

Key works

1981 *This Bridge Called My Back: Writings by Radical Women of Color*
1987 *Borderlands/La Frontera: The New Mestiza*
2002 *This Bridge We Call Home*

LEGALIZED PREJUDICE
SECTION 28 (1988)

During the 1980s, the UK, led by the Conservative government of Margaret Thatcher, was coming to terms with the emerging HIV/AIDS crisis. There was an undercurrent of homophobia in British society, with the British Attitudes Survey of 1987 reporting that 75 per cent of people thought homosexuality was "always or mostly wrong". Sections of the media referred to the crisis as the "gay plague" or "gay virus", with gay men in particular demonized for the spread of HIV. These homophobic attitudes came to a head in the infamous Section 28 bill, which became law on 24 May 1988.

Silencing and protest
Section 28 stated that a local authority should not "intentionally promote" homosexuality or the "acceptability of homosexuality as a pretended family relationship". This essentially prohibited all government-run schools from teaching same-sex relationships in any positive way. Ultimately no one was prosecuted under the act, partly because of a lack of legal clarity

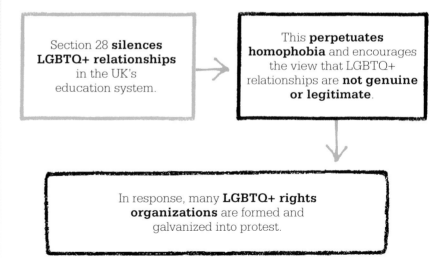

Section 28 **silences LGBTQ+ relationships** in the UK's education system.

This **perpetuates homophobia** and encourages the view that LGBTQ+ relationships are **not genuine or legitimate**.

In response, many **LGBTQ+ rights organizations** are formed and galvanized into protest.

See also: The Stonewall Uprising 190–95 ▪ LGBTQ+ parenting 228–31 ▪ Lesbians and Gays Support the Miners 242–43 ▪ Don't Ask, Don't Tell 272–75 ▪ Marriage equality 288–93

A march in Manchester, UK, to protest against the introduction of Section 28. The February 1988 event, attended by more than 20,000 people, also took aim at homophobic policing.

about what "promote" meant, but its impact was immense. Fearful of being targeted under the amendment, schools rolled back on any classroom discussion of LGBTQ+ relationships, silencing homosexual representation in the education system until Section 28 was repealed some 15 years later.

Section 28 was met with a fierce response from LGBTQ+ rights activists. On 2 February 1988, immediately after the UK's second chamber, the House of Lords, voted to support the law, four lesbian activists abseiled into its debating hall. Then on 23 May, a day before the law became active, protestors barged into a BBC studio during the Six O'Clock News and interrupted the live broadcast. A year later, a group of activists launched the influential Stonewall charity (see box, below).

Lasting impact

Although the bill was overturned in Scotland in 2000, and across the rest of the UK in 2003, its influence held back LGBTQ+ representation for years. It is only relatively recently that LGBTQ+ relationships have been discussed in schools, notably through the No Outsiders! charity, which teaches primary-school children about tolerance, diversity, and inclusion.

There is still much progress to be made: No Outsiders! founder Andrew Moffat received protests

and a death threat in 2019 and LGBTQ+ education remains a fraught topic around the world. There has been a resurgence of anti-LGBTQ+ laws governing education in several US states, and Florida's 2022 Parental Rights in Education (the "Don't Say Gay") Bill prohibits teachers from discussing "sexual orientation or gender identity" in a way that is "not age-appropriate". The bill does not outline what is "age-appropriate", but parents can still sue school districts if they feel that it has been breached. ▪

Stonewall's slogan "Some people are gay. Get over it!" was launched in 2007 as part of a campaign to tackle homophobic bullying in schools.

Stonewall

Founded on 24 May 1989 by a group of LGBTQ+ activists – including actor Sir Ian McKellen and *EastEnders* actor Michael Cashman – Stonewall is the UK's most influential LGBTQ+ charity. Named after the 1969 Stonewall Uprising, it was created in direct response to Section 28.

Stonewall lobbies for governmental and legal change, which today includes a strong focus on workplace equality. It has been successful in many of its campaigns, which have

focused on issues such as the laws surrounding adoption, equalizing the age of consent, and overturning the ban on lesbians and gay men serving in the armed forces.

Stonewall was picketed by transgender rights activists in 2008 after giving a Stonewall Award to a journalist who was critical of gender affirmation surgery. The organization has more recently explicitly stated support for trans people, but many are still concerned about how it supports the trans community.

OUT IN THE OP

1990–PRESENT

EN

Judith Butler's *Gender Trouble* and Eve Kosofsky Sedgwick's *Epistemology of the Closet* are published.

Don't Ask, Don't Tell is enacted by the US military to prevent LGBTQ+ service members from coming out.

Zoe O'Reilly's online essay "My Life as an Amoeba" describes her experience of asexuality.

Brazil bans conversion therapy, becoming the first nation in the world to do so.

1990   **1993**   **1997**   **1999**

1990   **1996**   **1998**   **2000**

The term "Two-Spirit" is coined at a conference in North America to describe gender-nonconforming Indigenous people.

The Inner Circle is formed as a support and activist group for LGBTQ+ Muslims in South Africa.

Matthew Shepard is murdered in Laramie, Wyoming; his killer blames "gay panic" for the crime.

In China, the artist and actress Shitou is the first woman to come out as a *lala* (a woman who desires women) in the mainstream media.

Today, the many letters of the LGBTQ+ acronym show a growing awareness that LGBTQ+ identities are more complex than a homosexual/ heterosexual or male–female binary. Bisexuality, pansexuality, and other multisexual identities are now well-established, and awareness of asexual (ace) and aromantic (aro) identities appears to be on the rise. Transgender identities, too, have received plenty of media attention in the 21st century – and terms such as "non-binary", "AFAB", and "AMAB" are more widely known. The term "queer", formerly a slur, has been reclaimed by many as a point of pride and resistance, and is now used in the academic disciplines of queer theory and queer history, which challenge the heteronormative status quo.

An expanding world

The 1990s were a decade of seismic innovation in technology, with the rise of the internet opening up a world of new possibilities for communication. During the 21st century, the internet has become a key site of identity-building. Isolated LGBTQ+ people have been able to find information and support from dedicated forums and other online communities.

The information age has not only shared knowledge, but also created it, as people have come together to discuss and shape new terminology to describe their lived experiences. Asexual and aromantic identities in particular have been explored and defined by online groups such as AVEN and AUREA. The increasing popularity of some of the new terms created has been

facilitated by social media, where people can not only share ideas but also explore these identities from the safety of an avatar, before bringing them into the physical world.

The queer frontier represented by the internet is not the only one to see progress. With more and more nations decriminalizing same-sex activity in the 21st century, new communities have begun to flourish out in the open. Technological advances have also been accompanied by scientific ones, leading to the refinement of gender affirmation surgeries and improved transgender healthcare.

Campaign successes

A number of the major projects of LGBTQ+ activism bore fruit in the late 20th and early 21st century: in 1999, Brazil became the first nation

Same-sex marriage becomes legal in the Netherlands – the first country to legalize marriage and not just civil unions.

2001

Robert McRuer's *Crip Theory* is published; it becomes a foundational text in queer disability theory.

2006

Kenyan writer Binyavanga Wainaina responds to the passing of new homophobic laws in Africa with his essay "I am a homosexual, Mum".

2014

Taiwan becomes the first Asian country to legalize same-sex marriage.

2019

2001

The Asexual Visibility and Education Network is formed by David Jay in San Francisco.

2008

Thomas Beatie makes headlines worldwide as a pregnant transgender man after appearing on *The Oprah Winfrey Show.*

2016

Forty-nine people are killed in a mass shooting at Pulse, an LGBTQ+ nightclub in Orlando, Florida.

2021

Blood donation restrictions for men who have sex with men are lifted in the UK and Germany.

to ban conversion therapy; and marriage equality was legalized in the Netherlands in 2001, triggering similar legislation around much of the world. Laws prohibiting blood donation for men who have sex with men have also begun to be lifted, with deferral times between sexual intercourse and donation being shortened or eradicated – as was the case for the UK and Germany in 2021, and France, Austria, Malta, and the Netherlands in 2022. The healthcare crisis created by the COVID-19 pandemic undoubtedly played a role in the timing of these legal changes.

One of the most visible successes of the 21st century has been the increased public nature of LGBTQ+ life through representation in film, books, news, and other media. LGBTQ+ culture now has clear mainstream appeal, from TV shows such as *RuPaul's Drag Race* to the cult followings of LGBTQ+ celebrities on social media and new generations of LGBTQ+ influencers on platforms such as Instagram, YouTube, and TikTok.

Still a way to go

The 2022 FIFA World Cup showed that, while many LGBTQ+ rights have been secured, there are still battles to fight. The host nation, Qatar, was awarded the prestigious tournament despite its laws criminalizing same-sex sexual acts. It is one of several countries where same-sex behaviour is punishable by death; others include Yemen, Sudan, Somalia, and Iran, where LGBTQ+ activists Zahra Sedighi-Hamadani and Elham Choubdar were sentenced to death in 2022.

LGBTQ+ life in the West, too, is not without its dangers. A 2021 Home Office survey showed hate crimes against transgender people on the rise in the UK, amid campaigns by transphobic activists to take away transgender rights such as gender-affirming healthcare. LGBTQ+ people have also been the victims of highly publicized murders – as in the case of Matthew Shepard in the US in 1998 – and terror attacks, such as America's Pulse nightclub shooting of 2016, one of a number of mass shootings to target victims in a gay bar.

While many challenges lie ahead for the LGBTQ+ community, queer theorists have nonetheless identified a trend towards what they call "queer futurity" – the belief in a more equitable and queer-affirmative future. ■

WE AWAIT THE DAY WHEN WE CAN LIFT THE CLOUDS
LGBTQ+ ACTIVISM IN ASIA (1990s)

IN CONTEXT

FOCUS
LGBTQ+ rights

BEFORE
1872 Influenced by Western culture, Emperor Meiji of Japan, where "boy love" flourished for centuries, criminalizes sodomy.

1933 Stalin recriminalizes same-sex acts in the USSR. Over 30 years after its fall in 1991, two former Soviet states in Central Asia retain the law.

AFTER
2016 China's National Radio and TV Administration bans any depictions of gay people being shown on television.

2019 Under international pressure, Brunei temporarily suspends its proposed death penalty for same-sex acts.

2021 Increasing violence against the LGBTQ+ community is reported following the Taliban takeover in Afghanistan.

During the 1980s, Taiwan was steadily evolving from a repressive one-party state to a democracy. Its president, Chiang Ching-kuo, ended martial law in 1987, and the Taiwanese population began to experience new freedoms.

Taiwan had never criminalized same-sex acts but was a largely socially conservative Chinese society. In the early 1990s, scholars returning from the West initiated daring public discussions on sex and sexuality. In 1995, this group of academics established the Center for the Study of Sexualities at the National Central University in Taoyuan City. Their activism would pave the way for Taiwan to legalize same-sex marriage in 2019 – the first Asian nation to do so.

Slow progress in Asia
Across Asia, LGBTQ+ activism has developed slowly, compared with the Western world. Although some regions of Asia have long histories of gender identities and sexual practices that could be viewed as queer by contemporary standards, a variety of factors has posed significant challenges to the advancement of LGBTQ+ rights. In East Asian countries such as South Korea, a combination of Confucian

Challenges confronted by LGBTQ+ activism in Asian regions

Homophobic interpretations of religions such as Islam and Christianity colour some nations' policies.

Autocratic governments reject the concepts of non-heterosexual orientation or identity.

Earlier British colonial rule has left some laws in place that suppress non-normative sexualities and genders.

See also: Hijras and British colonialism 108–09 ▪ Gender transgression in modern China 134–35 ▪ The decriminalization of same-sex acts 184–85 ▪ Kathoey in Thailand 220–21 ▪ Chinese *lala* communities 276–77 ▪ LGBTQ+ Muslims 278–79

LGBTQ+ activists celebrate in Bengaluru, India, in 2018, after the Supreme Court struck out the passage in Section 377 of India's Penal Code that criminalized same-sex sexual acts.

and Christian influences has strongly prioritized heterosexual marriage; only a third of South Koreans support same-sex marriage. China, which first criminalized same-sex acts in 1740, removed the vague crime "hooliganism"– used to prosecute same-sex acts – from criminal law in 1997, but its other LGBTQ+ rights are minimal.

In predominantly Muslim nations in the Middle East, stringent laws against same-sex sexual acts and gender nonconformism have contributed to a repressive climate. In Turkmenistan and Uzbekistan in Central Asia, same-sex acts are also still illegal. Kazakhstan, Kyrgyzstan, and Tajikistan decriminalized same-sex acts in 1998 but, as in Russia, where same-sex sexual relations became legal in 1993, few other LGBTQ+ rights exist.

New millennium

LGBTQ+ movements have achieved a few notable successes. In India, a 2001 petition received a favourable ruling in 2009 from the Delhi High Court, which rescinded the anti-sodomy wording in the Indian Penal Code's Section 377 – a colonial relic of England's 1533 Buggery Act. When this judicial victory was then overturned by a 2013 Supreme Court ruling, the reversal further galvanized India's LGBTQ+ activism. This led to a new Supreme Court judgement in 2018, which unanimously rescinded the original anti-sodomy statute.

Versions of the British penal code with its controversial Section 377 anti-sodomy wording were inherited by many other former British colonies in Asia and the Pacific, including Brunei, Hong Kong, Bangladesh, Malaysia, Fiji, and Singapore. In Hong Kong, the passage that criminalized same-sex acts was rescinded in 1991 and in 2010 in Fiji. In Singapore's parliament in 2007,

A Pink Dot supporter snaps the 2022 rally in Hong Lim Park, Singapore. Staged annually since 2009, Pink Dot events raise LGBTQ+ awareness.

prime minister Lee Hsien Loong acknowledged that "homosexuals are part of our society". In 2022, he finally announced the rescinding of the anti-sodomy provision; however, he also reaffirmed his continued opposition to same-sex marriage.

The struggle continues

In 2011, only 12 Asian nations supported the UN declaration for LGBT rights, and 24 opposed it. By 2022, same-sex sexual acts were still criminalized in 10 Asian nations, with a potential death penalty in eight, including Iran and Afghanistan. In Asia, only Cyprus, Israel, and Taiwan have legalized consensual same-sex intercourse and a few of Japan's municipalities are moving towards it; Thailand also took the first steps in 2022.

By early 2023, Taiwan was still the only nation in Asia to have legalized same-sex marriage. The island accounts for just 0.5 per cent of the continent's 4.5 billion population but continues to offer its most extensive LGBTQ+ rights. ▪

WE'RE HERE! WE'RE QUEER! GET USED TO IT!

RECLAIMING THE TERM "QUEER" (1990s)

IN CONTEXT

FOCUS
LGBTQ+ identity markers

BEFORE
c. **1500** The first recorded use of "queer", meaning "odd", appears in Scots poem "The Flyting of Dunbar and Kennedie".

1894 In Britain, the Marquess of Queensberry refers to Oscar Wilde and other society homosexuals as "snob queers".

1900s The adoption of "queer" as a slur spreads to the US.

1976 French philosopher Michel Foucault's *The History of Sexuality* puts forward ideas that later inspire queer theory.

AFTER
2000s Queer of colour theory and queer disability studies emerge as academic subjects.

2016 In the US, the Gay and Lesbian Alliance Against Defamation (GLAAD) officially recommends adding "Q" to the acronym "LGBT".

From the late Middle Ages, "**queer**" is used to mean "**unusual**" or "**strange**".

While still maintaining its original meaning, "queer" spreads as a **homophobic slur** from the early 20th century.

In the late 20th century, LGBTQ+ people **embrace the term** "**queer**" as a positive **identity marker**.

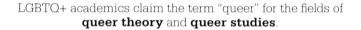

LGBTQ+ academics claim the term "queer" for the fields of **queer theory** and **queer studies**.

The origins of the word "queer" are not certain. It most likely derives from the German word *quer*, meaning "oblique" or "across", although it may also relate to Old Irish *cúar*, a word used to describe an object that was twisted or bent. The term has always meant something unusual or strange, such as "a queer fellow" or "feeling queer" – not feeling well. The first derogatory use of "queer" to mean homosexual appeared in 1894 in a letter from the 9th Marquess of Queensbury to his son, Lord Alfred Douglas. From there, "queer" – used particularly as a slur towards gay and feminine men – spread from Britain to the United States and persisted through much of the 20th century.

In the late 1980s, however, in the face of increased homophobia generated by the AIDS crisis,

Yeah, queer can be a rough word, but it is also a sly and ironic weapon we can steal from the homophobe's hands and use against him.
Queer Nation Manifesto

LGBTQ+ activists began to use "queer" to assert their identity and defuse attacks on their community. In 1990, AIDS activists in New York City formed the group Queer Nation, which handed out copies of its manifesto "QUEERS READ THIS!" at the city's Gay Pride Parade. In the manifesto, the group defiantly stated: "We've chosen to call ourselves queer. Using 'queer' is a way of reminding us how we are perceived by the rest of the world." Queer Nation groups soon spread to Atlanta, Houston, San Francisco, and other cities in the US.

"Queer" enters academia
In the early 1990s, "queer theory" and "queer studies" grew out of gender and sexuality studies to emerge as areas of research within academia, particularly in the US. The first recognized use of the term "queer theory" was in 1991 in the article "Queer Theory: Lesbian and Gay Sexualities", written by Teresa de Lauretis, a US-based Italian academic. De Lauretis suggested that it was possible to completely rethink the way gender and sexuality are understood and that this could be placed under the umbrella term "queer theory".

The basis for the theory lay in the work of French philosopher Michel Foucault (1926–1984). He argued that sexuality is not an innate aspect of humanity but instead a force that has been constructed and controlled across history through discourse and "state apparatus", such as the media, education, and forces of law and order. Developing Foucault's ideas, queer theorists questioned the structures that define sexual and gender identity and challenged the concepts of social "norms".

Widening acceptance
In 1999, the term "queer" moved from activism into the mainstream media with the release of the British television series *Queer as Folk* (a play on the old proverb "There's nowt so queer as folk"). The success of the series, chronicling the lives of three gay men, was repeated in 2000 in an American version of the same title.

While "queer" at first referred to gay, lesbian, bi, or trans people, it has since expanded its use to become, for many, a catch-all term for "non-heterosexual" or "gender nonconforming", encapsulating life outside a gendered or sexual binary. People now identify as queer in both sexual orientation and gender, using it as a single word or in combinations such as "genderqueer". The Q in LGBTQ+ denotes "queer" but can also mean "questioning" – covering those trying to determine their sexual orientation or gender identity.

Not all LGBTQ+ people agree with the reclamation of "queer". Some – particularly older members of the community who grew up enduring "queer" as a slur – push back against the use of the term, believing its history remains too painful to overcome. Some groups also claim that the all-embracing use of "queer" dilutes or overlooks identity categories such as "woman" and "bisexual". ▪

In New York City, activists on the 2020 Queer Liberation March carry puppet models of LGBTQ+ heroes, such as Black gay rights campaigners Bayard Rustin and Sylvia Rivera.

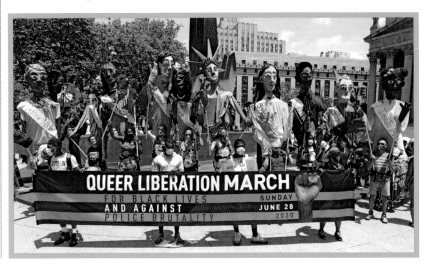

IT IS THE SPIRIT THAT IS YOUR GENDER

INDIGENOUS AMERICAN TWO-SPIRIT PEOPLE (1990)

FOCUS
Indigenous gender identity

BEFORE
1513 In what is now Panama, Spanish conquistador Vasco Núñez de Balboa kills 40 Cueva people who perform women's roles, calling them "sodomites".

17th century The derogatory term *berdache* for gender-non-conforming Indigenous people becomes entrenched in European discourse.

1880s Ohchiish, a Crow *badé* (non-binary AMAB person) is persecuted by US Agent E.P. Briscoe; Crow Chief Pretty Eagle defends them, ordering Briscoe to leave the reservation.

AFTER
2012 *The Tribal Equity Toolkit* is published, providing tribal legislators with legal guidance on issues affecting the treatment of Two-Spirit people.

Two-Spirit is an English translation of the Ojibwe words *niizh manitoag*, which denote a person with both feminine and masculine qualities. The Ojibwe, one of the largest Indigenous populations in the US and Canada today, traditionally nurtured young people whom they considered to be blessed with male and female spirits. As adults, these special people took on roles that helped strengthen kinship bonds within communities.

Before the European invasion of North America in 1492, many of its Indigenous nations had traditions of gender fluidity and/or sexual fluidity. For example, among the Laguna, in

See also: Intersex rights 48–53 ▪ Colonial Latin America 66–67 ▪ Transgender rights 196–203 ▪ Kathoey in Thailand 220–21 ▪ Māori gender and sexuality 236–37 ▪ The AIDS epidemic 238–41

Many North American Indigenous nations **accept and value** gender-nonconforming people, attributing them with both **male and female spirits**.

European colonizers impose heterosexual monogamy and **outlaw gender-nonconforming** people and behaviour.

Gender-nonconforming Indigenous people are **ostracized** by their own communities and **driven underground**.

Modern LGBTQ+ Indigenous people seek to reassert their **traditional status and power**, coining the term **Two-Spirit** to describe themselves.

---

the Southwest, a person assigned male at birth (AMAB) with a female identity was *kok'we'ma*; among the Lakota, in the Northern Plains, they were *winyanktehca*. Among the Diné people (also known as the Navajo) in the Colorado Plateau, *nadleehi* was an AMAB or AFAB (assigned female at birth) person "who changes". In these cultures, such people were honoured: they performed roles ranging from medicine people and priests to teachers and peacemakers.

A new name

The name Two-Spirit was coined in 1990 at the Third Annual Inter-tribal Native American, First Nations, Gay and Lesbian American Conference on the outskirts of Winnipeg, Canada, at the intersection of the Red and Assiniboine rivers. For more than 6,000 years, Indigenous people from nihi'wawin Cree, Dakota,

Ojibwe, Oji-Cree, and Diné language groups had gathered here to trade, negotiate, and share knowledge.

Since the 1970s, Indigenous North Americans have worked to reconnect with and revive the rich

and diverse histories, cultures, and languages that make up Indian Country. Among LGBTQ+ people in these communities, the question of naming had been a topic of debate for many years. They were unhappy with the way they were described by anthropologists, psychologists, and historians: for example, European anthropologists used the term *berdache* – a word derived from the Arabic *bardaj*, a term for "slave" or "kept boy" – which was viewed as a slur. Western terms such as gay, lesbian, or transgender were not considered offensive, but they did not capture the historical and cultural significance of the roles and identities that the delegates at Winnipeg felt they had inherited from their ancestors.

At the 1990 gathering, the name "Two-Spirit" was agreed upon. It enabled elders to draw attention to the important contributions that gender-nonconforming people have made, and continue to make, in Indigenous communities. It provided a framework for highlighting »

Accessing care for HIV/AIDS

When the HIV/AIDS epidemic exploded in the 1980s and 1990s, some North American Indigenous leaders dismissed it as a "white man's disease". As infection rates soared among Indigenous people, the need to address this myth and improve access to appropriate health care became urgent.

In 1987, the National Native American AIDS Prevention Center (NNAAPC) was founded by Indigenous people working in public health. Instrumental in this initiative was Choctaw

activist Ron Rowell. He was clear that homophobia was a painful reality within parts of Indigenous communities, and explained: "Trying to come to terms with our Indianness and our gayness ... has meant trying to look back into our past and ... understand who we are on the basis of our own traditional cultures."

The NNAAPC not only raised awareness about HIV/AIDS in Indigenous communities but also contributed to a renewed interest in Indigenous histories of gender and sexuality.

political priorities, and, above all, it fostered feelings of community and belonging. "We are everywhere," one delegate at the Winnipeg gathering proudly told a reporter. This sense of empowerment inspired Two-Spirit people to reclaim traditions specific to their tribal nations.

Deep histories

Scholars estimate that before the Europeans invaded, 150–200 tribal nations – around a third of the number recognized today in the US – had "Two-Spirit" traditions, integral to the meaning of kinship and to nurturing community. In the Southeast, the Chickasaw and Choctaw nations included people who were neither male nor female but both. The word *hatukiklanna* referred to an AMAB person who displayed the spirit and performed the roles of a woman, and people known as *hatukholba* were said to be AFAB but had the spirit of a man.

Within the Cree nation across the Northern Plains, a man who dressed as a woman was a *napêw iskwêwisêhot*, while *iskwêw ka napêwayat* referred to a woman who wore men's clothing. *Înahpîkasoht* described a person who was AFAB

We'Wha was a Zuni *lhamana* (an AMAB person who "behaves like a woman"). A skilled weaver and potter, We'Wha was taken to Washington, DC, in 1886, and treated as a woman.

The [Bureau of Indian Affairs] agent incarcerated the *badés*, cut off their hair, made them wear men's clothing … do manual labor.
Joe Medicine Crow
Historian (1913–2016)

but accepted as a man; *ayahkwêw* was an AMAB person who took on female roles and was accepted by their kin as a woman.

Blackfoot communities in the West, extending into what is today Canada, included *aakíí'skassi*, AMAB people who behave like women. An AFAB person who took on male roles was known as *saahkómaapi'aakííkoan.*

The colonial violence inflicted on Indigenous people had a devastating effect on traditional cultures. Nevertheless, archives from the 19th and 20th centuries show that scores of Indigenous nations worked to protect gender-nonconforming people from settler prejudices. One famed example from the late 19th century is of a Crow elder by the name of Ohchiish, who was a *badé* – a "not man, not woman". Subjected to homophobic and transphobic harassment by white Americans, Ohchiish was defended by their kin and tribe,

because they were loved, respected, and played important roles in Crow ceremonies.

Resistance and recovery

Five centuries of genocide, territorial dispossession, and US government efforts to "reeducate" Indigenous children in boarding schools resulted in the erosion of Indigenous language, traditions, and wisdom. To protect their history and culture, Indigenous nations often took their language and oral traditions underground, which also had the effect of some loss of knowledge. Furthermore, with the imposition of Christianity on Indigenous people by European settlers, Christian prejudices regarding gender identity and sexuality became internalized in Indigenous communities. Homophobia and misogyny crept into their cultures, and "Two-Spirit" people became ostracized.

From the late 1960s, a newly focused sense of political identity emerged within Indigenous nations, as the Red Power movement, a youth organization demanding self-determination for Indigenous people, highlighted their cause through social protest. In 1975, on this wave of change, a small group of gay and lesbian Indigenous people decided to reclaim their gender-fluid traditions: gay activists Barbara May Cameron and Randy Burns formed the gay rights organization Gay American Indians (GAI) in San Francisco. Cameron, a member of the Standing Rock Sioux, and Burns, a Northern Paiute, had travelled from their reservation communities to San Francisco to pursue their educations and careers. A generation of young Indigenous people had made similar moves, relocating to cities such as Los Angeles, Chicago, and Minneapolis.

Dancers perform at Arizona's first Two-Spirit powwow in Phoenix, in 2019. In traditional powwows, dances and competitions are gender-specific; here, they were open to everyone.

Cameron and Burns had initially organized GAI as a social club, but intense racism within the gay community, reflecting that in the wider population, meant that it quickly evolved into a politically oriented organization. GAI provided legal advice and social support to young gay Indigenous people who had recently arrived in San Francisco, and worked to increase the visibility of its members in gay and lesbian politics. During the peak of the HIV/AIDS epidemic in the late 1980s and early '90s, consciousness-raising work became a matter of life and death, because gay Indigenous men struggled to access medical services, especially care that was sensitive to their cultural traditions.

Across the US and Canada, galvanized by the HIV/AIDS crisis, Indigenous LGBTQ+ people began to mobilize. In New York City, Curtis Harris and Leota Lone Dog formed We'Wha and BarCheeAmpe, naming their group in honour of We'Wha – a famous *lhamana* of the Zuni tribe, in what is today New Mexico – and BarCheeAmpe, a 19th-century Crow warrior woman.

In Minneapolis, American Indian Gays and Lesbians was created; in Toronto, Gays and Lesbians of the First Nations; in Winnipeg, the Nichiwakan Native Gay Society.

Two-Spirit future

Today, Two-Spirit people continue to both reclaim and debate their place within the North American Indigenous community. For some, this has involved pressing tribal governments to recognize same-sex marriage. For others, it means reflecting on their relationship to the past through art, storytelling, or dance. Others work to decouple Indigenous concepts of gender and sexuality from Western ideas, or to explore the connections between Two-Spirit wisdom and a wide range of global issues. In ways both old and new, Two-Spirit people are contributing to the richness and complexity of Indigenous life. ∎

BAAITS

Bay Area American Indian Two Spirits (BAAITS) was formed in San Francisco in 1998. Building on the work of Gay American Indians (GAI) and other Indigenous LGBTQ+ groups, its mission is to provide a safe environment for Two-Spirit people to explore their cultural, spiritual, and artistic heritage. BAAITS helps to nurture a sense of community among Two-Spirit people not only in the San Francisco Bay Area but also across all of North America.

In 2012, BAAITS held the first-ever Two-Spirit powwow (an Indigenous people's traditional cultural celebration), with the aim of de-gendering Indigenous artistic traditions. This annual event brings people together in dance, song, drumming, and prayer. It is no longer the only Two-Spirit powwow, but it is the largest. Its prominence is indicative of the renewed awareness of Two-Spirit history and culture.

An attendee at the BAAITS powwow in 2020 holds a rainbow flag and an eagle staff. Traditionally, the staff is held at the event's start.

A WHOLE, FLUID IDENTITY

BISEXUALITY (1990)

IN CONTEXT

FOCUS
Sexual identities

BEFORE
1897 British psychologist Havelock Ellis declares that all "sexually functioning" people are heterosexual, homosexual, or bisexual.

1980–84 "Bicurious" is popularized as a term for heterosexuals who wish to experiment with people of their own gender.

AFTER
1999 Bi Visibility Day is first celebrated. The event is now observed around the world on 23 September.

2001 The *Bisexual Resource Guide* lists 352 bisexual and 2,134 bi-inclusive organizations in 68 countries, including Botswana, Colombia, Fiji, Lithuania, Namibia, Singapore, South Korea, and Uruguay.

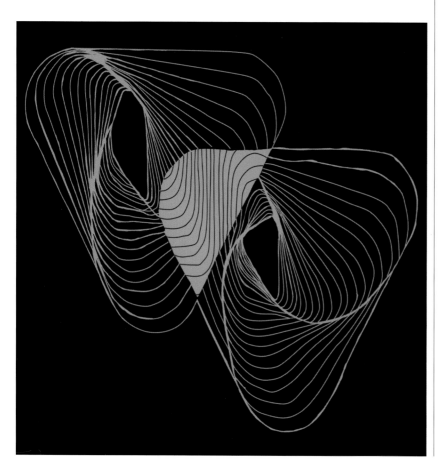

While many historical figures had relationships with more than one gender, "bisexual" is a modern label. Today, the most common definition is experiencing attraction to one's own and other sexes or genders, regardless of any preferences.

The San Francisco magazine *Anything That Moves: Beyond the Myths of Bisexuality* published its "Bisexual Manifesto" in 1990 – the first document by activists to conceptualize bisexuality as we now know it. Mindful of the diversity of bisexual opinions and experiences, the manifesto refused to offer one single definition. It mainly defined bisexuality in opposition to biphobic

This playful cover of an *Anything That Moves* issue shows a love triangle between Superman, Lois Lane, and Wonder Woman.

stereotypes that continue to this day: bisexuality is not binary, does not suggest there are only two genders, and does not lend itself to promiscuity or infidelity more than any other identity.

Sexology and theory

"Bisexual" has had many meanings. Sexologists in the late 19th century largely used "bisexual" to mean what we now call "intersex". Some cited the theory of primordial bisexuality, which argues that our ancestors had both male and female sexual characteristics. Attraction to multiple sexes was posited as a retrogression to this primordial state.

By the early 20th century, psychologists had begun to use "bisexual" to refer to the psyche rather than physical characteristics. Influenced by his surgeon friend Wilhelm Fliess, Sigmund Freud described "psychic bisexuality" as the natural state of having both masculine and feminine psychological traits, and suggested that all people were born with a

multiplicity of sexual feelings. In his 1940s and '50s reports on desire, American sexologist Alfred Kinsey did not use the term "bisexual" to describe sexuality, but today anyone between 2 and 5 on his "Kinsey Scale" might define themselves as such. Indeed, his research showed just how many Americans were attracted to more than one gender.

In the 1970s, the Kinsey Scale was improved upon by Austrian doctor Fritz Klein, whose Klein Sexual Orientation Grid (KSOG) explicitly includes "bisexual" as a sexual orientation. Klein became a major figure in the scientific study of bisexuality, founding the American Institute of Bisexuality in 1998.

Bisexual identification

By the 1960s and '70s, people in the West had begun to use the term "bisexual" as an identity and to seek out others who shared their experiences. Partly prompted by the failure of wider LGBTQ+ »

I realized that there must be bisexuals all over the world living in isolation, never meeting other bisexuals.
Gigi Raven Wilbur
American activist and co-founder of Celebrate Bisexuality Day

Lani Ka'ahumanu

Born in Edmonton, Canada, in 1943, Lani Ka'ahumanu married her high-school boyfriend at the age of 19 and became a self-confessed "suburban housewife". In the 1960s, she joined various civil-rights groups, working on causes from anti-war activism to antiracism and feminism. Divorcing her husband in 1973, Ka'ahumanu moved to San Francisco, where she helped found San Francisco State University's Women's Department. She came out as a lesbian in 1976 and became involved in the lesbian separatist movement, but a later relationship with a man led her to come out as bisexual in 1980.

Ka'ahumanu became a leading figure in the city's bisexual community, first as a founder of the campaigning group BiPOL and later as a member of the Bay Area Bisexual Network, which published *Anything That Moves*. A writer and poet in her own right, she co-edited a groundbreaking anthology, *Bi Any Other Name* (1991), with Loraine Hutchins.

Ka'ahumanu's activism extended across the US in 1990 when she co-organized the National Bisexual Conference. She was the only bisexual person to speak at the 1993 March on Washington, and later became the first bisexual person on the board of the National Gay and Lesbian Task Force. In the 1990s, she became a sex educator and body-positivity activist. She still serves on the board of the *Journal of Bisexuality*.

spaces to acknowledge bisexuality, activist groups proliferated. In 1972, a National Bisexual Liberation Group formed in New York City. In 1976, Maggi Rubenstein and Harriet Leve founded The Bisexual Center of San Francisco as a place to gather and receive support; after it closed in 1985, the Bay Area Bisexual Network (BABN) took its place, going on to become one of the most prolific bisexual activist groups in the US. San Francisco was also the home of BiPOL, the first bisexual political organization, which formed in 1983 in response to the AIDS crisis.

The BABN was influenced by the East Coast Bisexual Network (ECBN), which was founded in 1985 and later became the Bisexual Resource Center. The group notably published an International Directory of Bisexual Groups and the Bisexual Resource Guide, both of which were edited by bisexual scholar Robyn Ochs, who also co-edited (with Sarah E. Rowley) the anthology *Getting Bi: Voices of Bisexuals Around the World*.

In the 1980s, bisexual organizations also began to appear in the UK. The first to form was the London Bisexual Group (LBG), which formed in 1981 and organized the Bisexual Conference in 1984. The event, now known as BiCon, has continued to run annually and is the biggest bisexual political gathering in the UK. The LBG became inactive in 2003, but other groups remain, with Manchester-based BiPhoria, formed in 1994, the longest-running.

During the 1990s, bisexuality became more widely visible. The first International Conference on Bisexuality was held in Amsterdam in 1991, and ran every year until 2010. In 1990, the BABN published the first issue of *Anything That Moves: Beyond the Myths of Bisexuality*. The magazine, which ran until 2002, billed itself as part of a movement toward bisexual empowerment. 1990 also saw the publication of the influential *Bi Any Other Name: Bisexual People Speak Out*, edited by Loraine Hutchins and Lani Ka'ahumanu (see box, p.263), which acknowledged the multiplicity of bisexual experiences through fiction, poetry, and essays.

An academic turn

The growth of community networks and organizations coincided with the larger gay liberation movement, but bisexual groups had specific concerns, notably the absence of bisexual narratives in academia.

Earlier studies, in the late 1980s and 1990s, were often quantitative surveys proving the existence and breadth of bisexual experiences, while later works addressed key

The bisexual umbrella

The phrase "bisexual umbrella" encompasses many different non-monosexual people (those who experience attraction to more than one gender), who might also describe themselves as m-spec (on the multisexual spectrum) or bi+.

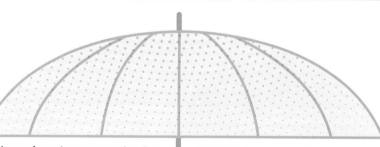

Bisexual people are attracted to their own and different genders, but may have a preference.

Pansexual people experience attraction to all genders without preference.

Polysexual people experience attraction to multiple, but not necessarily all, genders.

Fluid people can be attracted to any one or more genders at different points, without identifying with a fixed label.

Queer people who are attracted to more than one gender fall under the bisexual umbrella.

Omnisexual people experience attraction to all genders, but may have a preference.

Supporters of the community group amBi march with a bisexual flag at LA Pride in West Hollywood, Los Angeles in 2013.

problems such as biphobia and bisexual erasure (see box, below). The latter was explored by American legal scholar Kenji Yoshino, who claimed that homosexuals and heterosexuals come together in an "epistemic contract of bisexual erasure" to protect their sexual norms. Scholars have also noted the asymmetrical nature of acceptance for bisexuality; there is less stigma attached to being a bisexual woman than to being a bisexual man. These issues may mean that bisexuals are afraid to come out: in 2017, Pew Center polling suggested that only 19 per cent of bisexuals in the US are out to all or most of the important people in their lives, compared to 75 per cent of homosexuals.

Non-monosexuals and bi+
One key concept to arise from the scholarship of the 1990s is "monosexuality": sexuality oriented towards one gender. The term has been criticized, however, for creating a new binary that aligns gay, lesbian and heterosexual people in contrast with non-monosexuals. "Non-monosexual", on the other hand, is considered by some scholars to usefully describe all people who are attracted to more than one gender. Others refer to this group of people as being "bi+", or under the "bisexual umbrella", encompassing identities such as pansexual and multisexual.

The term "mononormativity", when used in the context of bisexuality, also derives from the idea of monosexuality. It describes a state in which monosexuality is considered normal and bisexuality is othered. In 2010, disability studies theorist Kate Caldwell used the term "compulsory monosexuality" to describe how bisexual people are assumed to be either homosexual or heterosexual at any given time based on the gender of their partner, rendering their bisexuality invisible.

Bisexuality today
Today, academic studies continue, with a new wave of interest coming from continental European scholars. Emiel Maliepaard and Renate Baumgartner's *Bisexuality in Europe* came out in 2020, forming a counterpoint to the dominance of Anglophone researchers.

Meanwhile, bisexual groups continue to advocate for the rights of bi+ people. Many organizations, such as the Bay Area Bi+ & Pan Network, have changed their names to be more inclusive of the growing number of people with pansexual, polysexual, multisexual, and other non-monosexual identities. ∎

Bisexual erasure

Visibility is a key issue for people under the bisexual umbrella, who often find their identity is invalidated or unrecognized by both homosexuals and heterosexuals.

"Bisexual erasure" describes the failure to make bisexuality visible, or to acknowledge that bisexuality exists. This erasure affects fields such as research, the law, and language. In 2008, for example, activist group Bialogue and the American Institute of Bisexuality argued that the language used around marriage should change: talking about "same-sex" rather than "gay" marriage acknowledges that bisexual people may also engage in these unions.

In 1999, the world's first Bi Visibility Day celebrations took place at the International Lesbian and Gay Association Conference in Johannesburg, South Africa. The event, which now stretches into a week of celebrations in some countries, acknowledges bisexual people, and their struggle against bisexual erasure.

NOBODY REALLY IS A GENDER FROM THE START

BUTLER'S *GENDER TROUBLE* (1990)

Society expects people to adopt **distinct male or female gender roles**.

→

People **perform such roles through repeated acts**: speech, body language, appearance, and behaviour.

↓

Nobody really is a gender from the start.

←

Gender is **not innate**; it is something that people **unwittingly copy** and **do**.

IN CONTEXT

FOCUS
Gender as performance

BEFORE
1966 French psychoanalyst Jacques Lacan publishes *Écrits* – 27 articles and lectures that influence Judith Butler when writing *Gender Trouble*.

1988 Butler first argues that gender is performative in the essay "Performative Acts and Gender Constitution".

AFTER
1995 American psychologist Sandra Bem calls for genders falling outside the binary to be made more visible.

2000 In *Sexing the Body*, American sexologist Anne Fausto-Sterling argues for new theories that allow for greater variations in human biology.

2018 Paul B. Preciado publishes *Counter-Sexual Manifesto*, further challenging conventional ideas about gender, sexuality, and desire.

In their 1990 book *Gender Trouble*, American philosopher Judith Butler reshaped the way that academics conceptualize and understand sex and gender, and their relationship to sexuality. Butler begins by questioning the category of "woman" in women, gender, and feminist studies, recognizing that it is complicated by other categorical factors, such as age, class, wealth, race, disability, or able-bodiedness.

Butler contends that classifying these varying factors into one category such as "woman", set against another such as "man" or "the patriarchy", obscures more specific acts of gender oppression in different cultures and locations. As a result, individual struggles become merely a political fight based on such singular – and thus reductive and inaccurate – identities.

Butler also argues against the then dominant feminist view that sex is biological and gender is social. Instead, they assert that it is impossible to separate sex from gender in that way, as both are socially constructed.

Gender as performative
Butler's most influential argument is that gender is performative and there is no innate identity that links gendered actions. Instead, Butler argues that it is gendered actions that create the gender. Acts so culturally ingrained that they go unnoticed are assigned to specific

See also: Transgender rights 196–203 ▪ Foucault's *History of Sexuality* 222–23 ▪ "The Straight Mind" 232 ▪ Heteronormativity 270–71

genders, creating the illusion that there is an innate "man" or "woman" identity that influences them, when in fact the acts produce the gender identity. The individual does not "be" a specific gender – instead they "perform" or "do" gender. If there is no specific gendered identity that influences actions, then people can "trouble" (disrupt) the idea of what gender is by performing differently.

Butler specifically references drag performance as one – very clear – example of "gender trouble". Through its use of parody and exaggeration of gender stereotypes, drag highlights the fact that gender itself is false and socially scripted, and that there is no innate identity connected to gendered actions. Butler contends that by destabilizing gendered norms and the assumption of innate gender identity, a new feminism may be established – built not on perceived identity, but instead on political ideals and collaboration.

Butler raises other important issues in the book, such as the concept of the "heterosexual

British singer David Bowie, whose stage acts expressed his gender fluidity, posed as a 1930s Hollywood actress on the cover of his 1971 *Hunky Dory* album.

There is no gender identity beyond the expressions of gender; that gender is performatively constituted by the very "expressions" that are said to be its results.
Judith Butler
Gender Trouble

matrix", the seemingly natural social norm that defines people as heterosexual until shown otherwise. In framing social interaction by default, this construct normalizes heterosexuality and the idea that everyone exists within a strict "natural" gender.

Gender under fire
Butler's work has influenced theorists such as Spanish-born philosopher and trans activist Paul B. Preciado, musical groups such as Russian feminist protest and performance art collective Pussy Riot, and artists such as American drag performer Sasha Velour.

Butler now writes more explicitly political texts but still comments and lectures on gender. In October 2021, in *The Guardian* newspaper, Butler launched a powerful critique of the many anti-gender movements now emerging across the world – often in countries with increasingly authoritarian governments, declaring that they are "not just reactionary but *fascist* trends". ▪

Judith Butler

Born in Cleveland, Ohio, US, in 1956, Judith Butler was raised in a Jewish household. After attending a Hebrew school, Butler studied philosophy at Yale University and was influenced by the works of figures such as French philosophers Michael Foucault and Jacques Derrida, and French feminists Simone de Beauvoir and Monique Wittig. Butler has held a number of university teaching positions, and is currently Distinguished Professor in the Graduate School of the University of California, Berkeley.

Politically active, Butler has commented on movements such as Occupy Wall Street and Black Lives Matter, and has opposed the wars in Iraq and Afghanistan, trans-exclusionary radical feminism, and Israel's illegal occupation of Palestinian lands. Butler's books have been translated into 27 languages. They live with their partner, political theorist Wendy Brown.

Key works

1993 *Bodies That Matter*
2004 *Precarious Life*
2004 *Undoing Gender*

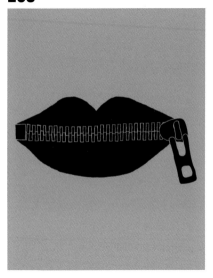

SEXUALITY CONSTITUTED AS SECRECY

SEDGWICK'S *EPISTEMOLOGY OF THE CLOSET* (1990)

IN CONTEXT

FOCUS
Queer identity

BEFORE
1869 Hungarian writer Karl-Maria Kertbeny is the first to use the term "homosexual".

1980 Michel Foucault analyses silence as a form of discourse in the first volume of *The History of Sexuality*.

1986 American historian David Halperin calls the period 1892–1992 "One hundred years of homosexuality", describing the historical importance of homosexuality as a new form of sexual identity.

AFTER
2005 In his essay "Beyond the Closet as a Raceless Paradigm", Black American professor Marlon Ross argues that Sedgwick's paradigm of the closet does not apply to racially marginalized groups.

One of the most pervasive metaphors in LGBTQ+ culture is that of the closet. While "coming out of the closet" describes an LGBTQ+ person disclosing their sexual orientation or gender identity, being "in the closet" means allowing others to presume that they are cisgender and heterosexual.

American academic Eve Kosofsky Sedgwick's 1990 book, *Epistemology of the Closet*, explores the metaphor as a way to analyse how Western ideas of identity create heterosexuals, who live in a state of openness and normativity, and homosexuals, who are othered and forced to live in constant negotiation with the unstable boundary between openness and secrecy. Epistemology is the study of knowledge and how we know what we think we know – in this case, the study of how we think we know things about homosexuality. For Sedgwick, the boundary between "being in" and "being out" of the closet is fundamentally unstable and involves a conflict between socially enforced silences, open secrets, and demands for public disclosure.

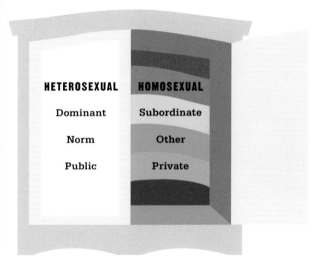

The binary nature of thinking about heterosexuality and homosexuality is heavily criticized in Sedgwick's work. She stresses that the two parts within this binary are not equal: homosexuality is subordinate and, historically, relegated to the closet; whereas homosexuals exist in a world built around and catering to heterosexual norms.

See also: Foucault's *History of Sexuality* 222–23 ▪ Butler's *Gender Trouble* 266–67 ▪ Heteronormativity 270–71 ▪ Don't Ask, Don't Tell 272–75

'Closeted-ness' itself is a performance initiated as such by the speech act of a silence.
Epistemology of the Closet

Such silences and assumptions about queer people have had negative effects on queer lives, particularly in such policies as the US military's edict of "Don't Ask, Don't Tell".

The homo–hetero divide

At the core of *Epistemology of the Closet* is Sedgwick's claim that Western thought since the end of the 19th century had been structured – and fractured – by what she calls an "endemic crisis of homo/heterosexual definition". As a result of 19th-century writing on homosexuality, individuals had become defined by their identity as either hetero- or homosexual. Before the concept of homosexuality entered public discourse, the concept of the "heterosexual" did not exist either. Sedgwick argues that binary approaches to sexuality are not helpful, and encourages more nuanced ways of thinking

Sedgwick also introduces two key categories of discourse that underscore contemporary understandings of sexuality. The first is minoritizing discourse, where homosexuals are discussed as a distinct and oppressed minority; the second is universalizing discourse, in which all humans are portrayed as having the potential for queer desire. Both discourses circulate simultaneously, creating conditions of incoherence that queer people are forced to navigate every day.

The Introduction to *Epistemology of the Closet* offers six axioms that have proved hugely productive for queer thought. From the observation that "People are different from each other" to a critique of what Sedgwick calls "the Great Paradigm Shift" in the history of homosexuality, her axioms have been used to develop queer approaches to ethical issues, methods of textual analysis, and the way that history is written. The book also offers interpretations of homosexuality in several late 19th-century literary texts, including Oscar Wilde's *The Picture of Dorian Gray* and Herman Melville's *Billy Budd, Sailor (An Inside Narrative)*. Sedgwick's book has received criticism mostly from those alarmed by her queer readings of beloved authors. ▪

… the deadly elasticity of heterosexist presumption means that… people find new walls springing up around them even as they drowse…
Epistemology of the Closet

Eve Kosofsky Sedgwick

Born in Ohio, US, in 1950, Eve Kosofsky showed great intellectual promise at a young age. The teenage Kosofsky helped her mother, an English teacher, to grade students' essays, and was accepted into Cornell University's exclusive Telluride House on a merit scholarship. She married Hal Sedgwick in 1969, and in 1971 began her PhD at Yale.

As a scholar, Sedgwick played an important role in the fields of English literature and queer theory. In 1985, she published *Between Men: English Literature and Male Homosocial Desire*, one of the first works to explore social bonds between men. Her *Epistemology of the Closet* was one of the 20th century's most influential works of queer theory. Diagnosed with cancer in 1991, Sedgwick died in 2009.

Key works

1985 *Between Men: English Literature and Male Homosocial Desire*
1990 *Epistemology of the Closet*
1997 *Novel Gazing: Queer Readings in Fiction*

FEAR OF A QUEER PLANET

HETERONORMATIVITY (1991)

Heteronormativity is a key concept in queer theory. The term was coined in 1991 by American academic Michael Warner, whose influential *Fear of a Queer Planet* explores "the pervasive and often invisible heteronormativity of modern societies". American scholar Lauren Berlant, who collaborated with Warner, wrote of "the institutions [and] structures of understanding …

Heteronormativity privileges some behaviours and punishes others, an idea explored by American anthropologist Gayle Rubin, who suggests that privileged acts and behaviours form a "charmed circle".

DISADVANTAGED
- LGBTQ+ people
- Single people
- Non-monogamous people
- People (particularly women) without children
- Non-normative (such as fetishistic or anal) sex acts

PRIVILEGED
- Heterosexual people
- Cisgender people
- People who are married or in long-term monogamous relationships
- People with children
- Conventional, or "vanilla", sex acts

So much privilege lies in heterosexual culture's exclusive ability to interpret itself as society.
Michael Warner
Fear of a Queer Planet

Homonormativity

The term "homonormativity" was popularized by LGBTQ+ theorists in the early 2000s. It refers to the assumption that LGBTQ+ people should integrate into heterosexual norms, with same-sex relationships fitting as closely as possible into the template of a heterosexual relationship, and thus becoming more socially accepted. A gay male couple, for example, might be interpreted as having "male" and "female" roles, could marry, and might have children via surrogacy or adoption.

Some LGBTQ+ people are happy enough with these norms, but others have argued that homonormativity is damaging because it upholds oppressive structures and forces LGBTQ+ people to adhere to heterosexual structures. In response, queer theory has privileged a stance of "antinormativity", in which LGBTQ+ people are encouraged to assert their queer identity.

that make heterosexuality seem not only coherent – that is, organized as a sexuality – but also privileged". Simply put, heteronormativity is the idea that society favours those who exist within "traditional" understandings of heterosexual life, and that heterosexuality is the "correct" default, with any deviation seen as less normal. It is reinforced through marriage laws, adoption rights, and social expectations regarding coupledom and monogamy.

Identity and expectations

Heteronormativity puts pressure on everyone and influences many daily decisions, albeit often in an invisible or subconscious way. For example, social pressure may be applied to a cis woman to marry a cis man, as their unmarried life threatens the heteronormative expectation that they should be in a "productive" heterosexual relationship – one that produces children.

The pervasiveness and power of heteronormativity means that the societal inclusion of LGBTQ+ people will not necessarily lead to

equality, as the structure of society itself favours those who are heterosexual. American philosopher Judith Butler's idea of a "heterosexual matrix" argues that society uses identifiable traits such as gender, sex, or sexuality as the basis for a series of heteronormative assumptions. For example, a person who presents as a man or woman may be assumed to be a cis individual of that gender or sex.

Heteronormativity applies social pressure not just to relationships, but also to gendered identities. Society assumes a cis-gendered body, and so public toilets are often categorized male or female, and assume specifically sexed bodies using these toilets; this excludes trans men who menstruate and non-binary identities. Gendered identities are often ascribed specific traits as well. People who adhere to these traits, such as a woman who is visibly a mother, are rewarded, while those who do not, such as a woman who does not bear children, may be socially excluded or otherwise penalized.

For Warner, "even when coupled with a toleration of minority sexualities, heteronormativity can be overcome only by actively imagining a necessarily and desirably queer world". Rejecting heteronormativity allows marginalized identities to exist on their own terms, and not be demonized for falling outside social norms. Yet despite legal and social changes, there is a long way to go before heteronormative frameworks are no longer the default position for understanding social interaction. ▪

… our biases against the other are empowered less by our assumptions of their otherness and more by our assumptions of our own normality.
Jamie Arpin-Ricci
Canadian LGBTQ+ activist

TO LIE IN ORDER TO SERVE

DON'T ASK, DON'T TELL (1993–2011)

IN CONTEXT

FOCUS
LGBTQ+ exclusion

BEFORE
1778 Lieutenant Frederick Gotthold Enslin is court martialled and discharged from the US Continental Army for attempting to have sex with a man.

1990 The World Health Organization (WHO) removes homosexuality from the International Classification of Diseases.

AFTER
2012 During the US presidential election campaign, several Republican candidates call for the restoration of DADT.

2014 The Hague Centre for Strategic Studies develops the LGBT Military Index, which ranks more than 100 countries on the inclusion of LGBTQ+ service members.

O n 21 December 1993, the US Department of Defense issued a new policy for non-heterosexual members of the US Military. Directive 1304.26, known as "Don't Ask, Don't Tell" (DADT), allowed homosexuals and bisexuals to serve in the military, provided they kept their orientation private. Personnel were not permitted to question or harass one another based on their sexuality. Openly gay individuals remained barred from service, and if a person "manifested" their orientation through conduct that was deemed "unacceptable" they would be subject to an investigation, usually followed by dismissal.

See also: AFAB people in combat 99 ▪ Transgender rights 196–203 ▪ Removal of homosexuality from the DSM 219 ▪ The assassination of Harvey Milk 226–27

Almost 13,000 military personnel were discharged from the US army between 1994 and 2008 due to the Don't Ask, Don't Tell policy.

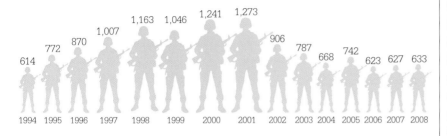

1994	1995	1996	1997	1998	1999	2000	2001	2002	2003	2004	2005	2006	2007	2008
614	772	870	1,007	1,163	1,046	1,241	1,273	906	787	668	742	623	627	633

The policy also set standards for how investigations into this conduct could take place to avoid "witch hunts", with the policy sometimes extended to "Don't Ask, Don't Tell, Don't Pursue". In theory, a service member would only be investigated if there was "credible information", and an investigation could not be carried out solely to determine someone's sexual orientation. What exactly the threshold for this evidence was and who was responsible for presenting or rebutting it remained unclear and controversial throughout the policy's duration, until its repeal in 2010.

It wasn't what I did or what I said or how good a citizen I was or how many awards I had gotten. Because I had a label, it didn't matter.
Margaret Witt

Although DADT attempted to end discrimination based on sexual orientation, it still punished same-sex acts. This made it unlike any other policy regarding LGBTQ+ people in the military in the world. Introduced by President Bill Clinton, it was the result of a compromise, attempting to please both those critical of and in support of bans on homosexuals serving in the military. DADT resulted in the discharge of around 13,000 people from the armed forces.

While on paper DADT may have represented a loosening of existing regulations, in reality it served as the latest evolution in a long history of LGBTQ+ service members being controlled and suppressed in military settings.

Exclusion takes shape
Until World War I, the treatment of LGBTQ+ people in the military largely mirrored a country's civilian laws. Same-sex acts, defined by many penal codes as "sodomy", would be grounds for court martial and dismissal. The focus was overwhelmingly on gay men, with other LGBTQ+ identities yet to be articulated and therefore often ignored in policymaking. Whether or not an LGBTQ+ service »

Witt v. Department of the Air Force

Serving as a major in the US Air Force, Margaret Witt kept her sexual orientation private until her partner's ex-husband outed her as a lesbian in 2004. The subsequent investigation into her homosexuality under Don't Ask, Don't Tell laid bare the contradictions that existed in the policy and what constituted "credible evidence".

Witt was informed in 2006 that discharge proceedings had been initiated. In response she filed a suit in the District Court, claiming that DADT violated due process and that there was no evidence that her orientation caused a problem in her conduct. The district dismissed the case, and Witt was discharged in July 2007. A year later, the Ninth Circuit Court of Appeals ruled that her claims would be reinstated, noting that the Air Force must ensure that dismissals relating to DADT are entirely necessary to uphold "good order, morale, and discipline". This became known as the "Witt standard", a vital step in paving the way for the repeal of DADT in 2010.

Margaret Witt joined the US Air Force in 1987. She received numerous awards and medals during her 20-year military career.

I'm living proof that the mere presence of an openly gay person … does not harm either cohesion or morale.
Zoe Dunning
Retired US Navy commander (1963–)

member was able to be comfortably out in the military varied, but it was historically a frequent cause for harassment and blackmail, with many attempting to keep their sexuality private.

Gradually, control of who was able to join the military became more institutionalized. In 1916, the US military introduced a new means to remove service members, known as the blue discharge. This was a discharge from service that was neither honourable nor dishonourable, allowing the impracticalities of a court martial requiring proof of "unacceptable" sexual acts to be avoided. Commanders used this to remove those they did not want from service. Homosexuals, women, and Black Americans are all known to have been subject to this practice, with the blue discharge quickly becoming a source of stigma.

In the 1940s, militaries across the world responded to the widespread pathologizing of

Thousands of flags displayed in Washington, DC, to protest against Don't Ask, Don't Tell on the 13th anniversary of its signing. Each flag represents a soldier discharged from military service.

LGBTQ+ identities, with many declaring them to be mental illnesses that were incompatible with military service and a danger to an effective military. The presence of gay men, specifically, in the military was feared as a distraction, and it was also recognized that they would be subject to ridicule and harassment, which would lower morale. Lesbians were largely ignored until 1944, when homosexuality became a reason for disqualification from the Women's Army Corps. Although the policy of excluding non-heterosexuals from the military based purely on sexual orientation took shape during World War II, it was not strictly enforced until the end of the war, when the need for soldiers became less pressing. And it was not until 1963 that transgender people were officially prohibited from joining the military for being mentally "unfit".

Interpretations and challenges

The disconnect between the aims of DADT and the reality of its implementation had serious consequences. The first issue to arise was known as the "rebuttable presumption". This was the process whereby the statement by a service member that they were homosexual or bisexual – or their forced outing by someone else – automatically created a rebuttable presumption that they engaged in same-sex acts or had intent to do so. This acted to immediately undermine the distinction Clinton had sought between orientation and acts, with an admission of orientation being read as effectively an admission of unacceptable conduct that was very difficult to prove or disprove.

The "live and let live" attitude of the policy also assumed a level of tolerance or acceptance towards LGBTQ+ people in the military that did not exist. In 1999, a review was ordered into the policy after 21-year-old soldier Barry Winchell was murdered following persistent and unchecked harassment due to him dating American trans performer Calpernia Addams. What began as a review around Winchell's murder soon developed into an investigation into what was a widespread atmosphere of harassment towards LGBTQ+ people in the military, despite DADT. It revealed that many had received

no training regarding the policy, and while broadly aware of it, did not understand it in any detail.

Legacy of DADT

Following the terrorist attacks of 11 September 2001, during the presidency of George Bush, discharges relating to DADT sharply dropped. Some speculate that this was due to growing acceptance of LGBTQ+ in the military, but it has also been attributed to an unwillingness by the military to lose able service members during the subsequent Iraq War.

The presence of DADT was increasingly viewed as antiquated when set against the global context. Following early lifts of bans in the Netherlands in 1972 and Denmark in 1979, Australia, New Zealand, and Canada all lifted bans in 1992, with Israel following in 1993. In the UK, the ban was lifted in 2000 after the European Court of Human Rights made a historic ruling in 1999 that the Ministry of Defence's ban on homosexuals was unlawful.

However, it would not be until 2010 under President Barack Obama that DADT would finally be repealed; it remained in effect until September 2011. The working group within the Department of Defense that implemented the repeal declared that "allowing gays and lesbians to serve openly will not harm the military". The American Civil Liberties Union filed for compensation, which was secured

… gender identity should not be a bar to military service, and … America's strength is found in its diversity.
White House statement
January 2021

LGBTQ+ veterans and activists handcuff themselves to the railings of the White House in 2010, calling for the repeal of the Don't Ask, Don't Tell policy. It was repealed in December that year.

for all those discharged since November 2004. Yet sodomy, even consensual, is still recognized by military law as criminal, alongside bestiality.

Transgender people remained disqualified from service in the US military following the repeal of DADT, with a 2012 instruction listing it as a "psychosexual condition". However, when a study by the RAND Corporation's National Defense Research Institute found no evidence of any impact to "operational effectiveness" in allowing trans people to serve, the ban was lifted in 2016. It was later reinstated by President Donald Trump in 2017, only to be reversed again once Joe Biden took office in 2021. Despite its good intentions, the policy of DADT became purely discriminatory. ∎

TOMBOYS AND WIVES
CHINESE *LALA* COMMUNITIES (1994)

IN CONTEXT

FOCUS
Same-sex desire in China

BEFORE
17th century Lesbian relationships feature in early Qing dynasty literary accounts of polygamous marriage.

19th century In southern China, *zishu nü* ("women who bind up their own hair") resist marriage and live together. Some practise same-sex relationships and share pledges in *nüshu* (women's script).

AFTER
1995 Held in Beijing, the UN's Fourth World Conference on Women has its first ever lesbian tent.

2018 Chinese social media giant Sina Weibo is criticized for its ban on LGBTQ+ content and reverses the policy, but censorship continues.

2020 China's National People's Congress acknowledges petitions for marriage equality.

*L*ala is a Chinese slang term that broadly includes cisgender or transgender women with same-sex desire, such as lesbian and multisexual women. It has its roots in *lazi*, a word first used by Taiwanese writer Qiu Miaojin in her 1994 novel *Notes of a Crocodile*.

Historically, *lalas* have been less subject to scrutiny than their male counterparts, who have been criminalized since the 18th century. *Lalas* were ignored largely because they were seen as less of a threat to the patrilineal family. This gendered erasure is sometimes misunderstood as tolerance. Yet, to this day, *lalas* face stigma and discrimination.

I wish I could fall in love with a man, but there are too many beautiful women.
Qiu Miaojin
Notes of a Crocodile, 1994

In the 1990s, *lala* communities started to form in cities such as Beijing and Shanghai, facilitated by the proliferation of *lala* bars and online forums. These important semi-public spaces, influenced by the more established LGBTQ+ culture of the West, enabled *lalas* to explore their identities and seek romance. Yet in their family life and work, *lalas* were often met with denial and rejection.

New gender roles
As the community has grown more confident, *lalas* have engaged in more open nonconformity by playing creative and transgressive gender roles and forming same-sex family units. The emergence of the masculine–feminine pairing of T–P is central to this shift: the roles of T ("tomboy") and P (*po* in Chinese means "wife"), were derived from the T–Po lesbian subculture in Taiwan. T–P relations have since evolved to include variations such as *niang T* ("sissy T") and dominant P, and developed into a foundational element of Chinese *lala* subculture.

Same-sex couples are unable to marry or adopt, and some *lalas* who do not want to come out publicly instead enter cooperative marriages

See also: Butch and femme 152–55 ▪ LGBTQ+ parenting 228–31 ▪ LGBTQ+ activism in Asia 254–55 ▪ Marriage equality 288–93

with gay men, although critics argue that this risks further compromising women's independence.

Activism and families

Lala activism was initially low key, with an informal group, Beijing Sisters, established in 1998. In 2005, three Chinese *lala* organizations set up in Beijing (Common Language and community magazine *les+*) and Shanghai (Shanghai Nvai). These groups and the Lala Alliance, which gathered grassroots activists from all over China for *lala* camps, have helped the community organize rapidly. Activists have also worked to bring queerness into the public

A *lala* **couple** pose for a wedding photo in Beijing in 2019. Same-sex marriages are not officially recognized in China, but that has not stopped increasing numbers of *lalas* from tying the knot.

sphere, with academics exploring gender inequality within the LGBTQ+ community and artists producing work that imagines a future beyond reproduction and heterosexual family units.

These hard-won developments have met with resistance. Xi Jinping became president in 2013, and his administration has tightened state control of civil society and increased the surveillance and censorship of rights-based groups and activists with international links.

Today, ideas of T-P and cooperative marriage are being contested by a new generation. With the availability of assisted reproductive technology, rainbow families that consist of two *lala* partners and a baby have emerged. However, negotiating same-sex relationships and *lala* lifestyles remains culturally stigmatized and unconventional in the eyes of both the authorities and many older Chinese people. ▪

Definitions of *lalas*	
Lala	A same-sex-desiring cisgender or transgender woman (e.g. lesbian or multisexual).
Tomboy (T)	A butch-leaning *lala*
Wife (P)	A femme-leaning *lala*
Bu fen (Unidentified)	A *lala* who opts out of the T–P binary.

Out *lalas*

In 2000, Hunan Satellite Television's *Let's Talk it Out* became the first Chinese TV show to discuss homosexuality; one of its guests, the artist and actress Shitou, became the first woman to come out as *lala* in the mainstream media. The episode was a watershed moment that gathered unprecedented attention and generated huge public debate.

Since then, more and more individuals have come out as *lalas* in China. One of the most prominent is Li Ying, a high-profile Chinese footballer, who announced her engagement to her girlfriend Chen Leilei on Sina Weibo in 2021. Li became the first Chinese sportswoman to come out, and her post went viral on the network before she deleted it – a move possibly prompted by China's censors, who still discourage LGBTQ+ content.

Footballer Li Ying came out as a *lala* in 2021, making her one of the most high-profile LGBTQ+ people in China. Li, a striker, has played more than 100 times for China's national team.

IT WAS NOT GOD THAT REJECTED ME

LGBTQ+ MUSLIMS (1996)

Nearly two billion people around the world are Muslim and around one in four countries has a Muslim majority. Attitudes vary hugely, but many LGBTQ+ Muslims face social stigma and legal barriers or persecution from often unsympathetic governments.

The Organization of Islamic Collaboration (OIC), which in 2022 counted 57 nations as members, has shown a broadly united front in attempting to block the inclusion of LGBTQ+ rights as human rights at the United Nations. Same-sex acts are punished with severe sentences in many countries and some, such as Egypt, actively entrap and persecute LGBTQ+ people. In others, including Lebanon and Turkey, same-sex intercourse is permitted and LGBTQ+ organizations are legally recognized. However, these organizations have tended to be secular and to work on civic issues, leaving a shortage of Muslim-specific bodies, including in the West, where Islamophobia and homophobia often need to be addressed in tandem.

Community organizations

While Islamic LGBTQ+ groups were rare for much of the 20th century, several influential organizations

---

The development of LGBTQ+ Muslim activism

Restrictive laws in many Islamic nations make community organization difficult.

Individuals instead start to correspond via online mailing lists and groups.

Mailing list members meet offline and form groups around the world.

LGBTQ+ activism continues via inclusive mosques, literature, music, art, and film.

See also: The Abbasid Caliphate 46–47 ▪ Ottoman gender and sexuality 62–63 ▪ Changing Ottoman society 104–05 ▪ LGBTQ+ activism in Asia 254–55 ▪ The LGBTQ+ struggle in modern Africa 306–07

> Islam does give us leeway to think. We can never change the Qu'ran, but we can change our interpretation of it.
> **Muhsin Hendricks**

have emerged in recent decades. As the internet spread in the 1990s, LGBTQ+ communities formed online. Many Muslims graduated from digital to face-to-face meetings, and some leveraged philanthropic grants to set up organizations.

In 1996, the Inner Circle emerged in Cape Town, South Africa from a series of study circles run by gay imam Muhsin Hendricks. Today, it is the world's longest-standing forum for LGBTQ+ Muslim activism. In 1997, the Al-Fatiha Foundation grew out of a mailing list for LGBTQ+ Muslims in 25 countries. This US-based activist group organized conferences and set up offices in the UK, Turkey, Spain, Canada, and South Africa, before disbanding in 2011. In 1999, the peer-support group Imaan appeared in London, UK.

Inclusive spaces

As LGBTQ+ Muslims met more in real life, the need for inclusive places for worship and marriage gave rise to several initiatives. In 2009, El-Tawhid Juma Circle, an inclusive prayer space and an offshoot of Salaam, opened in Toronto. Here,

people of all genders worship together, which is particularly helpful for trans and non-binary Muslims. In France, gay Algerian-born imam Ludovic-Mohamed Zahed opened an inclusive prayer room in Paris in 2012. That same year, the intersectional feminist Inclusive Mosque Initiative (IMI) was started in the UK. While IMI does not currently have a physical space, members meet virtually for prayers and celebrations.

In the US, gay imam Daayiee Abdullah founded the educational MECCA Institute in 2015 and began officiating same-sex marriage ceremonies. In Germany, an inclusive bricks-and-mortar mosque, the Ibn Rushd-Goethe Mosque in Berlin, was founded by Turkish-born female imam Seyran Ateş in 2017. Support for LGBTQ+ Muslims is growing in Australia too: in 2017, gay Somali-born imam Nur Warsame began holding regular meetings at the Victoria Pride Centre, and Sydney Queer Muslims (SQM) was founded, beginning as a clandestine social media group.

Activism and the arts

Non-profit organizing is not the only form of LGBTQ+ Muslim activism. The 21st century has seen a flourishing of LGBTQ+ activism and representation in scholarship, literature, art, film, and music.

Highlights include Junaid Jahangir and Hussein Abdullatif's rigorous scholarship on *Islamic Law and Muslim Same-Sex Unions* (US/Canada, 2018); *Are You This or Are You This?*, a memoir by Palestinian Jordanian Madian Al Jazerah (2021); Pakistani–Canadian Samra Habib's photo exhibit *Just Me and Allah* (2014) and her memoir *We Have Always Been Here* (2019); New York City-based Indian Parvez Sharma's documentary *A Jihad for Love* (2007); Lebanese–American Mike Mosallam's feature-length romantic comedy *Breaking Fast* (2020); and Lebanese indie band Mashrou' Leila's openly queer lyrics. ▪

Muslims attend Friday prayers at the Ibn Rushd-Goethe Mosque, a place of worship in Berlin that welcomes LGBTQ+ Muslims.

NOT A PUZZLE WITH A MISSING PIECE

THE AROMANTIC AND ASEXUAL SPECTRUM (1997)

IN CONTEXT

FOCUS
Widening sexual identities

BEFORE
1896 German sexologist
Magnus Hirschfeld calls
asexual people "anaesthesia-
sexual" in his pamphlet
Sappho und Sokrates.

1977 One of the first papers
on asexuality – "Asexual
and Autoerotic Women:
Two Invisible Groups" – is
published by American
sexologist Myra T. Johnson.

AFTER
2014 The first worldwide
Aromantic Awareness
Week takes place.

2019 In *Qwear Fashion*
magazine, British model
and activist Yasmin Benoit
introduces the hashtag
#ThisIsWhatAsexualLooksLike
in response to being told that
she does not look asexual.

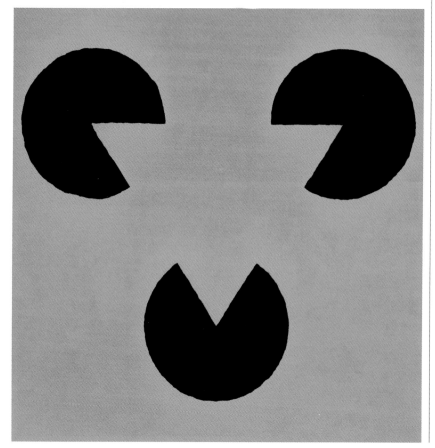

Before the publication of blogger Zoe O'Reilly's essay "My life as an amoeba" in 1997, there were virtually no spaces – real or online – for a community of asexual and aromantic people to gather. Psychologists and sexologists had attested to the existence of asexuals, who featured in scientific essays and models such as the Kinsey Scale of the 1940s and the Storms Sexuality Axis of 1980. There were signs, too, that the label was being used in everyday life. In a 1981 "Dear Abby" letter to American agony aunt Abigail Van Buren – berating her for suggesting that no man (or woman) could be happy and sexually abstinent – the writer spoke

See also: First recognition of asexuality 122–23 ▪ Sexology and psychoanalysis 132–33 ▪ Kinsey's research on sexology 164–65 ▪ *The Asexual Manifesto* 218

on behalf of the "forgotten minority" of the "genuinely asexual". Many asexual people, or those questioning their potential asexuality, worked through their identity alone. As American activist Julie Sondra Decker put it, asexuality was an "invisible orientation".

Community building

Online spaces played a key role in developing a sense of asexual community, and became a forum for discussions that helped to shape modern conceptions of asexuality and aromanticism. The comment section of Zoe O'Reilly's essay was one of the first such spaces. The use of the term "amoeba" reflected O'Reilly's view that the world tended to believe asexual organisms with more than one cell did not exist – amoebas being single-cell organisms that reproduce asexually. The comparison of asexuals with plants and amoebas became a common metaphor in asexual groups, although many in the asexual community now find it offensive.

In 2000, the first major asexual online forum was created – a Yahoo! Group named Haven for the Human Amoeba (HHA). HHA's founders defined asexual simply as "a person who is not sexual", but its members' discussions revealed a lack of consensus about what exactly made a person asexual.

One of the most significant milestones in asexual history was the founding in 2001 of the Asexual Visibility and Education Network (AVEN). As a way of defining asexuality, American activist David Jay, AVEN's founder, put forward the

> Sexuality is like any other activity. There are people for whom skydiving, chocolate cake, and soccer are their world. But some people don't like skydiving, chocolate cake, or soccer.
> **David Jay**

"collective identity model", in which anyone who identifies as asexual is part of the asexual community. This reflected the reality that members of the community all had different experiences of asexuality, and rejected the need for specific categories such as "no sexual attraction" or "no interest in sex".

Attitudes towards sex

Discussions on AVEN's online forums and their precursors created new language for the distinctions among asexuals. They could, for example, be described as "sex positive" or "sex favourable" if they had and enjoyed sex despite not experiencing sexual attraction. They could be "sex repulsed", with a strong aversion to the act as well as a lack of sexual attraction. Or they could be "sex neutral", with no strong feelings either way.

AVEN's members were largely of the opinion that sex was fine – for other people. However, some AVEN members held an antisexual »

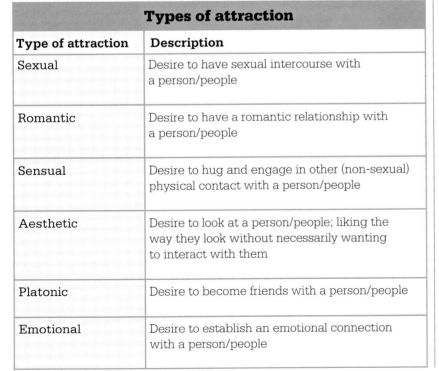

Types of attraction	
Type of attraction	**Description**
Sexual	Desire to have sexual intercourse with a person/people
Romantic	Desire to have a romantic relationship with a person/people
Sensual	Desire to hug and engage in other (non-sexual) physical contact with a person/people
Aesthetic	Desire to look at a person/people; liking the way they look without necessarily wanting to interact with them
Platonic	Desire to become friends with a person/people
Emotional	Desire to establish an emotional connection with a person/people

position – opposed to sex as a whole – for a variety of reasons, such as concerns about overpopulation and the environment; sharing feminist views on unequal power relations; and believing that sex is a base and nihilistic urge.

From ace to aro

Many early AVEN members were both asexual (ace) and what is now called aromantic (aro) – not experiencing romantic attraction. AVEN members initially used the term "asexual–asexual" to denote this dual identity. A 2003 poll on the AVEN website saw 302 people (nearly 17 per cent of respondents)

identify as asexual–asexual – as opposed to "straight–asexual", "gay–asexual", "bi–asexual", or "other" – and one of the earliest uses of the word "aromantic" on the AVEN forum was in a thread responding to the poll. In 2005, some members queried the meaning of asexual–asexual, and one commenter suggested "aromantic asexual" as a preferable alternative. The formation of aromanticism as an identity then moved from AVEN forums to those dedicated to aromantic people.

In 2010, a group of American college students founded the National Coalition for Aromantic Visibility (NCAV), one of the earliest

aromantic organizations. Its goal was to provide a space for all aromantics, and not just aromantic asexuals who might read about aromanticism in AVEN forums. Like AVEN, NCAV was both a community and an educational resource. Other forums, including *Aropocalypse* and the Aromantic-spectrum Union for Recognition, Education, and Advocacy (AUREA), emerged over the next decade, helping to widen the debate and establish that asexuality and aromanticism were not monolithic categories but spectrums (see below) that cover different degrees of attraction rather than an asexual/

Asexual and aromantic identities

Many identities fall within the asexuality and aromanticism spectrum. Below is a selection of some of the most common identities, each with the main flag it has adopted. Alternative flags also exist.

Asexual identities

Asexual
Experiences no sexual attraction.

Demisexual
Experiences sexual attraction only once an emotional bond has been formed.

Fraysexual
Sexual attraction fades after initially meeting someone.

Greysexual
Experiences sexual attraction rarely and/or under extremely specific circumstances.

Lithosexual
Also known as akoisexual or aposexual.
Experiences sexual attraction, but does not want it reciprocated.

Aromantic identities

Aromantic
Experiences no romantic attraction.

Demiromantic
Experiences romantic attraction only once an emotional bond has been formed.

Frayromantic
Romantic attraction fades after initially meeting someone.

Greyromantic
Experiences romantic attraction rarely and/or under extremely specific circumstances.

Lithromantic
Also known as akoiromantic or aporomantic.
Experiences romantic attraction, but does not want it reciprocated.

AVEN members join the 2016 London Pride celebrations. In 2012, London hosted the first World Pride Asexual Conference, which was addressed by AVEN founder David Jay.

alloosexual binary (allosexual meaning experiencing sexual attraction relatively frequently).

Research and challenges

Since the 2000s, researchers in areas such as psychology, sociology, and queer theory have developed new ways to understand and discuss asexuality and aromanticism. Much research has focused on how societies assert sexual and romantic attraction. In 2011, Polish–Canadian feminist scholar Ela Przybylo used the term "sexusociety" to describe a society that makes sexuality "compulsory". American philosophy professor Elizabeth Brake coined the term "amatonormativity" in 2012 to describe the belief that "everyone is better off in an exclusive, romantic, long-term coupled relationship", thus devaluing other kinds of relationship that might be more important to ace and aro people. Similarly, American academic Elizabeth Hanna Hanson used "erotonormativity" in 2014 to describe the expectation for people to experience sexual attraction and have sexual relations.

More recent studies have focused on aspects that intersect with asexuality, such as whiteness and autism. Non-white scholars have highlighted the whiteness of asexual spaces and the need to amplify Black, Hispanic, and Asian voices. Researchers in Italy and the US have also begun to investigate the prevalence of asexuality among autistic people, who are overrepresented in samples of asexual people in comparison to those who are neurotypical.

Even in the LGBTQ+ community, ace and aro people are ostracized by some who believe that these identities are not inherently queer. Some medical professionals still "treat" asexuality as a physical problem, and other asexual and aromantic misconceptions persist, such as the idea that asexuality must result from previous sexual trauma. However, representation of asexual and aromantic characters and people in the media has begun to combat such misconceptions, and aro-ace activists raise awareness in annual events such as the International Asexuality Day. ∎

A participant at the 2016 Helsinki Pride procession in Finland protests against the invisibility of ace and aro sexual orientations.

The split attraction model

Aromantic people are not necessarily asexual, and vice versa. The separation of the two into distinct identities is called the split attraction model. The model sets apart the concepts of romantic and sexual attraction so that a person can call themselves, for example, a biromantic asexual (romantically attracted to their own and different genders, but experiencing no sexual attraction towards them) or a greyromantic homosexual (experiencing little romantic attraction, but sexually attracted to people of their own gender).

While the split attraction model is largely used by people on the asexual and aromantic spectrums, it could also be used by anyone whose orientation includes a disparity in terms of romantic and sexual attraction. Some critics of the model believe that it places too much emphasis on romantic and sexual attraction as definable, separate experiences and ignores the ways in which they can overlap.

HIS LEGACY HAS INSPIRED US TO ERASE HATE

THE MURDER OF MATTHEW SHEPARD (1998)

IN CONTEXT

FOCUS
LGBTQ+ hate crime

BEFORE
1976 Matthew Shepard is born in Casper, Wyoming, US.

AFTER
December 1998 Judy and Dennis Shepard found the Matthew Shepard Foundation in memory of their son and to tackle homophobia.

2002 A film adaptation of *The Laramie Project* premieres at the Sundance Film Festival and is screened on American TV.

2016 For the first time in the US, a criminal charge is brought for selecting a victim because of their gender identity. Joshua Vallum is found guilty in 2017 of murder under the Matthew Shepard and James Byrd Jr. Hate Crimes Prevention Act, 2009.

2018 Shepard's remains are interred at Washington National Cathedral.

I n October 1998, Matthew Shepard, a young gay university student, was brutally attacked, tortured, tied to a fence, and left to die outside the city of Laramie, Wyoming, US. A local cyclist found Shepard tied to this fence a day and a half later, where he was comatose but alive. Shepard was taken to hospital in Fort Collins, Colorado, and put on life support, but he never regained consciousness. Candlelight vigils were held across the country while he lay in intensive care. He died six days after he was attacked, from the severe head injuries he had sustained.

Shepard was killed by Aaron McKinney and Russell Henderson, who had met him at a local pub and offered to give him a lift home. The attackers were charged with and

A candlelit memorial to Matthew Shepard in New York City in 1998. The vigil also remembered James Byrd Jr., a hate-crime murder victim who died four months before Shepard.

See also: Persecution during the Holocaust 156–61 ■ Transgender rights 196–203 ■ The assassination of Harvey Milk 226–27 ■ Don't Ask, Don't Tell 272–75 ■ The Pulse shooting 308–09

In 2020, 23.4% of hate crimes in the US, with 11,126 victims, were motivated by a single bias against sexual orientation, gender, or gender identity. (A further 346 victims were attacked because of more than one bias.) Matthew Shepard's legacy has ensured that these are counted as hate crimes.

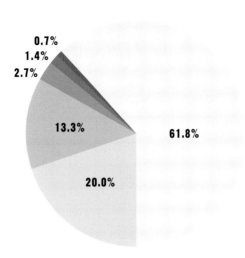

Key

- Race/ethnicity/ancestry
- Sexual orientation
- Religion
- Gender identity
- Disability
- Gender

convicted of first-degree murder, and both sentenced to two consecutive life terms in prison. Largely due to the violent nature of Shepard's killing, the case caused a national and international outcry.

Hate crime

During McKinney's trial, his defence tried to argue that he had been driven into a state of temporary insanity by unwanted sexual advances from Shepard. This is known as a "gay panic" defence, which derives from the homophobic idea that unwanted same-sex sexual advances are so traumatizing that the recipient of such advances cannot be held responsible for an assault that they commit as a self-defence response.

The culture of hatred underlying Shepard's murder was highlighted when his funeral was picketed by members of the bitterly homophobic Westboro Baptist Church. Unbowed, Matthew's parents, Dennis and Judy Shepard, founded the Matthew Shepard Foundation to combat homophobia and to lobby for the strengthening of US federal hate-crime legislation. In October 2009, President Barack Obama signed into law the Matthew Shepard and James Byrd Jr. Hate Crimes Prevention Act. Byrd was a Black American murdered by three white men in Texas in June 1998.

A hate crime is a crime in which the victim is targeted because they belong to a certain social group. This motivation is key to the nature of the crime and is a factor taken into consideration in the penalty for it. The first hate crime law in the US was passed in 1871, to combat racially motivated crimes after the Civil War, during a period known as Reconstruction. From 1968, US federal law recognized hate crimes to be crimes motivated by prejudice with regard to race, colour, religion, or national origin. In 1990, the concept was extended, for the purposes of data collection, to include prejudice regarding sexual orientation – with the proviso that federal funds were not to be used to "encourage homosexuality". In 1994, the definition of hate crime was extended further to include bias against persons with disability.

The 2009 legislation expanded federal hate crime law to include crimes motivated by a victim's gender (actual or perceived), sexual orientation, or gender identity. It also dropped the condition that the victim be engaged in a "federally protected activity", such as voting.

The Laramie Project

In 2000, Matthew Shepard's legacy was enshrined in *The Laramie Project*, a play by Moisés Kaufman and members of New York City's Tectonic Theater Project, created from interviews with Laramie residents about the murder. Along with its epilogue *The Laramie Project: Ten Years Later*, it is produced continually by school and community theatre groups in the US. It was made into a film, written and directed by Kaufman, in 2002.

The play has drawn controversy in parts of the US, with picketing by hate groups. In 2009, parents tried to stop a production at a high school in Las Vegas, but their request for an injunction was denied. ■

There doesn't need to be this kind of violence and hatred in our world.
Judy Shepard
The Meaning of Matthew, 2009

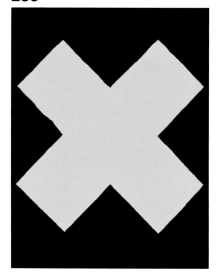

I DON'T NEED TO BE FIXED

CONVERSION THERAPY IS BANNED (1999)

IN CONTEXT

FOCUS
Ending abusive sexual "cures"

BEFORE
1860 The British introduce the Indian Penal Code. It penalizes "carnal intercourse against the order of nature", shaping laws across the British Empire.

1899 German psychiatrist Albert von Shrenck-Notzing is the first to claim that hypnosis can "cure" homosexuality.

1967 The UK government legalizes same-sex acts for men in England and Wales – extended to Scotland in 1980 and Northern Ireland in 1982.

AFTER
2003 Different-sex and same-sex sodomy are legalized in all US states.

2008 The United Nations' first Declaration on Human Rights, Sexual Orientation, and Gender Identity is supported by 66 nations.

Some 19th century doctors and psychiatrists begin to believe that homosexuality is a **"disease"** that **can be "cured"**.

LGBTQ+ protests emphasize the **ubiquity and normality** of different sexualities and identities.

Most medical authorities **declassify LGBTQ+ identities** as "disorders", but **lay conversion therapies persist**.

Western nations increasingly **ban conversion therapy**, but hard-line attitudes persist elsewhere.

In 1999, Brazil became the first country in the world to ban conversion therapy, which the UK LGBTQ+ charity Stonewall defines as "any intervention that seeks to change a person's sexual orientation or gender identity". Such practices began at least a century earlier and range from castrations and lobotomies to aversion therapy – inflicting considerable trauma on subjects.

Victims have included British mathematician Alan Turing, who had accelerated the end of World War II by deciphering codes produced by the German Enigma machine. After his conviction for "gross indecency" in 1952, he was compelled to undergo chemical castration and died by suicide in 1954, aged 41.

Not a "disease" but ...

From the early 1970s onwards, amid increasing protests from LGBTQ+ activists, the medical authorities in many countries that had deemed homosexuality a "disease" gradually acknowledged its normality. The American Psychiatric Association removed "homosexuality" from its list of mental illnesses in 1973, with the World Health Organization following suit in 1992.

See also: The decriminalization of same-sex acts 184–85 ▪ Transgender rights 196–203 ▪ Removal of homosexuality from the DSM 219 ▪ Heteronormativity 268–69

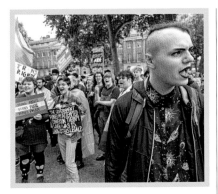

Trans activists staging protests in London (above) and in other major cities are forcing the UK government to rethink its exclusion of trans people from a proposed conversion therapy ban.

While medical interventions subsided, faith-based and other groups across Europe and the Americas have pursued aggressive conversion therapies that brand LGBTQ+ sexualities as "unnatural" and "sinful". Religious groups may employ humiliating prayer and deliverance sessions. In one long-standing "therapeutic" treatment, subjects are exposed to homoerotic content; if they express arousal, therapists induce nausea, vomiting, and electric shocks in an attempt to suppress same-sex desires. "Corrective rape" is a further extreme in parts of Africa.

In 2021, House of Rainbow, a Black, faith-based LGBTQ+ organization in the UK, conducted research into those who have undergone conversion therapy. The research found that avoiding such treatments can be especially challenging for LGBTQ+ members of ethnic minorities in tight-knit communities whose religious beliefs are rooted in rigid colonial Christian orthodoxy. When any deviation from heterosexuality is deemed "sinful",

that influence is difficult to resist. The research further reveals that LGBTQ+ ethnic minorities face greater obstacles than the general population when seeking help from law enforcement agencies or social services. House of Rainbow has urged the government to address these issues in future legislation.

Britain lags behind

Some 20 countries, including Canada in 2021 and France, New Zealand, Norway, and Greece in 2022, have now introduced laws banning conversion therapy. By mid-2022, 20 US states and 100 municipalities had also taken action to ban it for minors.

In Britain, legislation promised in 2018 has not yet materialized. In April 2022, the government's decision to exclude transgender people from its proposed conversion therapy ban was met with outrage and widespread protests. More than 100 LGBTQ+ groups and other organizations refused to attend the UK's first-ever international LGBT rights conference –"Safe To Be Me" – to be held two months later in June, forcing its cancellation. ▪

Being LGBTQIA+ is beautiful, and there is no place in our society for any so-called "interventions" that tell us otherwise.
Nancy Kelley
Chief executive of Stonewall

Jide Macaulay

Born in London, UK, in 1965 to Christian Nigerian parents, Jide Macaulay spent much of his youth in Nigeria. At the age of five, he knew he was gay but fought hard to hide it and change his sexuality. He married a woman in 1991, fathering a child in 1992, and also suffered conversion therapy in the form of prayer, exorcism, and even flogging – "beating the gay away".

In 1994, Macaulay came out as gay and four years later became a Christian minister. In Lagos, Nigeria, in 2006, he founded House of Rainbow as a weekly gathering for LGBTQ+ Christians. It was soon described as "Nigeria's first gay church", and death threats followed. Macaulay, also an HIV-positive activist, returned to London and developed House of Rainbow as a global organization to pioneer dialogue between LGBTQ+ people and religious leaders. It now has sister groups in 22 African and Caribbean countries. In 2022, Macaulay was also appointed chaplain of St Peter's House at Manchester University, UK, promoting equality, diversity, and inclusion.

LOVE WINS

MARRIAGE EQUALITY (2001)

IN CONTEXT

FOCUS
LGBTQ+ rights

BEFORE
1968 Rev. Troy Perry performs the first same-sex marriage ceremony in the United States at a church in Los Angeles.

1970 As the 1968 ceremony is deemed illegal, Perry files the first American lawsuit seeking to legalize same-sex marriage.

AFTER
2013 France, Uruguay, and New Zealand all legalize same-sex marriage.

2015 The Supreme Court case *Obergefell v. Hodges* legalizes same-sex marriage in the US.

2020 Same-sex marriage is legalized in Northern Ireland, in line with the rest of the UK.

2022 A bill designed to ensure federal protection for same-sex marriage clears its first hurdle in the US Senate.

Marriage is historically seen as **the union of a man and woman** for the purpose of procreation and shared economic concerns.

As progress is made on **LGBTQ+ rights and recognition**, pressure for **marriage equality** grows – initially in the West.

Some politicians and religious leaders **resist change**, claiming marriage equality would **harm "traditional" families**.

By 2022, same-sex marriage is **legal in 32 countries**. Support rises in some other nations, but in most **opposition remains**.

For most of human history, marriage has been primarily a socio-economic union – an alliance between families, and a matter of property and producing heirs. However, as love and affection became increasingly important components from around the late 17th century onwards, greater emphasis began to be placed on individuals' ability to select their own partners, which prompted a reassessment of how to understand the institution itself. Notably, as same-sex practice was increasingly decriminalized and depathologized in the latter part of the 20th century,

some advocates declared that to forbid a significant portion of the population from marrying on the basis of gender was indefensible and potentially illegal and that marriage – with all its legal rights – should be available to all couples regardless of gender. In 2001, the Netherlands became the first nation to legalize same-sex marriage.

Opponents, however, have often argued on religious grounds that marriage should be between a man and a woman, with an emphasis on procreation and bringing up children together. They claim that marriage between same-sex couples risks destabilizing a traditional institution.

First positive steps

European countries were the first to actively pursue and approve same-sex unions. In 1979, the Netherlands had recognized cohabiting same-sex partners for the purposes of rent law, and for inheritance tax two years later.

In 1989, Denmark became the first nation to legalize civil unions for same-sex couples. These were something of a midway point between traditional marriage and a looser category of domestic partnerships that existed in the US. They were designed to mirror formal marriages in many respects

Dutch lesbians Helene Faasen and Anne-Marie Thus, together with three gay male couples, became the world's first legally married same-sex couples on 1 April 2001 in Amsterdam.

Henk Krol

Born in 1950 in Tilburg in the Netherlands, Henricus Cornelis Maria "Henk" Krol graduated in psychology from the Free University Amsterdam in 1971 and pursued a career as a journalist and publisher. In 1980, he founded *Gay Krant*, a monthly magazine for the gay community, and was its editor-in-chief. The magazine was taken over by other gay media interests in 2013.

From 1978 until 1985, Krol was the principal spokesman for the People's Party for Freedom and Democracy in the Dutch House of Representatives. In the mid-1980s,

Krol was an early pioneer for same-sex marriage. Because of his political authority and media influence, his voice was heard, helping to make the Netherlands the first country to legalize same-sex marriage in 2001.

From 2016 to 2020, Krol led the 50Plus political party, which represents the interests of Dutch pensioners. After retiring from this post, Krol announced on NPO Radio 1 that he would go down on his knees to propose to his partner, former professional footballer Aldo Koning. The couple married in April 2021.

but without being marriages in name. Several countries in Scandinavia and Western Europe soon copied Denmark's example, followed by other nations and jurisdictions around the world.

However, even as civil unions were emerging as a popular alternative to formal marriage, many advocates viewed them as an imperfect compromise that conveyed neither the respect nor emotional investment of the term

Gay people must open up their windows, open up their doors, and show everyone who they are and how they're living.
Henk Krol

"marriage". Humanists, Unitarians, Quakers, and civil rights groups, together with LGBTQ+ bodies such as Stonewall, were among those who pressed for marriage to include same-sex unions.

From Europe to the US

In the mid-1980s, Dutch gay rights activist Henk Krol, head of *Gay Krant* magazine, had first called for the legalization of same-sex marriage. A commission was created in the Netherlands in 1995; a year later it concluded that marriage should be extended to same-sex couples. In 2000, the Dutch House of Representatives approved same-sex marriage by 109 votes to 33. Endorsed by the Senate, it passed into Dutch law in 2001. Belgium approved same-sex marriage in 2003, Canada and Spain in 2005, followed by South Africa in 2006 and a swathe of Western nations in later years.

In 1989, the year Denmark legalized civil unions, American polls indicated that some 70 per cent of the population opposed

same-sex marriage and 75 per cent believed that same-sex couples should not adopt children. That year, British–American writer and LGBTQ+ activist Andrew Sullivan argued powerfully for same-sex marriage in an article in the progressive American magazine *The New Republic*.

Making the case

Sullivan noted that some cities in the US had domestic partnership laws allowing non-married couples to derive some of the legal benefits of married couples and that these were potentially available to a wide range of cohabiting couples from "an elderly woman and her live-in nurse" to "two frat buddies". Such a broad category, he suggested, was open to abuse and eroded the prestige of traditional relationships. For a devoted same-sex couple, he contended, the commitment of marriage was far more appropriate than a domestic partnership.

A series of court battles relevant to Sullivan's argument played out in Hawaii from 1990. That year, three »

Types of partnership or marriage	
Civil union (or civil partnership)	A civil union gives same-sex couples many of the same legal rights as marriage. Some European countries have legalized gender-neutral civil unions. Heterosexual civil unions are possible in the UK, Canada, New Zealand, some US states and some European nations. In Australia, couples who register their relationship enjoy similar legal rights.
Same-sex marriage	Now legalized in more than 30 countries, including Australia, New Zealand, and 13 European nations, as of 2022, same-sex marriage confers most of the rights of opposite-sex marriage, although many nations exclude adoption rights.
Non-sexual same-sex marriage	Women in several African countries practise this form of marriage. In Kenya, 5–10 per cent of women are involved, primarily to secure an inheritance for families without sons. Such marriages are also permitted among Igbo women in Nigeria.
Genderqueer marriage	Non-binary marriages, like same-sex marriages, have been legal across the US since 2015, and are also legal in Australia and New Zealand. In the UK, transgender people can marry provided they have a gender recognition certificate. In the EU, rules around genderqueer marriage vary from country to country.

same-sex couples applied for marriage licences and were denied them. Their subsequent lawsuit, *Baehr v. Lewin*, claimed that limiting marriage to opposite-sex couples was unconstitutional. In 1993, the Supreme Court of the State of Hawaii ruled that under Hawaii's equal protection clause, refusing a marriage licence to same-sex couples constituted discrimination.

The Supreme Court, however, remanded the case back to the trial court, where in 1996, Judge Kevin Chang first ruled in favour of legalizing same-sex marriage, but the next day reversed his ruling. In 1998, Hawaii's voters approved a constitutional amendment that permitted only opposite-sex couples to marry. Same-sex couples were offered "reciprocal beneficiary registration", with limited rights.

Though unsuccessful, the Hawaii court battles helped lay the groundwork for the legalization of same-sex marriage in US states; Massachusetts was the first state to legalize same-sex marriage in 2004. It took a further 11 years before same-sex marriage was approved across the nation. According to a 2021 Gallup poll, more than 70 per cent of Americans now support same-sex marriage – up from around 12 per cent when Sullivan wrote his same-sex marriage article in 1989.

Approval and opposition

What was largely a Western phenomenon has become more widespread. In 2022, Cuba and Chile, together with Slovenia and Switzerland, joined the 29 other nations that have legalized same-sex marriage since 2001, bringing the global total to 33, with Andorra due to add its approval in 2023. In Cuba, an overwhelming majority voted in favour in a referendum that received vocal support from President Miguel Díaz-Canel and also Mariela Castro, daughter of former First Secretary Raúl Castro and niece of Fidel Castro, and an outspoken LGBTQ+ advocate.

Same-sex marriage has been legalized in nations accounting for a fifth of the global population, yet most countries – especially in Africa and Asia – remain firmly opposed. In 2022, the Church of England was still refusing to conduct or bless same-sex marriages, and European Union members such as Hungary, Poland, and Slovakia oppose both civil unions and same-sex marriage, despite an EU ruling in 2018 that same-sex marriages performed in one EU nation should be recognized throughout the EU.

In the US, where 13 states still criminalized same-sex activity in 2003, the issue of marriage equality has highlighted the rift between progressive supporters of LGBTQ+ rights and a significant number of conservative voters – largely in

This lesbian couple were allowed to marry at the district court in Gurgaon, India, in 2011, although the country does not recognize same-sex marriage.

Middle America. Their "traditional values", encouraged by the religious right and conservative politicians such as ex-president Donald Trump, risk becoming more entrenched.

LGBTQ+ questioning

Some LGBTQ+ academics have also questioned same-sex marriage, considering marriage to be, as Cuban American queer theorist José Esteban Muñoz wrote, a "suspect institution" symptomatic of a "corrupt and bankrupt social order". These critics link marriage to homonationalism and are sceptical of what they say is the increasing complicity of Western LGBTQ+ discourses – including the advocacy of marriage equality – with nationalist, capitalist politics.

Others believe that same-sex marriage is too narrow a category and think that its legalization has important implications for a broader range of non-binary individuals. If society discards the assumption that matrimony must be between a man and a woman, they query, why is there a need to insist that either partner must self-identify as a man or a woman? In her 2008 essay "Beyond Marriage", American academic Lisa Duggan, a self-described "commie, pink, queer feminist", argued that same-sex marriage is "a very narrow and utterly inadequate solution" for the problems that most queer people face and fails to provide the full equality and "expansively reimagined forms of kinship" that reflect actual LGBTQ+ lives. ∎

LGBTQ+ activists stage a flamboyant fashion show in Bangkok, Thailand, in a bid to legalize same-sex marriage. A parliamentary vote in favour in June 2022 was the first positive step.

Edith "Edie" Windsor

Born in 1929 in Philadelphia, Pennsylvania, Edie Windsor, née Schlain, gained a master's degree in mathematics from New York University in 1957. She worked for 16 years at IBM, marrying Saul Windsor in 1963; they divorced a year later. In 1965, Windsor began dating Thea Spyer, a Dutch-born psychologist. They lived together in New York City and later on Long Island. Windsor was now actively involved with LGBTQ+ organizations. In 2007, Windsor and Spyer married in Toronto, Canada.

Spyer, who had made Windsor executor and sole beneficiary of her estate, died in 2009, and Windsor claimed federal estate tax exemption for surviving spouses. When this was refused, she filed a lawsuit claiming that the 1996 Defense of Marriage Act (DOMA) discriminated against legally married same-sex couples. In 2013, the Supreme Court ruled in her favour and Section 3 of DOMA was declared unconstitutional. In 2016, a year after same-sex marriage was legalized in the US, Windsor remarried in New York City. She died in 2017.

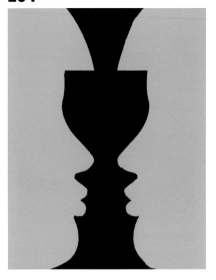

I LIKE THE WINE, NOT THE LABEL

PANSEXUALITY (2002)

In 2002, *The Guardian* published an article by British journalist Rose Rouse on the so-called "pansexual revolution" taking place among the sexually liberated. It described pansexuality as sexual fluidity – in which people stepped outside their assumed or self-proclaimed labels. An apparently gay man might date a woman, or a woman presumed to be heterosexual might sleep with another woman. Rouse gave several famous examples, but these people were not self-identifying pansexuals; she simply named individuals who had been presumed monosexual (only attracted to one gender) and were now seemingly not.

The term "pansexual" was not originally used to describe sexual orientation. One of the earliest references to pansexuality was in 1914, when "pan-sexualism" was used to describe Sigmund Freud's theory that all human behaviour is motivated by sex. Later in the 20th century, "pansexual" was also used to describe people who were active in the kink scene or were open to unconventional sex acts.

Sexual openness
From the 1970s, "pansexual" was increasingly used to describe openness in sexual orientation. In 1974, American rock singer Alice Cooper defined it as being able to "relate sexually to any human being". In 1982, American feminist Rita Mae Brown claimed she was expelled from her university in the '60s for being open to loving anybody – something she called

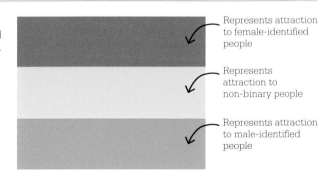

The pansexual flag has been used since 2010, when it was created and shared on Tumblr by British user Jasper V, who is non-binary.

Represents attraction to female-identified people

Represents attraction to non-binary people

Represents attraction to male-identified people

See also: Sexology and psychoanalysis 132–133 ▪ Kinsey's research on sexology 164–65 ▪ Transgender rights 196–203 ▪ The creation of the Pride flag 224–25 ▪ Bisexuality 262–65 ▪ Heteronormativity 270–71 ▪ Conversion therapy is banned 286–87

pansexuality. But takeup of the term was slow: Naomi Tucker's 1995 *Bisexual Politics: Theories, Queries, and Visions* notes that it was a label adopted by those seeking sexual liberation, but was not widely used.

A new century

The term's popularity skyrocketed in the 2000s and 2010s. Dutch actor and singer Peter Boom defined it in his 2002 essay on the "Theory of Pansexuality" as including all kinds of sexuality that could exist in a human. The Livejournal online community "I Am Pansexual" was created the same year, with its first post defining pansexuality as those who "love people of all genders". The community's founding post also defined pansexuality in opposition to bisexuality: it claimed that pansexuals, "unlike bisexuals", were also attracted to transgender, gender-fluid, and androgynous people. This, along with many definitions from the early 2000s focusing on transgender inclusion, contradicted many bisexuals' definitions of their sexuality, which

already encompassed people of all genders – including transgender and non-binary people. Most people now agree that while bi- and pansexuality broadly overlap, the key difference is that bisexuals can be attracted to their own and other genders, but are not necessarily attracted to all gender identities; pansexuals, on the other hand, are.

The number of pansexual people worldwide is not known. This may in part be due to the failure of many surveys to include pansexual as a possible orientation. For example, a 2020 Gallup survey of LGBTQ+ identity in the US gave respondents a choice of identifying as heterosexual, lesbian, gay, bisexual, transgender, and "other". However, we do know that pansexuality is on the rise, as more people discover and identify with it – often in online communities. In 2016, American psychologists Christopher Belous and Melissa Bauman found that web searches for "pansexuality" rose significantly in 2004 and 2012. Google Trends also shows that the topic's popularity has increased dramatically since 2019.

However one defines themselves, whether it's "they" or "he" or "she", I fall in love with the person – and that's that. I'm attracted to the person.
Cara Delevingne
British model and actor

In 2015, Dan Levy's character David in the Canadian comedy show *Schitt's Creek* used wine as a metaphor for attraction – he likes red wine, white wine, rosé, and "a merlot that used to be a chardonnay", seemingly a metaphor for transgender people. His conclusion, "I like the wine, not the label", resonated with many pansexual viewers. ▪

Layla Moran

Born in London in 1982, Layla Moran became Britain's first Member of Parliament of Palestinian descent when she was elected to represent Oxford West and Abingdon in 2017 for the Liberal Democrats. In 2020, she again broke new ground as Britain's first MP to come out as pansexual. In 2020, Moran announced her relationship with her partner Rosy Cobb in an interview with the LGBTQ+ publication *PinkNews*, explaining her sexuality as attraction that is "about the person themselves" rather than their gender. The

interview prompted interest in pansexuality, with articles appearing across British media.

Moran has used her political platform to criticize homophobia in Britain, and has described Parliament as a "weird, backwards place" for LGBTQ+ people. In 2021 and 2022, she accused the Conservative government of stalling on LGBTQ+ rights, calling on it to reform the Gender Recognition Act and ban conversion therapy for transgender people, who had been excluded from the government's proposed ban.

A QUEER PSYCHOLOGY OF AFFECT
AFFECT THEORY (2003)

IN CONTEXT

FOCUS
Queer theory

BEFORE
1962 Silvan Tomkins presents his affect theory in *Affect Imagery Consciousness*.

AFTER
2004 British-Australian scholar Sara Ahmed's *The Cultural Politics of Emotion* argues that emotions are social practices.

2009 *Cruising Utopia: The Then and There of Queer Futurity* by Cuban–American theorist José Esteban Muñoz explores the impulse to see and feel beyond the present.

2009 American theorist Heather Love's *Feeling Backward: Loss and the Politics of Queer History* focuses on "bad feelings" in queer histories.

2011 American scholar Lauren Berlant's *Cruel Optimism* examines the promises of capitalism and trauma theory.

Originating in the US with psychologist Silvan Tomkins, affect theory deals with feelings ("affects"). Tomkins identified nine affects: enjoyment, interest, anger, fear, surprise, disgust, shame, distress, and avoidance. These are psychological, have a physical impact, and are induced by social and political conditions.

Affect in queer theory
From the 1990s, American writer Eve Kosofsky Sedgwick, among others, brought affect into queer theory. In *Touching Feeling: Affect, Pedagogy, Performativity* (2003), Sedgwick described the role of shame in queer identities. Society introduces the idea of shame to infants very early, and it is fundamental in the development of behaviour and sense of self.

Also in 2003, American historian and queer theorist Ann Cvetkovich published *An Archive of Feelings: Trauma, Sexuality, and Lesbian Public Culture*, which told the previously undocumented stories

I think fine-grained accounts of affect are really important for addressing a whole host of non-normative and minoritarian experiences, queer, trans, or otherwise.
Heather Love
American queer theorist

of lesbian activists in New York City. According to Cvetkovich, "trauma" should be understood not just in a clinical sense but also as part of ordinary, intimate experience. The emotions arising from trauma – loss, grief, and mourning – are important and empowering, and should be valued rather than avoided. Queer history, says Cvetkovich, must reclaim a story not just of events but also of feelings. ∎

See also: Reclaiming the term "queer" 256–57 ▪ Sedgwick's *Epistemology of the Closet* 268–69

WE LEARNED TO BE QUARE, BLACK, AND PROUD
QUEER OF COLOUR THEORY (2004)

IN CONTEXT

FOCUS
Intersectionality

BEFORE
1977 The Combahee River Collective Statement is published in the US, arguing that Black women face a synthesis of oppressions.

1989 American civil rights scholar Kimberlé Crenshaw formalizes the theory of intersectionality, describing the combined effects of multiple factors of social identity.

2001 American sociologist E. Patrick Johnson coins the term "quare" – Black American vernacular for "queer".

AFTER
2008 The University of Chicago, US, hosts the first "Race, Sex, Power" annual conference on the subject of Black and Latine sexuality.

I n 2004's *Aberrations in Black*, American sociologist Roderick Ferguson formulated what he called "queer of color theory". The concept, also known as "queer of color critique", draws on theories of intersectionality to argue that in order to understand the lives of queer people – particularly queer people of colour – it is not enough to focus on sexuality alone. Instead, we must think about sexuality as intersecting with categories such as race, class, gender, and nationality.

The critique emerged in part as a resistance to the racism found in white queer communities and to the heterosexism found in communities of colour and in studies of ethnicity. Its origins can be traced back to 1970s Black feminist theory, which articulated the idea that different systems of oppression intersect, creating unique conditions for those living at the overlap of minority identities. Ferguson's ideas were developed by American queer theorists Chandan Reddy and Fatima El-Tayeb, and American Black studies scholar George Lipsitz.

Queer of colour theory questions the assumptions that underpin and distort mainstream concepts of identity – especially the perception of "whiteness" as neutral. It also strives to bridge the gap between theory and practice, pointing out that theory is useful only if it responds to the diverse realities of people's lives. It asks how "queer" a theory really is if it considers sexuality to be more important than other aspects of individuality. ∎

We have to encourage and develop practices whereby queerness isn't a surrender to the status quos of race, class, gender, and sexuality.
Roderick Ferguson
Interview in *Truthout*, 2018

See also: Black lesbian feminism 210–13 ▪ Ball culture 214–15 ▪ Reclaiming the term "queer" 256–57 ▪ Heteronormativity 270–71 ▪ Homonationalism 302–03

DISABILITY *IS QUEER,* QUEERER, THAN QUEER

QUEER DISABILITY STUDIES (2006)

IN CONTEXT

FOCUS
Queer disabled identities

BEFORE
1960s Disabled people begin to reclaim the word "crip" (derived from "cripple").

1970s Gay and lesbian studies are first taught at university level; the University of California, Berkeley is one of the first to offer a course.

1983 British disability rights activist Mike Oliver coins the term "social model of disability".

AFTER
2020 Queer disability theorists write extensively about the COVID-19 pandemic as perceived through a "crip" lens.

2021 The Queer Disability Studies (QDS) network is launched – an international online forum for sharing QDS contributions and comments.

In the 20th century, disability studies and queer studies were seen as unrelated academic fields. LGBT studies came first but, as new social theories of disability emerged, this too became a fertile area of academic interest, and the two found common ground. The publication of American theorist Robert McRuer's *Crip Theory* in 2006 then confirmed the birth of queer disability studies.

From activism to academia

Disability and queerness are both marginal positions that are subject to intense stigma. In the mid-20th century, both the disabled and LGBTQ+ communities generated social movements with the aim of

See also: Compulsory heterosexuality 233 ▪ Reclaiming the term "queer" 256–57 ▪ Butler's *Gender Trouble* 266–67 ▪ Sedgwick's *Epistemology of the Closet* 268–69 ▪ Affect theory 296

> My first experience of queerness centered not on sexuality or gender, but on disability. Early on, I understood my body to be irrevocably different from those of my … playmates …
> **Eli Clair**
> **American writer and activist (1963–)**

promoting their respective rights. Yet one group was often excluded from the other – largely due to discrimination, including fears that the stigma associated with each group might impede activist efforts.

As LGBTQ+ and disability rights movements gained momentum, scholarly fields associated with each movement emerged. These fields aim to explore the nature of each identity. They destigmatize them by challenging misunderstandings, and examine them within areas such as history, politics, and the arts, promoting the position of the respective community in academia. Both disciplines maintain close ties to the community activism from which they emerged, and many of their ideas originate in activist communities.

In disability studies, the social model of disability emerged in 1983. It contended that people are disabled by social barriers, such as discriminatory attitudes and poor accessibility, rather than by physical or mental impairments. The idea quickly gained traction and became prominent in disability policy, transforming the way that disability was understood. Queer theory was similarly influential. It emerged from women's studies and gay and lesbian studies in the early 1990s as a lens to deconstruct gender and sexuality, and challenge associated hierarchies. Under its influence, the field was increasingly referred to as "queer studies", expanding its focus beyond homosexuality.

Joining forces
Disability studies and queer studies are both interdisciplinary, drawing on ideas from multiple academic disciplines, and intersectional – they study how multiple aspects of identity overlap to create complex frameworks of social advantage and disadvantage. Thus, when both fields gained momentum in the late 1990s and early 2000s, scholars from each discipline began to examine ideas from the other, and queer disability studies emerged. The Queer Disability Conference in California in 2002 was the first ever international gathering of disabled people identifying as LGBTQ+.

Crip theory
For many, the term "crip theory" is synonymous with queer disability studies. Just as the LGBTQ+ community has reclaimed "queer" from its status as a slur, disabled people reclaimed the term "crip" (from "cripple") as the disability rights movement became more prominent. The term was first applied in an academic context »

LGBTQ+ and disability rights activists march at the 2020 Pride Parade in Taipei, Taiwan. More than 130,000 people took part.

I am yearning for an elsewhere ... in which disability is understood ... as political, as valuable, as integral.
Alison Kafer
Feminist, Queer, Crip, 2013

by American scholar Carrie Sandahl in a 2003 article entitled "Queering the Crip or Cripping the Queer?", which explained that disability studies could usefully build on theoretical ideas borrowed from other sources such as queer theory.

While scholars such as Sandahl first used queer ideas to write about disability, it was Robert McRuer's *Crip Theory* of 2006 that confirmed the birth of queer disability studies. It was the first extended exploration of how queer theoretical ideas could be used to inform disability studies, and how this might shape wider ideas about bodies and identities.

McRuer makes extensive use of an idea that American poet and writer Adrienne Rich outlined in her 1980 essay "Compulsory Heterosexuality and Lesbian Existence". Rich described how society suggests there is no viable alternative to heterosexuality, generating pressure for people to engage in heterosexual relationships. McRuer establishes a similar concept – compulsory able-bodiedness – in which being able-bodied is cast as normal and natural, while disability is framed as undesirable, abnormal, and deviant.

McRuer explains that compulsory heterosexuality and compulsory able-bodiedness both create highly idealized notions, to which disabled and LGBTQ+ people cannot match up. Disabled people can be understood as "queer" because not behaving sexually is often assumed in disabled people, so that any display of sexuality is deemed "inappropriate". Queer people can also be understood as "disabled" for being similarly labelled "defective" and subject to medical control, such as clinical diagnoses. Thus, compulsory heterosexuality and compulsory able-bodiedness are reliant on each other, both reinforcing the "queerness" of disabled and LGBTQ+ people.

Beyond *Crip Theory*

Following the publication of *Crip Theory*, queer disability studies expanded. Among several key works that developed earlier crip theoretical ideas and introduced new ones, *Feminist, Queer, Crip* (2013) by American scholar Alison Kafer has been especially influential. Kafer extends the idea of compulsory able-bodiedness and discusses compulsory able-mindedness too, stressing how cognitive impairment is framed as abnormal in a similar way to physical impairment. She also considers the relationship between disability and time, and explains how dominant understandings of time are based on able minds and bodies. Disabled people experience time differently, sometimes requiring more time to process ideas, perform tasks, or manage disruptions associated with their disability. For Kafer, a more flexible concept of time is required – "crip time" – a version of time that is adjusted to meet disabled needs.

From the work of Sandahl, McRuer, Kafer, and other crip theorists, certain key principles

Crip theory

Rejected assumptions	Alternative understandings
Disability is **based on flaws** in people's bodies or minds.	Disability is **socially constructed**.
Once established, disability is **fixed**.	Disability is **fluid**.
Disability and non-disability can be applied as **distinct categories**.	Disability and non-disability **cannot be clearly distinguished**.
Non-disability is the **normal, natural, ideal** identity.	It is **not possible** to apply labels of **normality or abnormality** around disability.

have emerged. For example, crip theory challenges the idea that disability is based on intrinsic flaws in certain people's bodies or minds. Instead, it underlines how society shapes our understanding of disability, creating its meaning, setting its boundaries, and labelling certain bodies and minds as disabled. Views of disability vary in different societies and also evolve, as public perceptions continually change. Disability itself may also be fluid, varying in nature or intensity over time, shifting alongside such contextual changes. These moving boundaries can make it difficult to clearly distinguish between disability and non-disability.

The 2016 marriage of disabled British YouTuber Jessica Kellgren-Hayes (seated) to former dentist Claudia Fozard is captured at the seafront in Brighton, UK.

Crip theory firmly rejects a further assumption – that disabled people are nonsexual. It highlights the potential of disabled people to enjoy relationships, be sexual, and experience and give pleasure. This was a topic that earlier disability studies tended to ignore as they viewed disability from a purely clinical perspective.

Crip theory's interpretation of such aspects of life has resonated throughout the disabled community, particularly with those who suffer chronic illnesses, who have both contributed to and taken up crip theoretical ideas.

Continuing debate

Recognizing the intersections between queerness and disability has been a key role of recent studies and one that has allowed many queer disabled people to better understand their identity. However, although many have welcomed the advent of queer disability studies, others suggest that it may be harmful. The term "crip" has been particularly contentious, as it was historically used as a highly offensive slur – as was "queer" – and sometimes still is. The label is also primarily associated with physically disabled people, so some also contend that its use in crip theory suggests a focus on physical impairment at the expense of cognitive impairment.

Certain scholars have also argued against the idea of viewing disability as a social construct. They believe that this could potentially weaken disabled people's political claims to greater rights, as such rights rely on understanding disability as fixed and material. They point out that blurring the boundaries between disability and non-disability creates potential for anyone to claim a disabled identity, and therefore invalidating those with "real" disabilities by universalizing and consequently trivializing disability.

Scholars are continuing to grapple with such criticisms as queer disability studies further develops and expands, spreading to academic centres across the globe. ∎

Rosie Jones performs live at the 2019 Latitude Festival in Suffolk, UK. The popular comedian has ataxic cerebral palsy and is gay.

Queer disability culture

The first years of the 21st century saw the emergence of queer disability culture. Known as crip culture, it loosely informs the principles of crip theory and has now entered mainstream culture, including television, fashion, and art. Its stars include disabled transgender Antiguan-American model Aaron Philip, British comic Rosie Jones, and American writer Ryan O'Connell, whose semi-autobiographical Netflix series *Special* explores the life of a gay man with cerebral palsy.

Such celebrities have made queer disabled people more visible. In the past, they were largely absent from mainstream culture where heterosexuality and non-disability tend to predominate. In 2016, only five per cent of disabled characters in the top ten American TV shows were played by disabled actors. Now, as scriptwriters pursue authenticity, disabled and LGBTQ+ characters are increasingly played by those who truly understand such roles.

THE VIOLENCE OF LIBERALISM
HOMONATIONALISM (2007)

IN CONTEXT

FOCUS
Exploiting LGBTQ+ rights

BEFORE
1980s The HIV/AIDS epidemic initially fuels homophobia in the US and Europe.

1996 The Defense of Marriage Act (DOMA) denies same-sex partners in the US all the rights enjoyed by heterosexual couples.

AFTER
2010 America's Don't Ask, Don't Tell Repeal Act enables gay, lesbian, and bisexual people to serve openly in the US Armed Forces. In 2021, the transgender ban is repealed.

2010 San Francisco-based QUIT (Queers Undermining Israeli Terrorism) accuses Israel of "pinkwashing" – promoting LGBTQ+ liberalism to distract from its actions in Palestine.

2015 The Supreme Court decision in *Obergefell v. Hodges* achieves full same-sex marriage equality in the US.

Since the mid-20th century, many countries have passed legislation boosting LGBTQ+ equal rights. Homonationalism is a complex concept that explores the effects that embracing this new "liberalism" has had on LGBTQ+ communities and domestic and world politics. American philosopher and queer theorist Jasbir Puar introduced the concept in *Terrorist Assemblages: Homonationalism in Queer Times* (2007), mainly with reference to the United States, which she accuses of weaponizing its "gay-friendly" status to further what some see as imperialist aims.

Rights and racism
Since the 1950s, multiple movements in the US have called for equal rights for LGBTQ+ people; this activism took deeper root from the 1980s. The 2003 US Supreme Court decision in *Lawrence v. Texas* meant that same-sex acts were finally decriminalized – decades after similar European rulings.

Puar outlines a subsequent rise in gay and lesbian representation in the US mainstream, with television shows such as *Queer Eye for the Straight Guy* (2003) and *The L Word* (2004). She then sets it against

Gay and lesbian rights discourses can risk slipping into Islamophobic and racist discourses.
Jasbir Puar
The Guardian, 2010

the racial backlash and rising Islamophobia prompted by the al-Qaeda terrorist attacks on 11 September 2001, which claimed 2,996 lives. Puar also explores how, during the post-9/11 "War on Terror", anti-Muslim racism played a role in the physical and sexual abuse of prisoners by US troops at Iraq's Abu Ghraib prison, exposed by the American media in 2004.

Puar's contention is that the US used its new sexually progressive multiculturalism to fuel racism and help justify foreign interventions in Muslim nations that are painted as homophobic and "less-civilized" – propaganda that leaves no place for

See also: Towards gay liberation 170–77 ▪ AIDS activism 244–45 ▪ Heteronormativity 270–71 ▪ Don't Ask, Don't Tell 272–75 ▪ LGBTQ+ Muslims 278–79 ▪ Marriage equality 288–93 ▪ Queer of colour theory 297

Homonationalism in practice

States use "progressive" LGBTQ+ equal rights to highlight "backwardness" in enemy powers that punish non-heterosexual citizens.

Gender recognition on passports allows nation states to make a claim to excellence and liberal tolerance.

Transnational adoption by same-sex couples implies that children can be offered a better life in Western nations than in their home country.

Emerging economies advance LGBTQ+ rights to promote and expand economic opportunities with new trading partners.

LGBTQ+ Muslims. Similarly, Puar suggests that Israel's gay-friendly stance parallels and "pinkwashes" its mistreatment of Palestinians.

Facet of capitalist power

Puar argues that homonationalism is not a question of good or bad but simply a modern phenomenon that now has a role in capitalist power play. In the US, fuelled by popular demand, it was a deliberate movement away from the idea that heterosexuality is the "right" and only option and that LGBTQ+ people should be punished. However, Puar

suggests that providing LGBTQ+ equal rights is of primary benefit to the state. The rights accorded to LGBTQ+ people who choose to live and work within a state's national framework can distract from those lost when states increase their power to scrutinize, detain, and deport "undesirable" individuals; an increase in LGBTQ+ rights can thus mask a shift to the nationalist right.

In *Out of Time: The Queer Politics of Postcoloniality* (2020), Indian writer Rahul Rao has expanded on Puar's ideas. His own theory of homocapitalism, a term

coined in 2015, explains that nations, international financial institutions, and high-profile LGBTQ+ activists support LGBTQ+ assimilation and progress because it is economically beneficial and furthers productivity. Yet, as Rao points out, involving LGBTQ+ individuals in capitalist objectives risks creating a divide between the "productive" and the "unproductive", posing a threat to queer anti-capitalist activists.

Homonationalism remains highly relevant in today's world, operating as a powerful force on national and international levels. ▪

A pinkwash protest in Tel Aviv, Israel, at its annual Pride Parade – the Middle East's largest – highlights policies that segregate Palestinians.

Pinkwashing

Closely linked to homonationalism is a trend called pinkwashing. It refers to ways in which people, organizations, and nations promote and embrace LGBTQ+ equal rights to indicate their progressive liberalism – with an ulterior motive. Governments often do it to mask societal inequalities or establish moral superiority over "less-civilized" foreign powers, while commercial interests may pinkwash their pursuit of profits with displays of LGBTQ+ inclusion.

A play on "greenwashing", the idea that companies become "eco-friendly" to enhance their appeal, pinkwashing was first used in 2010 by American political activists to refer to Israel's pro-LGBTQ+ public relations. A year later, American author and lesbian activist Sarah Schulman used the term in a widely read editorial in *The New York Times* to denote a feature of Israeli homonationalism. Others argue that, far from being a mere political tool, Israel's LGBTQ+ rights are the most progressive in the Middle East.

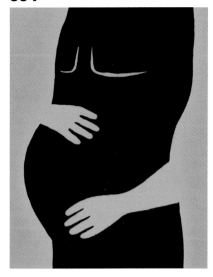

I SEE MYSELF AS MY OWN SURROGATE
TRANSGENDER PREGNANCY AND REPRODUCTIVE HEALTHCARE (2008)

IN CONTEXT

FOCUS
Transgender rights and medicine

BEFORE
1906 Karl M. Baer becomes the first documented trans man to undergo gender affirmation surgery, in Germany.

1930 Danish painter Lili Elbe is the first documented trans woman to undergo gender affirmation surgery.

AFTER
2014 In Australia, statistics that allow patients to nominate their own gender reveal that 54 babies have been born to trans men over the past year.

2017 The European Court of Human Rights rules that the requirement for sterilization for legal gender recognition is a violation of human rights.

2019 Sweden is the first European country to legally recognize trans men as fathers and trans women as mothers.

In 2008, American Thomas Beatie made headlines after appearing on *The Oprah Winfrey Show* while pregnant with his first child. Beatie had always wanted to have children, and as a transgender man he chose to keep his reproductive organs. He was able therefore to become pregnant, carry the baby, and give birth. He is legally recognized as a man and considers himself to be the child's father.

Beatie has spoken about the difficulties he faced with the healthcare system in the US during his pregnancy journey. He was turned away by doctors due to their

Wanting to have a biological child is neither a male nor female desire, but a human desire.
Thomas Beatie
Labor of Love, 2008

religious beliefs, deliberately addressed with the wrong pronouns, and made to see a psychologist to check he was mentally fit to raise a child. He and his then-wife Nancy went through nine different health professionals before they could access a sperm bank. To avoid any further obstacles, they then chose home insemination.

The media's reporting of Beatie's pregnancy aimed to shock. Some said it was a hoax, and claimed Beatie had only transitioned because he couldn't have a same-sex marriage with his wife. He became known as "the pregnant man" and entered the Guinness World Records as the "first married man to give birth", but he was far from the first transgender man to carry a child. American Matt Rice, who gave birth in 1999, was among the first trans men to share his pregnancy publicly. Rice had transitioned but retained his uterus and became pregnant via a sperm donor.

Despite the sensationalism, Beatie's story was immensely significant. It provided visibility to trans and non-binary pregnancy and helped bring about a positive shift in the social discourse around reproductive healthcare.

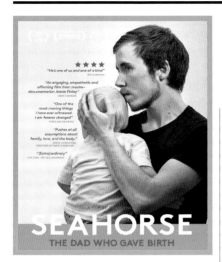

In the 2019 film *Seahorse*, British journalist Freddy McConnell movingly documents his path to parenthood, from preparing to conceive to the birth of his first child.

who menstruate are women, yet the period industry has excluded transgender and non-binary people by using terms such as "women's hygiene" and "feminine care", and hyper-feminine packaging. The blog and Twitter account, "People Who Menstruate", was started in 2020 to include trans men, non-binary, and intersex people in discussions about gynaecological healthcare.

In 2019, a new Twitter campaign #healthnothygiene sought to rename Menstrual Hygiene Day – a platform that works to improve access to menstrual products – to Menstrual Health Day. The idea behind the campaign was to remove the notion that periods are unhygienic and dirty, and to broaden the narrative around menstruation. In 2020, a petition called #RenameDontShame was launched, asking supermarkets

I felt isolated; everything about periods was tailored to girls, yet me, a boy, was experiencing this and nothing in the world documented that.
Kenny Ethan Jones
British transgender rights activist

in North America and the UK to alter their labelling from "feminine hygiene" or "sanitary products", to "period products" or "menstrual products" to be more inclusive, and to destigmatize periods as unclean. In New Zealand that year, the supermarket chain Countdown became the first to rebrand products; and in late 2021, the retailer Asda was praised for changing the name of its aisles to "period products" in the UK. ▪

More work to do

Conditions for transgender and non-binary pregnancies can improve: by reproductive options, such as gestational surrogacy or egg freezing, and better access to funded reproductive and fertility care; by the use of inclusive language such as "birthing parent" or "chestfeeding"; and by carrying out more research into transgender reproductive healthcare and challenging misinformation such as claims that taking testosterone causes infertility. Widening efforts to make midwifery care more inclusive of transgender parents – which has happened, for example, in some parts of the UK – would be another positive step, as would a change in the law to allow parents to choose the parental title registered on their children's birth certificates, which is the case in Iceland, Sweden, and Denmark.

Changing the discourse

Beatie's experience highlights the issues transgender men face in the healthcare system. For example, not all women menstruate, and not all those

Barriers to healthcare access

Beatie was not alone in his experience of the healthcare system in the US. In 2015, the US National Center for Transgender Equality produced the results of a survey of 28,000 respondents. According to the survey, 23% of participants did not see a doctor when they needed to because of their fear of being mistreated as a transgender person; 33% of respondents did not see a doctor due to economic reasons; this percentage increased for people of colour including multiracial (42%), Indigenous (41%), Black (40%), and Latine (37%) respondents, who were not likely to seek healthcare because of the intersection of racism and economic pressures. For people with disabilities, it rose to 42%.

The survey results demonstrate that access to healthcare for transgender people is affected by several factors, including race, immigration status, and economic resources, as well as transphobic stigma.

WE NEED OUR OXYGEN TO BREATHE

THE LGBTQ+ STRUGGLE IN MODERN AFRICA (2014)

Precolonial Africa is **largely tolerant of different sexualities**, orientations, and gender relations.

Western colonial powers, backed by Christian missionary doctrine, **criminalize same-sex relationships**.

In post-colonial Africa, **criminalization persists** in many independent nations.

I n 2014, Gambia's president Yahya Jammeh denounced homosexuals as "vermin" to be fought like malaria-carrying mosquitos. The same year, Nigeria's president Goodluck Jonathan signed the Same-Sex Marriage (Prohibition) Bill into law, prompting mob attacks against LGBTQ+ people. At the time, some 40 African nations had discriminatory anti-LGBTQ+ laws. These were strongly influenced by 19th-century Christian doctrine and first imposed by Western colonial powers to control any sexual behaviours and gender expressions considered to be "against nature" – in effect, those that were not heterosexual.

Colonial laws reinforced

Before European powers colonized Africa, its peoples had few official laws criminalizing LGBTQ+ people. African researchers have shown that expressions of gender, sex, and sexuality in precolonial times were varied and often did not conform to the West's heterosexual "norm".

In the 20th century, rather than revoking oppressive penal codes, most newly independent African

See also: The criminalization of sodomy 68–71 ▪ Gender nonconformity and colonial constraints in Africa 120–21 ▪ The decriminalization of same-sex acts 184–85 ▪ LGBTQ+ Muslims 278–79 ▪ Homonationalism 302–03

A **rainbow flag** held high celebrates the 2019 ruling by Botswana's High Court decriminalizing same-sex acts – upheld by an appeal court in 2021 that overturned a government challenge.

nations retained and reinforced them. LGBTQ+ people were often denied citizenship and were unable to obtain housing, healthcare, or employment. In some countries, the maximum penalty for same-sex acts was – and still is – death.

For years Ghana had imposed no prosecutions for same-sex relations, but when an LGBTQ+ centre opened in the capital, Accra, in 2021, abuse and threats from many, including Christian and Muslim leaders, quickly forced its closure, prompting the nation's politicians to discuss laws banning LGBTQ+ advocacy. In 2022, Sheila Adhiambo

Lumumba, a young non-binary lesbian, was raped and strangled in Kenya. The Kenyan National Gay & Lesbian Human Rights Commission says the murder is part of a pattern of violence against LGBTQ+ people in a country prejudiced by its official sodomy and indecency laws.

Fighting back

While LGBTQ+ rights still face setbacks in Africa, nine of its 54 nations have never criminalized same-sex relationships and 10 – including Angola, Botswana, and Mozambique – have repealed discriminatory legislation. When South Africa legalized same-sex marriage in 2006, it was only the fifth country in the world to do so.

African organizations, such as The Initiative for Equal Rights (TIERs) in Nigeria and the Gay and Lesbian Coalition of Kenya, provide

access to safehouses, specialized LGBTQ+ healthcare, and legal representation, and grapple with the varying factors that influence homophobic laws in different countries. While keen to foster transnational solidarity, such groups also recognize that the standards and politics of a now "liberal" West cannot be imposed on LGBTQ+ Africans; they must take action on their own terms. ▪

LGBTI+ Africans are … defying the demonization narrative that LGBTI+ people currently suffer in mainstream media depictions.
Ani Kayode Somtochukwu
Nigerian writer (1999–)

Binyavanga Wainaina

Born in Nakuru, Kenya, in 1971, Kenneth Binyavanga Wainaina studied commerce in South Africa and creative writing at the University of East Anglia, UK. In 2002, he won the Caine Prize for African Writing and used the prize money to found the Kenya-based literary magazine *Kwani?* In a widely read essay in 2005, he satirized the Western vision of a primitive, monolithic Africa.

Wainaina, who also worked as a writer and lecturer in the US, completed a memoir in 2011. In 2014, in response to new anti-gay laws passed in Africa, he wrote

"I am a homosexual, Mum", an essay announcing that he was gay – "Gay, and quite happy", he declared in a tweet. That year, *Time* magazine listed him among the "Most Influential People in the World". On World AIDS Day, 2016, he revealed he was living with HIV. Wainaina died in Nairobi in 2019.

Key works

2005 "How to write about Africa"
2011 *One Day I Will Write About This Place*

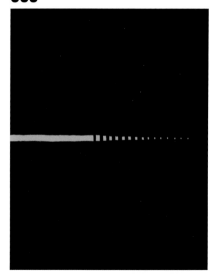

WHERE 49 LIVES WERE TAKEN, 49 LEGACIES BEGAN

THE PULSE SHOOTING (2016)

IN CONTEXT

FOCUS
Homophobic terrorism

BEFORE
1973 An arson attack on the Upstairs Lounge, a gay bar in New Orleans, kills 32 people.

1999 A nail bomb explodes in a homophobic attack on the Admiral Duncan pub in London, UK, killing three people and injuring 83 more.

2000 A gunman kills one person and wounds six more at the Backstreet Cafe gay bar in Roanoke, Virginia, US.

AFTER
2020 UK figures reveal that reported homophobic crimes have almost tripled since 2015.

2021 The US Congress designates the Pulse site a national memorial.

2022 Five people are killed and 25 are injured in a mass shooting at Club Q, an LGBTQ+ nightclub in Colorado, US.

In the early morning of 12 June 2016, Pulse, a popular LGBTQ+ nightclub in Orlando, Florida, US, was the target of a mass shooting. At around 2am, Omar Mateen entered the crowded club, which was holding its weekly Latin-themed night, and shot and killed 49 people, injuring a further 53, some critically. The police responded quickly, but the gunman retreated into the club and then barricaded himself in a toilet with a group of hostages.

During 911 emergency calls, the killer claimed allegiance to the Islamic terrorist group ISIL. He stated that he was acting in response to America's bombings in Iraq and Syria, leading the FBI to

The 49 victims of the Pulse shooting

Stanley Almodovar III • Amanda Lizzette Alvear • Oscar A. Aracena Montero •
Rodolfo Ayala Ayala • Antonio "Tony" Brown • Darryl Roman Burt II •
Angel Candelario-Padro • Juan Chavez Martinez • Luis D. Conde •
Cory James Connell • Tevin Eugene Crosby • Deonka "Dee Dee" Drayton •
Simón Adrian Carrillo Fernández • Leroy Valentin Fernandez •
Mercedez Marisol Flores • Peter Ommy Gonzalez Cruz • Juan Ramon Guerrero •
Paul Terrell Henry • Frank Hernandez • Miguel Angel Honorato •
Javier Jorge Reyes • Jason Benjamin Josaphat • Eddie Jamal Droy Justice •
Anthony Luis Laureano Disla • Christopher Andrew Leinonen •
Alejandro Barrios Martinez • Brenda Marquez McCool •
Gilberto R. Silva Menendez • Kimberly Jean Morris • Akyra Monet Murray •
Luis Omar Ocasio Capo • Gerardo A. Ortiz Jimenez • Eric Ivan Ortiz-Rivera •
Joel Rayon Paniagua • Jean C. Mendez Perez • Enrique L. Rios Jr. •
Jean Carlos Nieves Rodríguez • Xavier Emmanuel Serrano Rosado •
Christopher Joseph Sanfeliz • Yilmary Rodríguez Solivan • Eddie Sotomayor Jr. •
Shane Evan Tomlinson • Martin Benitez Torres • Jonathan A. Camuy Vega •
Juan Pablo Rivera Velázquez • Luis Sergio Vielma •
Franky Jimmy DeJesus Velázquez • Luis Daniel Wilson-Leon • Jerry Wright

See also: Persecution during the Holocaust 156–61 ▪ The Stonewall Uprising 190–95 ▪ The assassination of Harvey Milk 226–27 ▪ The murder of Matthew Shepard 284–85 ▪ Laws lifted against MSM donating blood 310–11

designate the shootings as a terrorist attack. Just after 5am, SWAT (special weapons and tactics) teams entered the club, and the gunman was shot dead. Owing to the club's theme that night, more than 90 per cent of his victims were of a Latine background. It was the deadliest terrorist attack in the US since the 9/11 attacks of 2001, and the deadliest assault to date on the nation's LGBTQ+ community.

Support and fundraising

The impact of the shooting was wide and instantaneous. Vigils were held around the world in memory of the victims, and many people voiced outrage at the attack on the LGBTQ+ community. US president Barack Obama called the shootings "an act of hate", and members of the United Nations Security Council denounced the attack for "targeting persons as a result of their sexual orientation". The two Orlando hospitals that treated the wounded waived all medical costs, and the city of Orlando offered free burial plots and funeral services for the 49 dead.

Gay clubs … were often the only safe gathering place and this horrific act strikes directly at our sense of safety.
Equality Florida
American LGBTQ+ civil rights organization

Millions of dollars were raised to support the victims and their families by organizations such as OneOrlando – founded by Orlando mayor Buddy Dyer – and Equality Florida, the state's largest LGBTQ+ rights group. NBCUniversal and the Walt Disney Company, who run resorts nearby, each gave $1 million to the OneOrlando fund. Profits donated from *Love is Love,* a comic book anthology that became a *New York Times* bestseller, added more than $165,000 to the fund.

The shootings also galvanized support for moves to overturn discriminatory, anti-LGBTQ+ policies, such as the blood donation ban for men who have sex with men, as many from the affected community wanted to give blood to help wounded victims. In 2020, the government's Federal Drug Administration (FDA) modified its rules, allowing blood donations after three months of sexual abstinence rather than a year.

In memoriam

Soon after the deadly shootings, the onePULSE Foundation was created to remember those who had lost their lives in the attack. Barbara Poma, the owner of the Pulse

The Pulse nightclub soon had an interim memorial wall and tribute garden, erected by Orlando's LGBTQ+ community and its supporters.

nightclub, was a founding member. The foundation provides educational scholarships reflecting the interests and careers of the 49 who died, such as art and healthcare. It is also creating a symbolic garden on the Pulse site, together with a museum and educational centre. The design includes a spiralling building, public plazas, vertical gardens, and a reflective pool. As a further tribute, 12 June has been dedicated as an annual "Orlando United Day – a day of love and kindness". ▪

To outlove hate is to win by loving.
Slogan of the onePULSE Foundation

SAFE, FAIR, AND SCIENCE-BASED

LAWS LIFTED AGAINST MSM DONATING BLOOD (2021)

IN CONTEXT

FOCUS
Inclusive medicine

BEFORE
1980s In Japan, thousands of haemophilia patients contract HIV due to blood products, in what becomes known as the "HIV-tainted blood scandal".

1985 The first blood test for detecting HIV is developed, but is too slow and prone to false negatives to be used for screening blood products.

2000s Wider availability of the nucleic acid test (NAT) allows for quicker, effective detection of HIV.

AFTER
2022 An open letter to the FDA criticizes the three month deferral of MSM donations in the US, as blood supplies reach a critical low.

2022 China and India, among other countries, retain indefinite deferrals for MSM donors.

The mandatory exclusion of men who have sex with men (MSM) from donating blood was implemented in countries across the world during the 1980s HIV/AIDS crisis. Governments justified these bans due to the early prevalence of HIV cases among gay men, and the thousands of transmissions that were occurring via blood transfusion due to the lack of reliable tests. Based solely on gender and sexuality, with no regard for individual risk, the ban was criticized as discriminatory. Many LGBTQ+ and HIV/AIDS activists argued that it served only to

… simply being a man who has sex with men is not a good enough reason to exclude someone from donating blood.
Ethan Spibey
Founder of the FreedomToDonate campaign

entrench the idea that AIDS was a problem for gay communities alone and that sexual relations between men carried an inherent danger.

Today, all donations can be screened for HIV, but there remains a "window period" following recent transmission during which positive cases may be missed. The existence of this risk has seen blanket bans on MSM donations upheld worldwide.

Origins of MSM blood bans

By 1983, American epidemiologists had found evidence that the transmission of HIV occurred due to the presence of the virus in the blood. The global response to this danger was rapid. What began as non-mandatory guidelines from the US Public Health Service in 1983 for those "at increased risk of AIDS" were revised to specifically exclude MSM blood donations in 1986. In 1992, the Food and Drug Administration (FDA) issued mandatory guidelines for a "lifetime deferral", effectively a ban, for MSM donors. This extended to trans women, controversially defined as "men who have sex with men".

Similar lifetime deferrals were soon introduced in many countries across the world. In China, all

The UK's 2021 blood donation law changed from a blanket deferral on MSM donating blood to an individualized risk assessment. All donors are asked about their sexual partners within the last three months. Anyone who has not had anal sex with a new partner in the last three months, or known exposure to an STI, can then donate.

✓ No sex or same sexual partner for the last three months.

✓ New sexual partner(s) in the last three months, but no anal sex.

✓ No known recent exposure to STIs (Sexually Transmitted Infections).

✗ Anal sex with new sexual partner in the last three months.

✗ Known recent exposure to an STI.

homosexuals were banned from donating, regardless of sexual activity. This is also the case in Iran, Thailand, Malaysia, Taiwan, and Sri Lanka.

Shortening of deferrals

By the new millennium, bans on MSM donations were subject to growing criticism. With effective testing for HIV and legal advances in protecting LGBTQ+ people from discrimination, the bans were seen as antiquated and discriminatory.

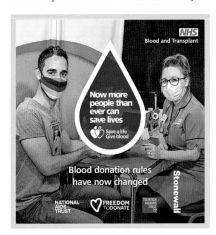

Campaign groups including FreedomToDonate highlighted that they were based on the stigma and fear so prevalent in the 1980s rather than scientific evidence. The initial response by governments was the shortening of lifetime deferrals. Since the 2000s, many countries have reduced their MSM deferrals to 12, six, and three months. Yet, any period of mandatory abstinence for MSM remains discriminatory.

Fairer alternatives

In 2001, Italy implemented a system of individualized risk assessments, allowing for the identification of "risky sexual practices" with no assumptions made based on sexuality or gender. Subsequent studies have proved the efficacy of this approach in maintaining a safe

This poster, issued by NHS Blood and Transplant, marks the change to the UK's blood donation rules in June 2021. Blood stocks dropped during the COVID-19 pandemic, spurring changes.

blood supply. Spain followed suit, introducing a similar system in 2005, and Mexico in 2012.

This system is championed as the most effective replacement for bans. In June 2021, the UK scrapped deferrals in favour of individual risk assessments, and France followed in March 2022. Both marked a shift that has seen MSM bans no longer the global norm, as progress, albeit slow, continues to be made. ▪

We are putting an end to an inequality that was no longer justified.
Olivier Véran
French health minister, 2022

DIRECTO

RY

DIRECTORY

The history of LGBTQ+ people and experiences encompasses a wealth of brave individuals and movements, including pioneers who were censored or forgotten, but later rediscovered and reassessed. As they cannot all be described in the main articles of this book, some further key figures are listed here. They range from early documented gender-nonconforming and intersex people to those who were more recently subject to fierce public speculation, such as actor James Dean, and those who continue to fight for LGBTQ+ rights, like American trans woman activist Miss Major. These examples demonstrate the numerous victories for LGBTQ+ rights across the world, but also the many battles for greater equality and recognition that are still to be won.

HYEGONG OF SILLA
758–80 CE

The only child of King Gyeongdeok and Queen Gyeongsu, Hyegong ascended the throne of the Korean kingdom of Silla in 765 CE aged just eight. From an early age, he was highly effeminate and chose to play with what were traditionally girl's toys. He was also said to have had relationships with men. The king's perceived weakness led to several rebellions, the last of which, in 780, ended in his assassination. Historians suggest that Hyegong was what would be known today as a trans woman.
See also: Favourites in Han China 28–29

JEAN II, BISHOP OF ORLEANS
1096

The scandalous appointment of Jean II as Bishop of Orleans in France in 1096, orchestrated by his lover Raoul II, Archbishop of Tours, was one of the first overt instances of same-sex activity in European ecclesiastical hierarchy. The consecration of Jean, nicknamed "Flora" after a Roman sex worker for his perceived sexual promiscuity, immediately prompted Ivo, Bishop of Chartres, to complain to Pope Urban II. The complaint mentioned Jean's promiscuity, but the primary objection was Jean's youth as he was not yet 30, the minimum age for a bishop required by canon law. The Pope did not consider this worth acting on, and Jean II remained bishop for almost 30 years.
See also: Sodomy and the medieval Catholic Church 42–45

ELEANOR RYKENER
14th century

A sex worker in 14th-century London, Eleanor Rykener – assigned male at birth (AMAB) and also known as John – was a rare documented example of gender nonconformity in late medieval England. In 1394, after being solicited for sex on Cheapside Road, Rykener was arrested and questioned by police. In court, Rykener spoke of being instructed how to present as a woman, have sex with men "in the manner of a woman", and take work as a woman, but also confessed to having sexual relations with nuns as a man.
See also: The criminalization of sodomy 68–71

TIBIRA DO MARANHÃO
Late 16th century–1614

A Tupinambá native of the Brazilian state of Maranhão, Tibira – a name meaning "homosexual" in the Tupi language – was the first person to be executed for same-sex activity in colonial Brazil. Sentenced to death by Capuchin monk Yves d'Evreux, Tibira was baptized and then strapped to a cannon, which was fired, killing him. In 2014, activist Luis Mott launched an unsuccessful campaign to declare Tibira a queer saint and martyr. In 2016, a monument honouring him was erected in Maranhão.
See also: The Spanish Inquisition 64–65 ▪ Colonial Latin America 66–67 ▪ Latin American LGBTQ+ movements 178–79

FELIPA DE SOUZA
1556–1600

The first recorded female–female relationship in colonial Brazil involved Portuguese former nun Felipa de Souza, who emigrated to the city of Salvador in Brazil. After love letters she had sent to another woman were handed over to the Catholic Inquisition, several other women came forward and testified to having had sexual relations with de Souza. When challenged, de Souza was unrepentant, proudly declaring that all the accusations were true. In an unusually severe punishment, she was publicly flogged, had her assets confiscated, and was exiled from the city.
See also: The Spanish Inquisition 64–65 ▪ Colonial Latin America 66–67

BENEDETTA CARLINI
1590–1661

Born in Italy in a remote village in the Apennines, Benedetta Carlini was a Catholic mystic and nun. In 1614, she reported her supernatural visions, which became increasingly vivid and allegedly involved visits from Christ. Her claims eventually attracted the attention of the Papal authorities, who launched several investigations. To support her in her battles with the devil, Carlini's superiors had assigned her a companion, Bartolomea Crivelli, who confessed to having sexual relations with the nun, although Carlini claimed she did so under the influence of an angelic entity called Splenditello. Carlini was imprisoned for the rest of her life. Her story was the subject of the 2021 film *Benedetta*.

See also: Sodomy and the medieval Catholic Church 42–45 ▪ Early modern lesbianism 74–79

CATHARINA/ANASTASIUS LINCK
1687–1721

The last recorded execution for "female sodomy" in Europe was that of Prussian Catharina/Anastasius Linck, who was assigned female at birth (AFAB) and presented alternately as a woman and as a man. In 1717, presenting as a man, Linck married 18-year-old Catharina Margaretha Mühlhahn. Linck used a leather dildo during sex and a leather-covered horn to urinate, which Mühlhahn's suspicious mother eventually handed over to the authorities, denouncing Linck as a woman impersonating a man. Although there was minimal contemporary legal guidance on punishments for sex between AFAB people, Linck was beheaded and Mühlhahn was imprisoned.
See also: Sodomy and the medieval Catholic Church 42–45 ▪ The criminalization of sodomy 68–71

PRINCESS ISABELLA OF PARMA
1741–63

The first child of Philip, Duke of Parma and Marie Louise Élisabeth of France, Isabella of Parma was married to Archduke Joseph of Austria at the age of 19. Dissatisfied with this match, and with court life in general, she became increasingly depressed and solitary but found some solace in a relationship with her new sister-in-law, Archduchess Maria Anna. For a brief period, the two were seen as inseparable, playing games together and constantly exchanging letters. Isabella openly expressed her love for Maria Anna, and some of those in court suspected they were having an affair, though historians debate the extent to which their relationship was sexual. Isabella died of smallpox, aged just 21.
See also: Early modern lesbianism 74–79 ▪ Erotic friendship in America and Europe 92–95

KARL DÜRRGE
1780–1835

Born in the Prussian city of Potsdam, Germany, and assigned female at birth (AFAB), Karl Dürrge – also known as Maria Dorothea Derrier – was admitted to hospital in 1801 with a skin condition. There, doctors discovered he was intersex. Dürrge chose to identify as a man, opting to live as a travelling medical specimen in exchange for food, lodgings, and money. The studies he took part in influenced the treatment of intersex people in Prussia, helping to establish medical guidelines for determining sex and the ability of adult intersex people to choose their gender identity.
See also: Intersex rights 48–53 ▪ Defining "homosexual" and "heterosexual" 106–07

LEVI SUYDAM
19th century

An intersex person living in 19th-century Connecticut, US, Levi Suydam was the subject of an early legal case that demonstrated the importance of sex determination. In 1843, property owners were eligible to vote only if male, which is how Suydam registered himself. On account of Suydam's feminine appearance, a charge of fraud was brought. Suydam was permitted to vote, however, when a subsequent medical examination declared his genitals to be "male". Suydam was later discovered to menstruate, but whether this discovery negated the vote he cast is unknown.

See also: Intersex rights 48–53

WALT WHITMAN
1819–1892

One of America's most influential poets, Walt Whitman is known as the "father of free verse" for pioneering a poetic style based on the cadence of natural speech. Writing before the medicalization of sexuality, Whitman's work, in particular *Leaves of Grass*, argued for a fluidity of gender and sexuality that he felt society repressed. The perceived homoeroticism of *Leaves of Grass* caused a backlash that led to libraries across the US banning the work. Although Whitman denied having relationships with men, biographers and writers, including Oscar Wilde, have suggested that he was bisexual or gay.

See also: Male–male love poetry 80–81 ▪ The trial of Oscar Wilde 124–25

MARY EDWARDS WALKER
1832–1919

Born in Oswego, New York, Mary Walker identified as female, but dressed in male clothes to work on the family farm and was educated as well as her brothers. In 1855, she graduated as a medical doctor – the only woman in her class. She volunteered for the Union Army in the American Civil War (1861–65), working as an unpaid field surgeon. She became the first and only woman to receive the Medal of Honor, and began to campaign for dress reform and women's suffrage. For much of her life, Walker preferred trousers to dresses, and later in life she wore a top hat, too.

See also: AFAB cross-dressers and "female husbands" 82–83

PYOTR ILYICH TCHAIKOVSKY
1840–93

Russian composer Pyotr Ilyich Tchaikovsky, known worldwide for his Romantic-era musical works such as the ballets *Swan Lake* and *The Nutcracker*, concealed his gay sexuality throughout his life, which may have contributed to his bouts of depression. His Symphony No.6 ("Pathétique"), completed nine days before his death, is seen by some as a suicide note. Tchaikovsky's sexuality became more widely known only after the discovery of letters following his death. Many of these were hidden by Soviet censors; some were published for the first time only in the 2010s.

See also: The criminalization of sodomy 68–71

ANITA AUGSPURG AND LIDA GUSTAVA HEYMANN
1857–1943, 1868–1943

Both major figures in the German women's movement, Anita Augspurg and Gustava Heymann were a lesbian couple who were among 13 cofounders of the *Verein für Frauenstimmrecht* (Society for Women's Suffrage). Augspurg was the first doctor of law in the German Empire, and Heymann had used her inheritance to found a women's centre and coeducational high school. In 1923, both Augspurg and Heymann called for Adolf Hitler to be expelled from Germany, and both moved to Switzerland once he came to power in 1933.

See also: Persecution during the Holocaust 156–61 ▪ Political lesbianism 206–07

SELMA LAGERLÖF
1858–1940

Author Selma Lagerlöf was born in Värmland, Sweden, to an army lieutenant and the daughter of a wealthy merchant. She enjoyed reading and writing from an early age and worked as a teacher while writing her first novels. In 1909, Lägerlof became the first woman to be awarded the Nobel Prize in Literature, and in 1914 she was the first woman granted membership of the Swedish Academy. She was a lesbian, but concealed her sexuality. Letters which, in accordance with her will, were made public only 50 years after her death revealed her long-term relationship with teacher Valborg Olander.

See also: Erotic friendship in America and Europe 92–95 ▪ Sapphism 98

ETHEL SMYTH
1858–1944

Born in Sidcup, Kent, British composer Ethel Smyth attended the Leipzig Conservatory in Germany, and later wrote a wealth of songs and chamber, orchestral, and choral works. Her opera *Der Wald* was staged at the Metropolitan Opera in

New York City in 1903 – the only opera by a female composer performed there in the 20th century. Smyth was also the first composer to be made a Dame of the British Empire. She had several passionate affairs with women and fell in love with novelist Virginia Woolf and suffragette Emmeline Pankhurst. An active campaigner for women's suffrage, Smyth served a two-month prison sentence for throwing stones at a politician's house.
See also: Erotic friendship in America and Europe 92–95

MARCEL PROUST
1871–1922

One of the 20th century's most influential authors, Marcel Proust was born in Paris into a wealthy family. Proust began his career writing for literary magazines before going on to write *À la recherche du temps perdu* (*In Search of Lost Time*); the seven volumes were published in France between 1913 and 1927. A reflection on his own early life in high-society France, it is considered one of the greatest novels of the era. Proust did not live openly as a gay man, but his works are often interpreted as his way of coming to terms with his sexuality; they feature several gay and bisexual characters.
See also: Belle Époque Paris 110–11

ELEANOR ROOSEVELT
1884–1962

American political figure and activist Anna Eleanor Roosevelt was America's longest-serving First Lady, during the presidency of her husband, Franklin D. Roosevelt, from 1933 to 1945. She defied the usual expectations of a first lady, campaigning for women's rights and racial equality even when her actions were at odds with her husband's policies. Roosevelt did not publicly identify as a lesbian or bisexual, but her close relationship with journalist and out lesbian Lorena Hickok is thought to have been romantic and sexual. The two exchanged many letters, the most explicit of which Hickok burnt.
See also: Erotic friendship in America and Europe 92–95 ▪ Bisexuality 262–65

LUCY HICKS ANDERSON
1886–1954

Born in Kentucky, US, Lucy Hicks Anderson was a socialite and owner of a boarding house in prohibition-era California. Assigned male at birth (AMAB), Anderson identified and presented as female from a young age. Doctors suggested that her parents allow this, making her one of the earliest documented Black American transgender people. After cases of venereal disease were linked to her establishment, a physical examination revealed that Anderson was AMAB. She was arrested and convicted of perjury for allegedly impersonating a woman on her marriage licence, as well as fraud for receiving payments as the wife of a soldier.
See also: Transgender rights 196–203

MARGARET ANDERSON AND JANE HEAP
1886–1973, 1883–1964

Born in Indiana, US, Margaret Anderson moved to Chicago where she met Jane Heap who had been born in Kansas and was studying at Chicago's Art Institute. They became partners in business and in love. Anderson founded and Heap edited *The Little Review*, an influential literary magazine that became notorious in 1918 when they began to serialize Irish author James Joyce's novel *Ulysses*. The US Post Office banned the book as obscene in 1920, and Anderson and Heap were convicted on obscenity charges a year later. Both later spent time with the ex-patriot community of writers and artists in Paris, France, where the magazine's last issue was published in 1929.
See also: Butch and femme 152–55

SYLVIA BEACH
1887–1962

American publisher and bookseller Sylvia Beach was born in Baltimore, US, before moving to Paris where she spent most of her life. While in Paris she met bookseller Adrienne Monnier and the two became lovers and business partners, establishing the bookstore and lending library Shakespeare and Company. They achieved fame for publishing Irish author James Joyce's controversial novel *Ulysses* (1922) in France after several publishers had rejected it as obscene.
See also: Ismat Chughtai's obscenity trial 162

DORA CARRINGTON
1893–1932

British artist Dora Carrington was born in Hereford and studied at the Slade School of Fine Art in London, where she encountered members of London's bohemian Bloomsbury Group. Carrington was known for

her androgynous appearance and had relationships with both men and women, most notably writer Lytton Strachey. Although her work was not well known during her lifetime, it has since been critically re-evaluated with major retrospective exhibitions in the UK.
See also: Sapphism 98

WILLEM ARONDEUS
1894–1943

Dutch artist and author Willem Arondeus was born in Naarden, the Netherlands. Working for an underground periodical led to him joining the Dutch anti-Nazi resistance movement, which blew up the Amsterdam public records office in a bid to prevent the Nazis identifying Dutch Jews. The group was arrested and sentenced to death. Arondeus lived openly as a gay man and before his execution made a point of publicly declaring both his sexuality and that of two other gay members of the group, in order to "tell the people that homosexuals can be brave!"
See also: Persecution during the Holocaust 156–61

CLAUDE CAHUN
1894–1954

Born in Nantes to a prominent intellectual and progressive Jewish family and initially known by their birth name, Claude Cahun, who adopted their name in 1914, was a French photographer and writer associated with the *Association des Écrivans et Artistes Révolutionnaires* and the Surrealist movement. Cahun was AFAB and identified as gender neutral, using their work in self-portraiture to adopt a variety of personae that deliberately blurred and played with gender distinctions.
See also: Belle Époque Paris 110–11
▪ Butler's *Gender Trouble* 266–67

FEDERICO GARCÍA LORCA
1898–1936

Spanish poet, playwright, and theatre director Federico García Lorca rose to international prominence as a member of the avant-garde Generation of '27. Throughout his career García Lorca struggled with the inability to live publicly as a gay man; his depression was exacerbated by the breakdown of his relationship with sculptor Emilio Aladrón Perojo and Salvador Dalí's rejection of his romantic advances. At the beginning of the Spanish Civil War, García Lorca was assassinated by Nationalist forces and his writing was banned – probably as a result of his socialism and his homosexuality.
See also: Persecution during the Holocaust 156–61

TAMARA DE LEMPICKA
1898–1980

Born in Warsaw, Poland, Tamara de Lempicka was a painter best known for her stylized Art Deco portraits and nudes, often completed for the rich and famous and incorporating themes of eroticism and seduction. Her artistic breakthrough came with the 1925 International Exhibition of Modern Decorative and Industrial Arts. Lempicka was bisexual and known for having numerous affairs. When she and her husband moved to Paris in 1918, she joined the city's burgeoning lesbian scene. She also began to sign her paintings with a masculine form of her name – Lempitzki. She remarried, and later lived in the US and Mexico.
See also: Belle Époque Paris 110–11
▪ Bisexuality 262–65

MICHEL-MARIE POULAIN
1906–91

French painter and performer Michel-Marie Poulain was a trans woman who wore traditionally feminine clothing from a young age. Between World War I and World War II, in which she served, Poulain worked as a cabaret performer under the name Micky. In the 1930s, she visited German doctor and trans advocate Magnus Hirschfeld, who offered her gender affirming surgery. She initially refused but later underwent several procedures and began to live more publicly as a woman, becoming a fashion model alongside her work in dance and cabaret.
See also: The first gender affirmation surgeries 136–41 ▪ Transgender rights 196–203

FRIDA KAHLO
1907–54

Born on the outskirts of Mexico City, artist Frida Kahlo had polio as a child, which left her with chronic pain, and aged 18 was in a serious bus accident that led to numerous surgeries. She taught herself to paint while recovering; her work frequently drew on her own experiences of pain and disability as well as her relationship with her Mexican identity. She lived openly as a bisexual, and during her marriage to the artist Diego Rivera, had affairs with men and women.
See also: Bisexuality 262–65

PAULI MURRAY
1910–85

Born in Baltimore, US, Pauli Murray became a civil rights lawyer after being arrested, along with a friend, for violating bus segregation laws. The first Black American to receive a Doctor of Juridical Science degree from Yale Law School, in 1965, Murray pioneered legal work on gender discrimination, serving on the Presidential Commission on the Status of Women, then cofounding the National Organization for Women. Later, they were drawn to religious work, becoming the first Black American AFAB person to be ordained as an Episcopal priest in 1977. Murray struggled with their sexual and gender identity, and some biographers have retroactively described them as transgender.
See also: Political lesbianism 206–07

TENNESSEE WILLIAMS
1911–83

Considered one of America's greatest 20th-century playwrights, Tennessee Williams was born in Mississippi to a travelling salesman. He found success relatively late in life with a string of plays including *The Glass Menagerie*, and the Pulitzer-prize winning *A Streetcar Named Desire* and *Cat on a Hot Tin Roof*. His melodramatic works were highly personal, exploring his troubled upbringing and depression, his sister Rose's struggles with schizophrenia, and his own difficulty in coming to terms with being a gay man. These experiences, combined with a poor reception for his later works, caused him to increasingly turn to alcohol and drugs, which eventually contributed to his death in New York City in 1983.
See also: The decriminalization of same-sex acts 184–85

BAYARD RUSTIN
1912–87

Born in Pennsylvania, US, Bayard Rustin was a Black American civil and gay rights activist. His arrest in 1942 for refusing to move on a racially segregated bus prompted him to be more open about the prejudice he also faced for being gay. He became an adviser to Martin Luther King, Jr., in 1956, and was a principal organizer of the 1963 March on Washington, an unprecedented mass rally in support of civil rights legislation pending in the US Congress. In 2020, Rustin was posthumously pardoned for his conviction as a sex offender after having sex with a man in 1953.
See also: Towards gay liberation 170–77 ▪ The decriminalization of same-sex acts 184–85

ALAN TURING
1912–54

Born in London, UK, Alan Turing was a gifted mathematician and computer scientist. During World War II, he worked for the Government Code and Cypher School at Bletchley Park, Britain's code-breaking centre. There he played a vital role in cracking codes produced by the German Enigma machine, helping the Allies to defeat the Axis powers. After the war, he designed early computers but was arrested and prosecuted in 1952 for his homosexuality. Instead of a prison sentence, Turing opted for hormonal treatment. Two years later, he died of cyanide poisoning – presumed to be suicide.
See also: Conversion therapy is banned 286–87

BENJAMIN BRITTEN
1913–76

Born in Suffolk, UK, composer and conductor Benjamin Britten was musically prolific as a child, composing some 800 works before the age of 18. In 1934, he met the tenor Peter Pears, who became his muse and romantic partner. Pears starred in many of Britten's works, including *Billy Budd*, which has homosexual undertones, and Britten's last opera, *Death in Venice*, which has a more overt homosexual theme. The two men lived relatively openly together and were buried together, too.

TOM OF FINLAND
1920–91

Finnish artist Touko Laaksonen, better known by his pseudonym Tom of Finland, produced highly stylized and homoerotic images. Focusing on fetishized subcultures such as leathermen, beefcakes, and soldiers, his depiction of gay strength and physicality had a profound impact at a time when male homosexuality was often depicted as passive and effeminate. At first more suggestive than explicit, his work became more erotic, commercially successful, and mainstream after the relaxation of censorship laws in the 1970s and has since featured in many films, exhibitions, and fashion collections. The Tom of Finland Foundation, established in 1984, promotes his and other homoerotic artwork.

See also: Towards gay liberation 170–77 ▪ The decriminalization of same-sex acts 184–85

JAMES McHARRIS
1924–after 1955

Born in Mississippi, US, James McHarris was assigned female at birth (AFAB) but lived his life as a man from an early age, working a variety of traditionally masculine jobs in the Midwest. In 1954, he was pulled over by police for having improper lighting, and a pat-down revealed his assigned gender. He was sentenced to 30 days in prison and shunned by the community but continued to live as a man. That year, his story gained greater publicity when an account was published in *Ebony* magazine, one of the most successful Black-oriented magazines in the US, but details of his later life are unknown.
See also: Transgender rights 196–203

GORE VIDAL
1925–2012

The grandson of a US senator, prolific novelist and essayist Gore Vidal was born in New York State. His third novel – *The City and the Pillar* (1948) – had a gay protagonist and was the first sympathetic and uncritical post-war representation of homosexuality in the US. It offended conservative book reviewers and shocked the public, but became a sensation and was reprinted in paperback in the 1950s. In his essays, Vidal wrote in favour of sexual freedom and against prejudice. In a later best-selling novel, *Myra Breckinridge* (1968), the main character undergoes gender affirmation surgery. Vidal himself was known to enjoy sex with men, but rejected the label "gay" and identified as bisexual.
See also: The Lavender Scare 166–67 ▪ The decriminalization of same-sex acts 184–85

OVIDA DELECT
1926–96

Communist poet and member of the French Resistance, Ovida Delect established a small resistance group while at school, leading to her arrest and imprisonment by the Gestapo. Delect survived the war, and in 1952 met her future wife Huguette. Assigned male at birth, Delect disclosed her identity as a trans woman to Huguette and to intimate friends. Aged 55, Delect started to live more openly as a trans woman, and publicly adopted her earlier private pen name Ovida. In 1986, Delect featured in the documentary film *Appelez-moi Madame*, one of the first to convey French trans women's experiences to a wider audience.
See also: Persecution during the Holocaust 156–61 ▪ Transgender rights 196–203

JACKIE FORSTER
1926–98

British actress, reporter, and activist Jackie Forster performed in London's West End and worked as a TV presenter before becoming a lesbian rights activist. Forster came out publicly in 1969 when she joined the Campaign for Homosexual Equality (CHE). In 1971, she took part in the UK's first Gay Pride March, and in 1972 she helped found the lesbian social club Sappho, which also published one of the UK's longest-running lesbian publications. In her later career, she played a crucial role in shaping the Lesbian Archive in Glasgow Women's Library, Scotland.
See also: Towards gay liberation 170–77

ANDY WARHOL
1928–87

A leading figure in the 1950s Pop Art movement, American artist Andy Warhol was born in Pittsburgh to Lemko immigrants from what is now Slovakia. Initially pursuing a career in illustration, he quickly became known as a visual artist, and his studio, The Factory, was an important site of bohemian culture in New York City. Living openly as a gay man before the Gay Liberation Movement began in the late 1960s, Warhol found that the work of closeted gay artists gained more acceptance than his own and felt frustrated. His early works were rejected by galleries for being too homoerotic, and his films would premiere in gay porn theatres. His works have since become some of the most widely known, and fetch among the highest prices at auction.
See also: Towards gay liberation 170–77 ▪ The Stonewall Uprising 190–95

JAMES DEAN
1931–55

Best known for his role in the 1955 film *Rebel Without a Cause*, American actor and cultural icon James Dean was born in Indiana. Dean's seemingly ambivalent attitude to sexuality and racy lifestyle caused public speculation both during his life and after his death, and many biographers have

since agreed that he was bisexual. Dean hoped to develop a career out of his motorsport hobby but died in a car crash in 1955, aged just 24.
See also: LGBTQ+ films 142–45

ANN BANNON
1932–

Born in Illinois, US, American author Ann Weldy is better known by her pen name Ann Bannon. Inspired by her own experiences growing up as a lesbian, she wrote a series of six lesbian pulp fiction novels, *The Beebo Brinker Chronicles*. The novels defied typical depictions of lesbians at the time, with the character of Beebo Brinker becoming an important reference point for butch lesbians and earning Bannon the title "Queen of Lesbian Pulp Fiction".
See also: Butch and femme 152–55

DAVID HOCKNEY
1937–

One of the most influential artists of his age, David Hockney was born in Bradford, Yorkshire, UK. He came out as gay aged 23, and celebrated his sexuality and the male form in works like *Domestic Scene* (1963), which depicts two men showering together, and *Peter Getting out of Nick's Pool* (1966), featuring his long-term boyfriend American artist Peter Schlesinger naked leaving a communal swimming pool in Los Angeles – both produced when sex between men was still illegal in the UK and US. His highly versatile output includes portraits, landscapes, stage sets, and videos.
See also: Towards gay liberation 170–77 ▪ The decriminalization of same-sex acts 184–85

JUDY GRAHN
1940–

Born in Chicago, American poet and writer Judy Grahn joined the US Air Force but was discharged for being a lesbian. Her experiences of homophobia for being a butch lesbian and a coma due to an illness at the age of 25 both influenced her desire to become a poet. Grahn became a central member of the West Coast feminist poetry movement in the 1970s and a member of the Gay Women's Liberation Group, using her poetry to explore issues of sexism, racism, classism, and homophobia. Later in life she moved into academia, and continues to teach.
See also: Butch and femme 152–55 ▪ Towards gay liberation 170–77 ▪ Don't Ask, Don't Tell 272–75

MISS MAJOR
1940–

A trans woman and activist for transgender rights, Miss Major Griffin-Gracy, often known as just Miss Major, grew up in Chicago, US, participating in drag balls and coming out as a trans woman in her late teens. The criticism she received from her peers and the violence faced by fellow trans women of colour fuelled her own activism, which started with her participation in the 1969 Stonewall Uprising. Moving to the San Francisco Bay Area, she became involved in grassroots community efforts, working for the Tenderloin AIDS Resource Centre and the Transgender Gender Variant Intersex Justice Project. In 2015, she was the subject of the documentary, *Major!*

See also: The Stonewall Uprising 190–95 ▪ Transgender rights 196–203

DEREK JARMAN
1942–94

British artist, filmmaker, costume designer, and gay rights activist Derek Jarman studied at the Slade School of Fine Art in London. He used his work, notably in film, to advocate for gay rights, campaigning against Section 28 (a law curbing alleged "promotion of homosexuality"), and raising awareness of the AIDS crisis. Jarman was diagnosed as HIV positive in 1986, prompting him to move to a remote cottage by the sea in Dungeness, Kent, where he continued to work on films and to cultivate a now famous garden. His final and best-known work, *Blue*, consists of a single shot of International Klein Blue set to audio narrations of his life and his experience of living with AIDS.
See also: LGBTQ+ films 142–45 ▪ The AIDS epidemic 238–41 ▪ AIDS activism 244–45 ▪ Section 28 248–49

JÓHANNA SIGURÐARDÓTTIR
1942–

Born in Reykjavik, Jóhanna Sigurðardóttir, a politician of the Social Democratic Alliance, was Iceland's 24th prime minister, between 2009 and 2013. Before entering politics, Sigurðardóttir worked for Icelandic Airlines and was active in the trade union movement. During her premiership, the Icelandic parliament passed a same-sex marriage bill, after which

Sigurðardóttir and her partner Jóanína Leósdóttir turned their civil union into a marriage, making them one of the first same-sex married couples in the country.
See also: Marriage equality 288–93

FREDDIE MERCURY
1946–91

Regarded as one of rock music's greatest figures, Freddie Mercury was born Farrokh Bulsara in the British protectorate of Zanzibar, off the coast of east-central Africa, to Parsi Indian parents, and spent most of his childhood in India. After the family moved to the UK, Mercury formed the band Queen with Roger Taylor and Brian May. While he quickly became known for his impressive four-octave vocal range, flamboyant persona, and theatrical performances, Mercury did not publicly label his sexuality but is considered to have been gay or bisexual. He was in a long-term relationship with Mary Austin, who left him because of his sexual relationships with men, although she remained his closest friend. He was diagnosed with AIDS in 1987, which he announced only the day before his death in 1991.
See also: Camp 180–81 ▪ The AIDS epidemic 238–41 ▪ AIDS activism 244–45

SALLY RIDE
1951–2012

American astronaut and physicist Sally Ride was born in Los Angeles and studied physics and English literature at Stanford University before joining NASA aged 27. In 1983, her first mission aboard the Space Shuttle Challenger saw her become the first American woman and the youngest American astronaut to fly in space, as well as the first astronaut known to be gay.

KEITH HARING
1958–90

Born in Pennsylvania, US, Keith Haring took an early interest in pop art and cartoon imagery, encouraged by his father, an engineer and amateur cartoonist. Haring moved to New York to study painting, first attracting public attention for his graffiti art on the city's subways, and later creating larger colourful murals, Haring soon rose to international fame and sought to make his work more accessible by opening his Pop Shop in 1986. In 1988, Haring was diagnosed with AIDS, and used his later work to explore political themes around anti-apartheid, safe sex, AIDS awareness, and gay rights until his death in 1990.
See also: The AIDS epidemic 238–41 ▪ AIDS activism 244–45

KIM JHO GWANG-SOO
1965–

One of South Korea's few openly gay film directors, Kim Jho Gwang-soo combines film with his work as an LGBTQ+ activist and has worked on several projects with LGBTQ+ themes. Gwang-soo and his partner David Kim Seung-hwan held a non-legal wedding ceremony in 2013, the first of its kind in South Korea, where same-sex marriages are still not legally recognized.
See also: LGBTQ+ films 142–45 ▪ LGBTQ+ activism in Asia 254–55 ▪ Marriage equality 288–93

KELLY HOLMES
1970–

Born in Kent, UK, Kelly Holmes won the English Schools 1,500 m race in 1983 and, aged 18, joined the British Army and became a physical training instructor. Taking up athletics full-time in 1997, she won gold medals in the 800 m and 1,500 m races at the 2004 Athens Olympic Games. Since retiring from professional athletics in 2005, Holmes has founded a charity to support young athletes and disadvantaged young people and been named president of Commonwealth Games England. She came out as gay in a newspaper interview in 2022, and revealed during a television documentary that she had known she was lesbian since 1988 but had feared being outed at a time when gay people were not allowed to serve openly in the British Army.
See also: LGBTQ+ sportspeople come out 208–09 ▪ Don't Ask, Don't Tell 272–75

SAGE
1978

Building on the momentum of the wider gay rights movement, Senior Action in a Gay Environment (SAGE) was founded in New York City, US, in 1978 specifically to address the concerns of older LGBTQ+ people and provided both advocacy and support groups for those living with HIV/AIDS. Now known as Services & Advocacy for LGBT Elders, it is still in operation, the largest and oldest non-profit organization in the US dedicated solely to the needs and concerns of the older LGBTQ+ community.

See also: The AIDS epidemic
238–41 ▪ AIDS activism 244–45

MARIELLE FRANCO
1979–2018

Born in a favela (slum) in Rio de
Janeiro, Marielle Franco was a
Brazilian politician and human
rights activist, elected to the city
council in 2016 campaigning for
the rights of Black women living in
the favelas. Franco identified as
bisexual, and throughout her career
also campaigned for LGBTQ+
rights. She was a fierce critic of
police brutality, and in March 2018
was shot and killed by two former
police officers while being driven
through Rio. Her murder was
universally condemned and
triggered nationwide protests.
See also: Latin American
LGBTQ+ movements 178–79

ALEXYA SALVADOR
1980–

Born in Brazil, Alexya Salvador
became the first transgender pastor
in Latin America when she was
ordained in 2019. She had begged
to be taken to church from an early
age, and joined a seminary, but
when she encountered LGBTQ+
prejudice in Catholic institutions,
she chose to sever her ties. Salvador
then discovered the Metropolitan
Community Church in São Paulo,
which welcomed her and where she
first served as an assistant pastor in
2015. In 2016, Salvador also became
the first trans woman to adopt in
Brazil, when she and her partner
Roberto adopted a transgender girl.
See also: Latin American LGBTQ+
movements 178–79
▪ Transgender rights 196–203

ARSHAM PARSI
1980–

Currently living in exile in Canada,
Arsham Parsi is an Iranian LGBTQ+
human rights activist who fled Iran
in 2005. Growing up gay in Iran, he
had felt alone until, as a teenager,
he discovered support on the
internet. In 2001, Parsi founded
the online Rainbow Group, later
renamed the Persian Gay and
Lesbian Organization (PGLO), to
educate people about the issues
facing sexual minorities in Iran;
a friend registered the website in
Norway. In 2006, Parsi founded the
Iranian Queer Organization in
Toronto, Canada, and in 2008 the
International Railroad for Queer
Refugees. His autobiography *Exiled
for Love* was published in 2015.
See also: Towards gay liberation
170–77 ▪ LGBTQ+ activism in Asia
254–55 ▪ LGBTQ+ Muslims 278–79

MOHSIN ZAIDI
c. 1985–

British author Mohsin Zaidi is best
known for his 2020 memoir *A Dutiful
Boy*, which describes the struggles
he faced growing up gay in a devout
Muslim household. It relates, for
instance, how Zaidi, as a young
Oxford University graduate, silences
a witch doctor brought to his home
to "cure" him of his homosexuality.
He also notes the racism he faced on
gay dating sites that declared "No
Asians". Zaidi joined the board of
the LGBTQ+ charity Stonewall in
2017, has worked as an attorney in
New York City and as a criminal
barrister in London, and became a
management consultant in 2021.
See also: LGBTQ+ Muslims
278–79

OUTRAGE!
1990–2011

Founded in response to the
homophobic murder of gay actor
Michael Boothe in 1990, OutRage!
was a British political group
created to advocate for LGBTQ+
rights through non-violent direct
action and civil disobedience.
Known for theatrical, witty, and
imaginative forms of direct action,
the group staged a "kiss-in"
at London's Piccadilly Circus,
protesting against the arrest of gay
men for kissing in public. OutRage!
lobbied for the age of consent for
sex between men to be brought in
line with that for different-sex
acts, and drew attention to what it
saw as religious homophobia in the
Church of England. The group also
successfully campaigned against
the conviction of the Bolton 7, a
group of gay and bisexual men
charged with gross indecency in
1998. OutRage! was dissolved
in 2011.
See also: Towards gay liberation
170–77 ▪ The murder of Matthew
Shepard 284–85

SAMUEL LUIZ
1997–2021

While on a night out in A Coruña,
Spain, on 3 July 2021, nursing
assistant Samuel Luiz was beaten
to death in a homophobic attack.
Luiz's death sparked nationwide
protests and prompted discussions
about the safety of LGBTQ+ people.
Public anger was exacerbated by
the reluctance of police and
politicians to label the attack
homophobic or a hate crime.
See also: The murder of Matthew
Shepard 284–85

GLOSSARY

In this glossary, terms defined within another entry are identified in *italic* type.

AFAB Assigned female at birth, usually on the basis of a child's external anatomy.

agender Describes a person who does not *identify* as any particular *gender*.

AIDS The abbreviation for acquired immunodeficiency syndrome, a chronic and potentially life-threatening condition that can occur as a result of *HIV*.

alloromantic Describes someone who experiences romantic attraction more frequently and/or under less specific circumstances than people who are on the *aromantic* spectrum.

allosexual Describes someone who experiences *sexual attraction* more frequently and/or under less specific circumstances than people who are on the *asexual* spectrum.

AMAB Assigned male at birth, usually on the basis of a child's external anatomy.

aromantic/aro Describes someone who does not experience *romantic attraction*.

asexual/ace Describes someone who does not experience *sexual attraction*.

ball culture An *LGBTQ+ subculture* in which Black and *Latine* people compete in events known as balls and often live together in family groups.

bicurious Describes *heterosexual* people who want to experiment sexually and/or romantically with people of their own *gender*.

bigender Describes someone who has more than one *gender identity*, for example identifies as both male and female.

binary The classification of a characteristic into two distinct and opposite categories. For example, the *gender* binary classifies *gender* into the distinct categories of male and female. See also *non-binary*.

biphobia Stigma, prejudice, and discrimination towards bisexuality or *bisexual* people.

bisexual/bi Describes someone who experiences attraction to their own *gender* and at least one other *gender*, but may have a preference.

butch Describes a *lesbian*, *bisexual* person, *non-binary* person, or *trans man* who exhibits a masculine *identity* and/or *presents* in a masculine way.

camp An aesthetic and cultural movement, commonly associated with *gay* men, that is characterized by exaggeration, theatricality, and femininity.

Chicane A *gender-neutral* term to describe American Mexican people. The "-e" ending of this term better reflects Hispanic languages than other gender-neutral terms such as "Chicanx". See also *Latine*.

cisgender/cis Describes someone who *identifies* as the *gender* they were assigned at birth. See also *AFAB*, *AMAB*, and *transgender*.

closeting Forcing an *LGBTQ+* person to hide their true *sexual orientation* or *gender identity*, so that others presume that they are *heterosexual*, *cisgender*, *allosexual*, and/or *alloromantic*.

colonialism The policy or practice of gaining political, social, economic, and/or cultural control over another country, occupying it with settlers, and exploiting it economically.

coming out Disclosing one's true *LGBTQ+ sexual orientation* or *gender identity*.

community A group of people who live in the same area and/or share a common interest, characteristic, attitude, and/or *identity*.

compulsory heterosexuality The pressure that society puts on people to experience opposite-*sex* desire and participate in *heterosexual* relationships.

conversion therapy An intervention, usually medical and/or psychological, that seeks to change a person's *sexual orientation* or *gender identity*.

cross-dressing Wearing items of clothing that are commonly associated with the opposite *gender* to the wearer.

DADT An acronym for Don't Ask, Don't Tell, an American policy, lasting from 1993 to 2011, that allowed *gay* and *bisexual* people to serve in the military as long as they kept their *sexual orientation* private.

deadnaming Calling a *transgender* person the name they were given at birth, rather than their chosen name.

demiromantic Describes someone who only experiences *romantic attraction* once an emotional bond has been formed.

demisexual Describes someone who only experiences *sexual attraction* once an emotional bond has been formed.

drag Performance that involves dressing and/or *presenting* in a way that exaggerates, comments on, and/or subverts a particular *gender* – often, but not always – different from the performer's everyday gender.

drag king A *drag* artist, usually female, who dresses in a masculine way and *presents* as a man in performance.

drag queen A *drag* artist, usually male, who dresses in a feminine way and *presents* as a woman in performance.

erasure Ignoring or dismissing *LGBTQ+* people, *identities*, histories, or cultures.

eunuch A historically and culturally specific term for an *AMAB* person who has been castrated. The term "eunuch" should not be used to refer to modern-day *trans women* who have had *gender affirmation* surgery.

feminism A wide range of social movements and ideologies based on the belief that women should have rights and opportunities equal to those of men.

femme Describes a *lesbian*, *bisexual* person, *non-binary* person, or *trans man* who exhibits a feminine *identity* and/or *presents* in a feminine way.

"fish" The Black *lesbian* counterpart of the *femme identity*.

gay A commonly used term meaning *homosexual* or a *homosexual* person, usually referring to men or male *homosexuality*.

gender A state or *identity* that is often expressed in terms of masculinity and femininity; socially constructed behaviours, roles, and activities that are connected to this identity.

gender affirmation An umbrella term for the actions that a person might take or support that they might access in order to live as their authentic *gender identity*.

gender dysphoria A feeling of unease, discomfort, or distress that a person might feel because of a mismatch between their *gender* assigned at birth and their *gender identity*. See also *AFAB* and *AMAB*.

gender expression The way in which a person expresses or *presents* their *gender identity*, typically through clothing, hair, make-up, mannerisms, and/or behaviour.

gender fluidity A change over time in, or a flexible approach towards, a person's *gender identity*.

gender identity An individual's personal sense of their own *gender*.

gender-neutral Not referring to any particular *gender* or making any distinctions between genders.

gender nonconformity The state of not conforming to society's "normative" male and female *gender* roles. See also *binary*.

greyromantic Describes someone who experiences *romantic attraction* rarely and/or under extremely specific circumstances.

greysexual Describes someone who experiences *sexual attraction* rarely and/or under extremely specific circumstances.

heteronormativity A concept or world view that promotes *heterosexuality* as the default *sexual orientation* and privileges those who exist within "traditional" understandings of *heterosexual* life, such as married people and people with children.

heterosexual Only experiencing attraction to people of one *gender* that is different from one's own gender. Heterosexuality has traditionally been defined in terms of the *gender binary*.

hijra 1) A *community* of *gender nonconforming* people mostly concentrated in Northern India but also in other parts of India, Pakistan, and Bangladesh. 2) A person from the hijra *community*.

HIV The abbreviation for human immunodeficiency virus, which can cause *AIDS*.

homonationalism A concept that explores the links between (mostly) Western nations embracing *LGBTQ+* rights and what some see as those countries' capitalist, nationalist, or imperialist ideologies, and the effect on LGBTQ+ *communities*.

homonormativity The assumption that *LGBTQ+* people should fit into *heterosexual* norms and that same-*sex* relationships should fit as closely as possible into the template of opposite-*sex* relationships.

homophile Advocating and supporting the rights and welfare of *homosexual* people.

homophobia Stigma, prejudice, and discrimination towards *homosexuality* or *homosexual* people.

homosexual Only experiencing attraction to people of one's own *gender*.

identity A person's sense of self; in the *LGBTQ+ community*, the term is often used to refer to a person's *sexual orientation* or *gender identity*.

intersectionality A concept that explores how different aspects of an individual's *identity* – such as race, ethnicity, *sexual orientation*, *gender*, *gender identity*, age, and class – create intersecting systems of discrimination and oppression.

intersex Describes a person born with *sex* characteristics – including genitals, gonads, and chromosome patterns – that do not fit *binary* notions of "male" and "female" bodies.

invert An early 20th-century term for a spectrum covering what we would now call *gay*, *lesbian*, *bisexual*, and *trans identities*.

kathoey A Thai *gender identity* that was historically applied to *intersex* people but now encompasses any *AMAB* person who defies conventional *gender* expectations.

Latine A *gender-neutral* term to describe Latin American people. The "-e" ending of this term better reflects Hispanic languages than other gender-neutral terms such as "Latinx". See also *Chicane*.

lesbian Describes a woman or a *non-binary* person who only experiences attraction to women.

lesbophobia Stigma, prejudice, and discrimination towards *lesbians*.

LGBTQ+ An acronym for *lesbian*, *gay*, *bisexual*, *transgender*, and *queer/ questioning*, with the + representing other non-normative sexual and *gender identities*. Longer acronyms, such as LGBTQIA+ and LGBTIQA+ also exist, with the "I" explicitly representing *intersex* identities and the "A" explicitly representing *aromantic* and *asexual* identities.

marriage equality A situation in which couples have the right to marry regardless of the *gender* of each partner.

molly An 18th-century term for men and *gender*-diverse *AMAB* people who have sex with men and/or desire men.

molly house The 18th-century equivalent of a modern *gay* bar or sex club and a relatively safe space for *mollies* to meet.

monosexual 1) A 19th-century term to describe people who do not have sex, only masturbate. 2) A term coined in the 1990s to describe people who only experience attraction to one *gender*.

MSM The abbreviation for men who have sex with men.

neopronoun A new *pronoun*, often created in an attempt to make language more *gender-neutral* and inclusive.

non-binary An umbrella term for *gender identities* that are neither exclusively male nor exclusively female. See also *binary*.

omnisexual Describes someone who experiences attraction to all *genders*, but may have a preference.

outing Disclosing someone else's *LGBTQ+ sexual orientation* or *gender identity* without their consent.

pansexual Describes someone who experiences attraction to all *genders*, without a preference.

passing Being perceived by others as a particular *gender* or *sexual orientation*; the term *passing* usually refers to *LGBTQ+* people being perceived by *heteronormative* society as *heterosexual* and/or *cisgender*.

patriarchy The social system in which men – particularly *cisgender* and *heterosexual* men – have most or all of the power, privilege, and value, and people of other *genders* are largely or completely excluded from this power.

pederasty In ancient Greece and ancient Rome, the practice of a sexual relationship between an older, bearded man (known as the *erastes*, or the lover) who is the active partner in the relationship and a younger, beardless man (known as the *eromenos*, or the beloved) who is the passive partner.

pinkwashing The way in which people, organizations, and nations promote *LGBTQ+* rights to indicate their progressive liberalism, but with an ulterior motive.

platonic Describes a close relationship that is affectionate, but not romantic or sexual.

political lesbianism The idea that *lesbianism* is a political choice and that women should reject romantic and sexual relationships with men as a means of resisting *patriarchal* oppression.

polysexual Describes someone who experiences attraction to multiple, but not necessarily all, *genders*.

presenting *Expressing* a *gender identity*, typically through clothing, hair, make-up, mannerisms, and/or behaviour.

pronoun A word that replaces a noun. Personal pronouns, such as "he", "she", and *gender-neutral* alternatives such as "they", are part of a person's *gender identity* and *gender expression*.

queer 1) A *homophobic* slur that has been reclaimed by many in the *LGBTQ+ community* as an *identity* marker. 2) An umbrella term for *LGBTQ+* people and the LGBTQ+ *community*.

queer theory An academic field that explores how *gender* and *sexuality* are understood. Queer theory questions, among other things, whether *identities* are fixed and whether gender and sexuality are *binary*.

questioning The process of exploring and/or determining one's *sexual orientation* and/or *gender identity*.

romantic attraction Desire to have a romantic relationship with another person/people.

romantic orientation The way in which a person experiences or does not experience *romantic attraction*, including the *gender*(s) to which they are or are not *romantically attracted*.

sapphism An 18th- and 19th-century term for same-*sex* relationships between women.

sapphist A woman who practises *sapphism*; an 18th- and 19th-century term for a woman who would today be known as a *lesbian*.

sex The way in which a given society classifies a person's physical and bodily characteristics – such as reproductive organs, chromosomes, and hormones – that usually determine the *gender* a person is assigned at birth. See also *AFAB* and *AMAB*.

sexology The study of human *sexuality* and sexual behaviour.

sexual attraction Desire to have sexual intercourse with another person/people.

sexuality The way in which people experience or express sexual feelings, thoughts, attraction, and/or behaviour.

sexual orientation The way in which a person experiences or does not experience *sexual attraction*, including the *gender*(s) to which they are or are not *sexually attracted*.

sodomy In the medieval period, any form of sexual activity without the potential for procreation within marriage. By the 15th century, sodomy was generally defined as same-*sex* activity, usually between men.

straight See *heterosexual*.

"stud" The Black *lesbian* counterpart of the *butch identity*.

subculture A group of people within a dominant culture whose beliefs, values, ideas, behaviour, and/or way of life differ from those of the dominant culture.

TERF Acronym for trans-exclusionary radical feminist, a *feminist* who believes that *trans women* are not "real women".

transgender/trans Describes someone who identifies as a different *gender* from the one they were assigned at birth. See also *AFAB*, *AMAB*, and *cisgender*.

transing A term used to describe behaviour – such as cross-dressing or living as a different *gender* from the one assigned at birth – that subverts *gender* norms. The term "transing" is particularly useful for talking about people from the past for whom the label *transgender* would be ahistorical. See also *AFAB* and *AMAB*.

transitioning The action that a *transgender* person might take to live as the *gender* with which they *identify*. This may or may not involve medical interventions such as hormone therapy and *gender affirmation* surgery. It may also involve *coming out* as transgender, *presenting* as one's chosen gender, and changing identity documents.

trans man An *AFAB* person who *identifies* as male.

transphobia Stigma, prejudice, and discrimination towards *transgender* people.

transvestism An alternative term for *cross-dressing*. Historically used in medical diagnoses, the term "transvestism" is considered derogatory and outdated in white Western cultures, but is still commonly used in many other cultures.

trans woman An *AMAB* person who *identifies* as female.

tribade A 17th-century term for a woman who desires other women.

Two-Spirit (2S) An umbrella term for *gender nonconforming* people in Indigenous American *communities*.

INDEX

Page numbers in **bold** refer to main entries.

QUOTE ATTRIBUTIONS

ACKNOWLEDGMENTS

Dorling Kindersley would like to thank Bonnie Macleod, Georgina Palffy, and Elise Solberg for editorial assistance; Freddy McConnell for authenticity reading; Steve Parker for additional consultancy; Prof Ruth Vanita for permission to use her translations from *Gender, Sex and the City* (2017), Valentino Vecchietti for permission to feature the Intersex-Inclusive Pride flag and advice on intersex inclusion and accuracy; Martin Copeland for picture research support; Oliver Drake for proofreading; Helen Peters for indexing; Gopika Gopakumar, for design assistance; Yogesh Kumar for administrative assistance; and the DK Diversity, Equity, and Inclusion team and Product and Content Working Group for their support and guidance.

PICTURE CREDITS

DK BIG IDEAS SIMPLY EXPLAINED

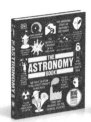

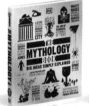

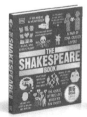

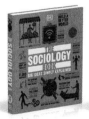

For the curious